Fodor's

BUENOS AIRES

3rd Edition

Fodor's Travel Publications   New York, Toronto, London, Sydney, Auckland

www.fodors.com

Portions of this book appear in *Fodor's Argentina*

FODOR'S BUENOS AIRES

Writers: Karina Martinez-Carter, Sorrel Moseley-Williams, Victoria Patience, Dan Perlman, Jessica Pollack

Editors: Heidi Leigh Johansen (lead editor), Laura M. Kidder, Maria Teresa Hart

Production Editor: Carrie Parker
Maps & Illustrations: David Lindroth, *cartographer;* Rebecca Baer, *map editor;* William Wu, *information graphics*
Design: Fabrizio La Rocca, *creative director;* Tina Malaney, Chie Ushio, Jessica Walsh, *designers;* Melanie Marin, *associate director of photography;* Jennifer Romains, *photo research*
Cover Photo: Tango, Caminito Street, La Boca district: Luis Padilla/age fotostock
Production Manager: Angela L. McLean

3rd Edition

ISBN 978–0–307–92836–8

ISSN 1941–0182

SPECIAL SALES

This book is available at special discounts for bulk purchases for sales promotions or premiums. Special editions, including personalized covers, excerpts of existing books, and corporate imprints, can be created in large quantities for special needs. For more information, write to Special Markets/Premium Sales, 1745 Broadway, MD 3-1, New York, NY 10019, or e-mail specialmarkets@randomhouse.com.

AN IMPORTANT TIP & AN INVITATION

Although all prices, opening times, and other details in this book are based on information supplied to us at press time, changes occur all the time in the travel world, and Fodor's cannot accept responsibility for facts that become outdated or for inadvertent errors or omissions. So **always confirm information when it matters**, especially if you're making a detour to visit a specific place. Your experiences—positive and negative—matter to us. If we have missed or misstated something, **please write to us.** Share your opinion instantly through our online feedback center at fodors.com/contact-us.

PRINTED IN CHINA

10 9 8 7 6 5 4 3 2 1

CONTENTS

Fodor's Features

MAPS

ABOUT
THIS BOOK

Our Ratings

At Fodor's, we spend considerable time choosing the best places in a destination so you don't have to. By default, anything we recommend in this book is worth visiting. But some sights, properties, and experiences are so great that we've recognized them with additional accolades. Orange **Fodor's Choice** stars indicate our top recommendations; black stars highlight places we deem **Highly Recommended**; and **Best Bets** call attention to top properties in various categories. Disagree with any of our choices? Care to nominate a new place? Visit our feedback center at www.fodors.com/feedback.

> For expanded hotel reviews, visit **Fodors.com**

Hotels

Hotels have private bath, phone, TV, and air-conditioning, and do not offer meals unless we specify that in the review. We always list facilities but not whether you'll be charged an extra fee to use them.

Restaurants

Unless we state otherwise, restaurants are open for lunch and dinner daily. We mention dress only when there's a specific requirement and reservations only when they're essential or not accepted—it's always best to book ahead.

Credit Cards

We assume that restaurants and hotels accept credit cards. If not, we'll note it in the review.

Budget Well

Hotel and restaurant price categories from ¢ to $$$$ are defined in the opening pages of the respective chapters. For attractions, we always give standard adult admission fees; reductions are usually available for children, students, and senior citizens.

Listings
★ Fodor's Choice
★ Highly recommended
✉ Physical address
✛ Directions or Map coordinates
✉ Mailing address
☎ Telephone
🖷 Fax
⊕ On the Web
✎ E-mail
✉ Admission fee
☉ Open/closed times
Ⓜ Metro stations
▭ No credit cards

Hotels & Restaurants
🏠 Hotel
↩ Number of rooms
⚲ Facilities
⑩ Meal plans
✗ Restaurant
⚱ Reservations
⚑ Dress code
⚲ Smoking

Outdoors
⛳ Golf
⛺ Camping

Other
☺ Family-friendly
⇨ See also
✉ Branch address
☞ Take note

Experience
Buenos Aires

1

BUENOS AIRES TODAY

They say the only thing certain in life is change, and no one knows it as well as *porteños* (citizens of Buenos Aires). While the world panics over stockmarket crashes and bailout packages, this city's inhabitants just yawn: when it comes to political uncertainty and financial instability, they've seen it all. But there's a lesson in hope here, too. From the ashes of economic burnout a vibrant, more progressive Buenos Aires has risen. At times uncertainty can be worrying. But it can be exciting, too.

Today's Buenos Aires . . .

. . . is getting a face-lift. Cobbled streets, wrought-iron billboards, and cafés that seem untouched since 1940 are all part of Buenos Aires' trademark time-warp look. But though porteños are nostalgic, even they've had enough of exquisite stone facades crumbling (sometimes plummeting) through lack of maintenance. Suddenly scaffolding is everywhere, as old buildings are revamped and savvy developers transform century-old mansions and warehouses into hotels—some boutique, others behemoth.

Controversy shrouds some makeovers: the city government was accused of selling the historic cobblestones they replaced with asphalt, and the restoration of the Teatro Colón went way over schedule and budget. Still, like other aging local beauties, Buenos Aires' historical buildings are looking younger by the minute.

. . . is coming to terms with the past. For years, sweeping things under the carpet seemed the official line on Argentina's last, and bloodiest, military dictatorship, which lasted from 1976 to 1983. But the current government has revoked pardons granted to high-ranking officers responsible for torture and disappearances, many of whom have been brought to justice. Memory is being inscribed on the cityscape, too. A former clandestine detention center has been transformed into a cultural center run by the Madres de Plaza de Mayo, and the city's official monument to the "disappeared," the Parque de la Memoria, is complete. The anniversary of the start of the dictatorship, March 24, has been made a public day of remembrance: thousands gather each year in Plaza de Mayo to mark it.

. . . is full of free speech. Forget writing to your political representatives when you've got a gripe with the system— in Buenos Aires you take to the streets. Strikes, marches, rallies, and *piquetes*

WHAT'S HOT IN BUENOS AIRES NOW

Argentineans have always been patriotic, but flags are flying higher and brighter than usual in the aftermath of the 2010 bicentennary of the May Revolution, which led to Argentina's independence. Celebrations culminated in five days of parades and musical performances attended by six million people on Avenida 9 de Julio, closed to traffic for the occasion.

Buenos Aires has more than its fair share of literary legends. UNESCO named the city World Book Capital for 2011 in recognition of the government's extensive books and reading program.

You can visit the spots that inspired Jorge Luis Borges, the Argentine writer, poet, and translator, on a themed walking tour or peruse his complete works over coffee at a dozen artsy cafés. If you

(road blocks) have long been fixtures of daily life. They reached new levels after December 19, 2001, when the country's economy crashed. The state froze private bank accounts, and ensuing demonstrations escalated into riots after violent police responses.

Although things have calmed since then, the Plaza and Avenida de Mayo still fill regularly with drum- and banner-toting crowds. Sometimes they're protesting or petitioning to change laws; other times they are celebrating victories both political and sporting.

. . . is going global. Argentina is a long, long way from a lot of places. In the years leading up to and immediately after the 2001 economic crisis, Buenos Aires felt very isolated: first, high prices and poor infrastructure kept people away, and then political instability did. Things couldn't have changed more. And though most porteños are descended from immigrants, they just can't get over the number of out-of-towners there are today. (Thankfully, the numbers are still small enough to keep sightseeing from being a competitive sport.)

And more and more of the visitors are staying: Buenos Aires has growing Asian and Latin American communities, the number of exchange students at city universities has soared, and there's a thriving English-language expat scene complete with how-to blogs and magazines. And the urban landscape is changing, too: The ultimate nod to globalization came in 2008, when Starbucks opened its first branches here. But some things never change: the city's time-honored cafés are as popular as ever.

Cafe Tortoni, Centro

don't read Spanish, the same tables are perfect for sitting down and starting a novel of your own.

Being out has never been this in. In 2010 Argentina became the first country in Latin America—and only the ninth in the world—to fully legalize same-sex marriage, sealing Buenos Aires' claim on the title of Latin America's gay capital. It's not just bars and clubs: we're talking travel agencies, tango schools, (tango dance halls), and Axel, a posh gay hotel. The Marcha del Orgullo Gay (Gay Pride March) attracts thousands of revelers each November.

BUENOS AIRES PLANNER

No Time Like the Present

Fabulous wine, endless nightlife, friendly locals, the best steak, rock-bottom prices... shaking off a stereotype can be hard. But when yours reads like a shopping list for indulgence, why bother? Whether they're screaming for a soccer team or enjoying an endless barbecue with friends, porteños are always living in the now.

Visitor Info

The Web site of the city tourist board, **Turismo Buenos Aires** (⊕ www.bue.gov.ar), has lively, downloadable MP3 walking tours in English. Information booths at the airports and seven other locations provide maps and have English-speaking staff. Hours can be erratic, but the booth at the intersection of Florida and Marcelo T. de Alvear is usually open during the day.

Get Around Just Fine

Intriguing architecture, an easy-to-navigate grid layout (a few diagonal transverses aside), and ample window-shopping make Buenos Aires a wonderful place to explore on foot. SUBE, a rechargeable swipe card, can be used on the subway, most city bus lines, and commuter trains.

Public Transit. Service on the *subte* (subway) is quick, but trains are often packed and strikes are common. Four of the six underground lines (A, B, D, and E) fan out west from downtown; lines C and H (only partly open) connect them. Single-ride tickets cost 1.10 pesos. The subte shuts down around 10:30 pm and reopens at 5 am.

Colectivos (city buses) connect the city's barrios and the greater Buenos Aires area. Ticket machines on board accept coins (fares within the city cost 1.20–1.25 pesos) or the SUBE card. Bus stops are roughly every other block, but you may have to hunt for the small metal route-number signs: they could be stuck on a shelter, lamppost, or even a tree. Stop at a news kiosk and buy the *Guía T*, a route guide.

Taxis. Black-and-yellow taxis fill the streets and take you anywhere in town and short distances into greater Buenos Aires. Fares start at 5.80 pesos with 58¢ per 650 feet. You can hail taxis on the street or ask hotel and restaurant staffers to call for them.

Safety

Although Buenos Aires is safer than most Latin American capitals, petty crime is a concern. Pickpocketing and mugging are common, so avoid wearing flashy jewelry, be discreet with money and cameras, and be mindful of bags and wallets. Phone for taxis after dark. Police patrol most areas where you're likely to go, but they do have a reputation for corruption.

Protest marches are a part of life in Buenos Aires: most are peaceful, but some end in confrontations with the police. They often take place in the Plaza de Mayo, in the square outside the Congreso, or along Avenida de Mayo.

Tours

The name says it all: **BA Free Tours** (⊕ *www.bafreetours. com*) runs two daily walking tours that won't set you back a penny (tipping the chirpy young guides is a nice gesture, though). To take part, you show up at a designated meeting spot Monday through Saturday.

Buenos Aires Bus (☎ *11/5239–5160* ⊕ *www. buenosairesbus.com*) is a hop-on hop-off service run by the city's official tourism body. It's an efficient way to tick off all the main tourist spots in the city. The colorful double-decker buses leave two to three times per hour and have bilingual guides aboard who point out landmarks.

The service—for tours in town and out—you get from Isabel at **Buenos Aires Tours** (⊕ *www.buenosaires-tours.com.ar*) is almost heroic.

For a local's perspective, contact the **Cicerones de Buenos Aires** (☎ *11/4330–0800* ⊕ *www.cicerones.org.ar*), a free service that pairs you with a porteño to show you parts of town you might not see otherwise.

Informed young historians from the University of Buenos Aires lead cultural and historical tours at **Eternautas** (☎ *11/5031–9916* ⊕ *www.eternautas.com*). It offers general city tours, themed private outings (e.g., Evita and Peronism, the literary city, Jewish Buenos Aires), and excursions outside town.

See Buenos Aires from the river on a 2½-hour sailboat tour with **Smile on Sea** (☎ *11/15–5018–8662* ⊕ *www. smileonsea.com*).

Large onboard screens make the posh minibuses used by **Opción Sur** (☎ *11/4777–9029* ⊕ *www.opcionsur.com. ar*) part transport and part cinema. Each stop on their tours of the city and the Tigre Delta is introduced by relevant historical footage (e.g., Evita rallying the masses at Plaza de Mayo).

See the major sights and get the lay of the land on the basic three-hour bus tours in English and Spanish run by **Travel Line** (☎ *11/4393–9000* ⊕ *www.travelline.com.ar*).

For tailor-made city tours, contact **Wow! Argentina** (☎ *11/5239–3019* ⊕ *www.wowargentina.com*) well in advance of your arrival in Buenos Aires. Enthusiastic Cintia Stella and her team also arrange excursions all over Argentina.

When to Go

Remember that when it's summer in the United States, it's winter in Argentina, and vice versa. Winters (July–September) are chilly. Summer's muggy heat (December–March) can be taxing at midday but makes for warm nights. During these months Argentineans crowd resorts along the Atlantic and in Uruguay.

Spring (September–December) and autumn (April–June), with their mild temperatures are ideal for urban trekking. It's usually warm enough for just a light jacket, and it's right before or after the peak seasons. The best time for trips to Iguazú Falls is August–October, when temperatures are lower and the falls are fuller.

Buenos Aires Temperatures

WHAT'S WHERE

1 Centro: Microcentro, Plaza de Mayo, Retiro, and Puerto Madero. Locals use "Centro" or "El Centro" as umbrella terms for several busy downtown districts. The heart of the city's heart is the chaotic Microcentro, which bursts with banks, offices, theaters (including the Colón), bars, cafés, bookstores, and crowds. The area around Plaza and Avenida de Mayo is the hub of political life and home to some of the city's oldest buildings. Posh hotels, gleaming skyscrapers, an elegant boardwalk, and the Museo Fortabat make up Puerto Madero.

2 San Telmo and La Boca. The tango was born in these southern barrios. Today antiques and hip clothing compete for store space along San Telmo's dreamy cobbled streets—ideal for lazy wandering and relaxing at bars or cafés. Just to the south, La Boca was the city's first port. Today visitors come for a snapshot of the colorful but tacky Caminito, and soccer fans fill the Boca Juniors stadium. The vibrant visuals don't end there: highbrow art is another attraction in both neighborhoods. Contemporary works fill the edgy galleries and revamped MAMBA in San Telmo, while in La Boca two small art museums—one traditional and one contemporary—look over the waterfront.

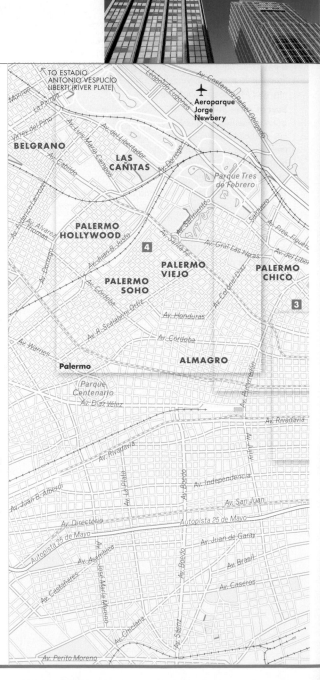

Recoleta and Almagro

Río de La Plata

0 ____ 1/2 mile
0 ____ 1/2 kilometer

Dársena F

Dársena E

oa Alcorta

9

RECOLETA

Av. del Libertador

Av. Santa Fe

Av. Córdoba

Av. Corrientes

Plaza del Congreso

Av. de Mayo

PLAZA DE MAYO

Av. Belgrano

Callao

Av. Julio

Terminal de Omnibus Retiro

Dársena A

RETIRO   Estación Retiró   **Centro and Environs**

Plaza San Martín

Antepuerto

Dársena Norte

CENTRO

Av. Leandro N. Alem

Dique 4

PUERTO MADERO

Dique 3

Plaza de Mayo

Dique 2

Reserva Ecológica

SAN TELMO

Av. Paseo Colón

Dique 1

Autopista 25 de Mayo

Av. Entre Ríos

Estación Constitución

Av. Martín García

Dársena Sur
Av. Pedro Mendoza

LA BOCA

Av. Amadeo Alcorta

Av. 9 de Julio (AU 1)

Av. M. Montes de Oca

Av. Reg. de Patricios

Brandsen

Brandsen

Irala

Vé el Sansfield

La Boca and San Telmo

3 Recoleta and Almagro.
The elite live, dine, and shop along Recoleta's gorgeous Paris-inspired streets. They're also often buried in the sumptuous mausoleums of its cemetery. Art galleries and museums—including the Museo Nacional de Bellas Artes—are also draws. Gritty, working-class Almagro is known for its fringe theater and tango scene, Peruvian restaurants, and the large Abasto shopping mall.

4 Palermo, Belgrano, Costanera Norte, and Las Cañitas. Large Palermo has many subdistricts. If it's cool, chances are it's in Palermo Viejo: boutiques, bars, restaurants, clubs, galleries, and hotels line the streets surrounding Plaza Serrano (also known to locals as Plazoleta Cortázar). There are two excellent museums (the MALBA and Museo Evita) in Palermo Chico, the barrio's northern end, also home to parks and the zoo. Clubs and bars line nearby Costanera Norte. It's also home to a golf course and the Jorge Newbery airport. Local celebs adore the shops and nightlife of Las Cañitas and Belgrano.

BUENOS AIRES TOP ATTRACTIONS

Museo Nacional de Bellas Artes

(A) Originally the city's waterworks, this russet-color columned building in Recoleta is your one-stop shop for Argentine painting and sculpture, especially modern and postmodern works. A surprisingly comprehensive collection of lesser works by European and North American masters, spanning the 13th century to the present, is an added boon.

Plaza de Mayo

(B) Since the city was founded, civic and political life has centered on this large, palm-shaded square in Centro. The favored stage of protesters and politicians alike, this was where Evita told a rally of thousands not to cry for her. Since the 1976–83 dictatorship, a group of mothers (now nongovernmental organizations called Madres and Abuelas de Plaza de Mayo) have been protesting their children's disappearances here each week. The presidential palace, a cathedral, the central bank, a colonial town hall, and the senate all flank the square.

Cementerio de la Recoleta

(C) The city's illustrious departed rest in mausoleums as sumptuous as their mansions. Heavily adorned with marble facades and dramatic statues, these second homes are arrayed along shaded avenues, forming an eerie but beautiful city of the dead. Residents include the must-see Evita, national heroes, sporting greats, writers, and several wandering ghosts—or so local legend goes.

Museo de Arte Latinoamericano de Buenos Aires (MALBA)

(D) Buenos Aires' first truly world-class museum is a luminous temple to the gods of 20th-century Latin American art. A vigorous acquisitions program means you see the latest talents as well as Frida Kahlo, Diego Rivera, and Fernando Botero. The architecture, rooftop views

over surrounding Palermo, and gift shop are excuses in themselves to stop by.

Parque Tres de Febrero (Los Bosques de Palermo)

(E) Porteños desperate for some green relief love this 200-acre Palermo park, which includes wooded areas, a rose garden, lakes, a planetarium, and a small art museum. Bask in the sun with a picnic and/or a book, or make like sporty locals and go for a run or a bike ride around its trails.

Caminito

(F) An entire postcard industry has been built on the Technicolor corrugated-iron constructions on this street in La Boca. A purpose-built tourist attraction, Caminito is unashamedly tacky and brash, but is still an exuberant must-see (and must-snap) on your first visit to Buenos Aires.

Plaza Dorrego

(G) Sunday sees this quiet San Telmo square transformed into the Feria de San Pedro Telmo, Buenos Aires' biggest antiques market. Junk, memorabilia, and, occasionally, genuine antiques are all part of the cult of nostalgia celebrated here in the shadow of century-old town houses. A beer or coffee at a traditional bar is an essential part of the experience.

Museo Evita

(H) Forget Madonna: for the true scoop on Argentina's most iconic citizen, come to this well-curated museum. Evita's life, works, and wardrobe are celebrated through insightful displays and original video footage, all housed in a gorgeous turn-of-the-20th-century mansion she requisitioned as a home for single mothers.

BUENOS AIRES LIKE A LOCAL

Pamper Yourself Like a Porteña

It's not just good genes that keep *porteñas* (women from Buenos Aires) looking fab: the *peluquería* (beauty salon) is a home away from home. Local women favor cheap, nondescript neighborhood salons where they can gossip and read trashy magazines. A normal Friday evening session might include *brushing* (blow-dry and styling, 35–50 pesos), usually with *planchita* (straightening irons), as most porteñas dislike curls.

A weekly *belleza de manos y pies* (manicure and pedicure, 20 and 50 pesos, respectively) is also standard. Local waxers are so good (and charge so little) that no porteña would dream of touching a razor. Most salons use the *sistema español*, involving thick, gloopy wax that's pulled off without fabric strips. Given the fierce rivalry between Argentina and its neighbor, all-out bikini waxing isn't called "a Brazilian." You can get the same effect by picking a combo of *cavado profundo* (regular bikini), *tira de pelvis* (a strip along the top, ideal for low-cut bikinis), and *tira de cola* (literally, "ass strip"— need we say more?). Expect to pay 40–50 pesos for the lot.

Llongueras (⊕ *www.llongueras.com.ar*) and **D'antuan** (⊕ *www.dantuan.com.ar*) are good-value chains with branches about town, and you usually don't need an appointment.

When local rockers want to trim their locks—or overhaul their looks—they go to **Roho** (✉ *Malabia 1931, Palermo*, ☎ *11/4833–7227* ⊕ *www.roho.com.ar*). The hip but friendly staffers are known for cuts as attention-grabbing as the neon-adorned salon front.

Travel Like a Porteño

For many porteños the run-down *colectivos* that rocket around in a cloud of exhaust are the only form of transport available. Hopping one of these buses can transport you from dolled-up tourist haunts to residential barrios in minutes.

Complex winding (and varying) routes make getting on a bus a leap into the unknown. If you're adventurous, try the first bus that comes along and see where it takes you. If you're a control freak, go to a news kiosk and buy a *Guía T*, which lists routes numerically at the back.

One route to try is that taken by Bus 60, which goes from Constitución through Congreso and Barrio Norte before branching into myriad subroutes, most through the northwest of Buenos Aires. Another good bet is Bus 126, which travels southwest from Plaza de Mayo through San Telmo, Boedo, Caballito, and Flores to the Feria de Mataderos market.

Romance Like a Porteño

They don't call Buenos Aires the Paris of the South for nothing. Palermo's Parque Tres de Febrero is perfect for a long afternoon of romance. Forget about a dozen red roses: at the **Paseo del Rosedal** (Rose Garden) you're surrounded by hundreds of blooms. The paths are made for wandering hand-in-hand. True, the pedal boats on the **Lagos de Palermo** (Palermo Lakes) aren't exactly Venetian gondolas, but there's plenty of tongue-in-cheek romancing to be had as you pedal in tandem.

Window-shopping along Palermo Viejo's cobbled streets is romantic in itself, but you can dress up the experience with a visit to local designer lingerie stores. Candlelit restaurants abound in the neighborhood, or you can add serious fuel to your

fire with a meal at aphrodisiac restaurant **Te Mataré Ramírez.**

You can't say you've made love like a porteño until you've checked into a *telo.* These hourly hotels are where privacy-deprived local parents, teenagers, adulterers, and just plain lovers come for some time alone. They're clean, safe, and cheesy rather than sleazy—think mirrored ceilings, water beds, Muzak, and mood lighting. At **Caravelle,** on the corner of Niceto Vega and Darwin, you get a two-hour slot for 90–180 pesos (depending on the level of luxury); if you check in after midnight on weeknights you can stay all night.

Go Out Like a Porteño

Porteños never have trouble finding an excuse to get together with friends, and not just on Friday and Saturday night. Wondering how they manage to combine a nightlife scene that doesn't kick off until 3 am with getting to work the next morning? We'll let you in on a secret: many don't. These days many head to an "after-office," an extended happy hour found in most bars in the Microcentro between 6 and 9 pm. Older couples and groups of friends prefer to catch a show or a play along Avenida Corrientes—most go wild over the lame jokes and sequin-and-feather-bedecked dancers of the big reviews, but there's plenty of highbrow theater on offer, too. If your heart's set on all-nighting, make like local clubbers and take a power siesta sometime after 10 pm.

Eat Fast Food Like a Porteño

Porteños are devoted to local fast food. One of the quickest lunches in town is a couple of slices standing at the bars of classic Microcentro pizzerias like Las Cuartetas and El Cuartito *(⇨ Chapter 5, Where to Eat).* Expect a doughy crust and lots of cheese.

UNDERCUTTING THE COMPETITION

People will often go to the ends of the earth to look good. The latest trend in special-interest tours to Buenos Aires is cosmetic surgery. Some visitors buy dedicated surgery packages (you know, flights, hotel, transfers, tummy tuck), while others combine treatments with a vacation.

Low prices are the draw, but Argentina's cosmetic surgeons also have a good international reputation. It's not all liposuction and boob jobs, either: dental implants, whitening, and laser eye surgery are also popular.

The truly porteño touch is to put a slice of *fainá* (baked garbanzo dough) on top of your pizza. For fast-fare alfresco, sink your teeth into a *choripán* or *vaciopán* (an oozing sandwich of chorizo or beef, respectively) from the stands that line the Costanera Sur walkway along the river south of Puerto Madero.

You might not be able to dial a dozen empanadas to your hotel room, but you could certainly do takeout: El Sanjuanino (☎ 11/4822–8080 ⊕ *www.elsanjuanino. com*) is a favorite among local connoisseurs. The idea is to eat them lukewarm straight from the paper wrapping, preferably washing them down with a beer or a Coke while watching bad TV programs in bed. For dessert: ice cream from chains like Persicco (⊕ *www.persicco.com*) or Un'Altra Volta (☎ 11/4783–4048 ⊕ *www. unaltravolta.com.ar*).

BUENOS AIRES' OLDEST AND NEWEST

Most buildings from the colonial era and the early days of the republic have long since been built over, but San Telmo still offers glimpses of bygone Buenos Aires. Adjacent Puerto Madero is the fastest-changing part of town, home to some of Latin America's most expensive real estate.

Time Travel in San Telmo

Start in **Plaza Dorrego**, the city's second-oldest square and the heart of San Telmo, and head north up Defensa. Late 19th-century town houses line the street—most now contain antiques shops or clothing boutiques. Detour left onto Estados Unidos to explore the **Mercado de San Telmo**, a produce market dating from 1897 (antiques now outnumber the apples on sale). Continue north up Defensa to Number 755, **El Zanjón de los Granados,** a restored 18th-century house and the tunnels under it. Turn right into Pasaje San Lorenzo, a cobbled alley. At Number 380 stands **Casa Mínima**, the city's thinnest building—about 8 feet wide—which once belonged to a freed slave.

Backtrack down Defensa and left onto Pasaje Giuffra, another quiet lane, then right onto Balcarce, lined with more old houses. Follow Estados Unidos east and over busy Paseo Colón. The huge neo-classical building is now the University of Buenos Aires' **School of Engineering**, but was the headquarters of Evita's social-aid foundation.

Watery Wonders

Cross Avenida Huergo onto Puerto Madero—Estados Unidos changes its name to Rosario Vera Peñaloza and becomes a wide boulevard with a leafy pedestrian median. Facing the end of the street is an ornate white fountain, **Fuente Las Nereidas**, sculpted by Argentinean Lola Mora in 1902. It was commissioned for Plaza de Mayo, but the nude nymphs were considered too scandalous to stand so close to the cathedral.

Wander north along the **Costanera Sur**: to your left are Puerto Madero's skyscrapers; to your right is a stretch of water separating Puerto Madero proper from the **Reserva Ecológica**. (The ecological reserve's entrance is through the trees behind Fuente Las Nereidas—a detour here will add gorgeous greenery and lots of extra mileage to your walk.) Be sure to try a *vaciopán* (steak sandwich) sold by the food carts along the Costanera.

Urban Renewal

Turn left onto Martha Lynch, which curves past the **Parque de las Mujeres Argentinas**, a small park, and ends at one of Puerto Madero's former docks, now home to Buenos Aires' newest buildings (and newest construction sites). The original redbrick warehouses over the water now house restaurants and offices.

Just ahead is Santiago Calatrava's sculptural pedestrian bridge, **Puente de la Mujer**. Continue up the side of the docks along Pierina Dealessi: the compact steel-and-concrete structure at the end of Dique 4 contains the **Colección Fortabat** art museum, which also has a stylish café.

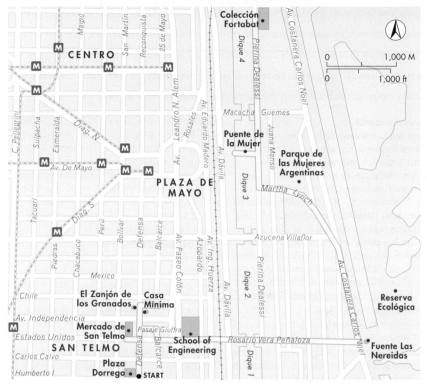

Where to Start:	Intersection of Defensa and Humberto I, Plaza Dorrego
Time/Length:	3 hours; just under 5 km (3 mi)
Where to Stop:	Colección Fortabat, intersection Pierina Dealessi and Mariquita Sánchez de Thompson
Best Time to Go:	After 11 am, Monday to Saturday
Worst Time to Go:	Sunday: the antiques market in Plaza Dorrego makes it impossible to move.
Highlights:	Plaza Dorrego, El Zanjón de Granados, Costanera Sur, Puente de la Mujer, Colección Fortabat

RECOLETA TO PALERMO: ART IN THE PARKS

Locals see busy Avenidas Figueroa Alcorta and Libertador as functional routes connecting downtown with the northern suburbs. But the parallel avenues also join Recoleta's major sights to Palermo's, and woven between them are beautiful green spaces. Use the avenues to get your bearings, but do your actual walking through the squares and parks.

Iconic Recoleta

From the **Cementerio de Recoleta** and **Centro Cultural Recoleta,** wind your way through Plaza Francia's market stalls (weekends) or past the couples lounging on the grass midweek and over Avenidas Pueyrredón and Libertador to the **Museo Nacional de Bellas Artes (MNBA),** with the world's biggest Argentine art collection. The colonnaded building behind it, over Avenida Figueroa Alcorta, is the University of Buenos Aires' **School of Law**—continue past it into Plaza Naciones Unidas and the giant metal flower sculpture **Floralis Generica.**

Art and Barrio Parque

Cross back over Avenida Figueroa Alcorta and weave through Plaza Uruguay and Plaza República de Chile. The white stone mansion on the other side of Libertador is the **Museo Nacional de Arte Decorativo.** Continue along Rufino de Elizalde, a curving cobbled street that's part of the Barrio Parque mini-neighborhood. Writer and socialite Victoria Ocampo commissioned the house at **Number 2831** as an homage to Le Corbusier. The architect, Alejandro Bustillo, also designed the French neoclassical building opposite it at **Number 2830,** now the Belgian embassy.

Other mansions line the rest of the street and adjoining Alejandro M. de Aguado, which leads you back to Avenida Figueroa Alcorta. The block-long brown building opposite is the **Palacio Alcorta,** built by an Italian, Mario Palanti, for an American automobile company, Chrysler, but now bearing a French name, the Museo Renault. Consecrated modern Latin American masters are on display next door at the **Museo de Arte Latinoamericano de Buenos Aires (MALBA),** and up-and-coming ones are at the **Daniel Maman** gallery at Libertador 2475, two blocks away down San Martín de Tours.

Los Bosques de Palermo

Steel yourself for two blocks along busy Avenida Libertador, then cross back into green space at Cavia: a diagonal route through Plaza Alemania takes you to the entrance of the **Jardín Japonés**—stop off to see the bonsai and carp. Then wander on through the **Parque Tres de Febrero** roughly following Avenidas Berro and Iraola to Infanta Isabel. Skirting the lake's south side takes you to the **Paseo del Rosedal,** a large rose garden. Stroll southeast through Plaza Holanda, parallel to Libertador. The white-marble column at the intersection with Sarmiento honors four Argentine regions (note the bronze allegories in the pool at the base), but is known as the **Monumento de los Españoles.** Turn right onto quiet República de la India, which flanks the **Buenos Aires Zoo**—you can glimpse century-old pavilions and some animals through the railings—or turn right when you hit Avenida Las Heras to the entrance on Plaza Francia.

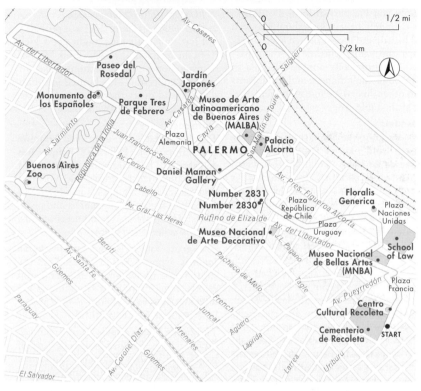

Where to Start:	Outside Cementerio de Recoleta at Junín 1760 in Recoleta
Time/Length:	3–5 hours (about 6 km/4 mi), depending on how many museums you visit
Where to Stop:	Entrance to Buenos Aires Zoo, intersection of Avenidas General Las Heras and Sarmiento, Plaza Francia
Best Time to Go:	Early morning if you're only interested in the parks, early afternoon to take in museums, too
Worst Time to Go:	When it's rainy or baking hot
Highlights:	First-floor galleries at MNBA and MALBA, Jardín Japonés, Paseo El Rosedal. In November: The mass of lilac-blue blossoms on the jacaranda trees.

BUENOS AIRES WITH KIDS

Family is a big part of local life. Porteños definitely believe kids should be seen and heard, and local children keep pretty much the same schedule as their parents. It's completely normal for kids to sit through adult dinners, and restaurants (and other diners) are fine with them dozing at the table.

Museums

Kids can go to the bank, shop at a supermarket, and play at adult jobs in the **Museo de los Niños** (Children's Museum) in Almagro. Although the museum is entirely in Spanish, activities like crawling through a large-scale plumbing system and operating a crane on a building site have universal appeal.

The motto of Recoleta's **Museo Participativo de las Ciencias** (Participative Science Museum) says it all—*Prohibido no Tocar,* or "Not touching is Forbidden." The colorful interactive displays—which explain how music, light, and electricity work—are hands-on enough for most kids to enjoy them despite the Spanish-only explanations. Better yet, it's on the first floor of the Centro Cultural Recoleta, so you can squeeze in some adult museum time, too.

Some of the dusty displays at the **Planetario Galileo Galilei** in Palermo's Parque Tres de Febrero seem almost as vintage as the gloriously retro building itself. Still, the night-sky projection room and the meteorite collection add up to a quick, fun outing. Cotton candy and popcorn machines near the duck ponds outside make for more earthly post-museum treats.

The few dinosaur skeletons at the **Museo Argentino de Ciencias Naturales** (*Argentine Museum of Natural Science* ✉ *Av. Angel Gallardo 470, Villa Crespo,*

☎ *11/4982–0306* ⊕ *www.macn.secyt.gov. ar* ✉ *5 pesos* ⊙ *Daily 2–7*) are probably old hat, but your kids might get a kick from the megafauna fossils (think 10-foot hamster bones). Some sections—like the mollusk collection—are housed in rooms so dark and dusty they're more likely to induce nightmares than curiosity.

Outdoors

The best place for unbridled running and jumping is Palermo's **Parque Tres de Febrero.** There are acres and acres of well-maintained greenery, and you can rent bicycles of all sizes (including ones with child seats), in-line skates, and pedal boats. There are also hamburger stands, balloon sellers, and clowns.

The gross factor is high at the **Jardín Japonés,** where you can actually pet the slimy koi carp swimming in ornamental ponds. Even more back-to-nature is the unkempt **Reserva Ecológica**—*guided* moonlight walks are an extra thrill.

The **Zoo de Buenos Aires** is home to pumas, tapirs, llamas, *aguarrá guazús* (a kind of wolf), and *yacarés* (caymans). And these are just some of the South American animals here that your kids might never have seen.

Adrenaline

The rides at **Parque de la Costa** (✉ *Vivanco 1509, Tigre* ☎ *11/4002–6000* ⊕ *www. parquedelacosta.com.ar* ✉ *80–100 pesos* ⊙ *Jan. and Feb., Tues.–Sun. 11–9; Mar.–Nov., Fri.–Sun. 11–7*), Buenos Aires' only theme park, are perfectly pitched for kids and tweens. The three most extreme roller coasters aren't the world's scariest, but they can keep older adrenaline junkies occupied for a while, and relatively small lines mean you can keep going back for more.

You know you'll never be able to beat your kids on the Playstation. Go retro and give yourself a sporting chance with a Scalectrix championship at **Añe** (⊠ *Scalabrini Ortíz 818, Palermo Viejo* ☎ *11/4775–5165* ⊕ *www.anie-slot.com. ar* ⊠ *6–16 pesos per 30 mins.* ☉ *Tues. and Thurs. 2–11 , Wed. and Fri. 2–6, Sun. 10 am–midnight*). There can be long waits for a turn on its five large-scale electric miniature car-racing tracks on weekends, so come midweek if your little racers are impatient.

Getting Around

Your kids might not be into the city's crowded subways, but there are other fun forms of travel in Buenos Aires. Horse-drawn carriages (called *mateos*) line up outside the Zoo de Buenos Aires and take you on a ride around the Parque Tres de Febrero.

Trams once ran through most of the city. The **Asociación Amigos del Tranvía** (⊠ *Emilio Mitre 500, at José Bonifacio, Caballito* ☎ *11/4431–1073* ⊕ *www.tranvia.org. ar* ☉ *Dec.–Feb., Sat. 5–8:30, Sun. 10–1 and 5–8:30; Mar.–Nov., Sat. 4–7:30, Sun. 10–1 and 4–7:30* Ⓜ *E to Emilio Mitre*) has saved some of the original carriages and operates free rides through the streets of the Caballito neighborhood on weekends.

For Treats

When it comes to rewarding—or bribing—their kids, porteño parents are unanimous: *helado* (ice cream) is the way to go. There are shops on nearly every block, but classy chains Freddo, Un'Altra Volta, and Persicco do the creamiest scoops. Children's menus aren't common in Buenos Aires: local kids usually eat the same as adults, in smaller portions. One exception to the rule is Canté Pri (⊠ *Charcas*

5216, Palermo ☎ *11/4777–7236* ⊕ *www. cantepri.com* ☉ *Fri. 4–8 pm, Sat. noon–midnight, Sun. noon–8 pm* Ⓜ *D to Palermo*), a kiddie café that also serves food to grown-ups.

Entertainment

You don't need Spanish-language skills to enjoy *circo* (circus), *títeres* (puppets), and *rock para chicos* (kiddie rock). For listings, check the "Chicos" section in the back of local papers or the online Spanish-language magazines *Revista Planetario* (⊕ *www.revistaplanetario.com.ar*) and *Kids en la Web* (⊕ *www.kidsenlaweb. com.ar*).

Street performers abound on squares and pedestrian malls and around outdoor markets. The Abasto and Solar de la Abadía malls have supervised playrooms where you can leave little ones while you shop.

FREE
(OR ALMOST FREE)

Free Art

It costs absolutely nothing to visit what is arguably the best collection of Argentine art in the world: Recoleta's **Museo Nacional de Bellas Artes** is free all week. Entrance to most other state-run museums is less than a dollar or two.

Take in art both old and new on Tuesdays, when you can gaze for free at the antique furnishings of the **Museo Nacional de Arte Decorativo** and the contemporary works at the **MAMBA**. Wednesdays and Saturdays, go for handicrafts at the **Museo de Artes Plásticas Eduardo Sívori**; it's in the middle of the Palermo Woods.

Check out colonial art downtown in Retiro free of charge on Thursday at the **Museo de Arte Hispanoamericano Isaac Fernández Blanco**. The one serious artistic saving you can make is at the **MALBA**, in Palermo, which reduces its 22-peso entry fee to 10 pesos on Wednesday—expect to compete for floor space, though.

Browsing the choice contemporary Argentine art displayed in galleries like **Galería Ruth Benzacar** in the Microcentro, **Daniel Abate** and **Rubbers** in Recoleta, and **Braga Menéndez** in Palermo Hollywood is totally free, although you'd fork out thousands to buy any of it. Try Palermo Viejo's **Galería Catena Foster** for contemporary photography, gratis.

Free History

It costs thousands to spend an afterlife in the **Cementerio de la Recoleta,** but nothing to spend an afternoon or morning there. San Telmo is the best barrio for a free local history lesson: churches and traditional houses (many now antiques shops) are some of the historic buildings open to the public.

Free Touring

The popular English-language walking tours operated by **BA Free Tours** (⊕ *www. bafreetours.com*) are totally gratis. You might want to tip the enthusiastic young guides at the end, however. To take part, join the group that gathers around the green-shirted guides Monday through Saturday at 11 am in Plaza del Congreso and 5 pm in Plaza San Martín, for the tours of El Centro and Recoleta, respectively.

Turismo Buenos Aires, the city's official tourism body, has a large range of self-guided walking tours (organized by neighborhood and by theme) on its Web site, ⊕ *www.bue.gov.ar*. Their detailed downloadable audioguides are free, too. Enthusiastic local volunteers are your guides on the free city tours run by Cicerones de Buenos Aires. The two-hour historical walks run by tour group **Eternautas** in different parts of town on alternate Saturdays cost only about 20 pesos.

Cheap Entertainment

During January and February there are free outdoor concerts and festivals in parks around the city. Wednesday is reduced-price day at every cinema in town; many also do cut-price tickets Monday through Thursday and for the first screening of each day.

Instead of forking out hundreds at a fancy "for export" tango show, head to a low-key *milonga* (⇨ *Tango in Chapter 4, After Dark)*. The cover charge is usually only around 25 pesos, drinks are cheap, and the dancing is excellent. Tangoing street performers also abound on Calle Florida, in Plazas Dorrego and Serrano, and around the Caminito.

MASTER CLASS

Buenos Aires has excellent universities and higher education establishments that accept foreign students.

Government-run Web site **Estudiar en Argentina** (⊕ *estudiarenargentina.siu.edu. ar*) contains information on exchange programs and long-term study.

Learn Spanish

Language schools are popping up all over town. Many advertise online or in the *Buenos Aires Herald,* but not all employ qualified teachers. The city tourism site (⊕ *www.bue.gov.ar*) has reliable school listings on the "Students" page of its "Profiles" section, and below are some we recommend.

Two of the most established Spanish schools are affiliated with the Universidad de Buenos Aires. Teaching levels at both are excellent, and prices are reasonable, but be aware that you generally need to enroll in advance and to be available for level testing several days before classes start.

The **Centro Universitario de Idiomas** (⊕ *www. studyinbuenosaires.edu.ar*) runs four-week (three hours per weekday) courses year round at ten different levels in several locations. Their one-week Buenos Aires Impact course is designed to give travelers survival Spanish. The school also organizes one-on-one sessions, homestays, volunteering opportunities, and cultural activities.

The classes at the **Laboratorio de Idiomas** (⊕ *www.idiomas.filo.uba.ar/extranjeros/ ingles/extranjeros.htm*) are popular with exchange students, but less practical for short-term stays. Semester-long courses of four hours per week start in March and August; intensive four-week courses of 15 hours per week start every two months.

They also run a Spanish certification program.

The approach at the nonprofit teaching organization **Asociación Argentina de Docentes de Español** (⊕ *www.espanol.org.ar*) is ideal if you're interested in grammar as well as communicating.

Private language school **Academia Buenos Aires** (⊕ *www.academiabuenosaires.com*) stands out for the range and flexibility of its classes. They also offer combination Spanish and tango courses.

The lively four-day courses at **Español Andando** (⊕ *www.espanol-andando. com*) take place on the streets: a lesson on transport culminates with getting real information from a ticket salesperson, for example. Beginner and intermediate group courses are available, and private classes at all levels.

If you want to practice your Spanish but don't fancy proper classes, consider a language exchange. There are extensive listings and activities on the **Spanglish Exchange** Web site (⊕ *www. spanglishexchange.com*).

Learn Food and Wine

A local chef runs Latin American cooking classes in English at **Try2Cook** (⊕ *www. try2cook.com*), based in the southern suburb of Adrogué (transport here is provided). Argentine options include making empanadas and doing a full-blown *asado* (barbecue).

Private wine-tasting classes in English can be arranged by contacting stellar local sommelier school **CAVE** (⊕ *www.cave. com.ar*) several weeks before your trip.

Alex Audisio organizes tailor-made tastings of Argentine wine at **Terroir Fine Wines** (⊕ *www.terroir.com.ar*), one of the city's best wine shops.

WHO ARE THESE PEOPLE?

Buenos Aires has some lively inhabitants. Here are a few things you can expect of them:

It's All in the Hands

Like their Italian ancestors, many porteños gesture, rather than speak, half of their conversation. Brushing your chin outward with your hand means "I have no idea." Bunching up your fingers is "What on earth are you talking about?" Pulling down the skin under one eye says "Watch out."

Getting Physical

Porteños greet each other with an effusive kiss on the cheek (always to the left) and look for other opportunities that allow displays of affection. Even men follow this pattern and laugh at foreign males who refuse to do so, saying that they're insecure in their masculinity.

Hey Good-Looking

Locals claim porteño women are the most beautiful in the world, and in tribute the men have perfected the *piropo* (catcall). Comments range from corny compliments to highly witty—and mildly offensive—wordplays. Follow local women's cues and take it in stride.

Sweets for the Sweet

Even the tiniest espresso arrives with four packets of sugar (or sweetener), just one testament to the local sweet tooth. *Dulce de leche* (a milk-caramel spread) is another. It's practically a food group. Not only does it come in many desserts, but porteños also spread it on toast and—in the privacy of their kitchens—eat spoonfuls straight from the jar.

A Different Language

Porteños speak a very local version of Spanish. Instead of *"tú"* for "you," the archaic *"vos"* form is used, and "ll" and "y" are pronounced like "sh." A singsong

> **DID YOU KNOW?**
>
> Roughly 85% of the Argentine population is of European origin. Indeed, Buenos Aires locals refer to themselves as *porteños* because many of their forebears arrived by ship to this *port* town.

accent owes a lot to Italian immigrants; indeed, an Italian-influenced slang—called *lunfardo*—is ever-present.

Puppy Love

Porteños are big dog-lovers. Professional *paseaperros* (dog walkers) wander with packs of well-dressed hounds anchored to their waists. Most porteños seem to have excellent poop radar, too: though the streets are filled with dog mess, you rarely see anyone step in it.

Driving You Crazy

Crossing the street is an extreme sport: roads are packed, traffic rules are openly flaunted, drinking and driving is practically a norm, and porteños think seat belts are for sissies. Sadly, traffic accidents are the biggest cause of death in the city, but that hasn't caused local habits to change.

Rules Are Made to Be Broken

Most porteños see laws, rules, and regulations as quaint concepts invented mainly to give them the satisfaction of finding a way to evade them. Displaying *viveza criolla* (literally "native cunning" but really "rule-breaking ingenuity") is a matter of national pride.

ALL OF THE COW BUT THE MOO

Argentina is the world's capital of beef, and Buenos Aires the capital of Argentina. So does Buenos Aires have the world's best steak?

It's hard to say no after your first bite into a tender morsel of deeply flavored beef carefully charred by an open fire. Indeed, aside from the *estancias* (ranches) on the pampas grasslands themselves, Buenos Aires is probably the best place to eat in a *parrilla* (steak house). That said, it can be difficult, upon a first glance at the bewildering menu of a parrilla, to know where to begin. Merely speaking Spanish isn't enough: entire books have been written attempting to pin down which cuts of meat in Argentina correspond to which ones in the United States and Europe. There's much disagreement. The juicy *bife de chorizo,* for example, the king of Argentine steaks, is translated by some as a bone-in sirloin, by others as a rump steak—and it's not as if "sirloin steak" is well defined to begin with.

Don't worry about definitions. If you order a *parrillada*—everything but the kitchen sink—a sizzling platter will be brought to you. Don't be timid about trying the more unfamiliar pieces. The platter will usually include a salty, juicy link or two of *chorizo* (a large, spicy sausage), and a collection of *achuras* (innards), which some first-timers struggle with. King among them is the gently spicy and oozingly delicious *morcilla* (blood sausage—like the British black pudding or the French *boudin noir*); give it a chance. Even more challenging are the chewy *chinchulines* (coils of small intestine), which are best when crisped on the outside, and the strongly flavored *riñones* (kidneys). Although *mollejas* (sweetbreads) aren't usually part of a parrillada spread (they're

more expensive), don't miss their unforgettable taste and fatty, meltingly rich texture, like a meatier version of foie gras. You'll also want to try the rich *provoleta* (grilled provolone cheese sprinkled with olive oil and oregano) and garlic-soaked grilled red peppers.

You can also skip the ready-made parrillada and instead order à la carte, as the locals often do. You might try the *vacio* (flank steak, roughly translated), a common cut that is flavorful but can also be tough, especially if overcooked. You may instead be seduced by the *lomo* (tenderloin or filet mignon), the softest and priciest cut, or the immortal *bife de chorizo,* always a safe bet. Both of those steaks are better when requested rare (*"vuelta y vuelta"*), or at the least medium-rare (*"jugoso"*).

But the true local favorite is the inimitable *asado de tira,* a rack of beef short ribs often cooked on a skewer over an open fire. Done properly, the asado brandishes the meatiest grass-fed flavor of all. For accompaniments, the classics are a mix-and-match salad and/or french fries. And don't forget that delicious Argentine red wine; Malbecs and Cabernets both pair well with the deeply flavored meat. And though the first time you visit a parrilla the mountain of meat might seem mind-bogglingly high, chances are that by the time you leave you'll be cleaning your plate and gnawing at the bones with the best of them.

—Robin Goldstein

ARGENTINA'S WINES

Argentina has transformed into an international wine powerhouse, becoming the fifth leading wine producer in the world. While most of Argentina's wine production is centered in Mendoza, a 12-hour car ride west of Buenos Aires in the Andes foothills, the coastal capital has its own wine attractions: boutique wine shops and wine bars, called *vinotecas*.

You may notice that wine shops and bars feature domestic wines almost exclusively. Why? Imported wine is often prohibitively expensive for Argentine consumers due to exchange rates. Fortunately for wine-loving travelers to the country, this means that excellent Argentine wines are available at bargain prices. It also means that you'll want to know something about the country's wines to help you make informed buying decisions.

A Little History

In the mid-19th century hundreds of thousands of Europeans immigrated to Argentina, bringing with them wine-grape vines, which they planted on the eastern flanks of the Andes Mountains in the region of Mendoza. Consumption of Mendoza's wine remained local for years, as the area was geographically isolated from big cities until late in the century. By the late 19th century a railroad connected Mendoza to Buenos Aires, and Mendoza's wine was traded throughout the country.

For the next 100 years vintners produced simple wines in accordance with local tastes and budgets. Finally, in the 1990s, the newly open economy sparked fresh interest in South American wines. Since then, big investments from France, Spain, Italy, the United States, and elsewhere have significantly improved growing and production practices, resulting in top-quality wines. Now there are more than 1,500 wineries in Argentina, and the country's wines are widely exported.

Growing Conditions

Argentina's wine band extends along the western border of the country, comprising 10 regions, from Salta in the north to the Rio Negro in Patagonia, at the country's southern end. The vineyards are clustered in irrigated plots in areas that would otherwise be desert. Most vines are planted at high elevations, between 2,000 and 3,000 feet above sea level. The climate here can be temperamental, so producers must be prepared for downpours, hailstorms, and scorching, dehydrating winds.

The most significant wine regions are Mendoza and San Juan, located in the middle of the country, which together account for about 90% of the country's wine production. Mendoza and San Juan are dry, temperate regions, with fewer than eight inches of rain per year, and temperatures that range from around 33°F in the winter to 94°F in the summer.

Wines to Try

Dozens of imported grape varieties—from popular Chardonnay to obscure Bonarda—are planted in Argentina. A large percentage of vineyard area is still planted with domestic grapes varieties like Criolla and Cereza, which yield basic table wines and grape juice. But international varieties are quickly replacing these historic grapes. Some of the most important types include the following:

Malbec: Just one sip of Argentina's most widely known wine evokes gauchos and tangos. Malbec is still a minor blending variety in France's Bordeaux wines, but the grape has become Argentina's signature varietal, and some say it finds its best expression here. Malbecs are deep-

colored, full-bodied wines, concentrated with plum and raspberry flavors.

Cabernet Sauvignon: Argentine Cabernets are full-bodied, with high acid and tannin, typically expressing bold black cherry and herbal notes. They're perfect with grilled steaks.

Red Blends: The red blends here may be mixtures of classic Bordeaux varietals—mainly Merlot, Cabernet Sauvignon, and Malbec—but they express the fruit-forward results typical of New World wines. Other red blends include nontraditional pairings like Italy's Sangiovese with Syrah.

Chardonnay: This international varietal can vary widely in its expression depending upon where it is grown. Some Argentina bottlings express citrus and honey flavors, while others are packed with tropical fruit. Most Chardonnays are oaked, so expect toasty, buttery notes as well.

Torrontés: Argentina's favorite white wine—considered an indigenous grape—has prominent aromatics of flowers and herbs in a full-bodied dry wine. Often tangy and lively, Torrontés is an excellent aperitif wine.

Wine Tasting Primer

Ordering and tasting wine—whether at a *vinoteca*, winery, or restaurant—is easy once you master a few simple steps.

Look: Hold your glass by the stem, raise it to the light, and take a close look at the wine in the glass. Note the wine's hue, color depth, and clarity. For white wine, is it greenish, yellow, or gold? For red wine, is it purplish, ruby, or garnet? For depth, is the wine's color pale, medium, or deep? Is the liquid clear or cloudy? (This is easiest to do if you can move the glass in front of a white background).

Sniff: Swirl the wine gently in the glass to intensify the scents, then sniff over the rim of the glass. What do you smell? Try to identify aromas like fruits (citrus, green fruit, black fruits), flowers (blossoms, honey), spices (sweet, pungent, herbal), vegetables (fresh or cooked), minerals (earth or wet stones), dairy (butter, cream), oak (toast, vanilla), or animal (leathery) notes. Are there any unpleasant notes, like mildew or wet dog that might indicate that the wine is "off"?

Sip: Take a first sip and swish the wine around your mouth for a few seconds to "prime" your palate, then swallow or spit it into a discard bucket. Then take another sip and begin to evaluate the wine. In the mouth, you experience sweetness on the tip of the tongue, acidity on the sides of the tongue, and tannins (an astringent, mouth-drying sensation) on the gums. Is the sipping experience pleasant, or is one of the wine's elements out of balance? Also consider the body—does the wine feel light in the mouth, or is there a sensation of richness? Are the flavors you taste consistent with the aromas you smelled? If you like the wine, try to pinpoint what you like about it, and vice versa if you don't like it. Most of all, take time to savor the wine as you're sipping it—the tasting experience may seem a little scientific, but the end goal is your enjoyment.

TANGO

"Life is a *milonga* (dance hall)," says one famous tango. "Life is an absurd wound," goes another. "I'm dying, dying just to dance," cries a third. When it comes to tango, emotions ride high. Whether you experience it through impassioned dancing or tortured lyrics, you'll find a mix of nostalgia, violence, and sensuality that reflects this city's spirit.

THE DANCE

At the turn of the 19th century, immigrants in the Buenos Aires neighborhood of La Boca began sharing rhythms and dance steps from their homelands. There's no consensus on what elements of tango come from where, but many agree it's a fusion of African-Uruguayan candombe, Spanish-Cuban habanera, and polkas and mazurkas.

Tango's mood is said to be one of nostalgia and loss. Indeed, those who learn tango in a dance school before they come to Buenos Aires may be homesick for the choreographed moves they learned; here tango is all improvisation and subtlety and the rules are always changing.

There are plenty of English-speaking instructors and pre-milonga practice sessions to get you up to speed on tango Buenos Aires style. When you're ready, choose a milonga depending on the atmosphere you're looking for. *For more, see "The Dance of Buenos Aires" feature, and Instruction and Milongas under Tango, in Chapter 4, After Dark.*

THE SHOWS

If you'd prefer a more passive appreciation of this fanciest of footwork, fear not: there are options that won't require significant coordination. For many, the tango experience begins and ends with *cena-shows*. These include drinks and a three-course dinner, and are entirely aimed at tourists (the only locals are businesspeople entertaining clients). Some are flashy affairs known as *tango de fantasía* in expensive, purpose-built clubs—expect sequined costumes, gelled hairdos, and high-kicking moves. Others are relatively lower-key in older venues that once catered to porteños before tango tourism took off.

Best Bets for Shows

Not all shows are created equal; below are a few suggestions to guide you. *For more details see Chapter 4, After Dark.*

Atmospheric surroundings: Bar Sur for the worn checkered floor and Old World bar; **Mansión Dandi Royal** for the art nouveau architecture.

Blowing the bank: Rojo Tango for the gorgeous surroundings—and tangoers; **Madero Tango** for varied, professional performances and first-rate food.

Least tacky: Querandí for classic café surroundings and polished shows; **El Viejo Almacén** for pedigree (founded by tango legend Edmundo Rivero) and high energy.

Shamelessly over-the-top: Señor Tango for fishnetted glitz and over-the-top embracing of stereotypes.

THE MUSIC

The average porteño is much more likely to go see tango musicians than tango dancers. Offerings range from orchestras churning out tunes as was done in Carlos Gardel's day to sexy, bluesy vocals from divas like Adriana Varela; from pared-down revisitings of the tango underworld by groups like 34 Puñaladas to anarchic young collectives like La Orquesta Típica

Fernández Fierro. For tango that packs a punch, look out for electronic tango fusion from groups like Gotan Project and Bajofondo Tango Club.

Best Bets for Music
The places below are reviewed fully in Chapter 4, After Dark.

Most laid back: La Maldita Milonga for a hip, clubby vibe; **Bar de Roberto** for gin-guzzling old-timers and impromptu performances; **Club Atlético Fernández Fierro** for the rootsy eponymous orchestra that runs it

Most traditional: Gran Café Tortoni for the historic setting and consistently excellent performances; **La Ideal** for the old-school orchestra and gorgeous surroundings.

Most modern: La Trastienda for performances by stellar soloists and the occasional electrotango show.

Tango Playlist
The tango never shook off its edgy origins: early lyrics ran the gamut from lewd to pornographic. Later songs are peppered with references to infidelity, crime, and cocaine. And there's tango's place in politics: some lyrics have encoded criticisms of the government, others are piercing social commentaries. For many, the richly metaphoric use of street slang elevates tango to a poetic form. Here's a selection to get you started. You can download most of them online.

Late 1800s–Early 1900s: "La morocha," Roberto Firpo y Su Quarteto Alma de Bohemio

1910s–20s: "La cumparsita," Juan D'Arienzo y Su Orquesta; "Caminito," Augustín Magaldi

1930s (The Golden Age): "El día que me quieras" "Por una cabeza," and "Volver,"Carlos Gardel; "Se dice de mí," Tita Merello; "Cambalache," Agustín Irusta

1940s–50s: "Naranjo en flor," Floreal Ruiz; "La última curda," Edmundo Rivero; "Que me van a hablar de amor," Julio Sosa

1960s–80s: "Adiós Nonino," Astor Piazzolla; "Balada para un loco," Roberto Goyeneche

Today: "Garganta con arena," Adriana Varela; "Santa María (del Buen Ayre)," Gotan Project; "Canción desesperada," Orquesta Típica Fernández Fierro

CARLOS GARDEL

Carlos Gardel (1887 or 1890–1935)

Toting his trademark fedora, the face of Carlos Gardel oozes charm on walls and signs all over Buenos Aires, where he grew up and became a tango superstar. Gardel died tragically on June 24, 1935, at the height of his fame, when his plane crashed in Medellín, Colombia. Thousands followed his funeral cortege along Avenida Corrientes. Pay *your* respects at his grave in the *Cementerio de Chacarita* or at *Museo Casa Carlos Gardel.*

GOOD MARKETING SKILLS

The array of open-air *ferias* (markets) in Buenos Aires testifies to the fact that locals enjoy stall-crawling as much as visitors do. Argentina holds its craftspeople, both traditional and contemporary, in high esteem. The selections include crafts, art, antiques, curios, clothing, jewelry, and housewares; stalls are often attended by the artists themselves. Bargaining isn't the norm, although you may get a small discount for buying lots of items.

The **Feria de San Pedro Telmo** packs a small San Telmo square every Sunday. Elbow your way through the crowds to pick through antiques and curios of varying vintages as well as tango memorabilia, or watch dolled-up professional tango dancers perform on the surrounding cobbled streets. The unofficial "stalls" (often just a cloth on the ground) of young craftspeople stretch several blocks up Defensa, away from the market proper. As it gets dark, the square turns into a milonga, where quick-stepping locals show you how it's done. ⊠ *Plaza Dorrego, Humberto I, and Defensa, San Telmo* ⊕ *www.feriadesantelmo.com* ⊙ *Sun. 10–dusk* Ⓜ *E to Independencia, then walk 9 blocks east along Independencia to Defensa. Alternatively, A to Plaza de Mayo, D to Catedral, or E to Bolívar, then walk 8 blocks south on Bolívar.*

In the heart of colorful La Boca, the **Feria de Artesanías de la Plaza Vuelta de Rocha (Caminito)** showcases local artists all week long. You can find attractive port scenes in watercolors as well as stylish photographs of the neighborhood's old houses, though don't expect any budding Picassos. The market expands on weekends with stalls selling handicrafts and tacky souvenirs. As shoppers here are almost exclusively tourists, prices tend to be overambitious—sometimes irritatingly so. ⊠ *Av. Pedro de Mendoza and Caminito, La Boca* ⊙ *Art market daily 10–dusk; craft market weekends 10–dusk.*

The sprawling **Feria Artesanal de la Recoleta**—known universally as Feria Plaza Francia—winds through several linked squares outside the Recoleta Cemetery. Artisans sell handmade clothes, jewelry, and housewares as well as traditional crafts. ⊠ *Avs. Libertador and Pueyrredón, La Recoleta* ⊕ *www.feriaplazafrancia.com* ⊙ *Weekends 11–dusk.*

The business conducted in hip Palermo Viejo's **Feria de Plaza Cortázar** (also known as Plaza Serrano) rivals that done in the neighborhood's trendy boutiques. In a small square—which is actually round—artisans sell wooden toys, ceramics, and funky jewelry made of stained glass or vintage buttons. This is also a great place to buy art: the railings around a playground here act as an open-air gallery for Palermo artists, and organizers control the quality of art on display. The feria continues on the sidewalks of Honduras and Serrano, which intersect at the square, and inside the bars on the square itself, which push their tables and chairs aside to make room for clothing and accessory designers: expect to find anything from cute cotton underwear and one-off T-shirts to clubbing dresses. Quality is often low, but so are prices. ⊠ *Plazoleta Cortázar (Plaza Serrano) at Honduras and Serrano, Palermo Viejo* ⊙ *Weekends 11–dusk.*

On the edge of Palermo Hollywood lies the large warehouse sheltering the **Mercado de las Pulgas** *(Flea Market)*, packed with furniture on its second (or third or fourth) time around. You won't come across any Louis XV, but original pieces from the 1940s, '50s, and '60s may turn

out to be (relative) bargain investments. Lighting up your life is a cinch: choose from the many Venetian-glass chandeliers, or go for a chrome-and-acrylic mushroom lamp. If your taste is more rustic, there's also a sizable selection of hefty farmhouse-style tables and cabinets in oak and pine. Don't be deceived by the stalls' simple-looking set-up: vendors are used to dealing with big-name local customers, and can often arrange overseas shipping. ⊠ *Alvarez Thomas between Dorrego and Concepción Arenales, Palermo Hollywood* ⊘ *Daily 10–dusk.*

On weekends upscale craftspeople transform a posh Belgrano square into the **Feria de Artesanías de Belgrano**. Nickel silver (a silver-colored alloy of copper and nickel) is a popular material here, for both jewelry and adornment on items like boxes for storing tea bags. You'll also find leather sandals and clogs, knitted ponchos, and wooden toys. Around Christmas this is a great place to buy nativity scenes and tree ornaments. ⊠ *Av. Juramento at Cuba, Belgrano* ⊘ *Weekends midday–dusk.*

Locavores, slow foodies, and socially conscious cooks stock their pantries at **El Galpón**, a bright yellow warehouse in Chacarita. It began as a barter market at the height of Argentina's 2001 financial crisis, but these days the organic veggies, fair-trade coffee, homemade preserves, and artisan cheeses are traded for hard currency. ⊠ *Federico Lacroze 4171, Chacarita* ⊕ *www.elgalpon.org.ar* ⊘ *Wed. and Sat. 9–6.*

The best handicrafts in town and a vaguely authentic gaucho atmosphere make the trek west to the traditional **Feria de Mataderos** well worth the effort. Stalls sell great-value matés, *asado* knives, *boleadoras* (gaucho lassos), and leather

goods, and there are usually traditional dance performances. Look out for real-life gauchos wearing woolen berets, scarves, and baggy pants wandering around with a horse or two in tow. Part of the experience is chomping through a *vaciopán* (dripping steak sandwich) from the immense barbecue; wash it down with a plastic beaker of *vino patero* (semi-sweet red wine). The subte (subway) doesn't go to Mataderos; take Bus 126 from outside Retiro train station, or take a taxi (about 35 pesos from downtown). ⊠ *Lisandro de la Torre at Av. de los Corrales, Mataderos* ⊕ *www.feriademataderos.com.ar* ⊘ *Sun. 10–dusk.*

FASHION FORWARD

The stars of Argentine fashion have much in common with the country's top soccer players: they're as highly trained and technically proficient as their European counterparts, but there's a freshness and flair to their game that the weary old countries just don't have. And, of course, getting them into your wardrobe (or onto your team) can be a relative bargain.

On the Runway

Technically speaking, **Buenos Aires Fashion Week** (⊕ *www.bafweek.com.ar*) is two fashion half-weeks. Fall–winter collections are presented in February, and spring–summer in August, at La Rural convention center. Entrance costs around 30 pesos, and there's a good chance of getting into most shows.

Each March local trendspotters and international buyers descend hungrily on the **Feria Puro Diseño** (⊕ *www.feriapurodiseno. com.ar*), an expo of works by up-and-coming local designers held at La Rural convention center. Clothing and accessories are the focus, but housewares, lighting, and textiles are also included.

Big in Buenos Aires

There's no question who makes the best little black dresses—and sharp black suits—in town. In fact just about every garment that comes off **Pablo Ramírez's** (⊕ *www.pabloramirez.com.ar*) cutting table is black, and they're also exquisitely tailored, with waspish waists and structured draping that ooze '40s Hollywood glamour. He regularly designs costumes for highbrow theater productions, and his clothes have been exhibited in three Buenos Aires museums.

Jessica Trosman (⊕ *www.trosman.com*) has shown collections in Paris, been pronounced one of the 250 most influential people in the future of fashion by *i-D* magazine, and had her work featured in Taschen's *Fashion Now 2* and Phaidon's *Sample* books. Her signature fabric is richly colored cotton T-shirting, which she transforms into highly draped tops and dresses whose futuristic simplicity is both chic and slightly strange.

It's not just fabulous clothes **Martín Churba** creates, but also the textiles they're made of (his brand name, **Tramando** [⊕ *www. tramando.com*], means both "weaving" and "plotting"). His pleats, floaty folds, and attention to detail recall the best Japanese designers.

Eye-popping colors, big prints, and unusual texture combinations characterize the light-hearted looks of **Benito Fernández** (⊕ *www.benitofernandez.com. ar*). Fans of his dramatic dresses include Sarah Jessica Parker, who requested that his Etnia collection be included in the *Sex and the City 2* wardrobe.

Her market presence is as subtle as the earthy neutrals she favors, but **Cora Groppo**'s (⊕ *www.coragroppo.com*) polished urban designs are quiet showstoppers. Her floaty dresses, skinny pants, and sleek overcoats marry ambitiously stark lines and unusual textures with eminent wearability.

Min Agostini (⊕ *www.minagostini.com.ar*) "builds" her designs on mannequins, and the results are tunics, dresses, and wraps that look like a *Star Wars* wardrobe collision between Princess Amidala and the whole Jedi crew. Her clothes have been displayed in the windows of Harrods of London.

THE SPORTING LIFE

Get Your Kicks

Tens of thousands of ecstatic fans jump up and down in unison, roaring modified cumbia classics to the beat of carnival drums; crazed supporters sway atop 10-foot fences between the stands and the field as they drape the barbed wire with their team's flags; showers of confetti and sulfurous smoke from colorful flares fill the air. The occasion? Just another day's *fútbol* (soccer) match in Argentina.

For most Argentineans soccer is a fervent passion. The national team is one of the world's best, and the World Cup can bring the country to a standstill as workers gather in cafés and bars to live out the nation's fate via satellite. Feelings also run high during the biannual local championships, when rivalry between *hinchas* (fans) gets heated. In a country where people joke that if soccer great Diego Maradona were to run for president he'd win hands down, fútbol is the subject of endless debate, fiery dispute, suicidal despair, love, and hate.

Matches are held year-round and are seriously exciting—and sometimes dangerous. You're safest in the *platea* (preferred seating area), which starts at around 60 pesos and increases depending on location and the importance of the match, rather than in the chaotic 25- to 30-peso *popular* (standing room) section. Be careful what you wear—fans carry their colors with pride, and not just on flags and team shirts. Expect to see painted faces, hundreds of tattoos, and even women's underwear with the colors of the best-known teams: Boca Juniors (blue and gold) and their archrivals River Plate (red and white), as well as Independiente (red), Racing (light blue and white), and San Lorenzo (red and blue). The

no-man's-land that separates each team's part of the stadium, the drum-banging antics of hooligan mafias known as the *barra brava,* and the heavy police presence at matches are a reminder of how seriously the game is taken.

You can buy tickets at long lines at the stadiums up to four days before matches or from the teams' official Web sites.

Skip the lines and the hassle by buying match packages through **Tangol** (☎ *4312–7276* ⊕ *www.tangol.com*). These include well-located platea seats, transport, and a soccer-loving guide. Expect to pay more to see the most popular teams.

Walls exploding with huge, vibrant murals of insurgent workers, famous inhabitants of La Boca, and fútbol greats splashed in blue and gold let you know that the **Estadio Boca Juniors** is at hand. The stadium that's also known as La Bombonera (meaning candy box, supposedly because the fans' singing reverberates as it would inside a candy tin) is the home of Argentina's most popular club. Boca Juniors' history is completely tied to the port neighborhood. The nickname, *xeneizes,* is a mangling of *genovés* (Genovese), reflecting the origins of most immigrants to the Boca area. Blue and gold bedeck the stadium's fiercely banked seating.

Inside the stadium is **El Museo de la Pasión Boquense** (The Museum of Boca Passion), a modern, two-floor space that chronicles Boca's rise from neighborhood club in 1905 to its current position as one of the world's best teams. Trophies, videos, shirts, match histories, and a hall of fame make up the rest of the circuit, together with a huge mural of Maradona, Boca's most beloved player.

The extensive stadium tour is worth the extra money. Lighthearted guides take

you all over the stands as well as to press boxes, locker rooms, underground tunnels, and the emerald grass of the field itself. ⊠ *Brandsen 805, at del Valle Iberlucea, La Boca,* ☎ *11/4309–4700 stadium; 11/4362–1100 museum* ⊕ *www. museoboquense.com* ▨ *Museum: 35 pesos. Museum and stadium: 50 pesos* ☽ *Museum daily 11–6 except when Boca plays at home; stadium tours hourly 11–5; English usually available, call ahead.*

Horse Around

Combine the horsey inclinations of Argentina's landed elite with the country's general sporting prowess, and what do you get? The world's best polo players. The game may be as posh as it gets, but most local sports fans take begrudging pride in the stunning athletic showmanship displayed by *polistas* like 10-goaler Adolfo Cambiaso or Ralph Lauren pinup Nacho Figueras.

Major polo tournaments take place at the **Campo Argentino de Polo** (*Argentine Polo Field* ⊠ *Av. del Libertador 4000, at Dorrego, Palermo*). Admission to autumn (March–May) and spring (September–December) matches is free. The much-heralded Campeonato Argentino Abierto (Argentine Open Championship) takes place in November; admission to the whole championship starts at 160 pesos. (They only sell admission to individual matches if there are leftover tickets.) You can buy tickets in advance through **Ticketek** (☎ *11/5237–7200* ⊕ *www.ticketek. com.ar*) or at the polo field on the day of the event.

Tour company **Tangol** (☎ *4312–7276* ⊕ *www.tangol.com*) offers ticket packages to the Argentine Open and other major polo matches, which include a guide and a shuttle to and from your hotel. You get even closer to the action on their all-day polo tours to a club on the outskirts of Buenos Aires, which include a visit to the stables, a polo demonstration, a horseback ride, and an asado lunch.

For polo match information, contact the **Asociación Argentina de Polo** (☎ *11/44777– 8005* ⊕ *www.aapolo.com*).

As well as polo players and polo ponies, Argentina also breeds swift racehorses, prized throughout the world.

Catch the Thoroughbreds in action at the **Hipódromo Argentino de Palermo** (⊠ *Av. del Libertador 4101, Palermo,* ☎ *11/4779– 2800* ⊕ *www.palermo.com.ar*). Major races like the Gran Premio Nacional (nicknamed the Argentine Derby and held in November) pull a crowd.

Tee Up

The 18-hole municipal course, **Campo de Golf de la Ciudad de Buenos Aires** (⊠ *Tornquist 6397, Palermo* ☎ *11/4772–7261*), is between Palermo and Belgrano. It's open Tuesday through Sunday from 7:30 to 5 for a 40-peso greens fee.

If you want a range with a view, **Costa Salguero Golf** (⊠ *Av. Costanera Rafael Obligado at Jerónimo Salguero, Palermo* ☎ *11/4805–4734*) is right on the river and includes a driving range (50 balls for 30 pesos), pitch 'n' putt (40 pesos for 18 holes), as well as club and ball hire.

For more information, contact the **Asociación Argentina de Golf** (*Argentine Golf Association* ☎ *11/4325–1113* ⊕ *www. aag.com.ar*).

A PASSIONATE HISTORY   by Victoria Patience

If there's one thing Argentinians have learned from their history, it's that there's not a lot you can count on. Fierce—often violent—political, economic, and social instability have been the only constants in the story of a people who seem never to be able to escape that famous Chinese curse, "May you live in interesting times."

Although most accounts of Argentinian history begin 500 years ago with the arrival of the conquistadors, humans have been living in what is now Argentina for around 13,000 years. They created the oldest recorded art in South America—a cave of handprints in Santa Cruz, Patagonia (c. 7500 BC)—and eventually became part of the Inca Empire.

Spanish and Portuguese sailors came in the early 16th century, including Ferdinand Magellan. The Spanish were forced out 300 years later by locals hungry for independence. Though autonomous on paper, in practice the early republic depended heavily on trade with Europe.

Conflict and civil war wracked the United Provinces of the South as the region struggled to define its political identity and the economic model it would follow.

Spanish and Italian immigrants arrived in the 20th century, changing Argentina's population profile forever. Unstable politics characterized the rest of the century, which saw the rise and fall of Juan Perón and a series of increasingly bloody military dictatorships. Nearly 30 years of uninterrupted democracy have passed since the last junta fell, an achievement Argentinians value hugely.

(left) Ferdinand Magellan (c. 1400–1521)
(right) Stamp featuring Evita

(top left) Cave paintings, Cueva de las Manos, Santa Cruz; (top right) Río de la Plata aboriginals, pictured by Hendrick Ottsen; (bottom) Relief detail, San Ignacio Miní Mission, Misiones Province.

PRE-1500
PRE-CONQUEST/ INCA

Argentina's original inhabitants were a diverse group of indigenous peoples. Their surroundings defined their lifestyles: nomadic hunter-gatherers lived in Patagonia and the Pampas, while the inhabitants of the northeast and northwest were largely farming communities. The first foreign power to invade the region was the Inca Empire, in the 15th century. Its roads and tribute systems extended over the entire northwest, reaching as far south as some parts of modern-day Mendoza.

1500—1809
BIRTH OF THE COLONY

European explorers first began to arrive at the River Plate area in the early 1500s, and in 1520 Ferdinand Magellan sailed right down the coast of what is now Argentina and on into the Pacific. Buenos Aires was founded twice: Pedro de Mendoza's 1536 attempt led to starving colonists turning to cannibalism before running for Asunción; Juan de Garay's attempt in 1580 was successful. Conquistadors of Spanish origin came from what are now Peru, Chile, and Paraguay and founded other cities. The whole area was part of the Viceroyalty of Peru until

1776, when the Spanish king Carlos III decreed present-day Argentina, Uruguay, Paraguay, and most of Bolivia to be the Viceroyalty of the Río de la Plata. Buenos Aires became the main port and the only legal exit point for silver from Potosí. Smuggling grew as fast as the city itself. In 1806–07 English forces tried twice to invade Argentina. Militia from Buenos Aires fought them off with no help from Spain, inciting ideas of independence among *criollos* (Argentinian-born Spaniards, who had fewer rights than those born in Europe).

(left) Julio Roca
(right) Monument to
General San Martín;

BIRTH OF THE NATION: INDEPENDENCE AND THE CONSTITUTION

1810—1860s

Early-19th-century proto-Argentinians were getting itchy for independence after the American Revolution. On May 25, 1810, Buenos Aires' leading citizens ousted the last Spanish viceroy. A series of elected juntas and triumvirates followed while military heroes José de San Martín and Manuel Belgrano won battles that allowed the Provincias Unidas de América del Sur to declare independence in Tucumán on July 9, 1816. San Martín went on to liberate Chile and Peru.

Political infighting marked the republic's first 40 years. The conflict centered on control of the port. Inhabitants of Buenos Aires wanted a centralist state run from the city, a position known as *unitario*, but landowners and leaders in the provinces wanted a federal state with greater Latin American integration. The federal side won when Juan Manuel de Rosas came to power: he made peace with indigenous leaders and gave rights to marginal social sectors like gauchos, although his increasingly iron-fisted rule later killed or outlawed the opposition. The centralist constitution established on his downfall returned power to the land-owning elite.

RISE OF THE MODERN STATE

1860—1942

Argentina staggered back and forth between political extremes on its rocky road to modern statehood. Relatively liberal leaders alternated with corrupt warlord types. The most infamous of these was Julio Roca, whose military campaigns massacred most of Argentina's remaining indigenous populations in order to seize the land needed to expand the cattle ranching and wheat farming. Roca also sold off services and resources to the English and started the immigration drive that brought millions of Europeans to Argentina between 1870 and 1930.

TIMELINE

Coup ends
privitization

Perón elected
president

1930

1940

1950

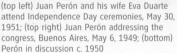

(top left) Juan Perón and his wife Eva Duarte attend Independence Day ceremonies, May 30, 1951; (top right) Juan Perón addressing the congress, Buenos Aires, May 6, 1949; (bottom) Perón in discussion c. 1950

THE RISE AND FALL OF PERONISM

1942–1973

A 1943 coup ended a decade of privatization that had caused the gap between rich and poor to grow exponentially. One of the soldiers involved was a little-known general named Juan Domingo Perón. He rose through the ranks of the government as quickly as he had through those of the army. Uneasy about Perón's growing popularity, other members of the military government imprisoned him, provoking a wave of uprisings that led to his release and swept him to the presidency as head of the newly formed labor party in 1946.

Mid-campaign, he quietly married the young B-movie actress he'd been living with, Eva Duarte, soon to be known universally as "Evita." Their idiosyncratic, his'n'hers politics hinged on a massive personality cult. Together, they rallied the masses with their cries for social justice, political sovereignty, economic independence, and Latin American unity. Then, while he was busy improving worker's rights and trying to industrialize Argentina, she set about press-ganging Argentina's landed elite into funding her social aid program. Their tireless efforts to close the gap between rich

and poor earned them the slavish devotion of Argentina's working classes and the passionate hatred of the rich. But everything began to go wrong when Evita died of uterine cancer in 1952. By 1955, the Marshall Plan in Europe reduced Argentina's export advantage, and the dwindling economy was grounds for Perón being ousted by another military coup. For the next 18 years, both he and his party were illegal in Argentina—mentioning his name or even whistling the Peronist anthem could land you in prison.

(top left) Leopoldo Galtieri led the last military dictatorship in Argentina. (top right) Argentina military junta during the Falkland's War; (bottom right) Argentine prisoners of war—Port Stanley;

DICTATORSHIP, STATE TERRORISM & THE FALKLANDS

1973–1983

The two civilian presidencies that followed both ended in fresh military coups until Perón was allowed to return in 1973. Despite falling out with left-wing student and guerrilla groups who had campaigned for him in his absence, he still won another election by a landslide. However, one problematic year later, he died in office. His farcical successor was the vice-president, an ex-cabaret dancer known as Isabelita, who was also Perón's third wife. Her chaotic leadership was brought to an end in 1976 by yet another military

coup widely supported by civil society. The succession of juntas that ruled the country called their bloody dictatorship a "process of national reorganization"; these days it's referred to as state-led terrorism.

Much of the world seemingly ignored the actions of Argentina's government during its six-year reign of terror. Throughout the country, students, activists, and any other undesirable element were kidnapped and tortured in clandestine detention centers. Many victims' children were stolen and given up for adoption by pro-military families after their parents' bodies

had been dumped in the River Plate. More than 30,000 people "disappeared" and thousands more went into exile. Government ministries were handed over to private businessmen. Massive corruption took external debt from $7 million to $66 million. In 1982, desperate for something to distract people with, the junta started war with Britain over the Islas Malvinas, or Falkland Islands. The disastrous campaign lasted just four months and, together with increasing pressure from local and international human rights activitsts, led to the downfall of the dictatorship.

TIMELINE   Menem elected| president   State of emergency declared| Cristina Kirchner re-elected
                                                                                                    Bicentenary|
|Falklands War   Economic revival|

INFLATION REACHES 3,000% 1990   ECONOMY IN TATTERS 2000   2010

(top) President Carlos Menem mobbed by the public; (top right) a revitalized economy brings new construction. (bottom) Argentine riot police drag away a demonstrator near the Casa Rosada in Buenos Aires.

1982—1999

RETURN OF DEMOCRACY

Celebrations marked the return to democracy. The main players in the dictatorship went on trial, but received relatively small sentences and were eventually pardoned. Inflation reached a terrifying 3,000% in 1988 and only stabilized when Carlos Menem became president the following year. Menem pegged the peso to the dollar, privatized services and resources, and even changed the constitution to extend his mandate. But despite an initial illusion of economic well-being, by the time Menem left office in 1999 poverty had skyrocketed, and the economy was in tatters.

2000—PRESENT

CRISIS & THE K YEARS

The longer-term results of Menem's policies came in December 2001, when the government tried to prevent a rush on funds by freezing all private savings accounts. Thousands of people took to the streets in protest; on December 20, the violent police response transformed the demonstrations into riots. President Fernando de la Rúa declared a state of emergency, then resigned, and was followed by four temporary presidents in almost as many days. When things finally settled, the peso had devaluated drastically, many people had lost their savings, and the future looked dark.

However, under the center-leftist government of Argentina's following president, Néstor Kirchner, the economy slowly reactivated. Kirchner reopened trials of high-ranking military officials and championed local industry. In a rather bizarre turn of political events, he was succeeded by his wife, Cristina Fernández. Her fiery speeches have inspired both devotion and derision, but her social and economic policies ensured her landslide re-election in 2011. Times may be better than a few years ago, but Argentinians have lived through so many political ups and downs that they never take anything for granted.

MADE IN ARGENTINA

There's no doubt that Argentinians are an inventive lot. And we're not talking about their skill in arguing their way out of parking tickets: several things you might not be able to imagine life without started out in Argentina.

Una *birome* (ballpoint pen)

BALLPOINT PEN

Although László Jósef Bíró was born in Hungary and first patented the ballpoint pen in Paris, it wasn't until he launched his company in Argentina in 1943 that his invention began to attract attention. As such, Argentinians claim the world's most useful writing instrument as their own.

BLOOD TRANSFUSION

Before ER there was Luis Agote, an Argentinian doctor who, in 1914, was one of the first to perform a blood transfusion using stored blood (rather than doing a patient-to-patient transfusion). The innovation that made the process possible was adding sodium citrate, an anticoagulant, to the blood.

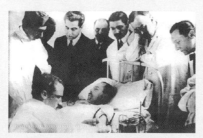

Luis Agote was one of the first to perform a nondirect blood transfusion, in Buenos Aires on November 9, 1914.

FINGERPRINTING

In 1891, Juan Vucetich, a Croatian-born officer of the Buenos Aires police force, came up with a system of classifying fingerprints. He went on to make the first-ever criminal arrest based on fingerprint evidence. Although his method has since been refined, it is still used throughout Latin America.

Huellas digitales (fingerprints)

■ Other useful Argentinian claims to fame include the first working helicopter (1916); the first one-piece floor mop (1953); and the first one-use-only hypodermic syringe (1989).

Buenos Aires Neighborhoods

WORD OF MOUTH

"Each day I walked in wider circles, discovering more places in San Telmo I wanted to know better—little theaters, the Spanish film club, hidden markets. I wanted to wake up again in this apartment with the French doors opening to . . . the sun, listening to the sounds of morning, sidewalks being washed, people on the way to work."

—santamonica

By Victoria
Patience

Incredible food, fresh young designers, and a thriving cultural scene—all these Buenos Aires has. Yet the less tangible lies at the heart of the city's sizzle—for one, the spirit of its inhabitants. Here a flirtatious glance can be as passionate as a tango; a heated sports discussion as important as a world-class soccer match. It's this zest for life that makes Buenos Aires one of Latin America's hottest destinations.

The devalued peso is still a draw, although prices are steadily rising. Equally attractive, if you're trying to escape the financial doom and gloom abroad, is the locals' attitude to the financial crisis—they've weathered so many here that this one is barely news.

A booming tango—and tango tourism—revival means dance floors are alive again. And camera crews are now a common sight on street corners: low production costs and "Old World generic" architecture—hinting at many far-off cities but resembling none—are an appealing backdrop for European commercials.

Women are taking more prominent social roles, not least in the form of the first female president, Cristina Kirchner, elected in 2007. (She's technically the second female president, though she's the first woman *elected* to the position. When Perón died, his third wife, Isabelita, took over for a disastrous couple of years.) Marriage and equal rights for same-sex partnerships and a thriving scene make Argentina a prime gay destination. And the country is finally seeking to bring the torturers of the 1976–82 dictatorship to justice.

Sadly, there are increasing numbers of homeless people, and protests about the city government's health and education policies are commonplace. Some things stay the same, though. Food, family, and *fútbol* (or fashion) are still the holy trinity for most *porteños* (as city residents are called). Philosophical discussions and psychoanalysis—Buenos Aires has more psychoanalysts per capita than any other city in the world—remain popular pastimes. And in the face of so much change, porteños still approach life with as much dramatic intensity as ever.

CENTRO AND ENVIRONS

Sightseeing
★★★★

Dining
★

Lodging
★★

Shopping
★★★

Nightlife
★

Porteños love to brag that Buenos Aires has the world's widest avenue (Avenida 9 de Julio), its best steak, and its most beautiful women. The place to decide whether they're right is the city's heart, known simply as "Centro" or "El Centro," where many things merit superlatives.

For a start, this is one of the city's oldest areas. Plaza de Mayo is the original main square, and civic buildings both past and present are clustered between it and Plaza Congreso. Though you probably know Plaza de Mayo best from the balcony scene in the 1996 film *Evita*, many of Argentina's most historic events—including revolutions, demonstrations, and terrorist attacks—took place around it. Bullet-marked facades, sidewalks embedded with plaques, and memorials where buildings once stood are reminders of all this history, and the protesters who fill the streets regularly are history in the making.

More upbeat gatherings—open-air concerts, soccer victory celebrations, post-election reveling—take place around the Obelisco, a scaled-down Washington Monument look-alike that honors the founding of Buenos Aires. Inescapably phallic, it's the butt of local jokes about male insecurity in this oh-so-macho city. It's even dressed in a giant red condom each year on AIDS Awareness Day.

The town's most highbrow cultural events are hosted a few blocks away in the spectacular Teatro Colón, and the highest-grossing theatrical productions line Avenida Corrientes, whose sidewalks overflow on weekends with dolled-up locals. The center of Argentina's biggest scandals, the judicial district, is Tribunales, the area around Plaza Lavalle.

Building buffs get their biggest kicks in this part of town, too. Architectural wonders of yesteryear—French-inspired domes and towers with Iberian accents—line grand avenues, as do dreamy art deco theaters and monumental Peronist constructions.

Contemporary masterpieces by such world-renowned architects as Sir Norman Foster and César Pelli fill adjacent Puerto Madero, a onetime port area that's now the city's swankiest district, with chic hotels, restaurants, and shops. A promenade along the old docks affords great views of developments across the water in Puerto Madero Este; cross via Santiago Calatrava's Puente de la Mujer, a bridge whose sleek white curves were inspired by tango dancers.

Office workers, shoppers, and sightseers fill Centro's streets each day. Traffic noise and driving tactics also reach superlative levels. Locals profess to hate the chaos; unrushed visitors get a buzz out of the bustle. Either way, Centro provokes extreme reactions.

TAKING IT IN

Crowds and traffic can make touring draining: try to do a few short visits rather than one long marathon. You can see most of the sights in the Plaza de Mayo area over the course of a leisurely afternoon; a late-morning wander and lunch in Puerto Madero is one good way to precede this.

Half a day in the Microcentro is enough to take in the sights, though you could spend a lot more time caught up in shops. Office workers on lunch breaks make the Microcentro even more hectic than usual between noon and 2. If you're planning on hard-core shopping, come on a weekend. The area is quiet at night, and a little dangerous in its desolation.

TOP ATTRACTIONS

Calle Florida. Nothing sums up the chaotic Centro better than this pedestrian axis through the Microcentro, which has fallen from grace and risen from its ashes at least as many times as Argentina's economy. During the week it's a riot of office workers, fast-food chains, boutiques, bookstores, and vendors selling (and haggling over) leather goods. You can wander it in less than an hour: start at the intersection with Diagonal Norte; a bench or patch of grass in shady **Plaza San Martín** will be your reward at the other end. A huge bronze statue of San Martín on horseback rears atop a plinth in the center of the square, and temporary outdoor art exhibitions often line its perimeter. It's overlooked by several ornate Italianate buildings and South America's tallest art deco structure, the Edificio Kavanagh.

Nestled in among the shops and offices are several noteworthy buildings. At ornate, cupula-topped **Edificio Bank Boston** (Number 99), attention tends to focus on the building's battered and paint-splattered 4-ton bronze doors—unhappy customers have been taking out their anger at *corralitos* (banks retaining their savings) since the economic crisis of 2001–02.

The restoration process at historic arcade **Galería Güemes** (⇨ *also Malls and Department Stores in Chapter 3, Shopping)* has left the soaring marble columns and stained-glass cupola gleaming. The tacky shops that fill it do nothing to lessen the wow factor. Witness Buenos Aires' often cavalier attitude to building preservation at Florida's intersection with Avenida Corrientes, where the neo-Gothic **Palacio Elortondo-Alvear** is now home to Burger King. Buy a soda and drink it upstairs to check out the plaster molding and stained glass.

Milan's Galleria Vittorio Emanuele served as the model for **Galerías Pacífico** (⇨ *also Malls and Department Stores in Chapter 3, Shopping)*, designed during Buenos Aires' turn-of-the-20th-century golden age.

GETTING ORIENTED

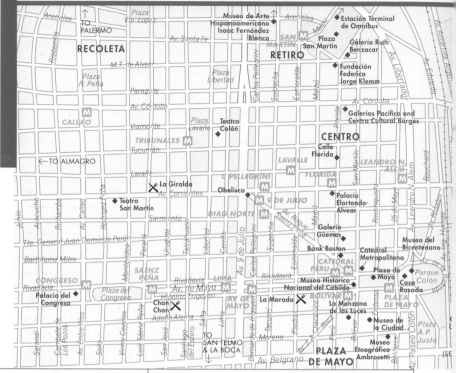

TOP EXPERIENCES

Reflecting: on Argentina's indigenous history at the Museo Etnográfico Juan B. Ambrosetti.

Witnessing: demonstrations in Plaza de Mayo, where Evita waved to crowds.

Descending: into the 17th-century tunnels the Jesuits built at La Manzana de las Luces.

Wandering: along Juana Manuela Gorriti and Pierina Dealessi to see Puerto Madero's "recycled" warehouses; Avenida de Mayo to visit 19th-century Europe; or Calle Florida for hustle, bustle, and souvenirs.

THE TERRITORY

The Microcentro (central business district) runs between Avenidas L. N. Alem and 9 de Julio and north of Avenida de Mayo. There are two axes: Avenida Corrientes (east–west) and pedestrian-only shopping street Calle Florida (north–south). Florida's northern end leads into Plaza San Martín in Retiro. South of the Microcentro lies Plaza de Mayo. From here Avenida de Mayo runs 12 blocks west to Plaza del Congreso. Puerto Madero borders the Centro to the east. Both it and its main thoroughfares, Avenida Alicia M. de Justo and Olga Cossentini, run parallel to the river.

SAFETY AND PRECAUTIONS

Be especially alert for "stain scammers" downtown: they squirt foul-smelling liquid on you surreptitiously, then "helpfully" offer to clean it off (as they pick your pocket). Use ATMs only during bank hours (weekdays 10–3); thieves target them after hours. Stay alert on Lavalle, a pedestrian street peppered with adult entertainment. At night, wander with care.

2

KEY

✗ Quick bites

Ⓜ Subte stops

QUICK BITES

Chan Chan. Peruvian dishes at bargain prices have made a name for Chan Chan. The spicy ceviches are ideal for stoking your sightseeing fires. ⊠ *Hipólito Yrigoyen 1390, Congreso* ☏ *11/ 4382–8492* ◷ *Tues.–Sun. noon– 4 pm and 8 pm–12:30 am.*

La Morada. Local office workers know that the best empanadas in the Microcentro are made by La Morada. ⊠ *Hipólito Yrigoyen 778, Plaza de Mayo* ☏ *11/4343– 3003* ⊕ *www.lamorada.com.ar* ◷ *Mon.–Thurs. 10–4; Fri.–Sat 10–4 and 6–midnight.*

La Giralda. Beret-wearing intellectuals love the retro café La Giralda. Its signature *choco- late con churros* (hot chocolate with crisp cigar-shaped donuts) are to die for. ⊠ *Av. Corrientes 1453, Centro* ☏ *11/4371–3846* ◷ *Mon.–Thurs. 7 am–midnight; Fri. and Sat. 7 am–2 am; Sun. 4 pm–midnight.*

GETTING AROUND

The quickest way into Centro is by subte. For Microcentro, get off at Florida (Línea/Line B) or Lavalle (C). Retiro and Plaza San Martín have eponymous stations on Line C. Stations Avenida de Mayo (A), Catedral (D), and Bolívar (E) all serve Plaza de Mayo. Line A has stops along de Mayo, including at Congreso. Lines B, C, and D intersect at Carlos Pellegrini/ Diagonal Norte/9 de Julio. Only change lines here if you're going more than one stop. Otherwise, walking is quicker. Puerto Madero is close to L. N. Alem on Line A, and is con- nected by the Tren del Este, a light-rail service running paral- lel to Avenida Alicia Moreau de Justo.

You can take a taxi or bus to the Microcentro, but walking is the best way to move within it. Bus 17 connects Centro and Recoleta; so do Buses 59 and 93. Bus 130 connects these areas with Puerto Madero. Buses 22 and 24 run between San Telmo and Microcentro.

2

Once the headquarters of the Buenos Aires–Pacific Railway, it's now a posh shopping mall and cultural center. Head to the central stairwell to see the allegorical murals painted by local greats Juan Carlos Castagnino, Antonio Berni, Cirilo Colmenio, Lino Spilimbergo, and Demetrio Urruchúa. The Centro Cultural Borges *(⇨ also Art Galleries, below)*, which hosts small international exhibitions and musical events, is on the mezzanine level. ✉ *Buenos Aires* Ⓜ *A to Plaza de Mayo, D to Catedral or B to Florida (southern end), C to Plaza San Martín (northern end).*

La Manzana de Las Luces *(The Block of Illumination)*. More history is packed into this single block of buildings southwest of Plaza de Mayo than in scores of other city blocks put together. Among other things, it was the enclave for higher learning: the metaphorical *luces* (lights) of its name refer to the "illuminated" scholars who worked within.

The Iglesia de San Ignacio is open to the public, but you can only visit the rest of Manzana de las Luces on guided tours led by excellent professional historians. Regular departures are in Spanish, but they provide brochures with English summaries of each stage; groups of over 20 people can call ahead to arrange English-language visits.

Procuraduría. The earliest occupant on La Manzana de Las Luces was the controversial Jesuit order, which began construction here in 1661. The only survivor from this first stage is the galleried Procuraduría, the colonial administrative headquarters for the Jesuits' vast land holdings in northeastern Argentina and Paraguay (think: *The Mission*). Historic defense tunnels, still undergoing archaeological excavation, linked the Jesuit headquarters to churches in the area, the Cabildo, and the port. Guided visits here include a glimpse of a specially reinforced section.

After the Jesuits' expulsion from Argentina in 1767 (the Spanish crown saw them as a threat), the simple brick-and-mud structure housed first the city's first school of medicine and then the University of Buenos Aires. Fully restored, it's now home to a school of luthiers and a rather tacky crafts market. ✉ *Corner of Alsina and Perú.*

Iglesia de San Ignacio de Loyola *(Saint Ignatius of Loyola Church)*. The Jesuits honored their patron saint at the Iglesia de San Ignacio de Loyola. The first church on the site was built of adobe in 1675; within a few decades it was rebuilt in stone. ✉ *Corner of Alsina and Bolívar.*

Casas Virreinales *(Viceroyal Houses)*. Argentina's first congress convened within the Casas Virreinales—ironic, given that it was built to house colonial civil servants. ✉ *Corner of Moreno and Perú.*

Colegio Nacional. The remaining historic building on the La Manzana de Las Luces block is the neoclassical Colegio Nacional, a top-notch public school and a hotbed of political activism that replaced a Jesuit-built structure. The president attends graduation ceremonies, and Einstein gave a lecture here in 1925. ✉ *Buenos Aires* ✉ *Entrance and inquiries at Perú 272, Plaza de Mayo* ☎ *11/4342–6973* ⊕ *www. manzanadelasluces.gov.ar* 🎫 *14 pesos* ☉ *Visits by guided tour only; Spanish-language tours leave weekdays at 3, and at 4:30, and 6 pm on weekends; call two weeks ahead to arrange tours in English* Ⓜ *A to Plaza de Mayo, D to Catedral, E to Bolívar.*

DID YOU KNOW?

La Puente de la Mujer, or "woman's bridge," connects Microcentro with Puerto Madero. The whole middle section of the bridge, including the skyward-reaching arm, swings like a door on a hinge to let boats pass.

Museo del Bicentenario. Today, the River Plate is nowhere in sight, but the humming traffic circle that overlooks this underground museum behind the Casa Rosada was once on the waterfront. The brick vaults, pillars, and wooden pulley mechanisms are the remains of the 1845 Taylor Customs House and jetty, discovered after being buried for almost a century. In honor of Argentina's 2010 bicentennary celebrations the structure was restored and covered with a glass roof.

Each vault has been assigned a segment of Argentina's political history, told through historic objects—often personal possessions of those who governed from the house overhead—paintings, photographs, film reels, and interactive screens.

Temporary art exhibitions run on the other side of the museum court-yard. However, the large glass structure in the center contains the real star of the show: a 360-degree masterpiece by Mexican muralist David Alfaro Siqueiros which originally covered the walls, floor, and ceiling of a basement room in a client's house. The house was demolished in the early 1990s, and the mural carefully removed in pieces, only to languish in a shipping container for 17 years. Thankfully, Siqueiros's innovative use of industrial paint meant that damage was minimal. Prompted by the campaigns of committed art activists, President Cristina Fernández intervened and the mural has now been fully restored and reassembled here. After donning protective shoes, you cross a small passageway into the work, which represents an underwater scene, against which the feet and faces of swimmers seem to press. The only male figure (swimming upwards on the wall opposite the entrance) is said to represent the artist.

A café at the back of the museum offers coffee, sandwiches, and salads, and a daily set lunch menu. ✉ *Paseo Colón 100, at Hipólito Yrigoyen, Plaza de Mayo* ☎ *11/4344–3802.*

★ **Museo Etnográfico Juan B. Ambrosetti** (*Ethnographic Museum*). Given that the 100-peso bill still honors General Roca, the man responsible for the massacre of most of Patagonia's indigenous population, it's not surprising that information on Argentina's original inhabitants is sparse. This fascinating but little-visited museum is a welcome remedy.

Begun by local scientist Juan Bautista Ambrosetti in 1904, the collection originally focused on so-called exotic art and artifacts, such as the Australasian sculptures and Japanese temple altar showcased in the rust-color introductory room. The real highlights, however, are the Argentine collections: this would be an eye-opening introduction to a visit to Argentina's far north or south.

The ground-floor galleries trace the history of human activity in Patagonia, with an emphasis on the tragic results of the European arrival. Dugout canoes, exquisite Mapuche silver jewelry, and scores of archive photos and illustrations are the main exhibits.

In the upstairs northwestern Argentina gallery the focus is mainly archaeological. Displays briefly chronicle the evolution of Andean civilization, the heyday of the Inca empire, and postcolonial life. Artifacts include ceramics, textiles, jewelry, farming tools, and even food: anyone for some 4,000-year-old corn?

2

The collection is run by the liberal Philosophy and Letters Faculty of the University of Buenos Aires. Although their insightful labels and explanations are all in Spanish, you can ask for a photocopied sheet with English versions of the texts. It's a pleasure just to wander the quiet, light-filled 19th-century town house that houses both the collection and an anthropological library. The peaceful inner garden is the perfect place for some post-museum reflection. ✉ *Moreno 350, Plaza de Mayo* ☎ *11/4345–8196* ⊕ *www.museoetnografico.filo.uba.ar* 🎟 *3 pesos* ⊙ *Tues.–Fri. 1–7, weekends 3–7* Ⓜ *Line A to Plaza de Mayo; Line D to Catedral; Line E to Bolívar.*

Fodor's Choice
★

Plaza de Mayo. Since its construction in 1580, this has been the setting for Argentina's most politically turbulent moments, including the uprising against Spanish colonial rule on May 25, 1810—hence its name. The square was once divided in two by a *recova* (gallery), but this reminder of colonial times was demolished in 1883, and the square's central monument, the Pirámide de Mayo, was later moved to its place. The pyramid you see is actually a 1911 extension of the original, erected in 1811 on the anniversary of the Revolution of May, which is hidden inside. The bronze equestrian statue of General Manuel Belgrano, designer of Argentina's flag, dates from 1873, and stands at the east end of the plaza.

The plaza remains the traditional site for ceremonies, rallies, and protests. Thousands cheered for Perón and Evita here; anti-Peronist planes bombed the gathered crowds in 1955; there were bloody clashes in December 2001 (hence the heavy police presence and crowd-control barriers); but the crowds were jubilant for Argentina's massive bicentenary celebrations in 2010. The white head scarves painted around the Pirámide de Mayo represent the Madres de la Plaza de Mayo (Mothers of May Square) who have marched here every Thursday at 3:30 for more than two decades. Housewives and mothers–turned–militant activists, they demand justice for *los desaparecidos*, the people who were "disappeared" during the military government's reign from 1976 to 1983, and welcome visitors to join in.

Casa Rosada. The eclectic Casa de Gobierno, better known as the Casa Rosada or Pink House, is at Plaza de Mayo's eastern end, with its back to the river. The building houses the government's executive branch—the president works here but lives elsewhere—and was built in the late 19th century over the foundations of an earlier customhouse and fortress. Swedish, Italian, and French architects have since modified the structure, which accounts for the odd mix of styles. Its curious hue dates from the presidency of Domingo Sarmiento, who ordered it painted pink as a symbol of unification between two warring political factions, the *federales* (whose color was red) and the *unitarios* (represented by white). Local legend has it that the original paint was made by mixing whitewash with bull's blood.

The balcony facing Plaza de Mayo is a presidential podium. From this lofty stage Evita rallied the *descamisados* (the shirtless—meaning the working class), Maradona sang along with soccer fans after winning one World Cup and coming second in another, and Madonna sang her filmed rendition of "Don't Cry for Me Argentina." Check for a small banner hoisted alongside the nation's flag, indicating "the president is in."

On weekends, hour-long guided tours take in some of the presidential offices and the newly opened *Galería de los Patriotas Argentinos del Bicentenario* (Bicentennial Gallery of Patriots), a pictorial who's who of Argentina's national heroes. The country's heroines have a room of their own here, which is often used for presidential press conferences. A impassioned Evita presides over black-and-white photographs of Argentina's other great dames. ⊠ *Balcarce 50, Plaza de Mayo* ☎ *11/4344–3714* ⊕ *www.presidencia.gov.ar/visitas-guiadas* 🎟 *Free* ⊘ *Weekends 10–6.*

Museo Histórico Nacional del Cabildo y de la Revolución de Mayo (*Cabildo*). The city council—now based in the ornate building over Avenida de Mayo—originally met in the Cabildo. It dates from 1765, and is the only colonial building on Plaza de Mayo. The epicenter of the May Revolution of 1810, where patriotic citizens gathered to vote against Napleonic rule, the hall is one of Argentina's national shrines. However, this hasn't stopped successive renovations to its detriment, including the demolition of the whole right end of the structure to make way for the new Avenida de Mayo in 1894 and of the left end for Diagonal Julio Roca in 1931. The small museum of artifacts and documents pertaining to the events of the May Revolution is less of an attraction than the building itself. As part of the 2010 bicentenary celebrations, a 3D video-mapping spectacular was projected onto the facade as an audience of thousands watched from Plaza de Mayo. Thursday and Friday from 11 to 6, an artisan fair takes place on the Patio del Cabildo. ⊠ *Bolívar 65, Plaza de Mayo* ☎ *11/4342–6729* 🎟 *4 pesos* ⊘ *Wed.–Fri. 10:30–5, weekends 11:30–6* Ⓜ *Line A, Plaza de Mayo; Line D, Catedral; Line E, Bolívar* ⊠ *Buenos Aires* Ⓜ *Line A to Plaza de Mayo; Line D to Catedral; Line E to Bolívar.*

Fodor'sChoice ★ **Teatro Colón.** Its magnitude, magnificent acoustics, and opulence (grander than Milan's La Scala) position the Teatro Colón (Colón Theater) among the world's top five opera theraters. An ever-changing stream of imported talent bolsters the well-regarded local lyric and ballet companies. After an eventful 18-year building process involving the death of one architect and the murder of another, the ornate Italianate structure was finally inaugurated in 1908 with Verdi's *Aïda*. It has hosted the likes of Maria Callas, Richard Strauss, Arturo Toscanini, Igor Stravinsky, Enrico Caruso, and Luciano Pavarotti, who said that the Colón has only one flaw: the acoustics are so good that every mistake can be heard. The theater was closed in 2008 for controversial renovations which ran way over schedule and budget, but reopened on May 24, 2010, to coincide with Argentina's bicentennary celebrations. Much of the work done was structural, but its stone facade and interior trimmings are now scrubbed and gleaming.

The theater's sumptuous building materials—three kinds of Italian marble, French stained glass, and Venetian mosaics—were imported from

The Casa Rosada sits on the eastern end of Plaza de Mayo.

Europe to create large-scale lavishness. The seven-tier main theater is breathtaking in size, and has a grand central chandelier with 700 lights to illuminate the 3,000 mere mortals in its red-velvet seats.

Nothing can prepare you for the thrill of seeing an opera or ballet here. The seasons run from April through December, but many seats are reserved for season-ticket holders. Shorter options in the main theater include symphonic cycles by the stable orchestra as well as international orchestral visits. Chamber music concerts are held in the U-shaped Salón Dorado (Golden Room), so named for the 24-karat gold leaf that covers its stucco molding. Underneath the main building is the ultra-minimal Centro Experimental, a tiny theater showcasing avant-garde music, opera, and dramatic performances.

You can see the splendor up close and get in on all the behind-the-scenes action with the theater's extremely popular guided tours. The whirl-wind visits take you up and down innumerable staircases to rehearsal rooms and to the costume, shoe, and scenery workshops, before letting you gaze at the stage from a sought-after box. (Arrive at least a half hour before the guided tour you want to take starts, as tours fill up very quickly.)

Buy tickets from the box office on Pasaje Toscanini. If seats are sold out—or beyond your pocket—you can buy 10-peso standing-room tickets on the day of the performance. These are for the lofty upper-tier *paraíso*, from which you can both see and hear perfectly, although three-hour-long operas are hard on the feet. ⊠ *Main entrance: Libertad between Tucumán and Viamonte; Box office: Pasaje Toscanini*

1180, Centro ☎ *11/4378–7100 tickets, 11/4378–7127 tours* ⊕ *www. teatrocolon.org.ar* 🖃 *Guided tours 60 pesos* ☉ *Daily 9–4, guided tours in Spanish every 15 mins., guided tours in English at 11, 12, 1, and 2* Ⓜ *D to Tribunales.*

WORTH NOTING

Buque Museo Corbeta Uruguay (*Uruguay Corvette Ship Museum*). The oldest of the Argentine fleet, bought from England in 1874, the ship has been around the world several times and was used in the nation's Antarctic campaigns at the turn of the 20th century. You can see what the captain's cabin and officers' mess looked like at that time; there are also displays of artifacts rescued from shipwrecks. A stroll around the decks affords views of the boat's structure and of Puerto Madero. ⊠ *Dique 4, Alicia M. de Justo 500 block, Puerto Madero* ☎ *11/4314–1090* ⊕ *www. ara.mil.ar/pag.asp?idItem=113* 🖃 *2 pesos* ☉ *Daily 10–7.*

Buque Museo Fragata A.R.A. Presidente Sarmiento (*President Sarmiento Frigate Museum*). The navy commissioned this frigate from England in 1898 to be used as an open-sea training vessel. The 280-foot boat used up to 33 sails and carried more than 300 crew members: the beautifully restored cabins afford a glimpse of what life onboard was like. Surprisingly luxurious officers' quarters include parquet floors, wood paneling, and leather armchairs; cadets had to make do with hammocks. ⊠ *Dique 3, Alicia M. de Justo 980, Puerto Madero* ☎ *11/4334–9386* ⊕ *www.ara. mil.ar/pag.asp?idItem=112* 🖃 *2 pesos* ☉ *Daily 10–7.*

Catedral Metropolitana. The Metropolitan Cathedral's columned neoclassical facade makes it seem more like a temple than a church, and its history follows the pattern of many structures in the Plaza de Mayo area. The first of six buildings on this site was a 16th-century adobe ranch house; the current structure dates from 1822, but has been added to several times. The embalmed remains of General José de San Martín, known as the Liberator of Argentina for his role in the War of Independence, rest here in a marble mausoleum lighted by an eternal flame. Soldiers of the Grenadier Regiment, an elite troop created and trained by San Martín in 1811, permanently guard the tomb. Guided tours (in Spanish) of the mausoleum and crypt leave Monday to Saturday at 11:45 am. ⊠ *San Martín 27, at Rivadavía, Plaza de Mayo* ☎ *11/4331–2845* ⊕ *www.catedralbuenosaires.org.ar* 🖃 *Free* ☉ *Weekdays 7–7, weekends 9–7:30* Ⓜ *A to Plaza de Mayo, D to Catedral, E to Bolívar.*

Colección de Arte Amalia Lacroze de Fortabat (Museo Fortabat). Argentina's richest woman, Amalia Fortabat, is a cement heiress, so it's not surprising that the building containing her private art collection is made mostly of concrete. It was completed in 2003, but after-effects from Argentina's 2001–02 financial crisis delayed its opening until 2008. Amalita (as she's known locally) was closely involved in the design, and the personal touch continues into the collection, which includes several portraits of her—including a prized Warhol—and many works by her granddaughter, Amalia Amoedo. In general, more money than taste seems to have gone into the project: the highlights are lesser works by big names both local (Berni, Xul Solar, Pettoruti) and international

(Brueghel, Dalí, Picasso), hung with little aplomb or explanation in a huge basement gallery that echoes like a high-school gym. The side gallery given over to Carlos Alonso's and Juan Carlos Castagnino's figurative work is a step in the right direction, however. So are the luminous paintings by Soldi in the glass-walled upper gallery. They're rivaled, however, by the view over the docks below—time your visit to end at sunset when pinks and oranges light the redbrick buildings opposite. Views from the dockside café come a close second. ⊠ *Olga Cossettini 141, Puerto Madero* ☎ *11/4310–6600* ⊕ *www.coleccionfortabat.org. ar* ⌦ *15 pesos* ⊙ *Tues.–Sun. noon–9.*

Museo de Arte Hispanoamericano Isaac Fernández Blanco (*Isaac Fernández Blanco Hispanic-American Art Museum*). The distinctive Peruvian neocolonial-style Palacio Noel serves as the perfect backdrop for this colonial art and craft museum, which was originally built in 1920 as the residence of architect Martín Noel. He and museum founder Fernández Blanco donated most of the exquisite silver items, religious wood carvings, inlaid furnishings, and paintings from the Spanish colonial period that are on display. Guided tours in English can be arranged by calling ahead. Shaded benches in the lush walled gardens provide welcome respite for your feet, and the rustling leaves and birdcalls almost filter out the busy Retiro traffic noises. The museum is an easy five-block walk from Estación San Martín on Línea C: from there go west along Avenida Santa Fe and then turn right into Suipacha and continue four blocks. ⊠ *Suipacha 1422, at Av. Libertador, Retiro* ☎ *11/4327–0228* ⊕ *www.museofernandezblanco.buenosaires.gob.ar* ⌦ *1 pesos, free Thurs.* ⊙ *Tues.–Fri. 2–7, weekends 11–7* Ⓜ *C to San Martín.*

Museo de la Ciudad. "Whimsical" is one way to describe the City Museum, which focuses on random aspects of domestic and public life in Buenos Aires in times past. "Eccentric" is probably closer to the mark for the permanent collection: an array of typical porteño doors. Historical toys, embroidery, religion in Buenos Aires, and garden gnomes (yes, really) have been some of the focuses of temporary exhibitions. Still, the peaceful building—which was restored in 2009—is worth a 10-minute wander if you're in the neighborhood. Downstairs, the Farmacia La Estrella sells modern medicine and cosmetics from a perfectly preserved 19th-century shop. ⊠ *Alsina 412, Plaza de Mayo* ☎ *11/4331–9855* ⊕ *www.museodelaciudad.buenosaires.gob.ar* ⌦ *1 peso, free Mon. and Wed.* ⊙ *Weekdays 11–7, weekends 10–8* Ⓜ *A to Plaza de Mayo, D to Catedral, E to Bolívar.*

Puente de la Mujer. Tango dancers inspired the sweeping asymmetrical lines of Valencian architect Santiago Calatrava's design for the pedestrian-only Bridge of the Woman. Puerto Madero's street names pay homage to famous Argentine women, hence the bridge's name. (Ironically its most visible part—a soaring 128-foot arm—represents the man of a couple in mid-tango.) The $6 million structure was made in Spain and paid for by local businessmen Alberto L. González, one of the brains behind Puerto Madero's redevelopment; he also built the Hilton Hotel here. Twenty engines rotate the bridge to allow ships to pass through. ⊠ *Dique 3, between Pierina Dealessi and Manuela Gorriti, Puerto Madero.*

Reserva Ecológica. The 865-acre Ecological Reserve was built over a landfill, and is home to more than 500 species of birds and a variety of flora and fauna. On weekends thousands of porteños vie for a spot on the grass, so come midweek if you want to bird-watch and sunbathe in peace or use the jogging and cycling tracks. A monthly guided "Walking under the Full Moon" tour in Spanish begins at 7:30 pm April through October and at 8:30 pm November through March. Even if you don't speak Spanish it's still a great way to get back to nature at night; otherwise avoid the area after sunset. It's just a short walk from the south end of Puerto Madero. ⊠ *Av. Tristán Achával Rodríguez 1550, Puerto Madero* 🕾 *11/4315–4129, 11/4893–1853 tours* ⊕ *www.buenosaires. gov.ar/areas/med_ambiente/reserva* 🖾 *Free* ☾ *Apr.–Oct., Tues.–Sun. 8–6; Nov.–Mar., Tues.–Sun. 8–7; guided visits in Spanish weekends at 10:30 and 3:30.*

ART GALLERIES

Centro Cultural Borges. There's something very low-key about this cultural center, despite its considerable size and prime location above the posh Galerías Pacífico mall. With a minimum of pomp and circumstance it has hosted exhibitions of Warhol, Kahlo and Rivera, Man Ray, Miró, Picasso, Chagall, and Dalí, as well as local greats Seguí, Berni, and Noé. Occasional mass shows focus on new local artists and art students. There are also small, independent theater and dance performances. ⊠ *Viamonte 525, at San Martín, Centro* 🕾 *11/5555–5359* ⊕ *www. ccborges.org.ar* 🖾 *15 pesos* ☾ *Mon.–Sat. 10–8:30, Sun. noon–8:30.*

Fundación Federico Jorge Klemm. You'd never guess that this sober, tastefully curated space was founded by one of Argentina's true eccentrics. The late Federico Jorge Klemm used his significant family fortune to amass a fabulous collection of local and international art—on display here, along with temporary exhibitions—and to start a prestigious local art prize, finalists for which are exhibited each year. Argentines remember Klemm best for his art-based TV program, which he presented dressed in exuberant outfits and wearing a trademark blond wig. ⊠ *Marcelo T. de Alvear 626, Centro* 🕾 *11/4312–4443* ⊕ *www. fundacionfjklemm.org* ☾ *Weekdays 11–8.*

LA BOCA AND SAN TELMO

Sightseeing
★★★★
Dining
★★★
Lodging
★★★★
Shopping
★★★★
Nightlife
★★★

"The south also exists," quip residents of bohemian neighborhoods like San Telmo and La Boca, which historically played second fiddle to posher northern barrios. No more. The hottest designers have boutiques here, new restaurants are booked out, an art district is burgeoning, and property prices are soaring. The south is also the linchpin of the city's tango revival, appropriate given that the dance was born in these quarters.

San Telmo, Buenos Aires' first suburb, was originally inhabited by sailors, and takes its name from their wandering patron saint. All the same, the mariners' main preoccupations were clearly less than spiritual, and San Telmo became famous for its brothels.

That didn't stop the area's first experience of gentrification: wealthy local families built ornate homes here in the early 19th century, but ran for Recoleta when a yellow-fever epidemic struck in 1871. Newly arrived immigrants crammed into their abandoned mansions, known as *conventillos* (tenement houses). Today these same houses are fought over by foreign buyers dying to ride the wave of urban renewal—the *reciclaje* (recycling), as porteños call it—that's sweeping the area and transforming San Telmo into Buenos Aires' hippest 'hood.

San Telmo has no major sights per se; it's the barrio itself that's the attraction. A few hours' gazing at its soaring Italianate town houses or writing in your travel journal over a drawn-out coffee is as much an insight into porteño life as any museum display. However, there's plenty of contemporary high culture on offer in the neighborhood's growing number of cutting-edge art galleries. All those cobblestones aren't just picturesque; they're useful, too, as they force you to slow down and enjoy the barrio.

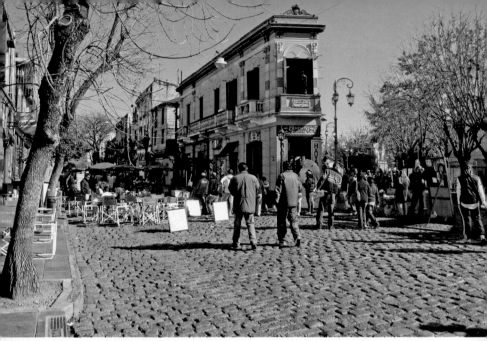

Caminito, the main pedestrian street in La Boca.

Although neighboring La Boca seems far more touristy, it shares much of San Telmo's gritty history. La Boca sits on the fiercely polluted—and thus fiercely smelly—Riachuelo River, where rusting ships and shipbuilders' warehouses remind you that this was once the city's main port. The immigrants who first settled here built their houses from corrugated metal and brightly colored paint left over from the shipyards. Today imitations of these vibrant buildings form one of Buenos Aires' most emblematic sights, the Caminito. Two quite different colors have made La Boca famous internationally: the blue and gold of the Boca Juniors soccer team, whose massive home stadium is the barrio's unofficial heart. Cafés, pubs, and general stores that once catered to passing sailors are now tourist traps dotting the partially renovated port. Whether your heart races over moves on the soccer field or the tango floor, over a fabulous building or a fabulous bargain, the south has plenty to spark your passions.

TAKING IT IN

San Telmo thrives on Sunday, thanks to the art and antiques market in Plaza Dorrego. During the week a leisurely afternoon's visit is ideal. Start with lunch in a café at the northern or southern end of San Telmo, then spend an hour or two wandering the cobbled streets. You still have time for some shopping before winding up with a coffee or a drink. In La Boca, allow two or three hours to explore Caminito and do a museum or two. It's busy all week, but expect extra crowds on weekends.

TOP ATTRACTIONS

★ **Calle Museo Caminito.**

See the highlighted listing in this chapter.

Estadio Boca Juniors and Museo de la Pasión Boquense.

See Get Your Kicks in "The Sporting Life" section of Chapter 1, Experience.

★ **Fundación Proa.** For more than a decade, this thoroughly modern art museum has been nudging traditional La Boca into the present. After major renovation work, its facade alone reads like a manifesto of local urban renewal: part of the original 19th-century Italianate housefront has been cut away, and huge plate-glass windows accented by unfinished steel stand alongside it. The space behind them now includes three adjacent properties. The luminous main gallery retains the building's original Corinthian-style steel columns, artfully rusted, but has sparkling white walls and polished concrete floors. With every flight of stairs you climb, views out over the harbor and cast-iron bridges get better. The first floor contains one of Buenos Aires' best art bookshops, including a strong collection of local artists' books and photography, which you can browse at trestle tables. On the roof is an airy café serving well-priced salads and sandwiches—bag one of the outdoor sofas around sunset and your photos will rival the work below. English versions of all exhibition information are available. They also run guided tours in English, with two days' notice. ⊠ *Av. Pedro de Mendoza 1929, La Boca* ☎ *11/4104–1000* ⊕ *www.proa.org* 🗐 *10 pesos; Tues. free* ⊙ *Tues.–Sun. 11–7.*

Pasaje de la Defensa. Wandering through this well-preserved house affords a glimpse of life in San Telmo's golden era. Behind its elegant but narrow stone facade, the house is built deep into the block around a series of internal courtyards. This type of long, narrow construction is typical of San Telmo, and is known as a *casa chorizo* (sausage house). Once the home of the well-to-do Ezeiza family, it became a *conventillo* (tenement), but is now a picturesque spot for antiques and curio shopping. The stores here are open daily 10 to 6. ⊠ *Defensa 1179, San Telmo* ☎ *No phone.*

★ **Plaza Dorrego.** During the week a handful of craftspeople and a few scruffy pigeons are the only ones enjoying the shade from the stately trees in the city's second-oldest square. Sunday couldn't be more different: scores of stalls selling antiques, curios, and just plain old stuff move in to form the Feria de San Pedro Telmo (San Pedro Telmo Fair). Tango dancers take to the cobbles, as do hundreds of shoppers (mostly tourists) browsing the tango memorabilia, antique silver, brass, crystal, and Argentine curios. Note that prices are high at stalls on the square and astronomical in the shops surrounding it, and vendors are immune to bargaining. ⚠ Pickpockets work as hard as stall owners on Sundays, so keep a firm hold on bags and purses or—wiser still—leave them at home. More affordable offerings—mostly handicrafts and local artists' work—are on stalls along nearby streets like Defensa. ■**TIP→** Be on the lookout for antique glass soda siphons that once adorned every bar

GETTING ORIENTED

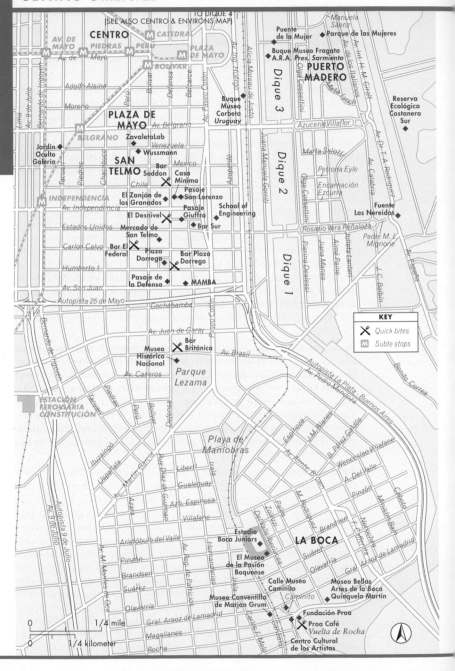

TO DIQUE 4
(SEE ALSO CENTRO & ENVIRONS MAP)

CENTRO   CATEDRAL

AV. DE
MAYO   PIEDRAS   PERÚ   PLAZA
DE MAYO

Av. de   Mayo

BOLÍVAR

Adolfo Alsina

Moreno

PLAZA DE
MAYO   Av. Belgrano

BELGRANO   ZavaletaLab

Jardín   Venezuela
Oculto   Wussmann
Galería

SAN   México
TELMO   Bar
Seddon   Casa
Mínima
Chile
El Zanjón de   Pasaje
los Granados   San Lorenzo
Pasaje
INDEPENDENCIA   Giuffra   School of
Engineering
Av. Independencia   El Desnivel   Bar Sur

Estados Unidos   Mercado de
San Telmo
Carlos Calvo   Bar El
Federal   Plaza
Dorrego   Bar Plaza
Humberto 1   Dorrego
Pasaje de
Av. San Juan   la Defensa   MAMBA
Autopista 25 de Mayo   Cochabamba

Av. Juan de Garay

Museo   Bar
Histórico   Británico
Nacional   Av. Brasil
Av. Caseros
Parque
Lezama

ESTACIÓN
FERROVIARIA
CONSTITUCIÓN

Playa de
Maniobras

Libert

Gualeguay

Azb. Espinosa

Villafane

Aristóbulo del Valle   Estadio   LA BOCA
Boca Juniors   Suárez
Pinzón   El Museo   Olavarría
de la Pasión
Brandsen   Boquense
Suárez   Calle Museo   Museo Bellas
Caminito   Artes de la Boca
Olavarría   Quinquela Martín
Museo Conventillo   Caminito
Gral. Araoz de Lamadrid   de Marjan Grum
Fundación Proa
Magallanes   Proa Café
Vuelta de Rocha
Rocha   Centro Cultural
de los Artistas

Manuela
Sáenz
Puente   Parque de las Mujeres
de la Mujer
Buque Museo Fragata
A.R.A. Pres. Sarmiento
PUERTO
MADERO
Buque
Museo   Reserva
Corbeta   Ecológica
Uruguay   Costanera
Sur
Azucena Villaflor

Marta Salotti

Petrona Eyle

Encarnación
Ezcurra
Fuente
Las Nereidas

Rosario Vera Peñaloza
Padre M. L.
Mignone

Dique 3

Dique 2

Dique 1

Autopista La Plata - Buenos Aires
Av. Pedro Mendoza

KEY	
✕	Quick bites
Ⓜ	Subte stops

0   1/4 mile
0   1/4 kilómetro

2

THE TERRITORY

San Telmo, south of the Centro, is bordered by Avenida Madero to the east, Avenidas Brasil and Caseros to the south, Piedras to the west, and—depending on who you ask—Chile or Belgrano to the north. The main drag is north–south Defensa, part of which is pedestrian-only. It forms one side of Plaza Dorrego, the area's tourist hub.

South of Avenida Brasil lies La Boca, whose westernmost edge is Avenida Patricios. The Riachuelo River forms a curving border; Avenida Don Pedro de Mendoza runs beside it.

GETTING AROUND

The subte takes you within about half a mile of San Telmo. The closest stations to the southern end are Independencia (Line C or E) and San Juan (Line C). Be prepared to walk nine blocks east along Avenidas Independencia, Estados Unidos, or San Juan to get to Defensa, the main street. To approach San Telmo from the north, get off at Bolívar (Line E) or Catedral (Line D) and walk eight blocks south along Bolívar. Buses 22, 24, 26, and 28 connect San Telmo to Centro. The same route by taxi costs 10–12 pesos.

There's no subte to La Boca, so taxi travel is a good bet, especially after dark: expect to pay 18–20 pesos to or from the Centro. Bus 29 runs between La Boca and the Centro; so do Buses 64 and 152, which continue to Palermo. Bus 53 connects La Boca and San Telmo.

SAFETY AND PRECAUTIONS

San Telmo's popularity with visitors has led to increased police presence in the busiest areas (especially near Defensa). Still, instances of petty crime are common. After dark, stick to busy, well-lighted streets close to Defensa.

La Boca is far sketchier, and you'd do best not to stray from the Caminito area. Avoid the neighborhood after dark, and take radio taxis if you must visit then.

TOP EXPERIENCES

Photographing: cobbled streets, then comparing them with the pro's work at ZavaletaLab or the MAMBA museum.

Descending: into El Zanjón de Granados's restored tunnels for a different perspective.

Drinking: in the atmosphere— and a *cortado* (coffee with a splash of milk)—at time-honored El Federal or La Perla cafés.

Watching: the sun set from Fundación Proa's roof café.

Wandering: Caminito (and adjacent Garibaldi and Magallanes), to tick the sightseeing boxes, or Defensa to cruise antiques stalls (on Sunday) and boutiques.

QUICK BITES

El Desnivel. El Desnivel is a classic parrilla (grill). Trimmings don't go beyond a mixed salad and fries, and surly waiters all but fling food at you. It's all part of the experience. ⊠ *Defensa 855, San Telmo* ☎ *11/4300–9081* ⊕ *www.parrillaeldesnivel. com.ar* ☯ *Mon. 7:30 pm–1 am; Tues.–Sun. noon–4:30 pm and 7:30 pm–1 am.*

Proa Café. Gorgeous port views await at the rooftop Proa Café, which does fresh juices and smoothies, salads, quiches, and pastas. ⊠ *Fundación Proa, Av. Pedro de Mendoza 1929, La Boca* ☎ *11/4104–1003* ☯ *Tues.–Sun. 11–7.*

CALLE MUSEO CAMINITO

✉ *Caminito between Av. Pedro de Mendoza (La Vuelta de Rocha promenade) and Olivarría, La Boca* 🎫 *Free* 🕙 *Daily 10–6.*

TIPS

■ "Caminito" comes from a 1926 tango by Juan de Dios Filiberto, who is said to have composed it while thinking of a girl leaning from the balcony of a ramshackle house like those here. It was chosen by local artist Benito Quinquela Martín (Falso Museo de Bellas Artes de La Boca Quinquela Martín), who helped establish the street as an open-air museum.

■ Expect to be canvassed aggressively by rival restaurant owners touting overpriced, touristy menus near the start of Caminito and along every other side street. Each restaurant has its own outdoor stage—competing troupes of stamping gauchos make meals a noisy affair. The best tactic to get by them is to accept their leaflets with a serene smile and "gracias."

■ The Caminito concept spills over into nearby streets Garibaldi and Magallanes, which form a triangle with it. The strange, foot-high sidewalks along streets like Magallanes, designed to prevent flooding, show how the river's proximity has shaped the barrio.

Cobblestones, tango dancers, and haphazardly constructed, colorful conventillos have made Calle Museo Caminito the darling of Buenos Aires' postcard manufacturers since this pedestrian street was created in 1959. Artists fill the block-long street with works depicting port life and tango, which is said to have been born in La Boca. These days it's painfully commercial, and seems more a parody of porteño culture than anything else, but if you're willing to embrace the out-and-out tackiness it can make a fun outing.

HIGHLIGHTS

Conventillos. Many of La Boca's tenements are now souvenir shops. The plastic Che Guevaras and dancing couples make the shops in the **Centro Cultural de los Artistas** (✉ *Magallanes 861* 🕙 *Mon.–Sat. 10:30–6*) as forgettable as all the others on the street, but the uneven stairs and wrought-iron balcony hint at what a conventillo interior was like. A sculptor owns the turquoise-and-tomato-red **Museo Conventillo de Marjan Grum** (✉ *Garibaldi 1429* 🎫 *10 pesos* ☎ *11/4302–2472*). The opening hours of this gallery–cultural center are erratic, but even the facade is worth a look.

Local Art. Painters, photographers, and sculptors peddle their creations from stalls along Caminito. Quality varies considerably; if nothing tempts you, focus on the small mosaics set into the walls, such as Luis Perlotti's *Santos Vega*. Another local art form, the brightly colored scrollwork known as *fileteado*, adorns many shop and restaurant fronts near Caminito.

Tangueros. Competition is fierce between the pairs of sultry dancers dressed to the nines in split skirts and fishnets. True, they spend more time trying to entice you into photo ops than actually dancing, but linger long enough (and throw a big enough contribution in the fedora) and you'll see some fancy footwork.

top in Buenos Aires. Classic colors are green and turquoise. Be sure to look up as you wander Plaza Dorrego, as the surrounding architecture provides an overview of the influences—Spanish colonial, French classical, and ornate Italian masonry—that shaped the city in the 19th and 20th centuries. ⊠ *Defensa and Humberto I.*

Fodor's Choice
★

El Zanjón de Granados. All of Buenos Aires' history is packed into this unusual house. The street it's on was once a small river—the *zanjón*, or gorge, of the property's name—where the first, unsuccessful attempt to found Buenos Aires took place in 1536. When the property's current owner—or custodian, as he prefers to be known—decided to develop what was then a run-down conventillo, he began to discover all sorts of things beneath the house: pottery and cutlery, the foundations of past constructions, and a 500-foot network of tunnels that has taken over 20 years to excavate. These were once used to channel water, but like the street itself, they were sealed after San Telmo's yellow-fever outbreaks. With the help of historians and architects, they've now been painstakingly restored, and the entire site has been transformed into a private museum, where the only exhibit is the redbrick building itself. Excellent hour-long guided tours in English and Spanish take you through low-lighted sections of the tunnels. The history lesson then continues aboveground, where you can see the surviving wall of a construction from 1740, the 19th-century mansion built around it, and traces of the conventillo it became. Expect few visitors and plenty of atmosphere on weekdays; cheaper, shorter tours on Sunday draw far more people. If you want to spend even more time here, you can rent the whole place (including an adjacent building reached via the tunnels) for functions. ⊠ *Defensa 755, San Telmo* ☎ *11/4361-3002* ⊕ *www.elzanjon.com.ar* ✆ *Guided tours 60 pesos (1 hr, weekdays only); 40 pesos (30 min, Sun. only)* ⊙ *Tours weekdays 11–3 on the hr; Sun. 1–6 every 30 min. Closed Sat.*

WORTH NOTING

Museo de Arte Moderno de Buenos Aires (MAMBA) (*Museum of Modern Art of Buenos Aires*). Some 7,000 contemporary artworks make up the permanent collection at this block-long museum. Once the site of a tobacco company, the MAMBA retains the original exposed-brick facade and fabulous wooden doors with wrought-iron fixtures. After being closed for more than five years of renovation work, these doors reopened in late 2010, although only a few galleries arre actually up and running. Eventually, most of wall acreage will contain a rotating selection of the museum's paintings, sculptures, and new media by 20th- and 21st-century artists both local and international. Since reopening, temporary exhibitions have included engravings by local great Antonio Seguí. Lectures and film screenings will form part of the program. ⊠ *Av. San Juan 350, San Telmo* ☎ *11/4341-3001* ⊕ *www.museos.buenosaires.gov.ar/ mam.htm* ✆ *1 peso* ⊙ *Weekdays 12–7, weekends 11–8.*

Museo de Bellas Artes de La Boca Quinquela Martín (*Quinquela Martín Fine Arts Museum of La Boca*). Vibrant port scenes were the trademark of artist and philanthropist Benito Quinquela Martín, the man who first

DID YOU KNOW?

Graffiti here can be political, whimsical, inspirational, or controversial, but it's technically always illegal. Popular targets like the Congreso building now sport graffiti-resistant paint for quick cleanup, reducing the incentive to paint.

Chile

400   500

SAN TELMO'S TRADITIONAL BARS

The best place for insight into traditional San Telmo is at the worn wooden tables of its vintage bars (most open from breakfast right through to the wee hours).

Bar Plaza Dorrego. Wood-paneled, dust-festooned Bar Plaza Dorrego is right on the main square. Sip your *cafecito* (espresso) or icy beer at one of its window tables for some prime people-watching, all the while shelling your pile of peanuts. ⊠ *Defensa 1098, at Humberto I* ☏ *11/4361–0141* ⊘ *Sun.–Thurs. 8 am–1 am, Fri.–Sat. 8 am–5 am.*

Bar Británico. When they tried to shut down ultravintage Bar Británico, the whole city rallied to its defense. Rub elbows with bohemian students and wizened old-timers as you perk up with a *cortado* (espresso "cut"

with a dash of milk) or unwind with a *ginebra* (ginlike spirit). ⊠ *Brasil 399, at Defensa* ☏ *11/4361–2107* ⊘ *Wed.–Mon., 24 hours.*

Bar El Federal. Veteran regulars assure that the *picadas* (snacks such as cold cuts and bread) at Bar El Federal are some of the best in town, and you can linger over them for hours, no questions asked. ⊠ *Carlos Calvo 599, at Perú* ☏ *11/4300–4313* ⊘ *Daily 8 am–2 am.*

Bar Seddon. Tango musicians often perform at Bar Seddon, an otherwise quiet bar with a beautiful checkered floor and old-fashioned cash register. ⊠ *Defensa 695, at Chile* ☏ *11/4342–3700* ⊘ *Sun.–Thurs. 10 am–3 am; Fri.–Sat. 10 am–5:30 am.*

put La Boca on the cultural map. His work and part of his studio are showcased on the third floor of this huge building, which he donated to the state for a cultural center in 1936. Don't be surprised to have to jostle your way in through kids filing into class: downstairs is an elementary school, something that the galleries' bland institutional architecture doesn't let you forget. Quinquela Martín set out to fill the second floor with Argentine art—on the condition that works were figurative and didn't belong to any "ism." Badly lighted rooms and lack of any visible organization make it hard to enjoy the minor paintings by Berni, Sívori, Soldi, and other local masters. Outside is a huge sculpture terrace with great views of the river and old port buildings on one side, with the Boca Juniors stadium and low-rise downtown skyline on the other. ⊠ *Av. Pedro de Mendoza 1843, La Boca* ☏ *11/4301–1080* ⊠ *8 pesos* ⊘ *Tues.–Fri. 10–5:30, weekends 11–5:30. Closed on days when Boca Juniors plays at home; call ahead.*

Museo Histórico Nacional. What better place for the National History Museum than overlooking the spot where the city was supposedly founded? The beautiful chestnut-and-white Italianate mansion that houses the museum once belonged to entrepreneur and horticulturalist Gregorio Lezama. It became a quarantine station when cholera and yellow-fever epidemics raged in San Telmo, before opening as this museum in 1897. At this writing, most of the museum is closed for some much-needed renovations, so be sure to check ahead of visiting. The Museo Histórico Nacional (National History Museum) sits in the shade of enormous magnolia, palm, cedar, and elm trees on the sloping hillside of **Parque Lezama,** also worth a visit on its own. ⊠ *Calle Defensa 1600, San Telmo* 🕾 *11/4307–1182* 🖼 *Free* ⊙ *Wed.–Sun. 11–6.*

ART GALLERIES

Jardín Oculto Galería. This collectively run gallery is known as much for its wild opening night parties as the unconventional works it favors. Federico Lanzi and San Poggio are two protégés whose fiercely colored pieces err on just the right side of the "But is it art?" line. ⊠ *Venezuela 926, San Telmo* 🕾 *11/4343–0179* ⊕ *www.jardinocultogaleria.com* ⊙ *Mon.–Sat. 1–7.*

Wussmann. It's hard to say which is more covetable at San Telmo's best-established gallery: the art or the building. A century-old house has been opened up into deep space, interrupted only by the original iron columns supporting the roof. The main exhibition space fronts the street; shows have included Nora Iniesta's large-scale collages; Roberto Plate's bold, semiabstract acrylics; and works by beloved local illustrator Liniers. Up-and-coming artists and photographers exhibit in a smaller first-floor gallery. Exquisite leather-bound notebooks and handmade paper fill the back of the space. ⊠ *Venezuela 570, San Telmo* 🕾 *11/4343–4707* ⊕ *www.wussmann.com* ⊙ *Gallery weekdays 2–8; shop weekdays 10:30–8, Sat. 10:30–2.*

ZavaletaLab. Formerly based in Recoleta, this is one of several galleries putting their money on San Telmo as Buenos Aires' new art hub. Although renovations have left the building as trendily stripped and bare as other nearby spaces, Zavaleta stands out for its impeccable taste. The focus is on contemporary painting and drawing that will weather changing art trends well. Exhibitions have included the bright, post-pop paintings of Daniel García and Alberto Passolini, and the sculptures and collages of contemporary local legend León Ferrari. ⊠ *Venezuela 567, San Telmo* 🕾 *11/4342–9293* ⊕ *www.zavaletalab.com* ⊙ *Weekdays 11–7, Sat. 11–2.*

2

RECOLETA AND ALMAGRO

Sightseeing
★★★★★

Dining
★★★

Lodging
★★★★

Shopping
★★★★

Nightlife
★★

For Buenos Aires' most illustrious families, Recoleta's boundaries are the boundaries of the civilized world. The local equivalents of the Vanderbilts are baptized and married in the Basílica del Pilar, throw parties in the Alvear Palace Hotel, live in spacious 19th-century apartments nearby, and wouldn't dream of shopping anywhere but Avenidas Quintana and Alvear. Ornate mausoleums in the Cementerio de la Recoleta promise an equally stylish afterlife.

Recoleta wasn't always synonymous with elegance. Colonists, including city founder Juan de Garay, farmed here. So did the Franciscan Recoleto friars, whose 1700s settlement here inspired the district's name. Their church, the Basílica del Pilar, was almost on the riverbank then: tanneries grew up around it, and Recoleta became famous for its *pulperías* (taverns) and brothels. Everything changed with the 1871 outbreak of yellow fever in the south of the city.

The elite swarmed to Recoleta, building the *palacios* and stately Parisian-style apartment buildings that are now the neighborhood's trademark. They also laid the foundations for Recoleta's concentration of intellectual and cultural activity: the Biblioteca Nacional (National Library), a plethora of top-notch galleries, and three publicly run art museums are all based here. Combine Recoleta's art and architecture with its beautiful parks and squares—many filled with posh pooches and their walkers—and sightseeing here becomes a visual feast. And despite the luxury around you, many sights are free (and so is window-shopping). An unofficial subdistrict, Barrio Norte, is one step south of Recoleta proper and one small step down the social ladder. Shopping is the draw: local chains, sportswear flagships, and mini-malls of vintage clothing and clubwear line Avenida Santa Fe between 9 de Julio and Puerreydón.

Almagro lies southwest of Recoleta but is a world apart. Traditionally a gritty, working-class neighborhood, it spawned many tango greats, including the legendary Carlos Gardel. The Abasto subdistrict has long been the heart of the barrio: it centers on the massive art deco building (at Corrientes and Agüero) that was once the city's central market. The abandoned structure was completely overhauled and reopened in 1998 as a major mall, spearheading the redevelopment of the area, which now has several top hotels and an increasing number of restaurants and tango venues. More urban renewal is taking place a few blocks away at Sarmiento and Jean Jaurés, where the Konex Foundation has transformed an abandoned factory into a cutting-edge cultural venue.

2

TAKING IT IN

You can blitz Recoleta's main sights in half a day, though you could easily spend a full morning or afternoon in the cemetery or cultural centers alone. Come midweek for quiet exploring, or on the weekend to do the cemetery and Plaza Francia crafts market in one fell swoop.

In Almagro a couple of hours will suffice to see all things Carlos Gardel—tango's greatest hero—and get a feel for the district. The mall gets busier than most on weekends because of the Museo de los Niños (Children's Museum).

TOP ATTRACTIONS

Basílica de Nuestra Señora del Pilar. This basilica beside the famous Cementerio de la Recoleta on Junín is where Buenos Aires' elite families hold weddings and other ceremonies. It was built by the Recoleto friars in 1732, and is considered a national treasure for its six German Baroque–style altars. The central one is overlaid with Peruvian engraved silver; another contains relics and was sent by Spain's King Carlos III.

Museo de los Claustros del Pilar. In the cloisters, which date from 1716, is the Museo de los Claustros del Pilar, a small museum of religious artifacts as well as pictures and photographs documenting Recoleta's evolution. There are excellent views of the cemetery from upstairs windows. ⊠ *Buenos Aires* 🎫 *5 pesos* 🕙 *Mon.–Sat. 10:30–6:15, Sun. 2:30–6:15* ⊠*Junín 1904, Recoleta* 🕿 *11/4806–2209* ⊕*www. basilicadelpilar.org.ar* 🎫 *Free* 🕙 *Daily 8 am–10 pm.*

Fodor's Choice **Cementerio de la Recoleta.**
★ *See the highlighted listing in this chapter.*

Centro Cultural La Recoleta. Art exhibitions, concerts, fringe theater performances, and workshops are some of the offerings at this major cultural center. The rambling building it's housed in was converted from the cloister patios of the Franciscan monks. ⊠*Junín 1930, Recoleta* 🕿 *11/4803–1040* ⊕ *www.centroculturalrecoleta.org* 🕙 *Mon.–Fri. 2–9, weekends 10–9.*

Museo Participativo de Ciencias. Kids love the Museo Participativo de Ciencias, a mini science museum inside the Centro Cultural La Recoleta complex whose motto, *Prohibido No Tocar* (Not Touching

GETTING ORIENTED

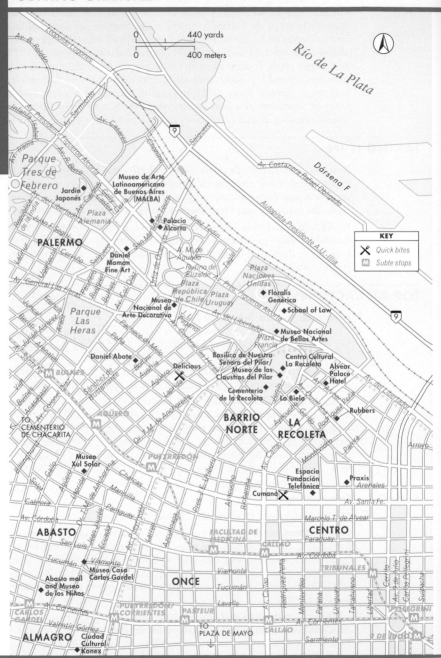

0 ——— 440 yards
0 ——— 400 meters

Río de La Plata

KEY
✕ Quick bites
Ⓜ Subte stops

Parque Tres de Febrero

Jardín Japonés

Museo de Arte Latinoamericano de Buenos Aires (MALBA)

Plaza Alemania

Palacio Alcorta

PALERMO

Daniel Maman Fine Art

A. M. de Aguado

Rufino de Elizalde

Plaza República de Chile

Museo Nacional de Arte Decorativo

Plaza Uruguay

Plaza Naciones Unidas

Floralis Genérica

School of Law

Parque Las Heras

Daniel Abate

Plaza Francia

Museo Nacional de Bellas Artes

BULNES Ⓜ

Delicious ✕

Basílica de Nuestra Señora del Pilar/ Museo de los Claustros del Pilar

Centro Cultural La Recoleta

Alvear Palace Hotel

TO CEMENTERIO DE CHACARITA

AGÜERO Ⓜ

Cementerio de la Recoleta

La Biela

BARRIO NORTE

LA RECOLETA

Rubbers

Museo Xul Solar

PUEYRREDÓN Ⓜ

Espacio Fundación Telefónica

Praxis

Cumaná ✕

Av. Santa Fe

ABASTO

FACULTAD DE MEDICINA

Marcelo T. de Alvear

CENTRO

CALLAO Ⓜ

Av. Córdoba

TRIBUNALES Ⓜ

Tucumán Ⓜ

Museo Casa Carlos Gardel

Abasto mall and Museo de los Niños

ONCE

Viamonte

Tucumán

Lavalle

CARLOS GARDEL Ⓜ

PUEYRREDÓN/ CORRIENTES Ⓜ

PASTEUR Ⓜ

Av. Corrientes

CALLAO Ⓜ

PELLEGRINI Ⓜ

ALMAGRO

Ciudad Cultural Konex

TO PLAZA DE MAYO

Sarmiento

9 DE JULIO

THE TERRITORY

The River Plate borders Recoleta to the north. Uruguay and Montevideo join to form the eastern border; the jagged western edge is made up of Mario Bravo, Coronel Díaz, and Tagle. The area between Juncal and Córdoba—Recoleta's southern boundary—is known as Barrio Norte, whose main thoroughfare is Santa Fe. In Recoleta proper, Avenidas Alvear and Quintana are the key streets.

Almagro is officially bordered by Avenidas Córdoba and Estado de Israel to the north, Río de Janeiro to the west, Independencia to the south, and Sánchez de Bustamente and Gallo to the east. The Abasto subdistrict, which centers on Gallo and Corrientes, stretches a few blocks farther east into neighboring Balvanera.

GETTING AROUND

True to its elite roots, Recoleta has no subway, so taxis are the best option. Expect to pay around 15 pesos from downtown or Palermo. Bus 17 runs from San Telmo and the Centro; the 92 connects Retiro and Recoleta, then continues to central Palermo and Almagro. Traffic can be slow within Recoleta and Barrio Norte—walking is fast and pleasant.

Heavy traffic means Almagro is best reached by subte. Line B runs along Avenida Corrientes through Almagro; Carlos Gardel station leads right into the Abasto mall. Bus 24 connects Almagro with Centro and San Telmo; the 168 goes west to Palermo Viejo.

SAFETY AND PRECAUTIONS

Recoleta and Barrio Norte are relatively safe in the daytime, but stick to well-lighted streets at night. Bag snatching is opportunist rather than systematic here: keep a firm grip on your purse in the crowded weekend market and in busy restaurants. Although Almagro is on the upswing, many streets near the Abasto mall are still run-down. Wander with caution.

TOP EXPERIENCES

2

Seeking: unusual statues in Cementerio de Recoleta.

Window-shopping: on Avenida Quintana for Argentine designs but buying more affordable ones on Avenida Santa Fe or in the Abasto mall.

Comparing: 19th-century Argentine and European art on the first floor of the Museo Nacional de Bellas Artes.

Wandering: Avenida Alvear for the gorgeous late-19th- and early-20th-century mansions.

QUICK BITES

Cumaná. The hearty stews, steaks, and empanadas at chaotic Cumaná are a far cry from Recoleta's European pretensions. Skip dessert (nearby ice-creameries are better). ⊠ *Rodríguez Peña 1149, Barrio Norte* 🖀 *11/4813–9207* ⊘ *Daily noon–1 am.*

Delicious. It's a hard name to live up to, but there's no doubt this casual café pulls it off. Delicious does super fresh sandwiches, salads, and smoothies, which you can eat in or pack into your picnic basket. An espresso and a portion of their Ultrachocolate cake contains the perfect dose of caffeine and sugar to get you back in the sightseeing saddle. ⊠ *Laprida 2015, Recoleta* 🖀 *11/4803–1151* ⊕ *www.deliciouscafe.com.ar.*

CEMENTERIO DE LA RECOLETA

✉ *Junín 1760, Recoleta*
☎ *11/4803–1594* 💲 *Free*
🕐 *Daily 7–6.*

The ominous gates, Doric-columned portico, and labyrinthine paths of the city's oldest cemetery (1822) may leave you with a sense of foreboding. It's the final resting place for the nation's most illustrious figures, and covers 13.5 acres that are rumored to be the most expensive real estate in town. The cemetery has more than 6,400 elaborate vaulted tombs and majestic mausoleums, 70 of which have been declared historic monuments. The mausoleums resemble chapels, Greek temples, pyramids, and miniature mansions.

HIGHLIGHTS

Evita. The embalmed remains of Eva Duarte de Perón, who made it (almost intact) here after 17 years of posthumous wandering, are in the Duarte family vault. Around July 26, the anniversary of her death, flowers pile up here.

Late Greats. If the tomb of brutal *caudillo* (dictator) Facundo Quiroga looks small, it's because he's buried standing—a sign of valor—at his request. Prominent landowner Dorrego Ortíz Basualdo resides in Recoleta's most monumental sepulcher, complete with chandelier. The names of many key players in Argentina's history are chiseled over other sumptuous mausoleums: Alvear, Quintana, Sáenz Peña, Lavalle, Sarmiento.

Spooky Stories. Rufina Cambaceres is known as the girl who died twice. She was thought dead after suffering a cataleptic attack, and was entombed on her 19th birthday in 1902. Rufina awoke inside her casket and clawed the top open but died of a heart attack before she could be rescued. When Alfredo Gath heard of Rufina's story he was appalled and commissioned a special mechanical coffin with an opening device and alarm bell. Gath successfully tested the coffin in situ 12 times, but on the 13th the mechanism failed and he died inside.

TIPS

■ The city government runs free guided visits to the cemetery in English on Tuesday and Thursday at 11; visits in Spanish operate Tuesday through Sunday at 9:30, 11, 2, and 4. Groups gather at the entrance.

■ If you prefer an independent tour, the administrative offices at the entrance can usually provide a free photocopied map, and caretakers throughout the grounds can help you locate the more intriguing tombs. These are also labeled on a large map at the entrance.

■ The cemetery had its blessing withdrawn by the Catholic Church in 1863, when president Bartolomé Mitre ordered that a suicide be buried there.

Cementerio de la Recoleta

Vicente López

Azcuénaga

Guido

Pueyrredón

Luis Ángel Firpo

Roque Sáenz Peña

Juan Lavalle

Vicente López

Evita

Rufina Cambaceres

Dorrego Ortiz Basualde

Domingo Faustino Sarmiento

Facundo Quiroga

Carlos M. de Alvear

Office

Capilla

Administration

Nuestra Señora de Pilar

Junín

Junín

ENTRANCE

Plaza Intendente Torcuato de Alvear

Guido

Pres. Roberto M. Ortiz

Av. Alvear

Ayacucho

| 0 | | 50 yards |
| 0 | | 50 meters |

Recoleta Cemetery is a good place for resting (both eternal and momentary).

Is Forbidden), says it all. ⊠ *Buenos Aires* ☎ *11/4807–3260* ⊕ *www. mpc.org.ar* ✉ *20 pesos, free for children under 4* ⊙ *Jan.–Feb., daily 3:30–7:30; Mar.–Dec., weekdays 10–5, weekends 3:30–7:30; winter school holidays (approx. mid-July–early Aug.), weekdays 12:30–7:30, weekends 3:30–7:30.*

La Feria de Plaza Francia. On weekends artisans' stalls line the small park outside the cultural center and cemetery, forming the open-air market known as La Feria de Plaza Francia. It's usually teeming with shoppers, who come for the quality crafts. Other souvenirs in the area include quirky homewares and designer clothing at the Buenos Aires Design Center, which you reach by following the walkway outside the cultural center into the adjacent Paseo del Pilar shopping mall. ⊠ *Buenos Aires* ⊕ *www.feriaplazafrancia.com*

★ **Floralis Genérica.** The gleaming steel and aluminum petals of this giant flower look very space age, perhaps because they were commissioned from the Lockheed airplane factory by architect Eduardo Catalano, who designed and paid for the monument. The 66-foot-high structure is supposed to open at dawn and close at dusk, when the setting sun turns its mirrored surfaces a glowing pink (sometimes the mechanism is out of order, however). The flower stands in the Plaza Naciones Unidas (behind El Museo Nacional de Bellas Artes over Avenida Figueroa Alcorta), which was remodeled to accommodate it. ⊠ *Plaza Naciones Unidas at Av. Figueroa Alcorta and J.A. Biblioni, Recoleta* ⊙ *Dawn–dusk.*

Museo Nacional de Arte Decorativo. The harmonious, French neoclassical mansion that houses the National Museum of Decorative Art is as much a reason to visit as the period furnishings, porcelain, and silver within it. Ornate wooden paneling in the Regency ballroom, the imposing Louis XIV red-and-black-marble dining room, and a lofty Renaissance-style great hall are some of the highlights of the only house of its kind open to the public in Buenos Aires. There are excellent English descriptions of each room, and they include gossipy details about the house's original inhabitants, the well-to-do Errázuriz-Alvear family. The museum also contains some Chinese art. Guided tours include the Zubov Collection of miniatures from Imperial Russia. ⊠ *Av. del Libertador 1902, Recoleta* ☎ *11/4801–8248* ⊕ *www.mnad.org* ☜ *5 pesos; free Tues. Guided tours in English 15 pesos* ☉ *Jan.–Feb., Tues.–Sat. 2–7; Mar.–Dec., Tues.–Sun. 2–7; guided tours in English Tues.–Sat. at 2:30.*

Fodor'sChoice **Museo Nacional de Bellas Artes.**
★ *See the highlighted listing in this chapter.*

WORTH NOTING

Cementerio de Chacarita. This cemetery is home to Carlos Gardel's tomb, which features a dapper, Brylcreemed statue and dozens of tribute plaques. It's treated like a shrine by hordes of faithful followers who honor their idol by inserting lighted cigarettes in the statue's hand. On June 24, the anniversary of his death, aging *tangueros* in suits and fedoras gather here to weep and sing. Fellow tango legends Aníbal Troilo and Osvaldo Pugliese are also buried in this cemetery, which is about equidistant from Palermo and Almagro. If you're heading from Almagro, hop subte Line B at the Carlos Gardel Station for a 10- to 15-minute ride west to the Federico Lacroze stop. Depending on where you are in Palermo, a cab here will cost you 20 to 30 pesos. ⊠ *Guzmán 680, at Corrientes, Chacarita* ☎ *11/4553–9338* ☜ *Free* ☉ *Daily 7 am–6 pm* Ⓜ *B to Federico Lacroze.*

Museo Casa Carlos Gardel. Hard-core tango fans shouldn't pass up a quick visit to the home of tango's greatest hero, Carlos Gardel. The front rooms of this once-crumbling *casa chorizo* (sausage house—that is, a long, narrow house) contain extensive displays of Gardel paraphernalia—LPs, photos, and old posters. The maestro's greatest hits play in the background. The back of the house has been restored with the aim of re-creating as closely as possible the way the house would have looked when Gardel and his mother lived here, right down to the placement of birdcages on the patio. Concise but informative texts in Spanish and English talk you through the rooms and the history of tango in general. Short guided visits in English are usually available on request on weekdays. ⊠ *Jean Jaurés 735, Almagro* ☎ *11/4964–2015* ⊕ *www.museocasacarlosgardel.buenosaires.gob.ar* ☜ *1 peso, suggested donation 10 pesos; Wed. free* ☉ *Mon. and Wed.–Fri. 11–6, weekends 10–7* Ⓜ *B to Carlos Gardel.*

Museo de los Niños. The real world is scaled down to kiddie size at this museum in the Abasto shopping mall. Children can play at sending letters, going to a bank, acting in a mini-TV studio, or making a radio program. You need to speak Spanish to participate in most activities, but the play areas and giant pipes re-creating the city's water system are

MUSEO NACIONAL DE BELLAS ARTES

✉ *Av. del Libertador 1473, Recoleta* ☎ *11/5288–9900* ⊕ *www.mnba.org.ar* 🎫 *Free* ⏱ *Tues.–Fri. 12:30–8:30, weekends 9:30–8:30.*

TIPS

■ Information about most works is in Spanish only, as are the excellent themed guided tours. For English information, check out one of the MP3 audio guides (35 pesos), or purchase a map (10 pesos) or guide (30 pesos) to the collection.

■ You wouldn't know it by looking at the museum's elegant columned front, but the building was once the city's waterworks. Famed local architect Alejandro Bustillo oversaw its conversion into a museum in the early 1930s.

■ The large modern pavilion behind the museum hosts excellent temporary exhibitions, often showcasing top local artists little known outside Argentina.

★ **Fodor's Choice** The world's largest collection of Argentine art is displayed in this huge golden-color stone building. Most of the 24 richly colored ground-floor galleries contain pre-20th century European art. The beautifully curated Argentine circuit starts in Room 22 with works from shortly after the country's independence. The plan is for the upper floor to encompass the museum's 20th-century collection.

HIGHLIGHTS

The Rest of the River Plate. Uruguayan artists like Rafael Barradas and Joaquín Torres García are the focus of the hushed Colección María Luisa Bemberg.

Picturesque Portraits. Gauchos cut evocative figures in Cesáreo Bernaldo de Quirós's oil paintings. The highly colorful depictions of port laborers in *Elevadores a Pleno Sol* are typical of the work of Benito Quinquela Martín, La Boca's unofficial painter laureate.

At the Cutting Edge. The huge final gallery shows the involvement of Argentine artists in European avant-garde movements before adopting homegrown ideas. Emilio Pettorutti's *El Improvisador* (1937) combines cubist techniques with a Renaissance sense of space, while Lino Enea Spilimbergo's *Terracita* (1932) is an enigmatic urban landscape.

Movers and Shakers. Contemporary Argentine art exhibits include geometric sculptures and the so-called *informalismo* (informalism) of the '60s. Its innovative use of collage is best exemplified in works by Antonio Berni. Psychedelic paintings, op art, and kinetic works from '60s gurus like Jorge de la Vega and Antonio Seguí follow.

internationally comprehensible. ⊠ *Abasto Shopping Center, Level 2, Av. Corrientes 3247, Almagro* ☎ *11/4861-2325* ⊕ *www.museoabasto.org. ar* 🖭 *Children over 2, 40 pesos Tues.–Fri., 45 pesos weekends; adults 20 pesos* ⊘ *Tues.–Sun. 1–8.*

ART GALLERIES

★ **Daniel Abate.** Most of Abate's artists have yet to reach their 30th birthday, yet they've got plenty of local prizes among them. Unusual media are a common denominator—look for Alita Olivari's Koons-like sculptures, Betsabee Romero's sculptures made of tires and car chassis, Lila Siegrist's high-color photos of diminutive model landscapes, and outlandish installations by Eduardo Novarro and Oligatega Numeric. Abate alternates individual and collective shows and most visitors to them are serious collectors planning to buy. ⊠ *Pasaje Bollini 2170, Recoleta* ☎ *11/4804–8247* ⊕ *www.danielabategaleria.com.ar* ⊘ *Weekdays noon–6.*

Espacio Fundación Telefónica. Spanish-owned phone company Telefónica is behind this slick gallery, which they've tried to make as technological as possible. Video art and new media are showcased on the huge flat screens of the Espacio Plasma, and there's a state-of-the-art media library. ⊠ *Arenales 1540, Barrio Norte* ☎ *11/4333–1300* ⊕ *www. espacioft.org.ar* ⊘ *Tues.–Sat. 2–8:30, guided tours 5 pm.*

Praxis. Choice contemporary Argentine painting and photography are the main emphases of this sparse gallery. Their discreet shows have attracted Argentine collectors for years—their branches in Miami and New York are now taking local work international. ⊠ *Arenales 1311, Recoleta* ☎ *11/4813–8639* ⊕ *www.praxis-art.com* ⊘ *Weekdays 10:30– 8, Sat. 10:30–2.*

Rubbers. The name may sound quirky, but this formidable gallery on Avenida Alvear is anything but. The list of artists it represents reads like a who's who of Argentine art, and includes grand masters Xul Solar, Berni, Spilimbergo, and Seguí; photographer Aldo Sessa; and abstract genius Luis Felipe Noé, who exhibits with Rubbers each year (sometimes at other Recoleta locations). ⊠ *Av. Alvear 1595, Recoleta* ☎ *11/4816–1864* ⊕ *www.rubbers.com.ar* ⊘ *Weekdays 11–8, Sat. 11–1:30.*

PALERMO

Sightseeing
★★★★

Dining
★★★★★

Lodging
★★★★

Shopping
★★★★★

Nightlife
★★★

Trendy shops, bold restaurants, elegant embassies, acres of parks—Palermo really does have it all. Whether your idea of sightseeing is ticking off museums, flicking through clothing racks, licking your fingers after yet another long lunch, or kicking up a storm on the dance floor, Palermo can oblige. The city's largest barrio is subdivided into various unofficial districts, each with its own distinct flavor.

Elegant boutiques, minimal lofts, endless bars, and the most fun and daring restaurants in town have made Palermo Viejo (also known as Palermo Soho) the epicenter of Buenos Aires' design revolution. Many are contained in beautifully recycled town houses built in the late 19th century, when Palermo became a popular residential district. Most shops and eateries—not to mention desirable properties—in Palermo Viejo fill the cobbled streets around Plazoleta Cortázar.

In neighboring Palermo Hollywood, quiet barrio houses and the flea market at Dorrego and Niceto Vega sit alongside sharp tapas bars filled with media types from the TV production centers that give the area its nickname.

Some say Palermo takes its name from the surname of a 16th-century Italian immigrant who bought lands in the area, others from the abbey honoring Saint Benedict of Palermo. Either way, the area was largely rural until the mid-19th century, when national governor Juan Manuel de Rosas built an estate here. Next, these grounds were turned into the huge patchwork of parks north of Avenida del Libertador. Their official name, Parque Tres de Febrero, is a reference to February 3, 1852, the day Rosas was defeated in battle. The park, which is more commonly known as Los Bosques de Palermo (the Palermo Woods), provides a peaceful escape from the rush of downtown. The zoo and botanical gardens are at its southern end.

GETTING ORIENTED

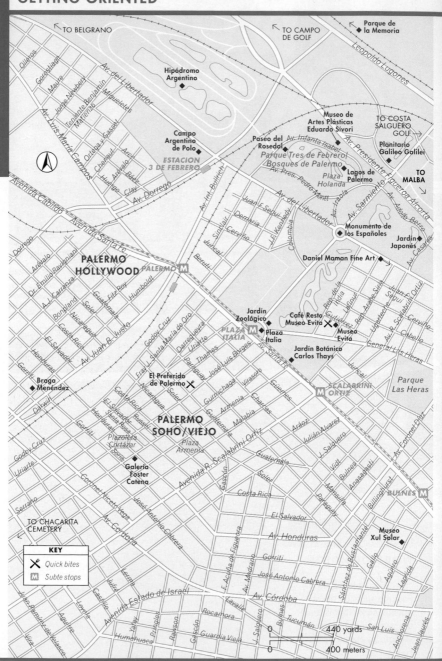

TO BELGRANO

TO CAMPO
DE GOLF

Parque de
la Memoria

Leopoldo Lugones

Hipódromo
Argentino

Av. del Libertador

Olleros

Gorostiaga
Maure
Jorge Newbery
Teniente Benjamin
Matienzo
Migueletes

Campo
Argentino
de Polo

ESTACIÓN
3 DE FEBRERO

Museo de
Artes Plásticas
Eduardo Sívori

TO COSTA
SALGUERO
GOLF

Paseo del
Rosedal

Av. Infanta Isabel

Planetario
Galileo Galilei

Parque Tres de Febrero
Bosques de Palermo

TO
MALBA

Av. Pres. Pedro Montt

Lagos de
Palermo

Plaza
Holanda

Av. Sarmiento

Av. Presidente Figueroa Alcorta

Av. del Libertador

Av. Tacza

Av. Adolfo Berro

Av. Luis María Campos

Ortega y Gasset
Arce
Chenaut
Arévalo
Báez
Huergo
Clay

Av. Dorrego

Av. Int. Bullrich

Juan F. Seguí

Demaria

Cerviño

Sinclair

Berutti

Monumento de
los Españoles

Jardín
Japonés

Avenida Cabildo

Avenida Santa Fe

Dorrego

Arévalo

Dr. Emilio Ravignani

A.J. Carranza

Bonpland

Nicaragua

Costa Rica

El Salvador

Honduras

Gorriti

Av. Luis María Campos

Soler

Guatemala

Humboldt

Av. Juan B. Justo

Godoy Cruz

Fray J. Santa María de Oro

Darragueyra

Uriarte

Thames

Paraguay

José Luis Borges

Gurruchaga

Juncal

Columbia

K. Kelliot

PALERMO
HOLLYWOOD

PALERMO Ⓜ

Daniel Maman Fine Art

Jardín
Zoológico

Café Resto
Museo Evita ✕

PLAZA
ITALIA Ⓜ

Plaza
Italia

Museo
Evita

Jardín Botánico
Carlos Thays

Rep. de la India

Av. Presidente Figueroa Alcorta

Rep. Árabe Siria

General Las Heras

Salguero

Juan María Ortiz

Cerviño

Cabello

Libertador

Parque
Las Heras

Braga
Menéndez

El Preferido
de Palermo ✕

Charcas

Guardia Vieja

SCALABRINI
ORTIZ Ⓜ

Av. Córdoba

Av. Coronel Díaz

Darwin

Cabrera

Serrano

Fitz Roy

El Salvador
Honduras
Gorriti
Costa Rica

Santa Rosa

Plazoleta
Cortázar

Soria

PALERMO
SOHO/VIEJO

Plaza
Armenia

Malabia

Armenia

Araoz

Av. Scalabrini Ortiz

Julián Álvarez

J. Salguero

Vidt

Bulnes

Mansilla

Paraguay

Anasagasti

Billinghurst

BULNES Ⓜ

Galería
Foster
Catena

Av. Raúl Scalabrini Ortiz

Gascón

Guatemala

Soler

Costa Rica

Godoy Cruz

Uriarte

Coronel Niceto Vega

José Antonio Cabrera

El Salvador

Av. Honduras

Gorriti

José Antonio Cabrera

Museo
Xul Solar

Gallo

Gascón

Mario Bravo

Sánchez de Bustamante

TO CHACARITA
CEMETERY

Av. Córdoba

Loyola

Juan Ramírez de Velasco

Aguirre

Castillo

Pierres

Lerma

Avenida Estado de Israel

F. Acuña de Figueroa

Av. Medrano

Zabala

José Antonio Cabrera

Av. Córdoba

Tucumán

San Luis

Anchorena

Laprida

Aráoz

Serrano

Humahuaca

Gascón

Guardia Vieja

J. Salguero

Bulnes

Rocamora

KEY

✕ Quick bites

Ⓜ Subte stops

| 0 | | 440 yards |
| 0 | | 400 meters |

THE TERRITORY

The city's biggest barrio stretches from Avenida Costanera R. Obligado, along the river, to Avenida Córdoba in the south. Its other boundaries are jagged, but include Avenida Coronel Díaz to the east and La Pampa and Dorrego to the west. Avenida Santa Fe cuts the neighborhood roughly in half. Palermo's green spaces and Palermo Chico lie north of it. To the south are Palermo Viejo and Palermo Hollywood, east and west of Avenida Juan B. Justo, respectively.

GETTING AROUND

Subte Línea (Line) D runs along Avenida Santa Fe, but doesn't always bring you to the doorstep of Palermo's attractions, so you may need to combine it with a taxi or some walking. Indeed, weekday traffic makes this combination a better idea than coming all the way from Centro by cab (which costs 20–30 pesos). Get off the subte at Bulnes or Scalabrini Ortíz for Palermo Chico; Plaza Italia for Palermo Viejo and the parks; and Ministro Carranza for Palermo Hollywood.

A more scenic route to Palermo Viejo and Hollywood from Centro is Bus 39 (Route 3, usually with a windshield sign "Palermo Viejo"). It runs along Honduras on the way to Palermo and Gorriti on the way back, and it takes 30–60 minutes. Once you're in Palermo, walking is the best way to get around: much of the district is leafy, and there's little traffic on its smaller streets.

SAFETY AND PRECAUTIONS

Pickpocketing is the biggest threat, especially on crowded streets on weekends. Palermo Viejo's cobbled streets aren't well lighted at night, so avoid walking along any that look lonely. Although locals usually hail cabs on the street, it's safer to ask a restaurant or bar to call one for you. The usual caveats about parks apply to the Palermo woods: don't linger after dark, and avoid remote areas at any time if you're female and alone.

TOP EXPERIENCES

Betting: on which up-and-coming artists at the Daniel Maman or Braga Menéndez galleries will end up in MALBA.

Exercising: your arms in Palermo Viejo carrying bags on a boutique crawl or lifting cocktails on a bar crawl.

Visiting: with Evita, getting to grips on the phenomenon that she was by taking in the Museo Evita.

Wandering: on the winding paths of Parque Tres de Febrero, to smell the roses, or along Honduras—east of Juan B. Justo for boutiques, west of it for bars and restaurants.

QUICK BITES

El Preferido de Palermo. Nothing changes the tall Formica tables of 1960s-general-store-meets-snackbar El Preferido de Palermo. A plate of cold cuts and pickles or sandwiches are the way to go. ⊠ *Jorge L. Borges 2108, Palermo Viejo* ☎ *11/4774–6585* ⊙ *Mon.–Sat. noon–4 and 8–12.*

Café Resto Museo Evita. The checkered floors and glossy black tables of Café Resto Museo Evita are as stylish as the great lady herself. ⊠ *J. M. Gutiérrez 3926, Palermo Botánico* ☎ *11/4800–1599* ⊙ *Mon.–Sat. 9 am–12:30 am, Sun. 9 am–7 pm.*

Palermo has two mainstream shopping areas. The streets around the intersection of Avenidas Santa Fe and Coronel Díaz are home to the mid-range Alto Palermo mall and many cheap clothing stores. There are more exclusive brands at El Solar de la Abadía mall and the nearby streets of Las Cañitas, Palermo's northwestern outpost. Its thriving, in-your-face bar-and-restaurant scene is the favorite of local models, TV starlets, and others dying to be seen. If a week away from your analyst is bringing on anxiety attacks, the quiet residential district around Plaza Güemes might bring some relief: it's nicknamed Villa Freud, for the high concentration of psychoanalysts who live and work here.

Plastic surgery and imported everything are the norm in Palermo Chico (between Avenidas Santa Fe and Libertador), whose Parisian-style mansions are shared out between embassies and rich local stars like diva Susana Giménez. Higher-brow culture is provided by the gleaming MALBA (Museo de Arte Latinoamericano de Buenos Aires, or the Museum of Latin American Art of Buenos Aires), whose clean stone lines stand out on Avenida Figueroa Alcorta.

TAKING IT IN

Palermo is so big that it's best to tackle it in sections. An even-paced ramble through Parque Tres de Febrero should take no more than two hours, though you could easily spend an entire afternoon at the zoo, Japanese Garden, and Botanical Garden. In architectural and geographic terms, Palermo Chico and the MALBA tie in nicely with a visit to Recoleta: allow at least a couple of hours for such an experience.

TOP ATTRACTIONS

ℭ **Jardín Japonés** (*Japanese Garden*). Like the bonsais in the nursery within it, this park is small but perfectly formed. A slow wander along its arched wooden bridges and walkways is guaranteed to calm frazzled sightseeing nerves during the week; crowds on the weekend make for a less-than-zen experience. A variety of shrubs and flowers frame the ponds, which brim with friendly koi carp that let you pet them should you feel inclined (kids often do). The traditional teahouse, where you can enjoy sushi, adzuki-bean sweets, and tea, overlooks a zen garden. ⊠ *Av. Casares at Av. Figueroa Alcorta, Palermo* ☎ *11/4804–4922* ⊕ *www.jardinjapones.org.ar* ☜ *8 pesos* ⊙ *Daily 10–6.*

★ **Museo Evita.**
See the highlighted listing in this chapter.

Fodor's Choice **Museo de Arte de Latinoamericano de Buenos Aires** (MALBA, Museum of
★ Latin American Art of Buenos Aires).
See the highlighted listing in this chapter.

★ **Parque de la Memoria.** Between 1969 and 1983, 30,000 civilians were illegally detained, tortured, and "disappeared" in Argentina by the 1976–83 military dictatorship and the paramilitary operations that preceded their coup. The 35-acre site of the country's first memorial park was chosen because it borders the River Plate, into which many of

MUSEO EVITA

✉ *Lafinur 2988, 1 block north of Av. Las Heras, Palermo* ☎ *11/4807-0306* ⊕ *www.museoevita.org* 🎟 *15 pesos; guided tours 35 pesos* ⏱ *Tues.–Sun. 11–7* Ⓜ *D to Plaza Italia.*

TIPS

■ Laminated cards with just-understandable English translations of the exhibits are available in each room and at the ticket booth.

■ Plan time for a post-museum coffee (or lunch) at the museum café's outside tables, shaded by classy black umbrellas. There's also a small gift shop.

■ The gray-stone mansion dates from 1909. It was purchased in 1948 by the Fundación de Ayuda Social Eva Perón (Eva Perón Social Aid Foundation) and converted into a home for single mothers, to the horror of the rich, conservative families living nearby.

■ The Evita myth can be baffling to the uninitiated. The museum's excellent guided visits shed light on the phenomenon and are available in English, but must be arranged by phone in advance.

Eva Duarte de Perón, known universally as Evita, was the wife of populist president Juan Domingo Perón. She was both revered by her working-class followers and despised by the Anglophile oligarchy of the time. The Museo Evita shies from pop culture clichés and conveys facts about Evita's life and works, particularly the social aid programs she instituted and her role in getting women the vote. Knowledgeable staffers answer questions enthusiastically.

HIGHLIGHTS

Photographic Evidence. The route through the collection begins in a darkened room screening footage of hundreds of thousands of mourners lining up to see Evita's body. Family photos and magazine covers document Evita's humble origins and time as a B-list actress. Upstairs there's English-subtitled footage of Evita's incendiary speeches to screaming crowds: her impassioned delivery beats Madonna's hands down.

Death Becomes Her. The final rooms follow Evita's withdrawal from political life and her death from cancer at age 33. A video chronicles the fate of Evita's cadaver: embalmed by Perón, stolen by political opponents, and moved and hidden for 17 years before being returned to Argentina, where it now rests in the Recoleta Cemetery.

Fabulous Clothes. Evita's reputation as fashion plate is reflected in the many designer outfits on display, including her trademark working suits and some gorgeous ball gowns.

MALBA

✉ *Av. Presidente Figueroa Alcorta 3415, Palermo* ☎ *11/4808-6500* ⊕ *www. malba.org.ar* 🎫 *22 pesos; Wed. 10 pesos* ⊙ *Thurs.–Mon. noon–8, Wed. noon–9.*

TIPS

■ MALBA also has a great art cinema showing restored copies of classics, never-released features, and silent films with live music, as well as local films of note.

■ Kids love hands-on kinetic works like Julio Le Parc's Seven Unexpected Movements, a sculpture with gleaming parts that move at the press of a button.

■ Leave time to browse the art books and funky design objects of the museum's excellent gift shop.

■ Young, enthusiastic guides give great tours of the permanent collection in Spanish on Wednesdays and Sundays at 4 pm.

■ Give your feet—and eyes—a rest on the first-floor sculpture deck, with views over Belgrano and Barrio Norte.

■ Córdoba-based studio AFT Arquitectos' triangular construction in creamy stone and steel is one of the museum's draws. The main galleries run along a four-story atrium, flooded in natural light from a wall of windows.

★ **Fodor's Choice** The fabulous Museum of Latin American Art of Buenos Aires (MALBA) is one of the cornerstones of the city's cultural life. Its centerpiece is businessman and founder Eduardo Constantini's collection of more than 220 works of 19th- and 20th-century Latin-American art in the main first-floor gallery.

HIGHLIGHTS

Europe vs. Latin America. Early works in the permanent collection reflect the European avant-garde experiences of painters like Diego Rivera, Xul Solar, Roberto Matta, and Joaquín Torres García. Soon the Latin American experience gave rise to works like *Abaporu* (1928) by Tarsila do Amaral, a Brazilian involved in the "cannibalistic" Movimento Antropofágico (rather than eating white Europeans, proponents of the movement proposed devouring European culture and digesting it into something new). Geometric paintings and sculptures from the 1940s represent movements such as Arte Concreto, Constructivism, and Arte Madí.

Argentine Art. Argentina's undisputed modern master is Antonio Berni, represented by a poptastic collage called *The Great Temptation* (1962) and the bizarre sculpture *Voracity or Ramona's Nightmare* (1964), both featuring the eccentric prostitute Ramona, a character Berni created in this series of works criticizing consumer society. Works by local greats Liliana Porter, Marta Minujín, Guillermo Kuitca, and Alejandro Kuropatwa form the end of the permanent collection.

Temporary Exhibitions. World-class temporary exhibitions are held on the second floor two or three times a year, and two small basement galleries show art by cutting-edge locals.

the *desaparecidos* (disappeared) were thrown, heavily drugged but still alive, from military aircraft. The park is designed to look toward the city skyline as a reminder of citizens' widespread collusion with the military government. The chilling stone walls slicing down through the park to the river form the **Monumento a las Víctimas del Terrorismo del Estado** (Monument to the Victims of State-Organized Terrorism). Engraved on it are the names of roughly 9,000 identified victims and their ages, organized by the year they disappeared. You reach the park and the monument via a square containing sculptures such as Roberto Aizenberg's untitled piece representing his three disappeared stepchildren, and Dennis Oppenheim's *Monument to Escape*. The small information booth usually has leaflets in English. ⊠ *Av. Costanera Norte Rafael Obligado 6745, Belgrano* ☎ *11/4787–0999* ⊕ *www.parquedelamemoria.org.ar* ▧ *Free* ☼ *Daily 10–6.*

☾ **Parque Tres de Febrero.** Known locally as Los Bosques de Palermo (Pal-
★ ermo Woods), this 200-acre green space is really a crazy quilt of smaller parks. Lush grass and shady trees make it an urban oasis, although the busy roads and horn-honking drivers that crisscross the park never let you forget what city you're in. South of Avenida Figueroa Alcorta you can take part in organized tai chi and exercise classes or impromptu soccer matches. You can also jog, bike, or in-line skate here, or take a pedal boat out on the tiny lake. The park gets crowded on sunny weekends, as this is where families come for strolls or picnics. If you'd like to picnic, take advantage of the street vendors who sell refreshments and *choripan* (chorizo sausage in a bread roll) within the park. There are also several posh cafés lining the Paseo de la Infanta (running from Libertador toward Sarmiento in the park).

Museo de Artes Plásticas Eduardo Sívori (*Eduardo Sívori Art Museum*). If you're looking for a sedate activity, try the Museo de Artes Plásticas Eduardo Sívori, which resides in the Parque Tres de Febrero. The focus of this collection is 19th- and 20th-century Argentine art, including paintings by local masters like Emilio Petorutti, Lino Eneo Spilimbergo, Antonio Berni, and the museum's namesake Sívori. The shaded sculpture garden is the perfect combination of art and park. ⊠ *Av. Infanta Isabel 555* ☎ *11/4774–9452* ⊕ *www.museosivori.org* ▧ *1 peso, Wed. and Sat. free* ☼ *Tues.–Fri. noon–8, weekends 10–8.*

Paseo del Rosedal (*Rose Garden*). Close to the Museo de Artes Plásticas Eduardo Sívori (within the Parque Tres Febrero) is the Paseo del Rosedal. About 12,000 rosebushes (more than 1,000 different species) bloom seasonally in this rose garden. A stroll along the paths takes you through the Jardín de los Poetas (Poets' Garden), dotted with statues of literary figures, and to the enchanting Patio Andaluz (Andalusian Patio), whose majolica tiles and Spanish mosaics sit under a vine-covered pergola. ⊠ *Avs. Infanta Isabel and Iraola* ▧ *Free* ☼ *Apr.–Oct., daily 9–6; Nov.–Mar., daily 8–8.*

Planetario Galileo Galilei (*Galileo Galilei Planetarium*). One of the city's most iconic buildings, the Planetario Galileo Galilei is a great orb positioned on a massive concrete tripod. Built in the early 1960s, it looks like something out of *Close Encounters of the Third Kind,* and it seems as though small green men could descend from its central staircase at any moment. At this writing, the inside was closed for renovation, but the authentic 3,373-pound asteroid remained in place at the entrance. The nearby pond with swans, geese, and ducks is a favorite with kids. ✉ *Avs. Sarmiento and Figueroa Alcorta* ☎ *11/4771–9393* ⊕ *www.planetario.gob.ar* ✆ *Free* ✉ *Bounded by Avs. del Libertador, Sarmiento, Leopoldo Lugones, and Dorrego* Ⓜ *D to Plaza Italia.*

WORTH NOTING

☙ **Jardín Botánico Carlos Thays.** With 18 acres of gardens and 5,500 varieties of exotic and local flora, the Carlos Thays Botanical Garden is an unexpected green haven wedged between three busy Palermo streets. Different sections re-create the environments of Asia, Africa, Oceania, Europe, and the Americas. Among the treasures is the Chinese "tree of gold," purportedly the only one of its kind. An organic vegetable garden aims to teach children healthy habits. Winding paths lead to hidden statues, a brook, and past the resident cats and dragonflies. The central area contains a beautiful greenhouse, brought from France in 1900, and the exposed-brick botanical school and library. ✉ *Av. Santa Fe 3951* ☎ *11/4832–1552* ⊕ *www.jardinbotanico.buenosaires.gob.ar* ✆ *Free* ☉ *Sept.–Mar., weekdays 8–7, weekends 9:30–7; Apr.–Aug., weekdays 8–6, weekends 9:30–6* Ⓜ *D to Plaza Italia.*

☙ **Jardín Zoológico.** The grandiose stone pens and mews—many dating from the zoo's opening in 1874—are as much an attraction at the 45-acre city zoo as their inhabitants. Jorge Luis Borges said the recurring presence of tigers in his work was inspired by time spent here. Today, the rare albino tiger may inspire you to pen a few lines of your own. South American animals you may not have seen before include the *aguará guazú* (a sort of fox), the *coatí* (a local raccoon), anteaters, and the black howler monkey. Some smaller animals roam freely, and there are play areas for children, a petting farm, and a seal show. *Mateos* (traditional, decorated horse-drawn carriages) stand poised at the entrance to whisk you around the nearby parks. ✉ *Avs. General Las Heras and Sarmiento, Palermo* ☎ *11/4011–9900* ⊕ *www.zoobuenosaires.com.ar* ✆ *32 pesos* ☉ *Tues.–Sun. 10–5* Ⓜ *D to Plaza Italia.*

Museo Xul Solar. Avant-garde artist, linguist, esoteric philosopher, and close friend of Borges, Xul Solar is best known for his luminous, semi-abstract watercolors. They glow against the low-lighted concrete walls of this hushed museum. Solar's wacky but endearing beliefs in universalism led him to design a pan-language, pan-chess (a set is displayed here), and the Pan Klub, where these ideas were debated. One of its former members, architect Pablo Beitia, masterminded the transformation of the town house where Solar lived and worked. Open stairways crisscross the space, an homage to one of Solar's favorite motifs. ✉ *Laprida 1212* ☎ *11/4824–3302* ⊕ *www.xulsolar.org.ar* ✆ *10 pesos, free Thurs.* ☉ *Tues.–Fri. noon–7, Sat. noon–6.*

Continued on page 102

ARGENTINIAN ICONS

SAINTS, SINNERS & PRODIGAL SONS by Victoria Patience

One minute Argentinians are cursing their country's shortcomings; the next they're waving a flag and screaming "Ar-gen-tina" as their soccer team chalks up a victory. But when it comes to their famous sons and daughters, most Argentinans are resolutely proud.

Were it not for the heroics of one man, José de San Martín, Argentina might not exist at all. Raised in Spain, he was a passionate believer in Latin American independence.

You could say that in modern Argentinian politics, it takes two to tango. The original political double act was Juan Domingo Perón and his wife, Evita, who were revered and reviled in equal measure.

Indeed, passionate hatred of Perón and serious literary genius were among the few things shared by two great Argentinian writers: erudite Anglophile Jorge Luis Borges and bearded bohemian Julio Cortázar.

Revolution was the passion of Ernesto Guevara, or rather, El Che. This middle-class med student was instrumental in the building of Castro's Cuba, and remains the figurehead of many left-wing student movements. You'll find Che's face tattooed on the arm of a different secular saint: Diego Armando Maradona, voted the 20th century's best soccer player by FIFA (International Football Association). The toughest local machos have been brought to tears by his goals.

(top) Eva Perón and Che Guevara posters. (bottom) Diego Maradona during the 1979 World Youth Championship in Japan.

POLITICAL FIGURES

AKA: El Libertador de America
BORN: February 25, 1778, in Yapeyú, Argentina
DIED: August 17, 1850, in Boulogne-sur-Mer, France
QUOTE: "Let us be free. Nothing else matters."
REMEMBERED: A national public holiday commemorates the anniversary of his death.

JOSÉ DE SAN MARTÍN

TOP 3 SAN MARTÍN SIGHTS

Plaza San Martín, named in his honor, contains a monument to the general, who looks dashing atop his horse.

Museo Histórico Nacional, which has recreated San Martín's bedroom at the time he died.

Catedral de Buenos Aires, home to his mausoleum.

BIO: Ironically, the man who freed Argentina from Spanish colonial shackles spent his formative years in Spain. But when news of Argentina's May 1810 revolution reached him, he abandoned an illustrious career in the Spanish army and rushed back to the country of his birth. His flamboyant military campaigns were instrumental in the independence of the Viceroyalty of the Río de la Plata (Argentina, Paraguay, Bolivia, and Uruguay). He then led his forces across the Andes to liberate Chile and Peru.

Today, San Martín's selfless idealism is universally lauded. However, he fell from favor in his lifetime by refusing to spill a fellow Argentine's blood and participate in Argentina's civil war. His military pension was never honored, and he died in France in severe financial straits, far from the country he'd fought so hard for.

POSTHUMOUS ADVENTURES: San Martín expressly requested in his will that his heart be buried in Buenos Aires. Political disagreements and red tape meant 30 years went by before his body was repatriated and he was finally laid to rest in a mausoleum in Buenos Aires Cathedral. The urn-like structure designed to contain his coffin was built too short, so he was placed in it on an angle (head down, local legend says) to fit.

(top) General José de San Martín engraving; (bottom) Monument to the Libertador General San Martín, by Frances Louis Joseph Daumes in Plaza San Martín, Buenos Aires, Argentina

2

AKA: El General; The Father of the Nation

BORN: October 8, 1895, in Lobos, Argentina

DIED: July 1, 1974, in Olivos, Argentina

QUOTE: "Better than saying is doing; better than promising, achieving."

REMEMBERED: Union members and fiercely loyal Peronists recreate the demonstrations in Plaza de Mayo that got Perón freed on October 17, 1945, the so-called Día de la Lealtad (Day of Loyalty).

POSTHUMOUS ADVENTURES: In 1987, thieves stole Perón's hands from his tomb in Buenos Aires' Chacarita Cemetery. Some say they demanded an $8 million ransom, others that they needed his fingerprints to access a bank deposit box in Switzerland. When the body was moved to a special mausoleum in 2006, scuffles between police and Peronist demonstrators led to 40 injuries.

JUAN DOMINGO PERÓN

BIO: Perón is a complex figure, even for Argentinians. Although he was an army general, Perón reached the presidency through a landslide election victory. He revolutionized worker's rights, nationalized Argentina's services, championed local industry, expanded the country's health and education, and instigated a huge social aid program. Despite these left-leaning policies, he loathed communism, and even secretly facilitated the entry of Nazi war criminals into Argentina.

The General and Evita were the people's pin-ups, but things began to fall apart after her death. Ousted by a coup in 1955, Perón went into an 18-year exile, during which Peronism was made illegal in Argentina. He made a glorious comeback in 1973, but party infighting soon soured things. He died in office in 1974 and was briefly and disastrously succeeded by the vice president, his third wife. Argentina's most horrific dictatorship soon followed. The Peronist party is riddled with contradictions—it spawned both the right-wing government of Carlos Menem and the center-left Kirchners—but Argentine politics still live in its shadow.

(top) Juan Domingo Perón (1895–1974), president of Argentina, addressing the parliament, May, 1952; (bottom) Perón and Evita

SANTA EVITA

AKA: Evita, mother of the nation, Spiritual Leader of the Nation, Santa Evita (Saint Evita), *esa mujer* (that woman)
BORN: May 17, 1919, in Los Toldos, Argentina
DIED: July 26, 1952, in Buenos Aires
QUOTE: "I have only one thing that counts, and I carry it in my heart. It burns my soul, it aches in my flesh, and it stings my nerves, and that is my love for the people and for Perón. I never wanted anything for myself, nor do I want it now. My glory is and will always be Perón and the flag of my people."
REMEMBERED: Loyal Peronists cover Evita's tomb with flowers and hold candlelight vigils on the anniversary of her death.

EVA MARÍA DUARTE DE PERÓN

BIO: Evita was revered long before musicals and Hollywood films made her internationally famous. Born in the provinces, she left home for Buenos Aires at 17, and soon became a B-movie actress. However, her loyalties switched from showbiz to politics upon meeting Perón, and they married during his first presidential campaign. Her campaign for female suffrage helped his re-election in 1951. Until her untimely death from cancer at the age of 33, Evita and Perón were a duo of unprecedented popularity. However, Evita is a contradictory figure: despite her designer frocks and perfect blonde chignon, her politics were radical, to the horror of the conservatives of the time. Her activism championed the working class as well as the poor and such marginalized groups as single mothers, and brought her millions of fanatical followers, who, more than 50 years on, still campaign for her to be made a saint.

POSTHUMOUS ADVENTURES: When a coup overthrew Perón in 1955, Evita's embalmed body was stolen by the opposition. The casket was stored in several army offices, hidden in an embassy garden in Bonn, buried under a false name in Italy, and put on display by Perón's third wife before it was finally laid in the family vault in Recoleta cemetery in 1977.

(top) 1950, Eva Perón being presented with an insignia by volunteer workers of the Institute for Work of Argentina

EVITA PILGRIMAGE

"¡Evita vive!" ("Evita lives"), her faithful followers never tire of saying. It's not just the national psyche she's left a lasting impression on: the city itself is full of places inextricably linked to her. Here's how to see them all during one day in Buenos Aires.

Start your pilgrimage in morbid Argentine style, at her tomb in **Recoleta Cemetery** (Junín 1760, Recoleta). If you come near the anniversary of her death, July 26, expect tearful crowds and piles and piles of flowers.

Intrigued? Catch a taxi or buses 37, 59, or 60 north along nearby Av. Las Heras to the 3900 block in Palermo to get the Evita 101 at the excellent **Museo Evita** (Lafinur 2988, 1 block north of Av. Las Heras, Palermo). Its classy, all-day restaurant is a good bet for coffee or lunch.

Then catch the subte from nearby Plaza Italia to Belgrano station on Línea C. Two 100-foot high portraits of Evita decorate the north and south faces of building in the center of Av. 9 de Julio. In 1951, Evita renounced her vice-presidential candidacy from a stage here before two million passionate supporters.

It's a short taxi ride or a 12-block walk east along Av. Belgrano then south on Paseo Colón to the monumental **Facultad de Ingeniería** (Faculty of Engineering; Paseo Colón 850, San Telmo). This rather totalitarian-looking building was originally designed for the Fundación Eva Perón, Evita's aid organization. Before being stolen by anti-Peronists, Evita's embalmed body lay in state for three years at the **Edificio de la CGT** (Building of the General Confederation of Labor; Azopardo 802, San Telmo), just around the corner from the Facultad de Ingeniería.

You can pick up Evita-print packing tape and other collectibles at **Tienda Palacio** (Defensa 926, San Telmo), two blocks west of the Edificio de la CGT along Av. Independencia and two blocks south along Defensa.

Next, head to Plaza de Mayo. Here, thousands of Perón's supporters protested his imprisonment in 1945 and were moved to tears by Evita's speeches from the balcony of the Casa Rosada.

Now the only thing left to do is throw back your head and sing "Don't Cry for me, Argentina."

(left) Burial plaque at Recoleta; (right) nursing school uniform at Museo Evita

LITERARY GIANTS

AKA: Georgie (his family nickname); H. Bustos Domecq (the pseudonym he and friend Adolfo Bioy Casares used for their collaborations).

BORN: August 24, 1899, in Buenos Aires

DIED: June 14, 1986, in Geneva, Switzerland

QUOTES: "To me it seems impossible that Buenos Aires once began / I judge her as eternal as the water and the air." "Reading . . . is an activity subsequent to writing: more resigned, more civil, more intellectual."

POLITICAL LEARNINGS: Extreme conservative, so much so that he initially praised the 1976 military coup, but ended up petitioning General Videla over disappearances.

DAY JOBS: Librarian; first in a small neighborhood library where his anti-Peronist sentiments got him fired; and eventually director of the National Library, courtesy of a military government he supported.

MARRIAGES: Two: Elsa Astete Millán, a one-time childhood sweetheart, in 1967. Borges described the marriage as "total incompatibility," and they divorced in 1970. María Kodama, a former student, 45 years his junior, shortly before his death in 1985. She had been his secretary, travel companion, and then partner for 10 years.

JORGE LUIS BORGES

BIO: Borges claimed all his life to belong far more to the 19th century than the 20th. A lifelong Anglophile, his conservative politics were probably what denied him the Nobel Prize many feel he deserved. His political ideas also earned him the passionate hatred of many Argentine intellectuals, although lots of them were eventually sufficiently overcome by his literary brilliance to forgive him.

LINGUISTIC TRIVIA: Legend has it Borges first read that greatest of Spanish works, *Don Quixote*, in English translation, and when faced with the Spanish original, thought it inferior. For, ironically, although Borges was a magician of the Spanish language, the first language he learned to read in was English, thanks to his English grandmother.

NOW READ ON: BORGES

- The Aleph and Other Stories
- Fictions
- Brodie's Report

Penguin

(top) Jorge Luis Borges, at home, Buenos Aires, 1983

AKA: Julio Denis, the pseudonym he published early work under.

BORN: August 26, 1914, in Argentine Embassy of Brussels, Belgium

DIED: February 12, 1984, in Paris, France

QUOTE: "Nothing is lost if we have the courage to admit that everything is lost and that we have to start again."

POLITICAL LEARNINGS: Very left-wing, he was a committed supporter of the Cuban revolution but was rejected by Castro when he protested the arrest of a Cuban poet for political reasons.

DAY JOBS: High-school teacher, but resigned when Perón came to power; translator for UNESCO; also translated Edgar Allan Poe and G.K. Chesterton, among others, into Spanish.

MARRIAGES: Three: Aurora Bernárdez, an Argentine translator, in 1955. Ugné Karvelis, a Lithuanian activist, whom he met in 1967. Carol Dunlop, a Canadian poet, in 1979.

JULIO CORTÁZAR

BIO: Cortázar's semi-surreal prose and flamboyant bohemian lifestyle have long made him the intellectual pin-up for idealistic students throughout Latin America. He began to publish in earnest after 1951, when a scholarship took him to Paris. He lived in that city for the rest of his life but always wrote in Spanish. His most famous works appeared in the 1960s, including the highly experimental *Hopscotch*, a story of Argentine beatniks afloat in Paris, the chapters of which can be read in any order. Stories from his several collections were published in English as *Blow-Up: And Other Stories*; Michelangelo Antonioni based his award-winning film on the title story. Jazz, boxing, and politics were also big passions, and he signed over the royalties of two books to Argentine political prisoners and the Sandinista movement in Nicaragua. Ironically for one who was also a brilliant translator, the English-language versions of his work have yet to gain him the respect he commands in Spanish.

LINGUISTIC TRIVIA: His early childhood in Belgium left him incapable of pronouncing the Spanish "r."

NOW READ ON: CORTÁZAR

- Hopscotch
- "Blow-Up": And Other Stories
- 62: A Model Kit

Pantheon

(left) June 1967, Paris, France; (right) Mature Cortázar and cat

SOUL STIRRERS

ERNESTO "CHE" GUEVARA DE LA SERNA

BIO: Ironically, this socialist figurehead started life in an upper-middle class family and was a keen player of rugby, considered a posh sport. Soon, his horror at the plight of Latin American peasants and workers and a chance meeting with the young Fidel Castro in Mexico led to his well-known participation in the Cuban revolution, first as a guerrilla and eventually as President of the National Bank and Minister of Industries.

Darker allegations also surround this time in Che's life: some say the trials—and executions—of Batista followers he oversaw in La Cabaña prison in 1959 were unfair. Che soon realized that he was more suited to fighting oppression than to pushing paper at the ministry. He led guerrilla campaigns in the Congo and Bolivia, where he was executed by Bolivian soldiers on October 9, 1967. His ideals, ascetic lifestyle, and, more than anything, a lot of very dramatic photographs have transformed him into a pop icon.

DID YOU KNOW?

Mario Terán, the Bolivian army sergeant who fired the shots that killed Che, benefited greatly from the Cuban health system. Just shy of the 40th anniversary of Che's death, Terán had cataracts removed by Cuban doctors in Bolivia as part of Operation Milagro, a program offering eye surgery to Latin Americans in need of free treatment.

(top left) Argentinian revolutionary portrait; (top right) posters; (bottom) Che Guevara and Fidel Castro

AKA: El 10 (Number 10), El Diego de la Gente (The Diego of the People), La Mano de Dios (The Hand of God).

BORN: October 30, 1960, in Buenos Aires

QUOTE: "It was the hand of God!" in defense of his supposed hand-goal in the 1986 World Cup.

SUPPORTS: Boca Juniors

DEFINING MOMENT: 1986 soccer World Cup quarter-final against England, when he scored his goal after dribbling down half the field and dodging round five players and the goalkeeper. FIFA voted it the Goal of the Century.

HEALTH PROBLEMS: Recurring cocaine addiction and obesity.

MARADONA SPOTTING

He might not be making the headlines, but you might see him . . .

■ . . . cheering on Boca Juniors or the Argentinian soccer team with his daughters from a special box. He's often in the crowds at international tennis and polo matches, too.

■ . . . in TV interviews giving his opinion on everything from soccer coaching to Latin American politics (in 2007 he was a guest on Venezuelan president Hugo Chávez's show, *Aló Presidente*).

DIEGO ARMANDO MARADONA

BIO: Ask any local soccer fan what nationality God is, and their answer will be "Argentinian," in clear reference to Diego Armando Maradona, whose status as national sporting idol can't get any higher. A football prodigy, Maradona grew up in one of Buenos Aires' shantytowns, but started playing professionally at the age of 10. He shot to fame in the early '80s playing for Boca Juniors and then Italian team Napoli, before his 1986 goal against England won the World Cup for Argentina and immortalized him for Maradona. Too much time at the top took its toll, though: after retiring Maradona's cocaine addiction bloomed and his weight skyrocketed, and for a while it looked like Argentina's greatest hero was on his way out. However, a clean, slimmed-down Maradona returned to become manager of the Argentina team for the 2010 FIFA World Cup. They only reached the quarter-finals but Maradona's status as national *fútbol* legend remains intact.

(top) Diego Maradona before the 1987 Xerox Super Soccer match in Tokyo, Japan; (bottom) World Cup, 1990

ART GALLERIES

★ **Braga Menéndez.** The sparse, warehouse-like space stewarded by Florencia Braga Menéndez showcases the work of bold Latin American rising stars. Her knack for backing those with staying power has made the gallery popular with independent collectors. Curious browsers get a warm welcome, and serious buyers get professional guidance. Artists in her care include Warhol's buddy Marta Minujín, Juan Tessi, and Sebastiano Mauri. ⊠ *Humboldt 1574, Palermo Hollywood* ☎ *11/4775–5577* ⊕ *www.galeriabm.com* ⊙ *Weekdays 11–8, Sat. 11–6.*

★ **Daniel Maman Fine Art.** This gallery space is stark, but its prime location on Avenida del Libertador (the local equivalent of New York's Fifth Avenue) hints of the riches within. The artists in Maman's collection read like a checklist of Argentinian art history: there are works by Quinquela Martín, Berni, Pettorutti, and Xul Solar, to name a few. As well as established contemporary greats like Liliana Porter and Guillermo Kuitca, expect avant-garde artists like the Mondongo collective, whose wacky collages mix resin-encased *fiambres* (cold cuts) and cookies, plasticine, and X-rated photos. London's Tate Modern and New York's MoMA both snapped up a work for their permanent collections. ⊠ *Av. del Libertador 2475, Palermo* ☎ *11/4804–3700* ⊕ *www.danielmaman. com* ⊙ *Weekdays 11:30–8, Sat. 11–3.*

Galería Foster Catena. Not content with bringing Argentina's best wines to the world, Ernesto Catena and his partners are determined to show off local photographic talent, too. In typical Palermo style, this clean white gallery is on the first floor of a recycled town house. Ultrarealist, high-color photography is a constant—think local answers to Nan Goldin, Martin Parr, and Rineke Dijkstra. ⊠ *Honduras 4882, 1st fl., Palermo Viejo* ☎ *11/4833–9499* ⊕ *www.fostercatena.com* ⊙ *Tues.–Sat. 1–7:30.*

Shopping

WORD OF MOUTH

"I live in Buenos Aires and shop now and then. Palermo Soho and Recoleta are excellent shopping neighborhoods; aside from having multitudes of wonderful shops, they are safe, pretty and interesting. I don't know if cheap, good leather is that available . . . As in all things, you pay for what you get. Have fun!

—Scarlett

By Sorrel
Moseley-
Williams

Whether you're looking for a unique handicraft, a fold-up cowhide chair, the latest boutique-vineyard Malbec, a one-off pair of rhodochrosite earrings set in silver, or jeans no one's got back home, you're sure to leave Buenos Aires with your bags full. Ever since Argentina's economic collapse in 2001, designers have had to inject a new level of creativity into their wares in order to survive. Innovation is key, and it can be found on every corner and at every street fair and upmarket boutique.

If you love the hustle and bustle, elbow your way to the stalls at the city's outdoor markets. Many artisans continue to set up around squares such as Plazas Francia, Armenia, and Serrano: sift through seed-bead necklaces, feathery dream catchers, and carved decorative nut bowls among vintage brooches and fabulously funky undergarments. On weekends in Palermo Soho, some artisans simply lay out handcrafted leather maté gourds or colorful aguayo hair clips symmetrically on the sidewalk, while Sundays at San Telmo's Plaza Dorrego turn into an outdoor theater show, with living statues and tango dancers jostling for space among the antiques.

At the other end of the scale, Buenos Aires certainly isn't lacking in high-end couture. Swank it up at the Paseo Alcorta mall or at a Recoleta boutique with security more stringent than an airport's. The city offers up its very own fashion week twice a year, giving its world-class designers who have made it on the global catwalk the chance to prove their worth locally.

Clothing bargains are harder to find than they once were, but that doesn't mean visitors should pay through the nose. Although haggling isn't really commonplace, do ask for a discount if paying in cash, especially if you decide to snap up leather wrist cuffs for all your cousins. Also look out for the tax refund sticker in many shop windows.

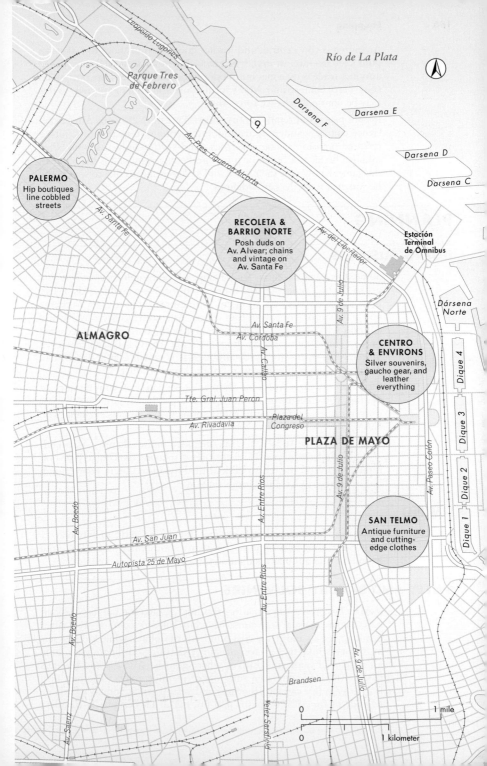

Río de La Plata

Darsena F

Darsena E

Darsena D

Darsena C

Leopoldo Lugones

Parque Tres de Febrero

9

Av. Pres. Figueroa Alcorta

Av. Santa Fe

Av. del Libertador

PALERMO
Hip boutiques line cobbled streets

RECOLETA & BARRIO NORTE
Posh duds on Av. Alvear; chains and vintage on Av. Santa Fe

Estación Terminal de Omnibus

ALMAGRO

Av. Santa Fe

Av. Córdoba

Av. Callao

Av. 9 de Julio

Dársena Norte

CENTRO & ENVIRONS
Silver souvenirs, gaucho gear, and leather everything

Dique 4

Dique 3

Dique 2

Dique 1

Tte. Gral. Juan Perón

Av. Rivadavia

Plaza del Congreso

PLAZA DE MAYO

Av. Paseo Colón

Av. Boedo

Av. Entre Ríos

Av. San Juan

Autopista 25 de Mayo

SAN TELMO
Antique furniture and cutting-edge clothes

Av. 9 de Julio

Av. Boedo

Av. Sáenz

Vélez Sarsfield

Brandsen

Av. 9 de Julio

0   1 mile

0   1 kilometer

Argentina is cow central, and leather goods—from shoes to jackets to polo saddles—are an excellent value. Buenos Aires' well-established antiques trade is thriving, but modern houseware shops are putting up some fierce competition. Many local wines still aren't exported, so this may be your only chance to try them.

It's not just about retail therapy, either. Part of the Buenos Aires experience can be wandering around and stepping, unexpectedly, into a restored mansion selling silk frocks and vertigo-inducing heels, then taking a break at a bistro or juice bar. People-watching is the name of the game. Known for their good looks, Argentineans like to watch and be watched from the café sidelines.

PLANNING

DOING BUSINESS

Some stores give discounts for paying cash (although check before you get to the till); others charge a premium for using credit cards. Carry both, and keep your options open. Tourist-area shops may try to charge you in dollars or euros what they charge Argentineans in pesos. Always confirm which currency you're dealing with. Bargaining is accepted only in some leather-goods shops on Calle Florida. Elsewhere—even in markets—prices are fixed, although it is worth asking for a small discount if you're buying several of the same product.

"Refund" is a dirty word. No shop will give you back your money just because you change your mind. Even if a product is faulty, exchanges or credit notes are the norm. Many shops won't process exchanges on Saturday.

Keep receipts: the 16% V.A.T. tax, included in the sale price, is refundable for purchases over AR$70 at stores displaying the Global Blue tax-refund sign. Visit the return desk at the airport to obtain your refund, but remember to have the goods on you.

TIMING

Malls open at 10 am; some boutiques in Palermo and San Telmo at 11 or noon, closing at around 8 pm. Many shops close on Sunday (and Monday), and although malls don't, they're usually packed.

SWEET AND SAVORY SOUVENIRS

Maté for Two. You might not adore this hot regional tea, but its paraphernalia makes unusual souvenirs. Marcelo Toledo's colonial-style silver drinking vessels and straw cost hundreds of dollars, while kid-size sets at Recursos Infantiles go for around AR$100. Coordinate your maté kit with your outfit at Positivo, where gourds (AR$50) and thermos flasks (AR$150) come in a rainbow of metallic colors. The best firm leather bags (for carrying thermos and vessel) sell at Sunday's Feria de Mataderos for AR$200 pesos and up, but at La Feria de la Recoleta simple gourds start at AR$25. You can even wear the drink: Elementos Argentinos sells hand-woven llama shawls dyed pale green using yerba maté (AR$260).

Salud! Although award winners from wineries such as Catena Zapata can cost hundreds of dollars a bottle, a great malbec starts at AR$40 at Winery. For AR$550 you can pick up a two-bottle leather carrying case from Grand Cru. In traditional restaurants specializing in regional cuisine, wine is served in a pingüino (penguin-shaped jug): get yours from Tienda Palacio for AR$28. If you're not fine with wine, how about showering in it? Universo Garden Angels does Malbec bath gel and body cream. Soothe your conscience at Fabro, which sells quirky tumblers made from recycled wine bottles.

Sweet Stuff. It's thick, sticky, and sickly sweet, but face it, you're addicted to dulce de leche (a spread made from sweetened condensed milk). All supermarkets and corner shops stock popular brands such as La Serenísima or posh glass jars of La Salamandra. Go to any Havanna coffee shop (one practically on every corner) for alfajores (chocolate-covered dulce-de-leche-filled cookies), a small and perfectly rounded taste of Argentina for friends and colleagues at home.

Where's the Beef? Can't kick your Argentine beef habit? Remind yourself of all those steaks with a traditional *asado* knife. Practical wood- or horn-handled knives are available at most markets from around 75 pesos; at Materia Urbana they come with a sturdy cutting board in a wooden carrying case. Silver and alpaca decorate the hilt and sheath of the more elaborate (and more expensive) knives at silversmiths such as Juan Carlos Pallarols Orfebre.

GET BUZZED IN

Locked shop doors are standard anti-theft practice. Don't be surprised (or intimidated) by having to ring a doorbell and be buzzed in. Furthermore, porteños take shopping seriously, and they dress for the occasion. You should, too: sloppily dressed customers usually get sloppy service. Ditch the sneakers and fanny pack, and look like you mean business.

BEST BUYS

The Beautiful Game. You've been to a live match at the stadium, you've chanted the songs, you've screamed at missed goals—all that's lacking is sporting your allegiance on your chest. Stock Center has a great range of all club shirts, or you could get your hands—or thumbs, rather—on Maradona's greatest moment with photo flipbook El Gol del Siglo. It shows his famous goal against England in the 1986 World Cup from Prometeo. Materia Urbana also stocks T-shirts showing the path of that very same goal which ensured his status as a legend forever.

Don't Cry for Me Argentina. Despite popping up at every political rally going on flags and banners, the country's most famous first lady is also quite the pop icon. Score a kitsch plastic bust of her at the Feria de San Pedro Telmo, which also sells packets of used stamps bearing her image. Evita screenprints in light blue or pink adorn notebooks on sale

at Papelera Palermo for AR$110, while silversmith Marcelo Toledo has a whole range of Evita-inspired jewelry, including replicas of pieces she wore. For a perfect finishing touch, invest in some Evita-print packing tape for AR$30 from Tienda Palacio to wrap your goodies in.

Holy Cow. If you can't take a real-life gaucho home with you, the next best thing is to accessorize your living quarters with some cowhide. Rugs are easily transportable, and at the leather wholesalers on Avenida Boedo's 1200 to 1400 blocks prices start at around AR$500. Beautiful cow-skin bags, laptop cases, and Birkenstock-style sandals from Humawaca start at around AR$600. Large illustrated editions of Martín Fierro, the national gaucho hero, come bound in leather or cowhide at El Ateneo. You can even get maté gourds made of polished cow hoof or horn: most outdoor markets sell them for around AR$60.

VALUE FOR MONEY

Clothing in Buenos Aires is cheap and plentiful, but bear in mind that the quality may match the price. Pay particular attention to seams and hems; stitching isn't always superlative. This is true even with international-brand items, which are often labeled "Made in Argentina."

Local brands come at even lower prices in the discount outlets on Avenida Córdoba (4400 to 5000) and in the unofficial new shopping zone, Palermo Outlets, between Malabia and Serrano—most chain stores have a branch here, as do Timberland, Lacroix, and Puma. End-of-season sales can work to your advantage, too—when summer is ending in Buenos Aires, it's just beginning in the United States and Europe.

CLOTHING SIZES

Porteños are, on average, smaller than Europeans and North Americans. Chic women's boutiques often don't have any clothes in sizes larger than a U.S. 8. It doesn't get any better for men: a porteño men's large will seem more like a small to many visitors, and trousers rarely come in different lengths.

CENTRO

BEAUTY

Universo Garden Angels. Despite the New Age brand name and emphasis on inner beauty, these cosmetics mix hard science with color and aromatherapy to create . . . aromacolortherapy. Home-grown goo like Patagonia Earth anti-age cream or the Malbec wine-therapy body cream are worthwhile Argentina-themed gifts for lotion-lovers. ✉ *Av. Santa Fe 917, Microcentro* ☎ *11/4325–0004* ⊕ *www.universogardenangels. com* Ⓜ *C to Gral. San Martín* ✛ *1:E2.*

CENTRO AND ENVIRONS

"It's not what it used to be," porteños whine about downtown. But although pickings might not thrill locals, the excellent selection of crafts, leather, and silver are reason enough for visitors to brave the crowds.

On pedestrian-only Calle Florida, local chain stores and boutiques abound; score international duds at Spanish megabrand Zara and clothes and housewares at Chilean Falabella. Argentine soccer shirts are best sellers at the many sports shops; no-brand leather jackets are another draw, and armies of salesmen are positioned outside shops. At Florida's north end established leather shops like Casa López and Prüne sell higher-quality bags and clothing.

All the office workers, street artists, and tourists make walking up Florida slow progress. Pickpockets are abundant, so keep your valuables close. When the crowds and exhaust fumes start to cause retail burnout, browse through big-name local stores inside the Galerías Pacífico Mall at Avenida Córdoba. Calmer still: browse the free-entry art galleries on Calle Arroyo north of Avenida Santa Fe.

Galerías Pacífico shopping Mall, Calle Florida at Avenida Córdoba

BEST TIME TO GO

Weekdays, but be warned that lunching office workers fill the streets between noon and 2:30. Things get sketchy at night, so don't linger too long after dark.

BEST SOUVENIR FOR CAFFEINE ADDICTS

Looking to wean a coffee junkie off the java (or hook them on another habit)? Gorgeous drinking sets for Argentina's national hot beverage, maté, come with silver trimmings at **Platería Parodi**. Leather specialists **Arandú** sell a variety of supple carrying cases for the gourd-and-thermos flask—they'd also make a stylish wine tote for picnics.

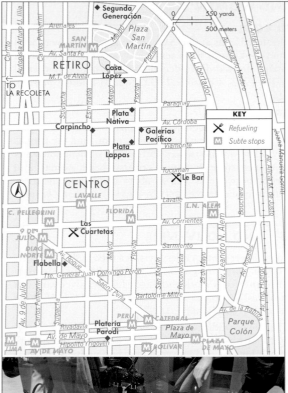

BEST FOR

SILVER

Plata Nativa: chunky jewelry inspired by native Argentine designs, from single-piece silver earrings to strings of gobstopper-size coral beads.

Platería Parodi: matés, belt buckles, knives—everything a gaucho needs, and more besides, in silver.

Platta Lappas: why shop for their classic tea sets, trays, and cutlery at Barney's or Saks 5th Avenue when you can get them from the source?

CLASSIC LEATHER

Carpincho: a cornucopia of gloves; many made from stippled capybara leather.

Casa López: beautiful leather briefcases, baguettes, clutches, totes, suitcases, and sports bags—whatever the shape, it's in the bag.

TANGO

Flabella: high-quality shoes in a range of designs make this the *tanguero* footwear favorite.

Segunda Generación: for hot custom tango wear.

REFUELING

Las Cuartetas. For the most quintessential *porteño* of refuels, head into classic pizzeria Las Cuartetas. Stand at the bar for a gooey slice, or get the whole pie at a Formica table. ⊠ *Av. Corrientes 838* ☎ *11/4326–0171* ✢ *1:E3.*

Le Bar. Leave the Downtown chaos behind with a truly zen moment at French-run Le Bar. A spacey interior, great lunch menus, and excellent cocktails are sure to perk you up in no time. ⊠ *Tucumán 422, Microcentro* ☎ *11/5219–0858* ✢ *1:F3.*

)THING — MEN'S AND WOMEN'S

CASUAL AND COOL

Ona Saez. The ultrafitted jeans at Ona Saez are designed to be worn with sky-high heels and slinky tops for a sexy night out. The menswear is equally slick, mixing dressed-down denim with cool cotton shirts and tees. ⊠ *Florida 789, #203, Centro* ☎ *11/5555–5203* ⊕ *www.onasaez. com* ✛ *1:C2.*

SPORTSWEAR

Stock Center. The official light-blue-and-white shirts worn by the Argentine soccer team, the Pumas (the national rugby team), and the Leonas (women's hockey team) are bestsellers and make excellent souvenirs from this sporting megastore. Pick up Converse, Nike, Adidas, and Puma clothing and footwear as well as über-trendy Gola sneakers. ⊠ *Corrientes 590, Microcentro* ☎ *11/4326–2131* ⊕ *www.stockcenter. com.ar* ✛ *1:E4.*

HANDICRAFTS, SILVER, AND SOUVENIRS

Plata Lappas. Classic silver trays, cutlery sets, tea sets, and ice buckets have been favorites on *porteño* high-society wedding lists for more than 110 years. Department stores worldwide stock Lappas silverware, but why pay export prices? ⊠ *Florida 740, Microcentro* ☎ *11/4325–9568* ⊕ *www.lappas.com* Ⓜ *B to Florida* ✛ *1:D2.*

Platería Parodi. This über-traditional store is chockablock with everything a *gaucho* about town needs to accessorize, all in top-quality silver. There are belt buckles and knives, and the no-nonsense Pampa-style women's jewelry would go great with Gap and Ralph Lauren alike. ⊠ *Av. de Mayo 720, Plaza de Mayo* ☎ *11/4342–2207* ⊕ *www. parodijoyas.com.ar* Ⓜ *A to Piedras* ✛ *1:E4.*

HOME DECOR

Falabella Hogar. A block away from Falabella (the excellent Chilean department store) is its home-ware branch, Falabella Hogar. It does a roaring trade in cheap 'n' stylish crockery, kitchenware, and textiles, mostly imported from China and India. It gets crowded with office workers from noon to 2:30. ⊠ *Florida 343, Microcentro* ☎ *11/5950– 5000* ⊕ *www.falabella.com.ar* Ⓜ *B to Florida; C to Lavalle; D to Catedral* ✛ *1:E4.*

JEWELRY AND ACCESSORIES

★ **Autoría Bs As.** After browsing the ready-to-wear women's collections by Mariana Dappiano and Vero Ivaldi, head to jewelry and accessories. Necklaces may be made of coiled silver by María Medici or crochet by Tatiana Pini. Some handbags have been fashioned from car tires, others are crafted from top-quality leather or organic wool. This is one of the few places to pick up a one-of-a-kind Manto Abrigo coat, handwoven in luminous colors in the north of Argentina. ⊠ *Suipacha 1025, Microcentro* ☎ *11/5252–2474* ⊕ *www.autoriabsas.com.ar* ✛ *1:E2.*

TANGO TO GO

Need we remind you that Buenos Aires is the best place in the world to stock up on tango music, memorabilia, and serious dance wear?

Flabella. Some of the best tango shoes in town, including classic spats, 1920s T-bar designs, and glitzier numbers for men and women are all made to measure and handmade at Flabella. ⊠ *Suipacha 263, Microcentro* ☎ *11/4322–6036* ⊕ *www.flabella.com* ⊹ *1:E4.*

Comme Il Faut. For foxier-than-thou footwear that's kicking up storms on *milonga* floors worldwide, head to Comme Il Faut; dedicated dancers love its combination of top-notch quality and gorgeous, show-stopping colors like teal or plum, usually with metallic trims. Animal-print suede, fake snakeskin, and glittering ruby take-me-home-to-Kansas

numbers are some of the wilder options. ⊠ *Arenales 1239, 3M, Barrio Norte* ☎ *11/4815–5690* ⊕ *www. commeilfaut.com.ar* ⊹ *1:D2.*

Segunda Generación. For custom-made, haute-couture tango wear and accessories, a trip to the family-run Segunda Generación is worth the effort. Also caters to teens and younger. ⊠ *Esmeralda 1249, Microcentro* ☎ *011/4312–7136* ⊕ *www.2gen.com.ar* ⊹ *1:E2.*

Zivals. Recordings by every tango musician under the sun can be found at Zivals. They stock CDs by classic and modern performers, and electro-tango as well as DVDs, sheet music, books, and T-shirts. ⊠ *Av. Callao 395, Congreso* ☎ *11/5128–7500* ⊕ *www. tangostore.com* Ⓜ *B to Callao* ⊹ *1:C4* ⊠ *Serrano 1445, Palermo Viejo* ☎ *11/4833–7948* ⊹ *3:C4.*

Cousiño. Veined pinky-red rhodochrosite comes both in classic settings and as diminutive sculptures at this second-generation goldsmiths specializing in Argentina's national stone. Cousiño's sculptures of birds in flight are also exhibited in the National Museum of Decorative Arts. ⊠ *Sheraton Buenos Aires Hotel, San Martín 1225, Retiro* ☎ *11/4318– 9000* ⊕ *www.rodocrosita.com* Ⓜ *C to Retiro* ⊹ *1:F2.*

★ **Plata Nativa.** This tiny shop in an arcade is filled with delights for both boho chicks and collectors of singular ethnic jewelry. Complex, chunky necklaces with turquoise, amber, and malachite—all based on original Araucanian (ethnic Argentine) pieces—and Mapuche-style silver earrings and brooches are some of the offerings. Happy customers include Sharon Stone, Pedro Almodóvar, and the Textile Museum in Washington, D.C. ⊠ *Galería del Sol, Shop 41, Florida 860* ☎ *11/4312–1398* ⊕ *www.platanativa.com* Ⓜ *C to San Martín* ⊹ *1:E3.*

LUGGAGE, LEATHER, AND HANDBAGS

Carpincho. Specializing in stippled *carpincho* leather from the capybara—the world's largest rodent, native to Argentina—which has super-soft skin, the main attraction are the gloves, which come in *carpincho* and kidskin and in many lengths and colors, from classic chocolate brown to tangerine and lime. ⊠ *Esmeralda 775, Centro* ☎ *11/4322– 9919* ⊕ *www.carpinchonet.com.ar* Ⓜ *C to Lavalle* ⊹ *1:E3.*

Casa López. Don't let the drab storefront put you off: you're as likely to find a trouser suit in floral-print suede as a staid handbag for grandma. A two-part store: the right-hand shop (Number 658) has totes in chestnut- and chocolate-color leather that looks good enough to eat; there are also classic jackets. More unusual fare include fur sacks with wool fringes, black cowhide baguettes, and tangerine purses next door at Number 640. ⊠ *Marcelo T. de Alvear 640 and 658, Centro* ☎ *11/4311–3044* ⊕ *www.casalopez.com.ar* Ⓜ *C to San Martín* ✛ *1:E2.*

La Martina. Feel part of the jet set when you browse the clothing line of Argentinian polo team La Martina. It's not just about boots and jodhpurs; there are also corduroy pants and cashmere sweaters perfect for lounging around your country house. To see what such a pad might look like inside, head to the huge Belgrano branch. Screen-printed tees—including the Argentine national polo-team shirt—are a must-have. ⊠ *Paraguay 661, Microcentro* ☎ *11/4311–5963* ⊕ *www.lamartina. com* Ⓜ *C to San Martín* ✛ *2:C1.*

MALLS AND DEPARTMENT STORES

Falabella. There's no love lost between Argentina and its neighbors, but when this Chilean department store opened, the low prices soon had locals swallowing their pride. The ground floor of this busy corner store contains accessories, international perfumes, and cosmetics such as MAC and Lancôme. Falabella has three clothing lines: Sybila does low-cost (and low-quality) street wear; University Club is preppier and harder-wearing; Basement includes better-quality casual and work clothes. The overworked staff at both Falabella and its nearby home-wares branch, Falabella Hogar, don't give much guidance, but the low prices make up for it. Avoid lunchtime. when it is packed with office workers looking for retail diversion. ⊠ *Florida 202, at Sarmiento, Microcentro* ☎ *11/0800–555–6684* ⊕ *www.falabella.com.ar* Ⓜ *B to Florida; C to Lavalle; D to Catedral* ✛ *1:E4.*

Galerías Pacífico. Upscale shops line the three levels of this beautiful building, designed during the city's turn-of-the-20th-century golden age. Stores are organized along four glass-roofed passages, which branch out in a cross from the central stairwell; the cupola above it is decorated by five Argentine greats such as muralist Antonio Berni. Top local, polo-inspired, menswear brands Etiqueta Negra and La Martina have large stores, while Ona Saez, Tucci, and Vitamina's collections are aimed at younger women. Check out Janet Wise and Claudia Larreta for more sophisticated looks among international brands such as Christian Lacroix. While the basement houses a bustling food court, head up to the second floor and the Centro Cultural Borges for tango shows: small international art exhibitions have featured Andy Warhol, Salvador Dalí, and Henri Cartier-Bresson. ⊠ *Calle Florida 737, at Av. Córdoba, Microcentro* ☎ *11/5555–5110* ⊕ *www.galeriaspacifico.com. ar* Ⓜ *B to Florida* ✛ *1:E3.*

WINE

Ligier. Ligier has a string of shops across town and lots of experience guiding bewildered drinkers through their impressive selection. Although they stock some boutique-vineyard wines, they truly specialize in the big names like Rutini and Luigi Bosca, as well as more modest mass-produced wines. ✉ *Callao 1111, Recoleta* ☎ *11/5353–8050* ⊕ *www.ligier.com.ar* Ⓜ *C to San Martín* ✢ *1:C2.*

SAN TELMO

3

ANTIQUES AND CURIOS

★ **Gabriel del Campo.** Gabriel's good taste means 50-year-old Louis Vuitton trunks don't look out of place beside wooden church statues or scale-model ships with canvas sails. Ceramic rubber-glove molds, one of his specialties, are some of the more accessible conversation pieces. The flagship store takes up a sizable patch of Plaza Dorrego shop front; there is also a branch on Defensa. ✉ *Bethlem 427, on Plaza Dorrego, San Telmo* ☎ *11/4307–6589* Ⓜ *C to San Juan (walk 6 blocks along Humberto I)* ✢ *1:E6.*

Gil Antigüedades. Sequined flapper dresses, dashing white-linen suits, and creamy lace wedding veils are some of the items you might stumble across in this pink *casa chorizo* (similar to a railroad apartment). Period accessories include Castilian hair combs and lacy fans that beg you to bat your lashes from behind them. ✉ *Humberto I 412, San Telmo* ☎ *11/4361–5019* ⊕ *www.gilantiguedades.com.ar* Ⓜ *C to San Juan (walk 6 blocks along Av. San Juan)* ✢ *1:F6.*

★ **HB Anticuario.** White-leather trefoil chairs and gleaming walnut side tables with black-lacquer details are among the many heavenly furniture items in this art-deco emporium. Much more packable (though not cheap) are the Clarice Cliff dinner services or a French rosewood cigar box. ✉ *Defensa 1016/18, San Telmo* ☎ *11/4361–3325* ⊕ *www.hbantiques.com.ar* Ⓜ *C or E to Independencia (walk 6 blocks along Estados Unidos)* ✢ *1:F6.*

La Candelaria. A Spanish-style house whose construction began in 1745 is the site of several choice shops. One is filled with enough miniature wooden furniture to fill several dollhouses; another sells golden-age Argentine cinema posters. Wind-up monkeys, brass fittings, old apothecary bottles, and old leather suitcases are other interesting finds. ✉ *Defensa 1170, San Telmo* ☎ *No phone* Ⓜ *C to San Juan (walk 6 blocks along Av. San Juan)* ✢ *1:F6.*

★ **Silvia Petroccia.** Despite being crammed with furniture, this corner store looks extravagant rather than chaotic. It's probably due to the alluring European collectibles, ranging from gilt-wood church candles to Louis XV–style chairs reupholstered in buttercup-yellow silk and terracotta amphoras. ✉ *Defensa 1002, San Telmo* ☎ *11/4362–0156* ⊕ *www.sp-antiques.com* Ⓜ *C or E to Independencia* ✢ *1:F6.*

SAN TELMO

"No es Palermo!" screams graffiti on a San Telmo shop front, a protest of the clothing boutiques muscling in on the barrio's traditional antiques trade. The "republic" of San Telmo is changing, but the quirky mix of age-old and brand-new is what makes this such an exciting place to shop.

It's entirely appropriate that the city's oldest neighborhood is *the* place to shop for timeless collectibles and curios. Along cobbled streets like Defensa, historic buildings house dozens of stores dealing entirely in antiques. But you're as likely to get a shirt as a chandelier: after decades as one of Buenos Aires' most marginal barrios, San Telmo suddenly looks set to be the next epicenter of *porteño* cool. Local fashion god Pablo Ramírez certainly thinks so: he has set up shop on Calle Perú.

Young designers yet to reach the dizzying heights of his fame (and price tags) share several multi-brand spaces closer to Plaza Dorrego. This plaza is the heart of the open-air Feria de San Pedro Telmo, a Sunday market.

BEST TIME TO GO

The market takes place on Sunday afternoon; it's packed, so don't expect to move much, let alone shop. For leisurely browsing and coffee stops, weekdays are a better bet (except Monday, when many stores are closed). Start with antiques shops, which open around 10 am, then move on to clothes.

BEST SOUVENIR FOR SOMEONE WITH IT ALL

High ceilings, parquet floors, curlicued stone fronts, and period fittings: what's not to like about San Telmo's beautiful old apartments? **Reynolds Propiedades** or **Ojo Propiedades** can set you up with one.

Find tailored duds for men and women, like these in Casa Rey boutique.

BEST FOR

SERIOUS ANTIQUES
Gabriel del Campo: something old, something new…the playful mix of decades is always in good taste.

HB Anticuario: art deco perfection in furniture and tableware.

TOP-NOTCH ARGENTINE DESIGN AND PRODUCTS
Fueguia: high-design apothecary meets B.A. chic.

Marcelo Toledo: silver jewelry inspired by Evita and maté gourds based on colonial designs.

Pablo Ramírez: the king of local couture favors nipped-in waists, hobble skirts, and perfectly cut Buster Keaton suits.

MULTIBRAND BOUTIQUES
Materia Urbana: high-quality souvenirs or affordable art objects? Either way, you're going to want them.

Un Lugar en el Mundo: the pioneer of the San Telmo clothing scene has been dealing the hippest togs in the barrio for years.

REFUELING

Nonna Bianca. Shopping can be hot work. The extra-creamy handmade ice creams at Nonna Bianca are a luxurious cool-off. If an ice-cold pint's more your thing, consider their beer sorbet (yes, really). Or try the frozen malbec in a cone. ✉ *Estados Unidos 407* ☎ *11/4362–0604* ✛ *1:F6.*

Territorio. Slip away from the crowds to the quiet tables of Territorio, where pick-me-ups come in many forms: homemade panini, moist cakes, local tea blends, or microbrewery beer. ✉ *Estados Unidos 500* ☎ *11/4300–9756* ✛ *1:E6.*

Soda syphons for sale in the San Telmo flea market in Plaza Dorrego

BOOKS

★ **Walrus Books.** A peaceful sanctuary away from the busy weekend street market, Walrus stocks more than 4,000 good quality books in English. American owner Geoff and his English-speaking staff are helpful yet unintrusive when it comes to selecting a translation of local masters or some contemporary literary fiction. Slide open the bargain drawer at the front of the store to uncover more reads perfect for whiling away time at airports. ⊠ *Estados Unidos 617, San Telmo* ☎ *11/4300–7135* ⊕ *www.walrus-books.com.ar* ✛ *1:E6.*

CLOTHING—MEN'S AND WOMEN'S

CASUAL AND COOL

Un Lugar en el Mundo. A trailblazer of San Telmo cool, this hip little store has been showcasing young designer streetwear for years. Named after the 1992 Argentine movie, the eminently wearable togs include plain but garishly bright dresses by Muda, quirky print tees for guys and girls, and Manos del Uruguay's exquisite knits from across the River Plate. Bolsas de Viaje's vinyl and canvas creations evoke the golden age of air travel, while Mir's satchels and totes in heavily stitched chestnut leather will convince you school is cool. ⊠ *Defensa 891, San Telmo* ☎ *11/4362–3836* Ⓜ *C or E to Independencia (walk 6 blocks along Estados Unidos)* ✛ *1:F6.*

HIGH DESIGN

Fodor's Choice
★
Pablo Ramírez. His tiny shop front is unadorned except for "Ramírez" printed on the glass over the door—when you're this big, why say more? Recently voted Argentina's best designer by the fashion blogger Scott Schuman, Ramírez's couture doesn't come cheap, but these perfectly tailored numbers are worth every *centavo*. He favors black or white for both waspishly waisted women's wear and slick gent's suits, though a few other shades are creeping in. ⊠ *Perú 587, San Telmo* ☎ *11/4342–7154* ⊕ *www.pabloramirez.com.ar* Ⓜ *E to Belgrano* ✛ *1:E5.*

CLOTHING—WOMEN'S

CASUAL AND COOL

María Rojo. This multibrand boutique takes up an entire traditional 1920s San Telmo *casa chorizo*. Each room opens out onto another to end with a kitsch café; all contain simple racks lined with different small designers' wares. Viotti and Arias Dorado do great-value chic cotton tops to accessorize with a pastel-colored Florencia Herraiz bag. The brighter clothes at the back include reversible T-shirts by Monoreversible, to which you could add far-out feet in multicolored Duvas sneakers and Pebeta Teta's mirrored bird-in-hoop earrings. ⊠ *Carlos Calvo 618, San Telmo* ☎ *11/4362–3340* Ⓜ *C to San Juan; C or E to Independencia (walk 6 blocks along Carlos Calvo)* ✛ *1:E6.*

HIGH DESIGN

Vicki Otero. With one recent collection focusing on milkmaids gone sexy, this favorite local designer who regularly shows her wares at Buenos Aires Fashion Week combines black and white with the occasional splash of grey to simple, saucy effect. Always with an eye on the feminine, Otero also holds design workshops. ⊠ *Carlos Calvo 516, San Telmo* ☎ *11/4300–8739* ⊕ *www.vickiotero.com.ar* ✛ *1:E6.*

HANDICRAFTS, SILVER, AND SOUVENIRS

Artepampa. An artist-and-architect duo is behind these singular works, which are inspired by native Argentine art. They use an unusual papier-mâché technique to create boxes, frames, tapestries, and freestanding sculptures. The primitive-looking pieces, a vision of rich rusts and earthy browns, make highly original gifts. ⊠ *Defensa 917 and 832, on Plaza Dorrego, San Telmo* ☎ *11/4362–6406* ⊕ *www.artepampa.com* Ⓜ *C San Juan (walk 6 blocks along Humberto 1)* ✛ *1:E6.*

Cualquier Verdura. Set up like the former 19th-century home it was, Cualquier Verdura gives the otherwise antique-dominating neigborhood a much-needed kitsch injection. The *casa chorizo* houses special objects which needed rescuing and includes furniture designed by Philippe Starck for Kartell, fun animal-shaped placemats, vinyl records, glow-in-the-dark toys, old-yet-functioning kitchen implements, and books by local photographers and artists calling out for a coffee table. ⊠ *Humberto Primo 517, San Telmo* ☎ *011/4300–2474* ⊕ *www. cualquierverdura.com.ar* ☾ *Closed Mon.–Wed.* ✛ *1:F6*

Juan Carlos Pallarols Orfebre. Argentina's legendary silversmith has made pieces for a mile-long list of celebrities that includes Frank Sinatra, Sharon Stone, Antonio Banderas, Bill Clinton, Nelson Mandela, the king and queen of Spain, and Princess Máxima Zorrequieta—a local export now integrated into the Dutch royal family. A set of ornate silver-handled steak knives is the perfect momento of cow country, although it will set you back a few grand. ⊠ *Defensa 1039, San Telmo* ☎ *11/4362–0641* ⊕ *www.pallarols.com.ar* Ⓜ *C or E to Independencia (walk 6 blocks along Estados Unidos)* ✛ *1:F6.*

Fodor's Choice
★ **Marcelo Toledo.** Sunlight and the smell of solder fill the rooms of this old San Telmo house, which doubles up as a store and open workshop for celebrity silversmith Marcelo Toledo. A huge silver mosaic of Evita gives away who Toledo's main muse is: he has created replicas of her own jewelry (and is the only silversmith authorized by her estate to do so) as well as pieces inspired by her. Eva Duarte Perón isn't the only crowd-pleasing politician Toledo's been associated with: a local magnate commissioned cuff links as an inauguration gift to President Obama. His most recent celebrated gift was a maté designed especially for Prince William and his bride Kate Middleton. ⊠ *Humberto I 458, San Telmo* ☎ *11/4362–0841* ⊕ *www.marcelotoledo.net* ✛ *1:F6.*

Materia Urbana. The quirky, postmodern souvenirs this store specializes in are a welcome variation from classic maté gourds or gaucho knives. Take the ubiquitous cow, which has been reformed into a leather

Marcelo Toledo is the place to go for beautifully crafted silver, like this *bombilla* (mate straw) set.

vampire-bat key holder or the piglet change purse. Beautiful bags, silver and steel bijouterie as well as tango-themed soaps are cute gift options. Pop upstairs to browse clothes by a variety of designers. ⊠ *Defensa 702, San Telmo* ☎ *11/4361–5265* ⊕ *www.materiaurbana.com* ✢ *1:F5.*

JEWELRY AND ACCESSORIES

Abraxas. "Yes" is pretty much guaranteed if you propose with one of the period engagement rings that dazzle in the window of this antique jewelers. If you're not planning on an "I do" anytime soon, surely you can find a home for some art deco earrings with the tiniest of diamonds or a gossamer-fine bracelet? ⊠ *Defensa 1092, San Telmo* ☎ *11/4361–7512* ⊕ *www.abraxasantiques.com* Ⓜ *C to San Juan (walk 6 blocks along Humberto I)* ✢ *1:F6.*

Midas Antigüedades. Everything a gentleman needs to accessorize like a lord is arrayed in the minimalist storefront. Vintage timepieces are the specialty: from turn-of-the-20th-century pocket watches to a 14k gold 1950s Longines wristwatch with a snakeskin strap. Jeweled tiepins, cuff links, cigarette cases, and even an evil dog-headed walking cane round out the stock. ⊠ *Defensa 1088, San Telmo* ☎ *11/4307–1314* ⊕ *www. relojeriamidas.com* Ⓜ *C to San Juan (walk 6 blocks along Humberto I)* ✢ *1:F6.*

DID YOU KNOW?

Traditionally made from fist-sized hollowed-out gourds, matés (MAH-tays) come in myriad shapes, sizes, and materials that look stunning on the shelf. For everyday use, however, stick with the original model.

RECOLETA

BOOKS

Ateneo. An imposing theater dating from 1919 is the rather fabulous backdrop to this bookshop. The former foyer holds a small selection of CDs and DVDs; the orchestra seating area includes fiction (including some in English) and art books; specialist subjects are arrayed in the circle; you pay at the box office. Argentine cookbooks, illustrated gaucho classics, and coffee-table photography tomes are some of the weighty souvenirs. There are similar offerings at the less dramatic store on Florida. ⊠ *Ateneo Grand Splendid, Santa Fe 1860, Barrio Norte* ☎ *11/4813–6052* ⊕ *www.tematika.com* Ⓜ *D to Callao* ✛ *1:E4.*

CLOTHING—MEN'S AND WOMEN'S

HIGH DESIGN
Giesso. A classic gents' tailor for well over a century, Giesso is pulling a Thomas Pink by adding jewel-color ties and shirts to its range of timeless suits and corduroy jackets. A women's line includes gorgeous linen suits and cashmere overcoats. ⊠ *Av. Alvear 1882, Recoleta* ☎ *11/4804–8288* ⊕ *www.giesso.com.ar* ✛ *1:D1.*

SPORTSWEAR
Topper. The cuts of their tank tops and sweatpants aren't quite as spacey as Nike or Reebok, but then this classic Argentine brand's prices are more down-to-earth, too. Tennis wear is a strong player, not surprising given that Topper sponsors '70s legend Guillermo Vilas as well as younger stars such as Facundo Arguello and Juan Ignacio Chela. There's off-court action, too: the black Converse-lookalike sneakers have been a fashion staple for teenage gig-goers for decades. ⊠ *Av. Santa Fe 1570, Barrio Norte* ☎ *11/4816–6964* ⊕ *www.topper.com.ar* ✛ *1:C2.*

CLOTHING—MEN'S

HIGH DESIGN
★ **La Dolfina.** Being the world's best polo player wasn't enough for Adolfo Cambiaso—he founded his own team in 1995, then started a clothing line which he also models for. If you thought polo is all about knee-high boots and preppy chinos, think again: Cambiaso sells some of the best urban menswear in town. The Italian-cotton shirts, sharp leather jackets, and to-die-for totes are perfect for any occasion. ⊠ *Av. Alvear 1751, Recoleta* ☎ *11/4815–2698* ⊕ *www.ladolfina.com* ✛ *1:D1.*

CLOTHING—WOMEN'S

HIGH DESIGN
Cora Groppo. A queen of the *porteño* haute-couture scene, Cora Groppo made her name designing flirty cocktail dresses with lots of cleavage and short flared or bell-shaped skirts, the main offerings at the Recoleta branch which have taken her designs to Italy and El Salvador. Her

RECOLETA AND BARRIO NORTE

Vuitton, Cartier, Hermès. Impeccable century-old town houses. Darkened limos ferrying stars and royalty from shops to hotels. Paris? Rome? Berlin? Wait—you *are* still in Argentina. Rest assured that Recoleta will do its utmost to convince you that you're not.

Argentina's high society has always looked to Europe for inspiration, nowhere more so than Recoleta—where the country's high society shops. Seriously big spenders needn't stray far from Avenida Alvear, where international designers rub shoulders with darlings of Argentine style like Martín Churba.

The linchpin of all this luxury is the Alvear Palace Hotel, home away from home for pop queens and blue-blooded queens alike. Patio Bullrich shopping mall is as elegant as the rest of Recoleta, but its stylish local chains make less of a dent in your credit card. Even humbler yet no less desirable offerings are at the Feria Artesanal de Recoleta, a weekend arts-and-crafts market.

BEST TIME TO GO

Mirror the platinum-card brigade and shop weekdays between lunch and afternoon tea (at the Alvear Palace Hotel, of course). High prices keep streets uncrowded. To hit the market, come on weekends between 2 pm and dusk.

BEST SOUVENIR FOR YOUR IN-LAWS

The handmade chocolate truffles at **El Viejo Oso** are sure to sweeten even the sourest mother-in-law. Go for the *dulce de leche* fillings. If they prefer liquid sustenance, head to **Grand Cru,** where staff can recommend a bottle of yet-to-be-exported boutique-vineyard Malbec.

The Alvear Palace Hotel, Calle Florida at Avenida Corrientes

BEST FOR

HORSEY CHIC

Arandú: exquisite leather hats, boots, saddles, and bridles—everything but the horse (though at these prices, you'll want a free one thrown in).

Cardon: the estancia look at high street prices.

La Dolfina: an edgier, Argentine take on Ralph Lauren.

AVANT-GARDE ARGENTINE DESIGN

Evangelina Bomparola: the limited-edition suits, funnel-neck coats, and A-line party dresses pay tasteful tribute to the 1960s.

Tramando, Martín Churba: Buenos Aires' answer to Issey Miyake weaves his wondrous, high-tech cloth into floaty masterpieces.

Trosman: made chiefly of T-shirting, Trosman's unusually draped garments are comfortable and flattering (if you're smaller than a size 6, that is).

KEY

✕ Refueling

REFUELING

El Sanjuanino. Very laid-back yet just a block from posh Avenida Alvear, El Sanjuanino is perfect for *empanadas* and hearty beef-and-bean stews from northern Argentina. ✉ *Posadas 1515* ☏ *11/4804–2909* ✛ *1:D1.*

Sirop Folie. The vibe is unashamedly French at Sirop Folie. Lunchtime dishes burst with fresh ingredients. The real stars here, however, are the painstakingly constructed patisseries. ✉ *Vicente López 1661, Shop 12* ☏ *11/4813–5900* ✛ *1:D2.*

Don't pass up the alfajores at the Alvear Palace Hotel's afternoon tea.

lower-key Palermo store sells skinny pants and shorts best accompanied by draped tops, although the whisper-thin cotton jersey most are made of doesn't do much for those without catwalk figures. ⊠ *Uruguay 1296, Recoleta* 🖃 *11/4815–8516* ⊕ *www.coragroppo.com* ✛ *1:D2.*

Evangelina Bomparola. Evangelina takes her clothes very seriously and it's easy to see why. Top-of-the-line materials and detailed attention to the way they hang means that although simple, her designs are far from boring. This is *the* place to come for a little (or long) black dress, but wilder items such as a '60s-style funnel-neck coat or a raw-silk jumpsuit also line the minimalist boutique's racks. ⊠ *Alvear 1920, Recoleta* 🖃 *11/4802–8807* ⊕ *www.evangelinabomparola.com* ✛ *1:D2.*

Fueguia. If you're the kind of person who has everything, then a visit to Fueguia's perfume and candle-making laboratory to make your own scent is a must. Named after the kidnapped native Indian nine-year-old girl from Patagonia who was abducted by HMS *Beagle* captain Robert FitzRoy, Fueguia offers more than 100 fragrances including Uruguayan jasmines, Tucumán lemons, and Neuquén roses to choose from. You can simply snap up a candle in the scent of Argentine author Borges: Biblioteca de Babel. ⊠ *Av. Alvear 1680, Recoleta* 🖃 *11/4311–5360* ✛ *1:D1.*

Marcelo Senra. Irregular natural linen, hand-knit sweaters, cow-hair boots—it's all about texture at Marcelo Senra, a long-established local designer. Loose, flowing evening dresses come in raw silk or satin, offset by belts or chunky wooden jewelry. Handwoven accessories complement the clothes' earthy palette, and are a reason in themselves to visit Senra's Barrio Norte showroom. ⊠ *Talcahuano 1133, Unit 3A, Barrio Norte* 🖃 *11/4813–2770* ⊕ *www.marcelosenra.com* ✛ *1:D2.*

★ **Tramando, Martín Churba.** This store's name means both "weaving" and "plotting": designer Martín Churba is doing plenty of both. Unique evening tops made of layers of draped and pleated sheer fabric adorned with circular beads and irregular embroidery look fit for an urban mermaid. Asymmetrical shrugs, screen-printed tees, and even vases are some of the other woven wonders in the hushed town-house store where art meets fashion. ⊠ *Rodríguez Peña 1973, Recoleta* 🖃 *11/4811–0465* ⊕ *www.tramando.com* ✛ *1:D1.*

Trosman. Highly unusual beadwork is the only adornment on designer Jessica Trosman's clothes. There's nothing small and sparkling about it: her beads are smooth, inch-wide acrylic orbs that look futuristic yet organic. You might balk at the price tags, considering that most of the clothes are made of T-shirting, but that hasn't stopped Tokyo or Paris from stocking her wares. The Palermo outlet carries jeans and tops from past seasons. ⊠ *Patio Bullrich Mall, Av. del Libertador 750, Store 1, Recoleta* 🖃 *11/4814–7414* ⊕ *www.trosman.com* ✛ *1:D1.*

★ **Varanasi.** The structural perfection of Varanasi's clothes is a clue that the brains behind them trained as architects. Find A-line dresses built from silk patchwork and unadorned bias cuts, some of the night-out joys that local celebs shop for. ⊠ *Juncal 1280, Recoleta* 🖃 *11/4812–4282* ⊕ *www.varanasi-online.com* ✛ *1:D2.*

Zitta. It's easy to pass by this unprepossessing Recoleta shop, but there's no way Fabián Zitta's evening dresses could go unnoticed. Local starlets

THE CHAIN GANG: HANDBAGS

Lázaro. Some are classic, others are beyond ultrahip, but Lázaro handbags and purses have in common simple lines, minimal adornment, and high-quality workmanship. Check out specific collections which include fabulous futuristic totes, document holders, and bandolier bags; plenty of inner divisions make them truly travel-worthy. Don't forget to try on some lace-up boots or brogues with a modern twist. ✉ *Buenos Aires, Buenos Aires* ⊕ *www.lazarocuero. com.ar.*

Prüne. Smart working chicks, busy moms, and older ladies who lunch all adore Prüne's chic yet practical leather bags, with thoughtful compartments and enough room for all your stuff. Colors tend to be rich and dark, while guest collections offer a brighter, quirkier deal. Details such as studs and steel rings linking bags to straps lend urban touches. Leather jackets, belts, boots and shoes are also on offer. ✉ *Buenos Aires, Buenos Aires* ⊕ *www.prune.com.ar.*

3

love his bold designs, notable for their volume. Think balloon skirts, puffball sleeves, or organic-looking ruffled tubes snaking over severely tight bodices. Each collection includes black, white, and one other (usually blinding) color. Brides-to-be must give his wedding collection a whirl. ✉ *Av. Quintana 10, Recoleta* ☎ *11/4811–2094* ⊕ *www. zittacostura.com* ✛ *1:D2.*

JEWELRY AND ACCESSORIES

Fodor's Choice **Celedonio.** Local boy Celedonio Lohidoy has designed pieces—often
★ with frothy bunches of natural pearls—for Kenzo and Emanuel Ungaro; his work has even been slung around Sarah Jessica Parker's neck on *Sex in the City.* He favors irregular semiprecious stones, set in asymmetrical, organic-looking designs such as butterflies and daisies. ✉ *Castex 3225, Recoleta* ☎ *11/4803–7598* ⊕ *www.celedonio.com.ar* ✛ *1:C1.*

Fahoma. This small boutique has enough accessories to make the rest of your outfit a mere formality. Berry-size beads go into chunky but affordable necklaces, and all manner of handbags line the back wall. ✉ *Libertad 1169, Recoleta* ☎ *11/4813–5103* ✛ *1:D2.*

Homero. Bright, playful acrylic and raw-looking black rubber offset diamonds and white gold in Homero's innovative necklaces and rings. Other pieces include cross pendants and silver-and-leather cufflinks. ✉ *Patio Bullrich, Av. Libertador 750, Third floor, Recoleta* ☎ *11/4812– 9881* ⊕ *www.homero-joyas.com.ar* ✛ *1:E1.*

LUGGAGE, LEATHER, AND HANDBAGS

★ **Arandú.** Selling everything you could possibly require to fill your country house needs, this three-storey Recoleta town house sells *asado* knives, *maté* gourds, chaps, silver-and-textile jewelry, and bridles. Racks stuffed with boots begging to be scuffed up gleam temptingly at the back of the shop, and if you find the supple canvas and leather sports bags too conventional, check out such novelties as leather rifle cases. Price tags are sky high, but the quality is superlative. ⊠ *Ayacucho 1924, Recoleta* ☎ *11/4800–1575* ⊕ *www.arandu. com.ar* ✛ *1:D3.*

Cardon. Pine floors, pine walls, and pine cabinets—it's all very country down at Cardon. The horsey set comes here for reasonably priced, no-nonsense sheepskin jackets, cashmere sweaters, and riding boots. Selections from the *talabartería* (traditional gaucho-style leather items) line, including cowboy hats and a new spin on traditional silver encasing handbags, make great gifts. ⊠ *Av. Alvear 1847, Recoleta* ☎ *11/4804–8424* ⊕ *www. cardon.com.ar* ✛ *1:D1.*

WORD OF MOUTH

"I have Prüne bags that are [still] fine. I just haven't bought anything there in a while and quality here does have a habit of bouncing around. My Lazaro bags have stood up to all kinds of beatings and look fine. I have bags from all over town! I am an Equal Opportunity Bag Lady."

—Scarlett

Rossi y Caruso. Top-quality workmanship and classic cuts are what have been bringing distinguished customers such as King Juan Carlos of Spain to Rossi y Caruso since 1878. The shop specializes in riding gear (think Marlborough fox-hunt rather than Marlboro man) but also sells luggage, leather jackets, and shoes. And should you need a saddle during your trip, those sold here are the best in town. ⊠ *Posadas 1387, Recoleta* ☎ *11/4811–1965* ⊕ *www.rossicaruso.com* ✛ *1:D1.*

MALLS AND DEPARTMENT STORES

Patio Bullrich. The city's most upscale mall was once the headquarters for the Bullrich family's meat-auction house. Inside, stone cow heads mounted on pillars still watch over the clientele. A colonnaded front, a domed-glass ceiling, and steel supports are reminders of another age. Top local stores are relegated to the lowest level, making way for the likes of Lacroix, Cacharel, and Calvin Klein. Urban leatherware brand Lazaro has a shop here, as does Palermo fashion princess Jessica Trosman, whose spare women's clothes are decorated with unusual heavy beadwork. The enfant terrible of Argentine footwear, Ricky Sarkany, sells dangerously pointed stilettos in colors that walk the line between exciting and kitsch. Named after the polo team, edgy but elegant menswear brand Etiqueta Negra has its first store outside the snooty northern suburbs here, while La Martina is giving them fierce competition. When the bags begin to weigh you down, stop for cake at Nucha, on the Avenida del Libertador side of the building. ⊠ *Enter at Posadas 1245 or Av. del Libertador 750, Recoleta* ☎ *11/4814–7400* ⊕ *www. shoppingbullrich.com.ar* Ⓜ *C to Retiro (walk 7 blocks up Av. del Libertador)* ✛ *1:D1.*

MUSIC

Notorious. Intrigued by some of the sounds you've heard on your trip? Take some home with you from Notorious, which has a strong selection of local rock, folk, jazz, and tango. Friendly staff will happily make suggestions. The shop is small, but there are plenty of listening stations so you can try before you buy. ⊠ *Av. Callao 966, Barrio Norte* ☎ *11/4813–6888* ⊕ *www.notorious.com.ar* Ⓜ *D to Callao* ✥ *1:C2.*

SHOES—MEN'S AND WOMEN'S

Guido. In Argentina loafers mean Guido, whose retro-looking logo has been the hallmark of quality footwear since 1952. Try on timeless handmade Oxfords and wing tips; there are also fun items like a tomato-red handbag or a cow-skin tote. Accessories include simple belts and suede wallets. ⊠ *Av. Quintana 333, Recoleta* ☎ *11/4811–4567* ⊕ *www.guidomocasines.com.ar* ✥ *1:D1.*

SHOES—WOMEN'S

Lonte. There's something naughty-but-oh-so-nice about Lonte's shoes. Chunky gold peep-toe heels are a dream, and the outré animal-print numbers are a favorite of local diva, TV presenter Susana Giménez. For more discreet feet there are patent-leather boots or classic heels in straightforward colors. ⊠ *Arenales 1272, Recoleta* ☎ *11/4813–3736* ⊕ *www.lonteshoes.com* ✥ *1:D1.*

Zapatos de María. María Conorti was one of the first young designers to set up shop in this area, and she's still going strong. Wedge heels, satin ankle-ties, and abundant use of patent leather in pumps and boots are the trademark touches of her quirky designs. Head to the basement at the back of the store for discounted past seasons. ⊠ *Libertad 1665, Recoleta* ☎ *11/4815–5001* ⊕ *www.zapatosdemaria.com.ar* ✥ *1:D1.*

WINE

★ **Grand Cru.** Incredibly savvy staff, some trained as sommeliers, will guide you through Grand Cru's peerless selection—high-end wines from small vineyards predominate—and they can FedEx up to 12 bottles anywhere in the world. ⊠ *Rodríguez Peña 1886, Recoleta* ☎ *11/4816–3975* ⊕ *www.grandcru.com.ar* ✥ *1:D1.*

ALMAGRO

MALL

Abasto. The soaring art deco architecture of what was once the city's central market is as much a reason to come here as the three levels of shops. Although Abasto has many top local chains, it's not as exclusive as other malls, so you can find relative bargains at the 250 shops such as Ver, Yagmour, and Markova. You can also dress up at Ayres, Paula Cahen d'Anvers, Akiabara, Rapsodia, or the Spanish chain Zara, famous for its cut-price versions of catwalk looks. Levi's, Billabong, Puma, Gola, and Adidas are among the casual international offerings; for something smarter, there's Yves Saint Laurent. Men can hit such trendy shops as Bensimon and Old Bridge or go for the *estanciero* look with La Martina polo wear. Take a break in the top-floor food court beneath the glass panes and steel supports of the building's original roof. The mall also has 12 movie screens and two 3D ones and hosts the annual Bafici independent international film festival in April; you can also pick up tickets for live entertainment around town at the Ticketek booth near the food court. ⊠ *Av. Corrientes 3247, Almagro* ☎ *11/4959–3400* ⊕ *www.abasto-shopping.com.ar* Ⓜ *B to Carlos Gardel* ✛ *2:G6.*

PALERMO

BEAUTY

Epoca Bella. Step back in time and get your soapy wares sliced and weighed before splashing the cash. Try the super-fresh Oceánico bubble bath or Té de Hojas Verdes, a warm and comforting room spray you'll wish came as a perfume. ⊠ *Gorriti 5037, Palermo Viejo* ☎ *011/4834–6306* ✛ *3:C3.*

Sabater Hermanos. Third-generation Spanish soap makers are behind this shop that sells nothing but—let's come clean about it—soap. Get into a lather over the trays of no-nonsense rectangles that come in heavenly sandalwood, chocolate, old lavender, and tea rose, to name a few. You can also buy your soap in brightly colored petals and with messages such as "don't wash away your conscience." ⊠ *Gurruchaga 1821, Palermo Viejo* ☎ *11/4833–3004* ⊕ *www.shnos.com.ar* ✛ *3:F3.*

BOOKS

Boutique del Libro. If you don't feel inspired to put pen to paper for your epic novel after wandering around this book boutique, it simply isn't meant to be. Stuffed with artsy coffeetable books and travel guides, wander through to the café at the back with your purchase. ⊠ *Thames 1762, Palermo Viejo* ☎ *11/4833–6637* ⊕ *www.boutiquedellibro.com. ar* ✛ *3:D2.*

CLOTHING—MEN'S AND WOMEN'S

CASUAL AND COOL

Antique Denim. Burberry meets Diesel at Antique Denim, where smart, dark jeans are paired with colorful tweed jackets with leather elbow patches. The denim cuts are sharp and tailored, made for cruising the town. ⊠ *Gurruchaga 1692, Palermo Viejo* ☎ *11/4834–6829* ✛ *3:E3.*

Refans A+. Footballers, soap-opera stars, clubbers: everyone seems to be wearing one of Refans's trademark T-shirts. They come in ultrabright colors, emblazoned with quirky Italian phrases like "*siamo fuori*" ("we are out," a reference to the FIFA World Cup). Lucas Castromán, a local football star himself, is behind the brand. Anoraks, hoodies, jeans, and messenger bags round out the offerings. ⊠ *El Salvador 4577, Palermo Viejo* ☎ *11/4833–9689* ⊕ *www.refans.net* ✛ *2:E2.*

HIGH DESIGN

Kostüme. It's all very space odyssey at Kostüme, a B.A. Fashion Week fave. Extra-brief dresses might be made of netting or bunched-up nylon and worn over drainpipe trousers. Many tops are asymmetrical, and pants come with saddlebag-like protrusions. Check out the Vader boots, a collaboration with Pony. ⊠ *Gurruchaga 1585, Palermo Viejo* ☎ *11/4831–4203* ⊕ *www.kostumeweb.net* Ⓜ *D to Plaza Italia* ✛ *2:G3.*

Nadine Zlotogora. Bring a sense of humor to Nadine Zlotogora when you fight your way through giant knitted cacti to rifle through her way-out designs which are playful yet exquisitely put together. Sheer fabrics are embroidered with organic-looking designs, then worn alone or over thin cotton. Even the menswear gets the tulle treatment: military-look shirts come with a transparent top layer. ⊠ *El Salvador 4638, Palermo Viejo* ☎ *11/4831–4203* ⊕ *www.nadinez.com* ✛ *3:F4.*

CLOTHING—MEN'S

CASUAL AND COOL

Bokura. Wooden shelving and layers of Persian rugs make Bokura look part general store and part 1,001 nights. Levi's-style jeans are reasonably priced; match them with slick leather jackets, shirts, and screen-printed, aged tees. There's also a branch in San Telmo at Defensa 891. ⊠ *El Salvador 4677, Palermo Viejo* ☎ *11/4833–3975* ⊕ *www.bokura. com.ar* ✛ *3:F4.*

Bolivia. *Porteño* dandies know that Bolivia is *the* place for metrosexual fashion. Expect floral prints on shirts, leather belts, even Filofaxes. Aged denim, top-quality silk-screen T-shirts, vintage military jackets, and hand-knit slippers are among the items that fill this converted Palermo town house to bursting. There's also a bright and breezy Palmero store at Costa Rica 4672. ⊠ *Gurruchaga 1581, Palermo Viejo* ☎ *11/4832–6284* ⊕ *www.boliviaonline.com.ar* ✛ *3:D4.*

Félix. Waxed floorboards, worn rugs, exposed brick, and aging cabinets are the backdrop to the shop's cool clothes. Beat-up denim, crisp shirts, and knits that look like a loving granny whipped them up are among the many delights. ⊠ *Gurruchaga 1670, Palermo Viejo* ☎ *11/4832–2994* ⊕ *www.felixba.com.ar* ✛ *3:E3.*

Hermanos Estebecorena. The approach at this trendy street-wear store is 100% practical: all the flat-front shirts, pants, and rain jackets have pockets, seams, and buttons positioned for maximum utility, designed by the siblings who are industrial designers. Everything looks good, too, and the product range, including footwear and underwear, makes this a one-stop guy shop. ⊠ *El Salvador 5960, Palermo Hollywood* ☎ *11/4772–2145* ⊕ *www.hermanosestebecorena.com* ✛ *2:C3.*

HIGH DESIGN

★ **Balthazar.** Everything a modern gent needs—and plenty he didn't know he wanted—lies in this discreet Palermo town house. Find top-notch shirts, suits, cuff links, and even driving gloves. Best sellers are

PALERMO

The hungry gazes of fashionistas on the prowl, the bloodthirsty competition for a town-house shop front, the sheer number of boutiques per cobbled block: there's no question that this is the heart of Buenos Aires' fashion scene.

Shops cluster around three hubs: Palermo Viejo (the heart of the action), Palermo Hollywood, and el Botánico. Take your time—the whole point of Palermo is to wander and be seduced.

Long home to small designer shops, Palermo Viejo, southeast of Avenida Juan B. Justo, now sees local chains vying for space as well. Honduras, El Salvador, Gurruchaga, and Malabia are the main drags. Shops come and go all the time, so keep an eye out for closing sales. Craftspeople and low-end designers sell on weekends from stalls on Plaza Serrano, and several dedicated covered spaces fronting the plaza operate week-round.

To the west is Palermo Hollywood; rents are sending smaller, quirkier boutiques here, while exclusivity-minded designers favor quiet Botánico, north of Santa Fe.

BEST TIME TO GO

You can do Plaza Serrano (Plazoleta Cortázar) and the shops in one very crowded go on Saturday. Shops keep odd hours Sunday and Monday; for wandering, go Tuesday through Friday—though half the shops don't open before midday.

BEST SOUVENIR FOR BACK HOME

Bring the sparkle back to your sister's eyes with the original but reasonably priced jewelry at **Metalistería**, or help her wind down with mini handmade soaps or bath petals, which come in funky boxes at **Sabater Hermanos**.

Affordable style rules the day in shops like this one in Palermo Soho.

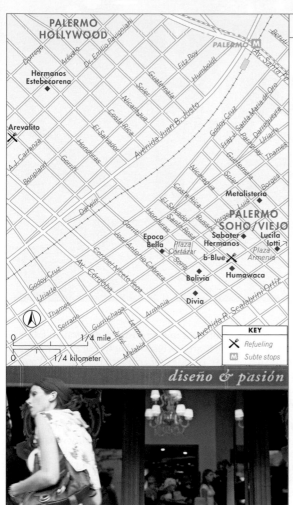

diseño & pasión

REFUELING

Arevalito. The delicious salad of the day at tiny Arevalito restores energy and keeps you light enough on your feet to continue shopping. Equally refreshing are the huge jugs of homemade lemonade. ⊠ *Arévalo 1478* ☎ *11/4776–4252* ✢ *2:C3.*

b-Blue. Check out fellow shoppers' bags over an organic blueberry smoothie. This deli's tasty sandwiches and delectable cakes are served all day. ⊠ *Armenia 1692* ☎ *11/4831–7024* ✢ *3:F4.*

BEST FOR

HIP MENSWEAR
Bolivia: the shirts are floral and the vintage jackets come with appliqués— wallflowers steer clear.

Hermanos Estebecorena: even the boxer shorts have been engineered at this stylish but ultra-pragmatic store.

FOXY SHOES AND SPACEY BAGS
Divia: there's something very retro about these limited-edition party shoes, which often combine metallic, stippled, and patent leathers.

Humawaca: from their cute round cowhide backpacks to stylish laptop totes, Humawaca's designs are some of the edgiest in town.

Lucila Iotti: the two-tone patent-leather lace-ups with tapering heels kick up a storm in all seasons.

BEAUTY
Epoca Bella: for a vintage slice of perfumed goods.

Some of Palermo's stores feature large windows or open-air designs, like diseño & pasión, pictured here.

Stop in for a browse at Félix in Palermo.

handwoven alpaca scarves. Balthazar imports English and Italian fabric for many of their shirts, which are correspondingly pricey, but there is a 20% discount if you pay cash. ✉ *Gorriti 5131, Palermo Viejo* ☎ *11/4834–6235* ⊕ *www.balthazarshop.com* ✢ *1:F6.*

CLOTHING—WOMEN'S

CASUAL AND COOL

Allô Martínez. Trashy but nice is the best way to describe Allô Martínez's full-on designs. Skinny satin pants and studded layered tees with plenty of leopard print will get you ready to rock, but you could go glam or formal in full-skirted, slightly Gothic ball gowns. ✉ *Honduras 4725, Palermo Viejo* ☎ *11/4831–3733* ⊕ *www.allomartinez.com* ✢ *3:E5.*

Desiderata. The curving wooden deck outside this store is inviting, but get inside for light and airy shirts, dresses, and tees. The well-cut jeans are merciful on both wallet and hips: unusually for Palermo, they go up to a size 12 (that's an Argentine 5). ✉ *Honduras 4733, Palermo Viejo* ☎ *11/4833–3883* ⊕ *www.desiderata.com.ar* ✢ *3:E4.*

Didi Bandol. The A-line coats and dresses, shiny fabrics, and blocks of primary colors are clearly a nod to the '60s. But combine them with perfect drainpipe pants and an overlength T-shirt for a look that's very now. The deal maker? Quality that's higher than most places in Palermo, at prices that are lower. ✉ *Gurruchaga 1767, Palermo* ☎ *11/4831–8041* ⊕ *www.bandol.com.ar* ✢ *3:E3.*

Lupe. The '80s are alive and well at Lupe, whose bright T-shirt dresses are all about draping and plunging necklines, with plenty of animal prints. Subtler options include sexy, semitransparent muslin. ⊠ *El Salvador 4657, Palermo Viejo* ☎ *11/4833–9205* ⊕ *www.lupeba.com.ar* ✛ *3:F4.*

Mäda. This store hails from posh Uruguayan beach resort Punta del Este, so it's no surprise that bikinis (think flower appliqués, glitter, and ruffles) are the main attraction. Slinky tank tops and T-shirt dresses round out the collection. ⊠ *El Salvador 4865, Palermo Viejo* ☎ *11/4833–9622* ⊕ *www.madastore.com.ar* ✛ *3:E3.*

María Aversa. There's a touch of gypsy in María Aversa's colorful knitwear, and the two-story town-house shop gives you plenty of room to roam. Summer collections involve Mexican-inspired embroidered cheesecloth, but there are also plenty of beautifully tailored cotton shirts (many with discreetly puffed sleeves) and smart but feminine drill and woolen jackets in mint green or rich red. ⊠ *El Salvador 4580, Palermo Viejo* ☎ *11/4833–0073* ⊕ *www.mariaaversa.com.ar* ✛ *3:F4.*

María Cher. Let the yards of racks draw you into this lanky shop, where simple cuts and swaths of natural fabrics make urban working clothes feel a touch Jedi-like. The earthy, deconstructed look is heightened by details such as unfinished hems or exposed seams. ⊠ *El Salvador 4724, Palermo Viejo* ☎ *11/4832–3336* ⊕ *www.maria-cher.com.ar* ✛ *3:E4.*

Objeto. Creative use of fabrics and quirky crafting make the everyday clothes here something special. Their feminine T-shirts are textile collages combining silk screening and appliqué techniques; skirts and jackets might mix new materials with original '60s off-cuts. Check out the waterproof jackets cut from gingham-print tablecloths complete with photos of food you'll be ready to bite into. ⊠ *Gurruchaga 1649, Palermo Viejo* ☎ *11/4953–1648* ⊕ *www.deboradistilio.com* ✛ *3:E4.*

Pesqueira. The young at heart and their mini-me counterparts can thrill together at the quirky use of animals on Pesqueira's signature pieces, including jumpsuits, bags, purses, and accessories. Don't leave without at least picking up the leather bear-face sling purse. ⊠ *Gurruchaga 1750, Palermo Viejo* ☎ *11/4833–7218* ⊕ *www.pesqueiratm.com* ✛ *3:E3.*

Seco. Singing in the rain is encouraged at Seco, where all the clothes are designed to get wet but keep you dry. See-through plastic numbers come with matching rain hats worth risking a soaking for. Pick up a pretty umbrella that will weather for any unexpected shower. ⊠ *Armenia 1646, Palermo Viejo* ☎ *11/4833–1166* ⊕ *www.secorainwear.com* ✛ *3:E4.*

HIGH DESIGN

★ **Cecilia Gadea.** The simple, almost stark, cuts Gadea favors are the perfect canvas for riotously pretty texture work. One dress might be adorned with hundreds of hand-embroidered petals, another made of an open, modern take on embroidery. Feast further on her skirts, suits, and well-cut cotton tops. High-heeled patent Mary Janes, designed specially for her by Belocca, are part girly, part sophisticated. ⊠ *Ugarteche 3330, Palermo Botánico* ☎ *11/4801–4163* ⊕ *www.ceciliagadea.com* ✛ *2:G3.*

María Lizaso. A rising star on the style scene, young designer Maria Lizaso recently opened her first boutique in the most fashionable of hubs. Her ready-to-wear and brides' collections speak for themselves in store, as does her British seaside apparel—think nautical stripes. Fall for one of her sassy LBDs that has walked the walk at Berlin Fashion Week and features in boutiques such as Lola y Maria in New York. ✉ *Armenia 1471, Palermo Viejo* ☎ *011/3971–0788* ⊕ *www.marializaso.com* ✛ *3:D5.*

Mariano Toledo. Draping is Mariano Toledo's forte: party dresses hang in toga-like folds, accentuated by futuristic harness-style belts. Colors like electric blue and lime—often overlaid with bold prints—are arresting. ✉ *Armenia 1450, Palermo Viejo* ☎ *11/4137–7777* ⊕ *www. marianotoledo.com.ar* ✛ *3:D5.*

★ **Min Agostini.** Acres of skirts, structured wraps with oversize funnel necks, and loads of layers: yes, it's all very Yamamoto. These party clothes maxing out on volume are the result of architect-turned-designer Jazmín Agostini's "building" her garments on mannequins, rather than using patterns (her cutting table is the centerpiece at the Palermo shop). Also check out the Recoleta store at Libertad 1532. ✉ *Julián Álvarez 1419, Palermo Viejo* ☎ *11/4833–7563* ⊕ *www.minagostini.com.ar* ✛ *1:D1.*

Vero Ivaldi. Unlike other heralded local designers, Vero Ivaldi sells gorgeous garments that flatter even less-than-perfect figures at scandalously accessible prices. Dresses and skirts come in bold tones such as tomato-red or ocher, and are often built of different-textured panels and strips. ✉ *Gurruchaga 1585, Palermo Viejo* ☎ *11/4832–6334* ⊕ *www. veroivaldi.com* ✛ *3:D4.*

HANDICRAFTS, SILVER, AND SOUVENIRS

★ **Elementos Argentinos.** A fair-trade agreement links this luminous Palermo town house to a team of craftswomen in northwest Argentina who spin, dye, and weave the exquisite woolen goods sold here. Some of the handmade rugs, blankets, and throws follow traditional patterns and use only natural pigments (such as *yerba maté* or beetroot juice); others are contemporary designs using brighter colors. Packable souvenirs include sheep-wool table runners, alpaca scarves, and knitted cacti. Ask about designing your own rug. ✉ *Gurruchaga 1881, Palermo Viejo* ☎ *11/4832–6299* ✛ *3:F3.*

Tienda Palacio. The slogan here is "Cool Stuff," and it's spot on. From dress-up refrigerator magnet sets of Evita and Che to traditional penguin-shaped wine jugs, Tienda Palacio is full of the nifty Argentine paraphernalia with a heavy emphasis on kitsch meeting tongue in cheek. Also check out the San Telmo branch at Defensa 926. ✉ *Honduras 5272, Palermo Viejo* ☎ *11/4833–9456* ✛ *3:B2.*

HOME DECOR

★ **Arte Étnico Argentino.** Naturally dyed weavings and hand-hewn wooden basins are some of the things made by indigenous craftsmen at this shop-slash-gallery, which is a socially responsible business. Owner Ricardo Paz handpicks items such as tables carved from a single tree trunk; exquisite woolen rugs are the most transportable of the shop's temptations. ⊠ *El Salvador 4656, Palermo Viejo* ☎ *11/4832–0516* ⊕ *www.arteetnicoargentino.com* ✥ *3:F5.*

Calma Chicha. The simple but fun household items in this warehouse-like shop are proudly Argentine: quirky cowhide chairs, patchwork placemats, and geometric cushions nestle alongside mini-parrillas (barbecues), maté gear, and retro *pingüino* penguin-shaped wine jugs. Signature pear-shaped bean bags are signature living-room chilling items, but a fun and funky leather rug is infinitely more packable. ⊠ *Honduras 4925, Palermo Viejo* ☎ *11/4831–1818* ⊕ *www.calmachicha.com* ✥ *3:D4.*

Casa Chic. With a double identity of boutique and hotel, this beautiful homewares store offers up luxurious and rustic chic goods. There's an emphasis on lace, velvet, and crocheted textiles; snap up a woolen rug or wonderfully potent handmade lavender soap. ⊠ *El Salvador 4786, Palermo Viejo* ☎ *011/4897–2040* ⊕ *www.casa-chic.com* ✥ *3:G4.*

Pehache. A price is tagged to everything, except on the stairway's coiled rope banisters, despite one eager client trying to take it home with them. The classic Palermo Soho two-story house replicates a private home, with eye-catching wares sourced from 80 Argentine designers, including kitchen goods such as hand-painted penguin wine jugs or chunky wool rugs for living room quarters. Wander upstairs to discover one-off jewelry pieces in the boudoir. ⊠ *Gurruchaga 1418, Palermo Viejo* ☎ *011/4832–4022* ⊕ *www.pehache.com* ✥ *3:C4.*

JEWELRY AND ACCESSORIES

Compañia de Sombreros. For all your headwear needs, whether it's a Panama for the blazing sun, or a flat cap complete with ear flaps for a rough winter, this spacious store has it all. An authentic Argentine touch would mean snapping up a tartan *boina* for an urban gaucho look. ⊠ *Armenia 1587, Palermo Soho* ☎ *11/4833–9116* ⊕ *www. companiadesombreros.com.ar* ✥ *3:E4.*

Infinit. Infinit's signature thick acrylic eyeglass frames are favored by graphic designers and models alike. If the classic black rectangular versions are too severe for you, the same style comes in a range of candy colors and two-tones. Bug-eye shades and oversize '70s-inspired designs are other options. ⊠ *Thames 1602, Palermo Viejo* ☎ *11/4831–7070* ⊕ *www.infinit.la* ✥ *3:C3.*

La Mercería. This sumptuous haberdashery is a shrine to texture. Piles of floaty Indian scarves, ostrich-feather fans, and fur-lined leather gloves beg to be touched. Even more hands-on are the reels of lace trims and sequined edging that line the walls. ⊠ *Armenia 1609, Palermo Viejo* ☎ *11/4831–8558* ✥ *3:E4.*

Manu Lizarralde. Forget diamonds. In Manu Lizarralde's hands it's uncut emeralds, topaz, and rough tourmaline that are a girl's best friend. His trademark chunky rings and heavy necklaces combine irregular semi-precious stones in geometric silver settings. ⊠ *Gorriti 5078, Palermo Viejo* ☎ *11/4832–6252* ⊕ *www.manulizarralde.com* ✥ *3:C3.*

3

Life Before Malls

No shopping trip is complete without browsing one of the city's many *galerías*. These quirky shopping arcades are the precursors of malls and were mostly built in the 1960s and '70s. Their boxy architecture often includes gloriously kitsch touches, and the unpredictable retail offerings of their small stores could include designer gear, no-name brands, used books, sex toys, cigars and pipes, tattoos, imported vinyl records, and other wonders. Though many galerías have closed down, they're still thick on the ground along Avenida Santa Fe (800 to 1500) and Avenida Cabildo (1500 to 2200). For an underground experience, try Paseo Obelisco Sur. Set up by an eccentric millionaire, it runs under the 9 de Julio avenue.

Galería Bond Street. A prerequisite cool hangout with teenagers

and clubbers alike is Galería Bond Street. Downstairs stores sell club wear, punky T-shirts, and band pins. The top floor has the slightly classier pickings of local designers who aren't big enough to move to Palermo, while those with the urge for a tattoo can take their pick from a large selection of ground floor studios. ⊠ *Av. Santa Fe 1607, Barrio Norte* ☎ *11/4812–8744* ⊕ *www.xbondstreet.com.ar* ✣ *1:C2.*

Galería Quinta Avenida. Vintage vultures should swing by the Galería Quinta Avenida, which has a host of dusty boutiques ideal for a few hours of rack-roaming. There's a particularly good selection of leather jackets, as well as accessories like specs from the 1950s and '60s. ⊠ *Av. Santa Fe 1270, Recoleta* ☎ *11/4816–0451* ✣ *1:D2.*

María Medici. Industrial-looking brushed silver rings and necklaces knitted from fine stainless-steel cables are some of the attractions at this tiny shop. Architect and sculpturist María Medici also combines silver with primary-color resin to make solid, unusual-looking rings. ⊠ *Niceto Vega 4621, Palermo Viejo* ☎ *11/4773–2283* ⊕ *www.mariamedici.com.ar* ✣ *3:D6.*

★ **Metalistería.** Seriously fun jewelry rules at this multidesigner boutique. As well as the silver, steel, and aluminum the store's name suggests, quirky pieces can include leather, wool, cotton, acrylic, laminated newspaper cuttings, or even papier maché. ⊠ *Jorge Luis Borges 2021, Palermo Viejo* ☎ *11/3151–2777* ⊕ *www.metalisteria.com.ar* ✣ *3:F1.*

Positivo. Among the kitsch offerings at Positivo are button-covered satin handbags and metallic *maté* vessels and thermos-flasks in enough garish colors to match them to any outfit. ⊠ *Honduras 4866, Palermo Viejo* ☎ *11/4831–8559* ⊕ *www.positivodesign.com.ar* ✣ *3:E4.*

LUGGAGE, LEATHER, AND HANDBAGS

Doma. Doma's leather jackets are both hard-wearing and eye-catching. Military-style coats in olive-green suede will keep you snug in winter while cooler summer options include collarless biker jackets in silver, electric blue, or deep red. ⊠ *El Salvador 4693, Palermo Viejo* ☎ *11/4831–6852* ⊕ *www.doma-leather.com* ✣ *3:E3.*

Big Spenders

If you're a shopper who just isn't satisfied by small-fry spending, why not splash out on something a little more extravagant, like, say…a new home?

Reynolds Propiedades. More than 40 years' experience have made Reynolds Propiedades a fail-safe option for foreign buyers. Reynolds works with other real estate agents to increase the number of properties it can offer, such as vineyards, new developments, or farms, and then guides you through the paperwork. Staffers can even help you furnish your house once you're done. ⊠ *Junin 1655, 3A, Recoleta* ☎ *11/4801–9291* ⊕ *www.argentinahomes.com* ✛ *1:C1.*

Ojo Propiedades. If you feel guilty about taking the property out of the hands of locals, you can go easy on your conscience at Ojo Propiedades, where all profits go to the Red Cross.

This hip outfit deals primarily with Palermo properties although it does have offerings in surrounding Villa Crespo, Belgrano as well as Chacarita, and has lots of foreign customers. ⊠ *Serrano 1503, Palermo Viejo* ☎ *11/4832–4040* ⊕ *www.ojopropiedades.com* ✛ *3:C4.*

Gateway To South America. This real estate broker specializes in giving advice about Argentina and its neighboring countries and deals with vacation rentals as well as residential and commercial properties, with an emphasis on farms. With a Buenos Aires office run by various native English speakers, GTSA helps perspective buyers with economic reports and also offers agri tours. ⊠ *Basavilbaso 1350, Office 706, Retiro* ☎ *11/5254–3415* ⊕ *www.gatewaytosouthamerica.com.*

Fodor's Choice
★ **Humawaca.** Their innovative bag shapes and funky colors keep this brand at the top of Buenos Aires design icons. The trendiest leather name in town also makes stylish laptop totes and travel bags, which come with a handy magazine-carrying strap. Cowhide is a favorite here, as are lively combinations like milk-chocolate-brown leather and moss-green suede, or electric blue nobuk with a floral lining. Price tags on the bags may make you gulp, but there are wallets, gloves, and pencil cases, too. ⊠ *El Salvador 4692, Palermo Viejo* ☎ *11/4832–2662* ⊕ *www.humawaca.com* ✛ *1:D1.*

★ **Uma.** Light, butter-soft leather takes very modern forms here, with geometric stitching the only adornment on jackets and asymmetrical bags that might come in rich violet in winter and aqua-blue in summer. The top-quality footwear includes teetering heels and ultrasimple boots and sandals with, mercifully, next to no elevation. Ultra-tight jeans and tops are also on offer. ⊠ *Paseo Alcorta Mall, Shop 1005, Jerónimo Salguero 3172, at Av. Figueroa Alcorta, Palermo* ☎ *11/0800–888–8862* ⊕ *www.umacuero.com.ar* ✛ *2:H2.*

MALLS AND DEPARTMENT STORES

Alto Palermo. A prime location, choice shops, and a pushy marketing campaign have made Alto Palermo popular. Giggly teenage hordes are seduced by its long, winding layout. Ladies who lunch sip espresso in the cafés on the top-level food hall. The 154 shops are strong on local street-wear brands such as Bensimon and Bowen for the boys and Akiabara, Ona Sáez, Las Pepas, and Rapsodia for the girls. Check out trendy local designers María Vázquez, Isabel la Católica, and AY Not Dead for way-out party clothes, and Kill for simple yet effective staples. Paruolo, Sibyl Vane, and Lázaro are the best of many good shoe and handbag shops. Surf-and-skate store Cristobal Colón does board shorts and All-Stars; local versions of Puma and Adidas footwear disappear fast despite high price tags. ⊠ *Av. Santa Fe 3253, at Av. Colonel Díaz, Palermo* ☎ *11/5777–8000* ⊕ *www.altopalermo.com.ar* Ⓜ *D to Bulnes* ✛ *2:G4.*

★ **Paseo Alcorta.** If you're a serious shopper with only enough time to visit one mall, make it this one. Local fashionistas favor it for its mix of high-end local chains and boutiques from some of the city's best designers. Trendsetters such as Trosman, Jazmín Chebar, and Allô Martinez make cool clothes for women, while María Cher and Chocolate offer more classic chic. The men can hold their own at Etiqueta Negra and Felix. Both girls and boys can break the bank at Tramando or save at Zara. There's even a personal shopper service if it all gets too overwhelming. The international presence is strong, too, with stores from Swarovski, Lacroix, and Cacharel, as well as the usual sports brands. Free transfers from hotels, a classy food hall, and Wi-Fi round off the reasons to come here. ⊠ *Jerónimo Salguero 3172, at Av. Figueroa Alcorta, Palermo* ☎ *11/5777–6500* ⊕ *www.paseoalcorta.com.ar* ✛ *2:H2.*

PAPER AND STATIONERY

★ **Papelera Palermo.** Making paper funky, piles of handmade sheets and envelopes, leather-bound diaries, and vintage notebooks are arrayed on simple trestle tables. Writing implements range from old-world pens to chunky pencils. The store often showcases work by top engravers and graphic artists, who return the favor by designing the covers of sketchbooks. Also holds workshops. ⊠ *Honduras 4945, Palermo Viejo* ☎ *11/4833–3081* ⊕ *www.papelerapalermo.com.ar* ✛ *3:D3.*

SHOES—MEN'S AND WOMEN'S

28Sport. These leather bowling sneakers and boxing-style boots are the heart and, er, sole of retro. All the models are variations on a classic round-toed lace-up, but come with different-length legs. Plain black or chestnut uppers go with everything, but equally tempting are the two-tone numbers—in chocolate and orange, or black with curving white panels, for example. Even the store is a nod to the past, kitted out like a 1950s living room. ⊠ *Gurruchaga 1481, Palermo Viejo* ☎ *11/4833–4287* ⊕ *www.28sport.com* ✛ *3:C4.*

SHOES—WOMEN'S

Divia. Step out in a pair of limited-edition Divias and it doesn't really matter what else you've got on. Designer Virginia Spagnuolo draws inspiration from travels to India, her own vintage shoe collection, and even her cat. The results are leather collages—suede, textured metallic, or patent leathers—in colors such as teal, ruby, or plum. Order à la carte and commission a custom-made pair. ✉ *Armenia 1489, Palermo Viejo* ☎ *11/4831–9090* ⊕ *www.diviashoes.com* ✛ *3:D5.*

Josefina Ferroni. Thickly wedged heels and points that taper beyond reason and are some of Ferroni's trademarks. Stacked heels in dark textured leather with metallic trim look like a contemporary take on something Evita might have worn. If all that height brings on vertigo, fear not: the three-tone boots and ballet pumps are pancake-flat. ✉ *Armenia 1687, Palermo Viejo* ☎ *11/4831–4033* ⊕ *www.josefinaferroni. com.ar* ✛ *3:D5.*

★ **Lucila Iotti.** Two or three swathes of shockingly bright citrus patent leather combined with thick tapering heels in another flashy color: these shoes are showstoppers. *Sex and the City* stylists certainly agree: they ordered a dozen pairs. The open-toed but arch-covering sandals Iotti favors have a definite whiff of Carnaby Street about them. ✉ *Malabia 2212, Palermo* ☎ *11/4833–0206* ⊕ *www.lucilaiotti.com* ✛ *2:F4.*

Mishka. At this longtime Palermo favorite, your feet will go to the ball in high-heel lace-ups, kick some butt in metallic boots, or feel like a princess sporting ballet pumps. Footwear comes in leather as well as in fabrics like brocade; most styles run narrow. Check out the new store in San Telmo (Balcarce 1011). ✉ *El Salvador 4673, Palermo Viejo* ☎ *11/4833–6566* ⊕ *www.mishkashoes.com.ar* ✛ *3:F4.*

TOYS

Recursos Infantiles. This cultural kiddie store has been designed with little ones in mind, right down to the menu at the in-store café. Mini musical instruments and most other toys are made of wood; little ones would look adorable playing with them dressed in bright knitted ponchos. The small-scale maté sets by D'ak come in a colorful bag. ✉ *Jorge Luis Borges 1766, Palermo Viejo* ☎ *11/4834–6177* ⊕ *www. recursosinfantiles.com.ar* ✛ *3:E2.*

WINE

Rogelio Wine Store & Art. Spacious yet not cavernous, this new addition on the Palermo wine scene takes pride in boutique and more commercial labels, offers private tastings, and has a wide range of Champagne on hand for special occasions. ✉ *Gorriti 4966, Palermo* ☎ *11/4897–2186* ⊕ *www.rogeliowinestore.com.ar* ✛ *3:C4.*

Fodor's Choice **Terroir.** A wine-lover's heaven is tucked away in this white stone Palermo ★ town house. Expert English-speaking staffers are on hand to help you make sense of the massive selection of Argentine wine, which includes collector's gems such as the 1999 Angélica Zapata Cabernet Sauvignon. They even arrange private wine-tasting courses to get you up to speed on local vintages: call a week or two before you arrive. Terroir ships all over the world. ✉ *Buschiazzo 3040, Palermo* ☎ *11/4778–3443* ⊕ *www. terroir.com.ar* ✛ *2:F2.*

BELGRANO

HANDICRAFTS, SILVER, AND SOUVENIRS

★ **Fundación Silataj.** This small handicraft shop is run by a non-profit organization that trades fairly with around 30 indigenous communities in Argentina. The shop smells like the aromatic palo santo wood used to make the trays, platters, cutting boards, and hair combs they carry. Other offerings include carnival masks, handwoven textiles, beaten tin ornaments, and alpaca jewelry. Prices, though higher than in markets, are reasonable; quality is excellent, hence the name in the Wichi Indian language which means "the best"; and you know your money is going to the artisans. Note that the store closes for lunch. ⊠ *Vuelta de Obligado 1933, Belgrano* ☎ *11/4785–8371* ⊕ *www.fundacionsilataj. org.ar* Ⓜ *D to José Hernández* ✛ *2:C1.*

Buenos Aires Shopping & After Dark Atlas

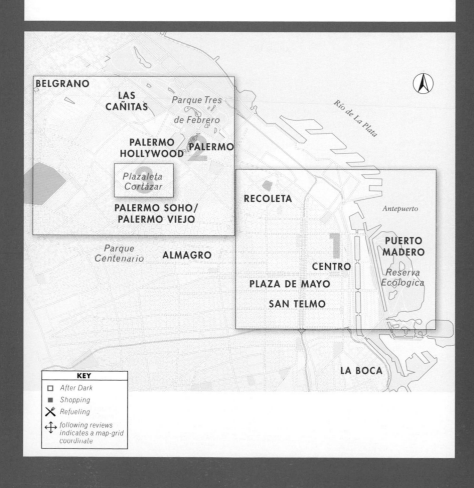

BELGRANO

LAS
CAÑITAS

*Parque Tres
de Febrero*

PALERMO
HOLLYWOOD

PALERMO

Río de La Plata

*Plazaleta
Cortázar*

RECOLETA

PALERMO SOHO/
PALERMO VIEJO

Antepuerto

*Parque
Centenario*

ALMAGRO

1

CENTRO

PUERTO
MADERO

*Reserva
Ecológica*

PLAZA DE MAYO

SAN TELMO

LA BOCA

KEY

☐ *After Dark*
■ *Shopping*
✕ *Refueling*
⟨↕⟩ *following reviews
indicates a map-grid
coordinate*

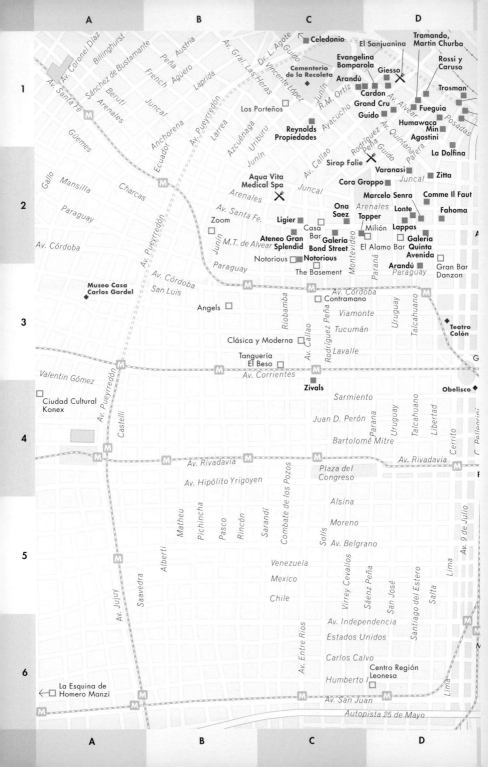

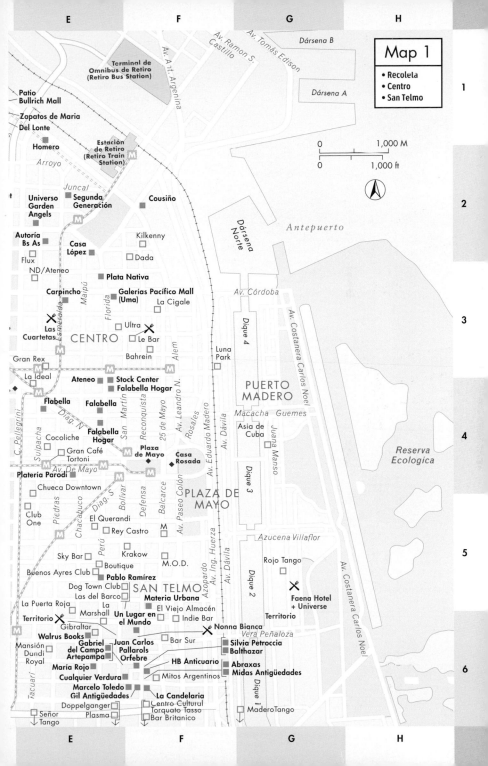

Map 1
- Recoleta
- Centro
- San Telmo

E F G H

Av. Ramon S. Castillo
Av. A 1t. Argentina
Av. Tomás Edison

Dársena B

Dársena A

1

Terminal de Omnibus de Retiro (Retiro Bus Station)

Patio Bullrich Mall
Zapatos de Maria
Del Lonte
Homero

Estación de Retiro (Retiro Train Station)

Arroyo

Juncal

Antepuerto

Dársena Norte

2

Universo Garden Angels
Segunda Generación
Cousiño

Autoria Bs As
Casa López
Kilkenny

Flux
ND/Ateneo
Dada

Plata Nativa

Carpincho
Galerías Pacífico Mall (Uma)
La Cigale

Av. Córdoba

3

Maipú
Florida
Esmeralda

Las Cuartetas
CENTRO
Ultra
Le Bar
Bahrein

Dique 4

Av. Costanera Carlos Noel

Luna Park

Gran Rex
La Ideal

Ateneo
Stock Center
Falabella Hogar

Alem

PUERTO MADERO

4

Flabella
Falabella

Diag. N
San Martín
Reconquista
25 de Mayo
Rosales

Macacha Guemes

Cocoliche
Falabella Hogar
Gran Café Tortoni
Plaza de Mayo
Casa Rosada

Asia de Cuba

Reserva Ecológica

Av. Eduardo Madero
Av. Dávila
Juana Manso

Platería Parodi
Av. De Mayo

Chueca Downtown
C. Pellegrini
Sulpacha
Piedras
Chacabuco
Diag. S
Bolivar
Defensa
Balcarce
Av. Paseo Colón

PLAZA DE MAYO

Dique 3

5

Club One
El Querandi
Rey Castro

Azucena Villaflor

Sky Bar
Krakow
M.O.D.
Rojo Tango

Buenos Ayres Club
Boutique
Pablo Ramírez

Dog Town Club
SAN TELMO
Materia Urbana

Av. Ing. Huerza
Av. Dávila
Azopardo

Dique 2

La Puerta Roja
Las del Barco
El Viejo Almacén
Indie Bar

Faena Hotel + Universe

Territorio
La Marshall
Un Lugar en el Mundo
Territorio

Gibraltar
Nonna Bianca
Vera Peñaloza

Mansión Dundi Royal
Walrus Books
Bar Sur

Gabriel del Campo
Artepampa
Juan Carlos Pallarols Orfebre
Silvia Petroccia
Balthazar

Maria Rojo
HB Anticuario
Abraxas
Midas Antigüedades

Cualquier Verdura
Mitos Argentinos

6

Marcelo Toledo
Gil Antigüedades
La Candelaria
MaderoTango

Tacuari
Doppelganger
Plasma
Centro Cultural Torquato Tasso

Señor Tango
Bar Britanico

Dique 1

0   1,000 M
0   1,000 ft

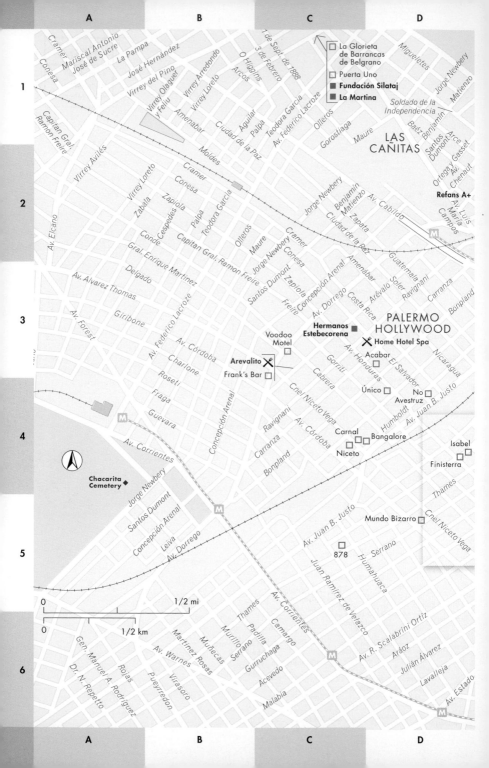

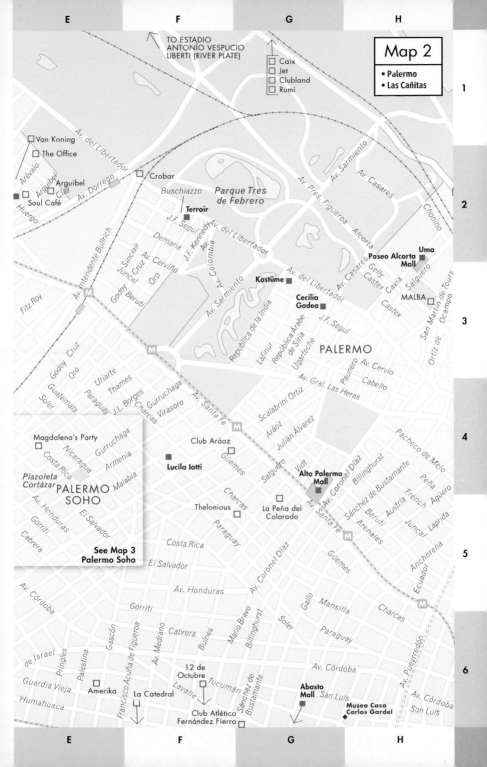

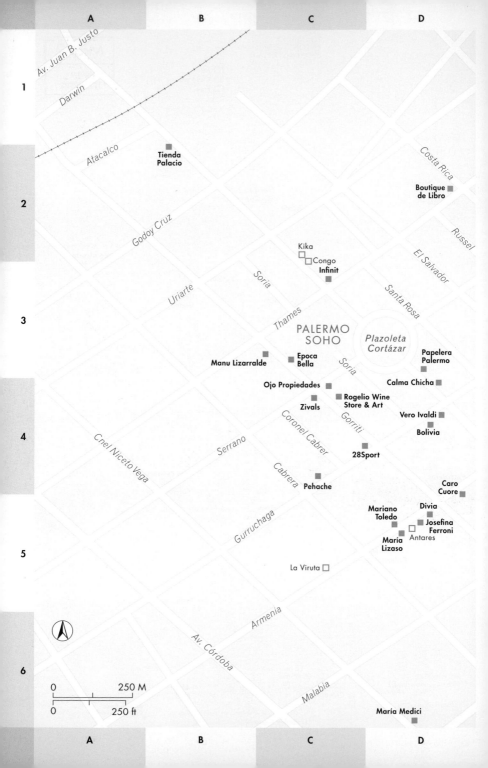

Nightlife

WORD OF MOUTH

"In most cases, a tango show will take up the whole evening. Be extremely wary of cabs waiting in line outside touristy spots. Have a cab called, or be sure the driver sees you write down his license plate, which should be hanging from the front seat. If said info is not there, get off the cab! Have a great time!"

—avrooster

By Sorrel
Moseley-
Williams

Preparing for an evening out in Buenos Aires has an element of marathon training to it. Rest up with a siesta, chow down some carbs, and drink plenty of fluids before, during, and after. That's right, the key to nightlife *porteño* style is longevity, where an early night means hailing a taxi at 6 am.

Good times lie ahead at a glossy cocktail bar, an old-school jazz café, a classic tango haunt, or on a packed dance floor. Whatever your preferences are, you'll find a space that suits.

Painting Buenos Aires red means looking sharp, going with the flow as you bar-hop the evening away, and not challenging new local buddies to indulge in raucous drinking games. Porteños adore going out and being with their friends, and it's not uncommon to see a large group sharing a liter bottle of beer and swigging from the same glass. Lightweights? Not at all—this is just how they do it.

As an increasing number of expatriate-run bars flourish in Palermo and San Telmo, with them come happy hours starting at around 9 pm that often stretch way beyond an hour. Downtown drinking establishments kick off even earlier to lure workers to part with hard-earned pesos, spawning the Wednesday "after-office" across the city, which is now a nightlife fixture.

Hours are relaxed, but there are general guidelines: theater performances begin around 9 pm and the last movie begins after midnight. Lines to get into popular bars start forming by midnight while clubs aren't buzzing until 4 am. If in doubt, turn up later than you consider reasonable if you're meeting a local; being 30 minutes late is the norm. The subte closes by 10:30 pm and opens at 5:30 am, so taking a cab to and from home is generally a good idea. It's also quicker than waiting for a colectivo bus.

In a nutshell, adhere to this Buenos Aires checklist: look good enough to eat, take enough cash for the evening, and have a pair of sunglasses handy for when the sun rises—because you'll need them if you're going to be doing things the porteño way.

PLANNING

WHAT IT COSTS

Wines are generally very good value: wine lists in reputable bars start around the 45-peso mark, while beer sets you back around 25 pesos for a pint and soft drinks approach the 15-peso mark. Cocktails, usually around 25 pesos and up, arc also popular, and mixologists take pride in making original concoctions. Concert admission can be 150 pesos or more for established international acts. Nightclubs can charge a cover of around 20–30 pesos, which usually includes a drink; fancier nightclubs charge more. Tips are roughly 10% on top of the bill. A taxi ride from Palermo to Centro is around 25 pesos, but fares rise between 10 pm and 6 am.

4

WHAT ARE THE OPTIONS?

Whatever your yen for the evening, start your planning with a look at daily paper Buenos Aires Herald's "Get Out!" section for up-to-date information on gigs, theater and music shows and tango, as well as **What's Up Buenos Aires** (⊕ *www.whatsupbuenosaires.com*).

Bars: Porteños may not be big drinkers, but they excel at everything else involved with spending time in bars—talking at length, seeing and being seen, and staying out all night. Expect a great variety of late-night bars and very little drunken behavior. Although Argentina's wines may be big business these days, its wine bars are still generally small, earnest spaces where the sacred grape is what matters. The late schedule of porteño nightlife means that even the busiest cocktail bars spend a good part of each evening empty. This has led to the rise of happy hours with half-price or two-for-one drink offers often stretching for three or four hours until midnight. Late-night bars—while late-night by most rational standards—should not to be confused with the *late* late-night bars known as "afters" (⇨ *When the Sun Comes Up, below*). Spending the wee hours at one (or several) of these places is like the evening's main course, so hold back some energy for it.

Tango: The passion, drama, and nostalgia of tango is the most concise expression of the spirit of Buenos Aires—and a *milonga* (tango dance hall) should definitely be on every visitor's itinerary. Many offer reasonably priced early-evening classes for all levels. Whether you eventually join in or not, spend some time at a floor-side table to appreciate the ritual (⇨ *The Dance of Buenos Aires, below*).

While we're on the subject, it's important to know that a milonga is more an event than a place. The same venue can host different milongas on different nights; conversely, the same milonga can take place at different venues on different nights. Reservations are usually essential. Most of our listings are for venues, but also include contact details for specific milongas: these are nearly always the cell phones or the home phones of the organizers, many of whom don't speak English.

Live Music: *Rock Nacional* (Argentine rock) makes up the majority of live music; it's highly derivative and of limited interest to most outsiders. Fortunately, there are also the small but lively jazz scene, a buzzing indie/electro-pop circuit, a digital cumbia scene to get static feet moving and—for those who need reminding they're in South America—folk peñas (meeting places), where guitars, pan pipes, and unpretentious singers conjure the spirit of the Andes and the north of the country in the urban jungle.

Dancing the Night Away: An influx of foreign DJs may be affecting the exclusivity of Buenos Aires' electronic music scene, but it's also supporting a more diverse range of club nights. There's plenty to please you here, especially if you like your house music progressive and your dress code smart.

Gay and Lesbian: With a city-wide gay-friendly attitude (enhanced by the national gay marriage bill, which became law in 2010), Buenos Aires has a whole network of bars and clubs, meeting points, and milongas. Many free gay guides, found in hotels and boutiques, help you navigate the scene; GayBA (⊕ *www.gay-ba.com*) is available in bookshops and kiosks. Also look out for the useful G Maps (⊕ *www.gmaps360.com*), or visit ⊕ *www.thegayguide.com.ar.*

> **SAFETY**
>
> Buenos Aires is relatively trouble-free, but incidents do occur. At night it's best to avoid La Boca, deserted areas of Montserrat and downtown, and parts of Abasto. Don't carry more money than you need; leave behind valuables that would be safer in your hotel. Keep handbags and purses about your person at all times. Take taxis, especially for getting between neighborhoods or through unlighted streets: they're cheap, plentiful, and don't increase their fares at night.

CENTRO

Downtown is chaotic on weekdays, but can be deserted at night and on weekends. If you know where to look, there are some great bars and nightclubs.

BARS

COCKTAIL BARS

★ **Dada.** Cozy and colorful, Dadá has a short but sweet cocktail list and an ideal bar to perch at while sipping one of the classics. With its owners doubling up as bar staff, Dadá attracts an eclectic mix of locals and visitors popping in for dinner, a drink, or both. Grab a booth at the back for extra privacy. ⊠ *San Martin 941, Centro* ☎ *11/4314–4787* ✢ *1:F2.*

The Kilkenny. A popular pub that spawned a whole street of imitators, the Kilkenny serves surprisingly good Irish food and has Guinness on draft. Celtic or rock bands play every night, entertaining the after-work crowd from nearby offices that comes for the extended happy hour and stays into the small hours. ⊠ *Marcelo T. De Alvear 399, Centro* ☎ *11/4312–7291* ⊕ *www.thekilkenny.com.ar* Ⓜ *C to San Martín* ✢ *1:F2.*

Le Bar. Le Bar is a stylish stalwart of the Centro's drinking scene. Up the stairs from the cocktail lounge is a clever sunken seating arrangement; farther still is a smokers' terrace. Office workers get the evening started; hot DJs spin sounds until late while it's also a great spot to catch cool local indie bands. ⊠ *Tucuman 422, Centro* ☎ *11/5219–8580* ⊕ *www. lebarbuenosaires.blogspot.com* ✛ *1:F3.*

LATE-NIGHT BARS

La Cigale. After moving two blocks down the road, La Cigale has undergone a serious upgrade, proving that size does matter. Take advantage of happy hour until 10 pm at its curvaceously seductive first-floor bar which leads to the street-side balcony. Another flight of stairs winds up to the stage, ready and waiting for local indie, jazz, and acoustic bands any night of the week. ⊠ *25 de Mayo 597, Centro* ☎ *11/4893–2332* Ⓜ *B to L.N. Alem* ✛ *1:F3.*

DANCE CLUBS

Fodor's Choice
★

Bahrein. Sheik—er, *chic* and super-stylish, this party palace is in a 100-year-old former bank. Head straight to the ground floor's Funky Room, where beautiful, tightly clothed youth groove to pop, rock, and funk. The downstairs Excess Room has electronic beats and dizzying wall visuals. Consistently good and popular with North American visitors is Tuesday night's drum-and-bass night run by local vegetarian DJ hero, Bad Boy Orange. ⊠ *Lavalle 345, Centro* ☎ *11/4315–2403* ⊕ *www.bahreinba.com* Ⓜ *B to Alem* ✛ *1:F3.*

Cocoliche. Cocoliche enjoys cult status in both the straight and gay communities. Upstairs is a diverse art gallery big on young locals; downstairs, underground house and techno drives one of the city's darkest dance floors, while DJs with huge followings line up to take on the decks. ⊠ *Rivadavia 878, Centro* ☎ *11/4342–9485* ⊕ *www.cocoliche. net* Ⓜ *A to Piedras* ✛ *1:E4.*

GAY AND LESBIAN SPOTS

Chueca Downtown. With a restaurant, a bar, and a yacht in Puerto Madero, the Chueca group is rapidly expanding. Their infamous cabaret show in Spanish but peppered with English is now based in the center of town, where the bar is open all day and serves as a "pre-dance" venue for neighboring Club One on Friday nights. ⊠ *Alsina 975, Centro* ☎ *11/4331–5330* ⊕ *www.chueca-restobar.com.ar* ✛ *1:E4.*

Contramano. It's been around since 1984, when it was the city's most popular and pioneering gay disco. Today Contramano operates more as a laid-back small bar with an older, male-only clientele. Occasionally there's live music and male strippers. ⊠ *Rodríguez Peña 1082* ☎ *No phone* ⊕ *www.contramano.com* Ⓜ *D to Callao* ✛ *1:C3.*

Flux. It took a couple of expats to realize the gap in the market for early-evening gay bars. Their creation, Flux, is a smart, friendly, and sociable basement club that gets going for happy hour and keeps on until after midnight with decent pop music and a good cocktail menu.

4

TIPS FOR A GOOD NIGHT OUT

Don't be afraid to stand in line outside. Lines are generally quick and painless, and if there isn't one, the place might not be worth the wait.

Be prepared to buy a ticket or make a reservation. For concerts, shows, and club events, people often buy tickets in advance, as many events do fill up or sell out, especially international ones.

Go late—really. Otherwise you'll miss out on the atmosphere and find it a bit boring. If necessary, help smooth the adjustment with a merienda (a snack of coffee and croissants at around 6 pm) and a "disco siesta."

Find out what's on and where. Scour flyers, Internet sites, ticket agencies, and magazine listings for up-to-date information. There's a lot more going on than you can find out from any single source.

Look sharp. Porteños like to dress up, like to wear their finery, although they err on the conservative side and only dress to impress on a big night out. With the exception of one or two scruffy bars in San Telmo, you'll never feel overdressed.

Never imagine you've seen it all. Private parties and last-minute underground events are where it's at. Finding out about them isn't easy, but keep an ear out and tell people you're looking and you might luck out.

✉ *Marcelo T. de Alvear 980, Centro* ☎ *11/5252–0258* ⊕ *www.fluxbar. com.ar* ✛ *1:E2.*

Palacio Alsina. Despite changing its name (from Palacio Alsina), this enormous downtown club never fails to churn out excellent nights, especially when world-famous DJs rock into town. Attracting a mixed-age gay and lesbian crowd on Fridays and Sundays for pop tunes, Saturdays, sees hard electronica for the dance mad. ✉ *Alsina 940, Centro* ☎ *11/4331–3231* ⊕ *www.clubonebsas.com.ar* Ⓜ *A to Piedras* ✛ *1:E5.*

MUSIC

ROCK

Gran Rex. Exquisite art deco theaters line Avenida Corrientes, but the Gran Rex is a favorite venue for rock, pop, and jazz musicians. Recent acts that have tested its great acoustics include legendary guitarist Peter Frampton and Coldplay. Tickets are available through Ticketek. ✉ *Corrientes 857, Centro* ☎ *11/4322–8000* ◷ *Box office daily 10–10* Ⓜ *B to Carlos Pellegrini* ✛ *1:E3.*

Luna Park. The indoor stadium is located at the very beginning of Corrientes Avenue and for more than 75 years, it has hosted boxing events, ice-skating spectaculars, political rallies, and international and national rock and pop concerts. Tickets normally need to be bought well in advance from the box office or from Ticketportal. ✉ *Av. Madero 420, Centro* ☎ *11/5353–0606* ⊕ *www.lunapark.com.ar* ◷ *Box office Mon.–Sat. 10–10* Ⓜ *B to L.N. Alem* ✛ *1:F3.*

ND/Ateneo. This spacious theater and cultural space mainly invites mid-level local bands, showmen, and comedians entertain you. Get tickets from the box office from noon to 8 pm Monday through Saturday, or through Ticketek. ✉ *Paraguay 918, Centro* ☎ *11/4328–2888* ⊕ *www. ndateneo.com.ar* ✛ *1:E3.*

★ **Ultra.** The owners of this dynamic space for art and live music have run an independent record label for more than a decade. On weekends they throw big parties until daybreak, and on most weeknights there's a strong line-up of local bands and even small festivals. ✉ *San Martin 678, Centro* ☎ *11/4312–5605* ⊕ *www.ultrapop-ar.blogspot. com* ✛ *1:E3.*

TANGO

4

MILONGAS

★ **La Ideal.** Soaring columns, tarnished mirrors, and ancient chandeliers are part of La Ideal's crumbling Old World glamour, along with rather pungent musty smell. The classic tearoom hosts milongas organized by different groups in its first-floor dance hall every day of the week. Some are held during the afternoon and evening, others late at night, like the popular Unitango Club (☎ *11/4301–3723*), held on Fridays. Many include live orchestras. ✉ *Suipacha 384, Plaza de Mayo* ☎ *11/4328–7750* ⊕ *www.confiteriaideal.com* ✛ *1:E4.*

Tanguería El Beso. The standard of dancing is usually high at this club, which belongs to La Academia del Tango Milonguero, one of the city's best tango schools. Intermediate dancers can get their footwork up to speed at the daily classes before putting themselves to the test at the milongas, run by different organizers Tuesday through Sunday. ✉ *Riobamba 416, Congreso* ☎ *11/4953–2794* ✛ *1:C3.*

MUSIC CLUBS

Gran Café Tortoni. Excellent local musicians put on daily performances of tango classics in the downstairs salon of this famous café, but note that ticket prices can be steep. There's jazz sometimes on weekends, too. ✉ *Av. de Mayo 829, Plaza de Mayo* ☎ *11/4342–4328* ⊕ *www. cafetortoni.com.ar* ✛ *1:E4.*

PUERTO MADERO

A business district whose star has risen over the past decade, the formerly dilapidated dock of Puerto Madero has adjusted well to its face-lift. Centrally located and home to some of the city's most expensive hotels, restaurants, and bars, the scene here is poised to keep getting better although can be lacking in soul.

BARS

LATE-NIGHT BARS

Asia de Cuba. Once *the* spot to be seen sipping Champagne and eating sushi, Asia de Cuba still draws local celebrities, though it's now lost some of its white-hot luster. The candlelight and red-and-black Asian

CLOSE UP

When the Sun Comes Up

Clubs starting so late means that regular cafés are open for a hard-earned *cortado* (coffee cut with a drop of milk) and *medialunas* (croissants) by the time you stumble out of clubs in the morning, but Buenos Aires does have a couple of alternative options for sunrise, too. The first is to head to the Costanera for a *choripan* (chorizo sausage and chimichurri sauce on a roll) from the 24-hour stands lining the river. If you're not already near the Costanera, sharing a taxi with friends to get there is part of the fun. The more hard-core option is to keep dancing at one of the many "afters"—clubs that start at 9 am and go until around 3 pm. The best-known is **Caix** (⊠ *Centro Costa Salguero, Av. Rafael Obligado y Salguero, Centro* ☎ *11/4806–9749* ✛ *2:G1*), but there are many others opening and closing all the time; any hardened clubber can take you through the options.

decor set the mood for an exotic evening—by local standards. Grab a booth to watch and be watched. ⊠ *Pierina Dealessi 750, Puerto Madero* ☎ *11/4894–1329* ⊕ *www.asiadecuba.com.ar* ✛ *1:G4.*

TANGO

DINNER SHOWS
Madero Tango. Local businesspeople looking to impress international clients invariably choose this showy concept restaurant. A night here may break the bank, but you get varied, highly professional performances often starring Argentine celebrities. Prices vary depending on how close you are to the stage. ⊠ *Alicia Moreau de Justo at Brasil, Puerto Madero* ☎ *11/5239–3009* ⊕ *www.maderotango.com* ✛ *1:G6.*

Fodor'sChoice ★ **Rojo Tango.** Five-star food, musicians, choreography, and glamour: you wouldn't expect anything less from the Faena Hotel + Universe. Crimson velvet lines everything from the walls to the menu at the Cabaret, and tables often hold celebs both local and global. The implausibly good-looking troupe puts on a tango-through-the-ages show, which includes jazz-tango, semi-naked numbers, and even the tango version of Roxanne from *Moulin Rouge*. It's worth breaking the piggy bank for. ⊠ *Martha Salotti 445, Puerto Madero* ☎ *11/5787–1536* ⊕ *www.rojotango.com* ✛ *1:G5.*

SAN TELMO

An immigrant neighborhood, San Telmo continues to be revamped with establishments popping up to cater to the latest wave of visitors to the city—backpackers, short-term expats, and tango hunters. Now home to dozens of trendy bars, the bohemian district is coming into its own again. La Boca to the south, on the other hand, is still best avoided at night.

BARS

COCKTAIL BARS

Dog Town Club. Space-wise one of San Telmo's largest bars, Dog Town has literally gone to town with its mixology, rustling up delights such as passionfruit mojitos. There's also an extensive whisky menu. Hidden at the back is a pool table. Pop music mash-ups make this a decent watering hole to start an evening. ⊠ *Bolivar 673, San Telmo* ☎ *11/4300–2859* ✛ *1:F5.*

★ **Doppelganger.** With a list of 100 cocktails and an excellent menu to match, this corner bar on the edge of San Telmo is a hidden gem. The music, the choice of books on the shelf, and the quotations in the menu show that the concept has been thought through down to the finest details. But your focus should be on the carefully made martinis, bitters, and vermouth, and having a good time. Take advantage of its happy two hours from 7 to 9 Tuesday through Friday. ⊠ *Avenida Juan de Garay 500, San Telmo* ☎ *11/4300–0201* ⊕ *www.doppelganger.com.ar* ✛ *1:E6.*

LATE-NIGHT BARS

Bar Británico. This traditional corner bar opposite Parque Lezama is one of San Telmo's most iconic spots and still stands more than 90 years after it opened. Day and night it's full of characters and passionate discussions, and serves up drinks and snacks until all hours. Named after the English who helped build the railway lines in nearby Constitución, its original owners were in fact Spanish. ⊠ *Brasil 399, San Telmo* ☎ *11/4361–2107* ✛ *1:F6.*

Gibraltar. A traditional British boozer in the heart of San Telmo, Gibraltar has ditched its expat refuge label to become a regular watering hole for locals and foreigners alike. A classical wooden bar with decent ales as well as fish and chips on the menu, it also sports a pool table in its smoking room, an outdoor terrace, and standoffish staff to boot. Those in the know should hire out the upstairs Library Bar—quintessentially English. ⊠ *Perú 895, San Telmo* ☎ *11/4362–5310* ✛ *1:E6.*

Indie Bar. An underrated corner watering hole on the eastern edge of San Telmo, this modern pub serves up decent drinks under mood lighting. Attracting a predominantly local crowd, Indie will lure you in for an early-evening cocktail; happy hour ends by 9 pm. ⊠ *Paseo Colón 843, San Telmo* ☎ *11/4307–0997* ⊕ *www.indiebar.com.ar* ✛ *1:F6.*

Krakow. Owned by a Polish expat with one of the lengthiest bars in the neighborhood, Krakow has a great selection of beers on tap as well as a big screen for those all-important soccer matches. One of the few bars to offer Wii games in the city. ⊠ *Venezuela 474, San Telmo* ☎ *11/4342–3916* ⊕ *www.krakow-cafe.com.ar* ✛ *1:F5.*

La Puerta Roja. Pass through its scarlet entrance and clamber the stairs to this trendy yet friendly bar which often has a decent happy hour. There's a wide selection of spirits and beers on tap, plus a pool table, and a sociable mix of locals and expat regulars. ⊠ *Chacabuco 733, San Telmo* ☎ *11/4362–5649* ✛ *1:E5.*

Las del BarCo. Get down with the hipsters who spill out onto the San Telmo sidewalk rain or shine when Las del BarCo gets too full. Pull up a love seat and grab a pint, and check out the ever-changing art exhibitions. Fun and frivolous, this hot spot has already attracted a dedicated following and not just for its 300 minutes of happy hour. ⊠ *Bolivar 684, San Telmo* ⊕ *www.lasdelbarcobar. blogspot.com/* ✦ *1:F5.*

M. Pull up a red velvet stool at the ground floor bar for an impeccable cocktail, or reserve your place at the cava downstairs for a wine-tasting session. Don't forget to peek at the tunnel which former president Juan Perón used to escape from Government House. With a huge ivy "M" marking the spot, M also houses Samsung Studio, San Telmo's latest tiny yet trendy live music venue. ⊠ *Balcarce 433, San Telmo* ☎ *11/4331–3879* ⊕ *www.mbuenosaires.com.ar* ✦ *1:F5.*

> ### FOLK MUSIC
>
> Argentine folk comes from the northwest of the country; is heavy on vocal harmonies, drums, and wind instruments; and is celebrated in *peñas folkloricas* (informal music halls specifically for folk music) set up by communities from the northwest. Most are far from the center and difficult to find, but Palermo now has a few of its own, such as La Peña del Colorado and La Paila.

DANCE CLUBS

Boutique. As it was designed by G. Eiffel (of the tower fame), the club formally known as Museum, which has seen substantially glitzy refurbishment, likes to talk up its history. This enormous three-dance floor club is all about fun, flirting, and feeling feisty—especially on Wednesday after-office nights when it becomes a meat market, and not of the steak variety. ⊠ *Perú 535, San Telmo* ☎ *11/4654–1774* ⊕ *www. clubmuseum.com.ar* Ⓜ *C to San Juan* ✦ *1:E5.*

Rey Castro. Just because this Cuban restaurant-bar gets a little wild on weekends doesn't mean things get out of hand: the bouncers look like NFL players. It's a popular spot for birthday parties and great mojitos. After the nightly live dance show, DJs crank up the Cuban rhythms; you're likely to learn some sexy new moves. ⊠ *Perú 342, San Telmo* ☎ *11/4342–9998* ⊕ *www.reycastro.com* Ⓜ *A to Perú* ✦ *1:E5.*

GAY AND LESBIAN SPOTS

M.O.D. Variete Club. Mainly attracting men keen for a pick-up, Friday cabaret nights at M.O.D. are buzzing in San Telmo. It's glamorous and fun, with plenty of dancing to indie, rock, and 80s. Slip into the VIP area to get close to the stars of the show. ⊠ *Balcarce 563, San Telmo* ✦ *1:F5.*

Sky Bar. Open to the elements—and the gazes of guests at the hetero-friendly Axel Hotel—the Sky Bar works well by day (Sunday pool parties) and by night (Friday pre-dance sessions) and has quickly become key to the trendy sector of the Buenos Aires gay scene. It's international, very cool, and a six-pack of finely honed abs is a prerequisite in the summer months from October to April. ⊠ *Venezuela 649, San Telmo* ☎ *11/4136–9393* ⊕ *www.axelhotels.com* ✛ *1:E5.*

MUSIC

ROCK

La Trastienda. A San Telmo institution, La Trastienda is one of Buenos Aires' most popular venues for local and international artists, so grab a table at this cabaret-style club and enjoy an intimate performance for 900. This is the place to catch electrotango or new tango groups, although the club takes pains to promote local artists as well. Check out national pop and rock legends, as well as local rock, reggae, and funk. ⊠ *Balcare 460, San Telmo* ☎ *11/4342–7650* ⊕ *www.latrastienda.com* Ⓜ *A to Bolivar* ✛ *1:F5.*

Mitos Argentinos. A little rock bar with heroic ambitions, since the mid-1990s Mitos Argentinos has been celebrating rock nacional by providing space for bands to play covers and their own additions to the genre. Entry is cheap, inside it's cheerful, and if the band's no good there's always another due on in a few songs' time. ⊠ *Humberto I 1489, San Telmo* ☎ *11/4362–7601* ⊕ *www.mitosargentinos.com.ar* Ⓜ *C to San Juan* ✛ *1:F6.*

Plasma. A few blocks from San Telmo and opposite the large headquarters of *Clarín* newspaper, Plasma is a little cradle for alternative and talented live bands with a savvy crowd and a relaxed vibe. Up the stairs is the main room, open from Wednesday to Sunday, and on weekends another band plays in the smaller space downstairs, too. The music's good, and so is the atmosphere. ⊠ *Piedras 1856, Barracas* ☎ *11/4307–9171* ⊕ *www.sitioplasma.com.ar* ✛ *1:E6.*

TANGO

MILONGAS

Buenos Ayres Club. Rousing live orchestras keeps even non-dancers entertained at the nontraditional milongas that are this club's hallmark. La Orquesta Típica El Afronte provides the music for two versions of the same milonga, La Bendita and La Maldita (*11/4560–1514*), on Mondays and Wednesdays, respectively. The vibe is clubby on Sundays for La Milonga Andariega (☎ *11/4362–3296*), while Tuesday's Tango Queer (☎ *11/15–3252–6894* ⊕ *www.tangoqueer.com*) draws both gay and straight dancers looking to escape the confines of more conservative local dancefloors. ⊠ *Perú 571, San Telmo* ☎ *011/4331–1518* ⊕ *www. buenosayresclub.com* ✛ *1:E5.*

Centro Región Leonesa. This Belle Époque–style building's vast wooden dance floor is the place to be late on Thursday night, when it hosts Niño Bien (☎ *11/15–4147–8687*), one of the most popular milongas in town (reservations are essential). The mix of older couples and younger dancers means you see very different styles in one place; all respect the traditional *cabeceo* (nonverbal invitation to dance) and partnership rules. Other milongas are held on Friday and Saturday nights. Note that Centro Región Leonesa is in the Constitución district but just four

The *Señor Tango* show in San Telmo. Photo by laubenthal, Fodors.com member

or five blocks outside San Telmo. ✉ *Humberto I 1462, Constitución* ☎ *11/4304–5595* ✛ *1:D6.*

★ **La Marshall.** A refreshing exception to the sometimes suffocatingly macho world of tango, this is *the* gay milonga. The main night is Wednesday, when a cool set of guys and girls, both gay and straight, look to break with the "he leads, she follows" doctrine. It also runs on Friday at Riobamba 416 (at Av. Corrientes) in the Congreso district. ✉ *Av. Independencia 572, San Telmo* ☎ *11/5458–3423* ✛ *1:E6.*

DINNER SHOWS

Bar Sur. Once a bohemian haunt, this bar went international after serving as a major location for Wong Kar-Wai's cult indie film *Happy Together.* The move to the mainstream has led to glitzier dancing and increasingly bad food and indifferent service. Still, the worn checkered floor and Old World bar make for a charming backdrop. ✉ *Estados Unidos 299, San Telmo* ☎ *11/4362–6086* ⊕ *www.bar-sur.com.ar* ✛ *1:F6.*

El Querandí. The polished shows at this classic café trace the history of the tango. The dancing and costumes are great, although the stagy interludes might make you wince. ✉ *Perú 302, at Moreno, San Telmo* ☎ *11/5199–1770* ⊕ *www.querandi.com.ar* ✛ *1:E5.*

★ **El Viejo Almacén.** This place was founded by legendary tango singer Edmundo Rivero, but he wouldn't recognize the slick outfit his bar has become. Inside the colonial building lurks a tireless troupe of dancers and musicians who perform showy tango and folk numbers. ✉ *Balcarce 786, at Independencia, San Telmo* ☎ *11/4307–6689* ⊕ *www.viejo-almacen.com.ar* ✛ *1:F6.*

BEST HOTEL BARS

Algodon Mansion. Whether its poolside at the Sky Bar or choosing a cigar in the venerable Frank's & Cognac Bar, the fresh new Algodon is modern chic at its finest.

Alvear Palace Hotel. At the grande dame of Recoleta, the Lobby Bar has Old World charm in spades; it's the perfect vantage point for watching the comings and goings of high society.

Faena Hotel + Universe. These could easily be the most opulent hotel bar options; Philippe Starck–designed choices include the Pool Bar, the racy tango show at El Cabaret, and the decadent charm of the Library Lounge.

Fierro Hotel. One of the few places serving up a summery Pimm's—enjoy it as wander through to the back garden to your very own lush urban jungle.

Home Hotel. Now synonymous with Palermo and good living, its bar rocks out on Fridays in summer when electronic pumps out around the pool until midnight.

La Esquina de Homero Manzi. La Esquina was once a traditional café favored by the barrio's old men—indeed, the famous 1948 tango "Sur" begins by mentioning its location on the corner of San Juan and Boedo, the heart of the low-key Boedo neighborhood, 30 blocks west of San Telmo. It's had the Disney-tango treatment, and is now a kind of 1940s concept bar—though its checkered floor and original bar remain. Performances are showy but reasonably priced. ⊠ *San Juan 3601, Boedo* ☎ *11/4957–8488* ⊕ *www.esquinahomeromanzi.com.ar* ✛ *1:A6.*

Mansión Dandi Royal. The unashamedly theatrical show at this tango-concept hotel dances you through the history of tango. It's a fascinating look at how the dance evolved, and the hotel's art nouveau architecture is pretty fantastic, too. ⊠ *Piedras 922, San Telmo* ☎ *11/4361–3537* ⊕ *www.mansiondandiroyal.com* ✛ *1:E6.*

Señor Tango. It doesn't get much glitzier—or much tackier. Performed daily, the unashamedly tourist-oriented shows are so eager to cash in on stereotypes that they even include a number from *Evita* (shock, horror). Still, you can't fault the fishnetted dancers on their footwork. Rather less glam is its location south of San Telmo, in the Barracas neighborhood, which can be sketchy: take a taxi here and back. ⊠ *Vieytes 1655, Barracas* ☎ *11/4303–0231* ⊕ *www.srtango.com* ✛ *1:E6.*

MUSIC CLUBS

Centro Cultural Torquato Tasso. Here classic trios and quartets share the stage with young musicians performing hip tango and folk sets. There are also milongas on weekends. ⊠ *Defensa 1575, San Telmo* ☎ *11/ 4307–6506* ⊕ *www.torquatotasso.com.ar* ✛ *1:F6.*

RECOLETA

Though upscale Recoleta isn't the nightlife spot Palermo and San Telmo are, there's still plenty here and just west in Barrio Norte to warrant exploration. You can find everything from swanky after-office spots to neighborhood watering holes—just avoid the seedier places near Recoleta Cemetery.

BARS

COCKTAIL BARS

Gran Bar Danzon. If Carrie Bradshaw lived in Buenos Aires, she'd probably frequent this first-floor hot spot where local business sharks and chic internationals sip cocktails and eat sushi by candlelight. It's extremely popular during happy hour, but people stick around for dinner and the occasional live jazz shows, too. The wine list and appetizers are superb, as is the flirting. ⊠ *Libertad 1161, Recoleta* ☎ *11/4811–1108* ⊕ *www. granbardanzon.com.ar* Ⓜ *C to Retiro* ✛ *1:D2.*

★ **Milión.** One of the city's most stunning bars spread across three floors, this perfectly restored French-style mansion is packed on weekends for its drinks and cool vibes. The sweet of tooth should try a basil daiquiri. Don't be surprised if the resident black cat drops in for petting. When the back garden fills on balmy summer nights, squeeze onto the marble steps with the beautiful people. ⊠ *Paraná 1048, Recoleta* ☎ *11/4815–9925* ⊕ *www.milion.com.ar* Ⓜ *D to Callao* ✛ *1:D2.*

LATE-NIGHT BARS

Casa Bar. This beautifully restored French mansion oddly puts an emphasis on being a sports bar but if balls aren't your bag, perch at the bar for a drink well made with imported liquor. Casa Bar not only lures in year-abroad students keen for an NFL fix but an older foreign crew keen to get some spicy wing action as well as local businessmen and pretty young things. ⊠ *Rodriguez Peña 1150, Recoleta* ☎ *11/4816–2712* ⊕ *www.casabarbuenosaires.net* ✛ *1:C2.*

El Alamo Bar. From the outside, it's only the signs asking patrons to leave quietly that suggest this isn't the demure bar it appears to be. The generous drinks promotions (ladies drink free until midnight Fridays) add substantial rowdiness, and it turns into a proper little party zone on weekends. A sports bar at heart, El Alamo also hosts bikini competitions—just so you know. ⊠ *Uruguay 1175, Recoleta* ☎ *11/4813–7324* ⊗ *24 hrs* ✛ *1:D2.*

Los Porteños. A traditional Buenos Aires bar with plenty of *fileteado* (colorful, swirly graphic embellishments) and wooden tables, Los Porteños serves coffee and snacks all day and stays open late into the night; it doesn't shut at all on Saturday. It's one block from Recoleta Cemetery and a good option when the dives on Vicente Lopez get to be too much. ⊠ *Av. Las Heras 2101, Recoleta* ☎ *11/4809–3548* ✛ *1:C1.*

Continued on page 171

The Dance of Buenos Aires

by Victoria Patience

"THE TANGO IS MACHO, THE TANGO IS STRONG. IT SMELLS OF WINE AND TASTES LIKE DEATH."

So goes the famous tango "Why I Sing Like This," whose mix of nostalgia, violence, and sensuality sum up what is truly the dance of Buenos Aires. From its beginnings, tango and its two-four beat marked and reflected the character of Buenos Aires. You may hear strains of tango on the radio while sipping coffee in a café, see high-kicking sequined dancers in a glitzy dinner show, or listen to musicians in a darkened cabaret. But one of the most memorable ways to experience the best of this broody, melancholic, impassioned art form is through dancing it yourself.

DANCING THE TANGO

Many milongas now kick off with group dance classes which usually last an hour or two and cost 15–20 pesos; some lessons are free, though chaotic. These classes are great for getting over nerves and getting you in the mood. However, most *milongueros* (people who dance at *milongas*, or tango dance halls) take tango very seriously and don't look kindly on left-footed beginners crowding the floor. We recommend you take a few private classes first—they can make a huge difference to your technique.

English-speaking private teachers abound in Buenos Aires; classes generally last 1½ hours and prices can range from $20 to $80 a class. Complete beginners should plan on at least three or four classes before hitting a milonga. Many private instructors organize milonga outings with groups of their students (usually for a separate fee). Others even offer a so-called "taxi dance service": you pay for them to dance with you all night. See the end of this feature for a rundown of some of the best options for lessons and milongas.

DANCE STYLES

Tango milonguero, the style danced at milongas and taught in most classes in Buenos Aires, is quite different from the so-called salon or ballroom tango danced in Hollywood movies and in competitions outside Argentina. Ballroom tango is all fixed steps and staccato movements, and dancers' backs arch away from each other in a stiff embrace. Tango milonguero is a highly improvised style built around a variety of typical movements, not fixed steps. Dancers embrace closely, their chests touching. There are other, historical tango styles, but it's

less common to see them on milonga floors. (Confusingly, "milonga" refers both to traditional tango dance halls and to a style of music and dance that predates the tango; though similar to tango, it has a more syncopated beat and faster, simpler steps.)

AT THE MILONGA

Dancers of all ages sit at tables that edge the floor, and men invite women to dance through *cabeceo* (subtle eye contact and head-nodding), a hard art to master. Note that women sitting with male partners won't be asked to the floor by other men.

Dances come in sets of three, four, or five, broken by a *cortina* (obvious divider of non-tango music), and it's common to stay with the same partner for a set. Being discarded in the middle is a sign that your dancing's not up to scratch, but staying for more than two sets with the same partner could be interpreted as a come-on.

To fit in seamlessly, move around the floor counterclockwise without zigzagging, sticking to the inside layers of dancers if you're a beginner. Respect other dancers' space by avoiding collisions and keeping your movements small on crowded floors. Don't spend a long time doing showy moves on the spot: it holds up traffic. Finally, take time to sit some out, catch your breath, and watch the experts.

TANGO TALK

Abrazo: the embrace or stance dancers use; in tango, this varies from hip-touching and loose shoulders to close chests and more fluid hips, depending on style.

Abrazo

Barrida: literally, "a sweep"; one partner sweeps the other's foot into a position.

Caminada: a walking step that is the basis of the tango.

Barrida

Camir ada

Canyengue: style of tango dancing with short and restricted steps; from the 1910s and '20s when tight hobble skirts were popular.

Ocho: eight; a criss-crossing walk.

Parada: literally a "stop"; the lead dancer stops the other's foot with his own.

Petitero: measured style of tango developed after the 1955 military coup, when large tango gatherings were banned and the dance relegated to small cafés.

MILONGA STYLE

Parada

Wearing a fedora hat or fishnet stockings is as good as a neon sign reading "beginner." Forget what on-stage tango dancers wear and follow a few basic rules.

Go for comfortable clothes that allow you to move freely; a sure bet are breathable, natural fabrics with a bit of stretch. Be sure it's something that makes you feel sexy. If in doubt, wear black. Avoid showy outfits: it's your footwork that should stand out. It's also smart to steer clear of big buckles, studs, stones, or anything that might catch on your partner. Try not to wear skirts that are too long or too tight. Also a bad idea are jeans or gymwear.

A good example of what to wear for men would be black dress pants and a black shirt; for women, two of many options are a simple halter-neck dress with a loose, calf-length skirt or palazzo pants with a fitted top.

As for your feet: look for dance shoes with flexible leather or suede soles that allow you to glide and pivot. The fit should be snug but comfortable. Note that rubber-soled street shoes or sneakers mark the dance floor and are often forbidden. High heels are a must for women; the most popular style is an open-toed sandal with an ankle strap (which stops them coming off). Black lace-ups are the favorite among men, so leave your two-tone spats at home.

TANGO THROUGH TIME

The tango and modern Buenos Aires were born in the same place: the *conventillos* (tenement houses) of the port neighborhood of La Boca in the late 19th century, where River Plate culture collided with that of European immigrants. The dance eventually swept from the immigrant-quarter brothels and cabarets to the rest of the city; rich playboys took the tango to Paris on their grand tours, and by the 1920s the dance had become respectable

Carlos Gardel

enough to fill the salons and drawing rooms of the upper class in Argentina and abroad. In the 1930s, with the advent of singers like Carlos Gardel, tango music became popular in its own right. Accordingly, musical accompaniment started to come from larger bands known as *orquestas típicas*.

By the '40s and '50s, *porteños* (people from Buenos Aires) celebrated tango as the national music of the people, and tango artists lent Evita and Perón their support. The military coup that ousted Perón in 1955 forbade large tango dances, which it saw as potential political gatherings, and (bizarrely)

encouraged rock 'n' roll instead. Young people listened, and tango fell out of popular favor.

The '90s saw a huge revival in both traditional *milongas* (dance halls) and a more improvised dance style. Musical offerings now include modern takes on classic tangos and electrotango or *tangofusión*. Even local rock stars are starting to include a tango or two in their repertory.

And since 1998, thousands of people from around the world have attended the annual fortnightlong Festival de Tango in Buenos Aires (⊕ *www.tangobuenosaires.gob.ar*), held late winter or spring.

Whether you decide to take in a show or take up dancing yourself, sit down for a classic concert or groove at an electrotango night, there are more ways to experience tango in Buenos Aires than anywhere else on earth.

4

IN FOCUS

DID YOU KNOW?

■ Tango so horrified Kaiser Wilhelm and Pope Pius X that they banned the dance.

■ In 1915, before he was famous, Carlos Gardel was injured in a barroom brawl with Ernesto Guevara Lynch, Che's father.

■ One of Gardel's most famous numbers, "Por Una Cabeza," is the tango featured in *Schindler's List, Scent of a Woman,* and *True Lies.*

■ The coup of 1930 prompted composers like Enrique Santos Discépolo to write protest tangos.

■ Finnish tango has been a distinct musical genre since at least mid-century and is still one of the most popular in Finland; there's even an annual *Tangomarkkinat* (tango festival) in Seinäjoki, complete with the crowning of a Tango King and Queen.

NEXT STEPS

TOURS & HOTELS

If you're serious about the dance of Buenos Aires, get in touch with the Web-based company **Argentina Tango** (⊕ www.argentinatango. com). Run by a British devotee, it offers highly organized, tailor-made tango tours.

SHOPS WITH TANGO GEAR

Head to shoe shop **Comme Il Faut,** for colorful, handcrafted high heels so gorgeous they're worth taking up tango for.

If you'd like high quality and classic designs, check out **Flabella.** At **Tango Brujo,** you'll find a variety of well-made footwear, clothing, how-to DVDs, and other tango merchandise.

Your best bet for milonga-worthy duds is regular casual clothing stores. (For more information, ⇨ see Shoes and Clothing in Shopping.)

SCHOOLS & INSTRUCTORS

Some schools we like are **La Escuela del Tango** (⊠ San José 364, Constitución ☎ 11/4383–0466 ⊕ www.laescueladeltango. com.ar), **La Academia de Tango Milonguero** (⊠ Riobamba 416, Centro ☎ 11/3166–4800 ⊕ www.laacademiatango.com), and **Estudio DNI Tango** (⊠ Bulnes 1011, Almagro ☎ 11/4866–3663 ⊕ www.dni-tango.com).

Private instructors **Ana Schapira** (☎ 11/ 4962–7922 ⊕ http://anamariaschapira.bloog. it), **Claudia Bozzo** of La Escuela de Tango, and **Susana Miller** (⊕ www.susanamiller.com.ar) of La Academia de Tango Milonguero are worth their salt.

The **Academia Nacional de Tango** (⊕ www. anacdeltango.org.ar) runs highbrow seminars on tango culture and history.

MILONGAS

For a novice-friendly floor, try **La Ideal or La Viruta. La Nacional** and **Niño Bien** at El Centro Region Leonesa are popular with locals.

The hippest tangueros flock to **La Catedral** and **Parakultural at Salón Canning.**

For breaking the "he leads, she follows" rule, head to **La Marshall.** (For more information, ⇨ see Milongas in After Dark.)

For the latest list of milongas, and instructors, look for the English-language publication **El Tangauta** at newsstands (you can also download it for free at ⊕ www.eltangauta. com). The website ⊕ www.milmilongas.com has listings of most milongas in town.

(above) Milonga in Buenos Aries.

DANCE CLUBS

The Basement. This rowdy nightspot downstairs at the Shamrock pub is owned by an Irish father-and-son duo and is popular with expats and young upwardly mobile *porteño* party people. Stop first for a Guinness at the bar upstairs, where you can yap away in English and easily forget you're in South America. Follow the techno beats to the downstairs dance club, to find Argentina's finest DJs burning up the decks. ⊠ *Rodríguez Peña 1220, Recoleta* ☏ *11/4812–3584* Ⓜ *D to Callao* ✛ *1:C3.*

GAY AND LESBIAN SPOTS

Zoom. Half a block from the very cruisey section of Santa Fe, between Avenidas Callao and Coronel Díaz, Zoom offers a good lounge bar, a maze, video cabins, and plenty of dark corners. It can get pretty intense, but there's good security. ⊠ *Uriburu 1018, Recoleta* ☏ *11/4827–4828* ⊕ *www.zoombuenosaires.com* Ⓜ *D to Pueyrredón* ✛ *1:B2.*

4

MUSIC CLUBS

JAZZ

Clásica y Moderna. It's not just a jazz club but a restaurant and bookshop besides. An older, artsy crowd gathers here for dinner, drinks, philosophy, and live jazz. The program makes good use of their grand piano; singers take on bossa nova, tango, and bolero. ⊠ *Av. Callao 892, Recoleta* ☏ *11/4812–8707* ⊕ *www.clasicaymoderna.com* Ⓜ *D to Callao* ✛ *1:C3.*

★ **Notorious.** A jazz bar, restaurant, and record shop rolled into one, some of the area's best musicians, such as guitarist Walter Malosetti and vocalist Ibrahim Ferrer Jr., play here often. You can also listen to the club's extensive music collection on the CD players at each table. ⊠ *Av. Callao 966, Recoleta* ☏ *11/4813–6888* ⊕ *www.notorious.com.ar* Ⓜ *D to Callao* ✛ *1:C2.*

ALMAGRO

GAY AND LESBIAN SPOTS

Angels. Angels is technically in the otherwise business-oriented barrio of Once (pronounced On-say), adjacent to the Almagro neighborhood, and is situated just behind the magnificent Palacio de Aguas Corrientes building in easy reach of Recoleta and Centro. It has several dance floors that play electronica, pop, and Latin music. It attracts a primarily gay male and transvestite clientele, but heterosexuals are welcome, too. ⊠ *Viamonte 2168, Onze* ☏ *No phone* ⊕ *www.discoangels.com.ar* Ⓜ *D to Facultad de Medicina* ✛ *1:B3.*

ROCK

Ciudad Cultural Konex. A mixed bag of live music, film screenings, wild parties, and Pecha Kucha (sort of like a poetry slam but with performance art) make for an interesting lineup at this huge converted factory.

It's socially acceptable to linger at your table for hours, even alfresco (like at Stranger Café, *above*).

The outdoor space in summer turns into an inner-city beach complete with hammocks while the winter months see DJs and bands hash it out indoors. ⊠ *Sarmiento 3131, Abasto* ☎ *11/4864–3200* ⊕ *www. ciudadculturalkonex.org* Ⓜ *B line to Carlos Gardel* ✛ *1:A4.*

TANGO

MILONGAS

La Catedral. Behind its unmarked doors is a hip club where the tango is somehow very rock. There are classes and milongas every evening, although Tuesdays are the most popular. It's a cool night out even if you're not planning to dance. ⊠ *Sarmiento 4006, Almagro* ☎ *11/15– 5325–1630* ⊕ *www.lacatedralclub.com* ✛ *2:F6.*

MUSIC CLUBS

★ **12 de Octubre.** Cobweb- and dust-covered bottles line the walls of this tiny venue, with maybe the most authentic tango music in town. It's known by all as "El Bar de Roberto" after its owner, who presides from behind the heavy wooden bar, dispatching *ginebra* (a local gin) to the old-timers and icy beer and cheap wine to the student crowd. When the singing gets going at 2 or 3 am it's usually so packed there's no room to breathe, but the guitar-and-voice duos manage gritty, emotional versions of tango classics all the same. ⊠ *Bulnes 331, Almagro* ☉ *Thurs.–Sat. after midnight* ✛ *2:F6.*

★ **Club Atlético Fernández Fierro.** The brains behind this laidback venue is a scruffy young tango collective—the eponymous Orquesta Típica Fernández Fierro, known for its rock-like take on the 2/4 beat. You can usually catch them at least one night a week; edgy young musicians and the occasional classic quartet perform other nights. ⊠ *Sánchez de Bustamante 764, Almagro* ☎ *No phone* ⊕ *www.caff.com.ar* ✛ *2:G6.*

PALERMO AND BELGRANO

Palermo Soho and Palermo Viejo—divided by the train tracks alongside Avenida Juan B. Justo—are the absolute pulsating heart of porteño nightlife. Cool and diverse, the many bars that stay open all night are for socializing and drinking more than dancing, though some of the best clubs are here, too. Belgrano isn't a big destination for nightlife, but on Friday and Saturday in La Glorieta de Barrancas park it *is* home to our favorite outdoor milongas.

BARS

COCKTAIL BARS

Acabar. This is an offbeat bar in the heart of Palermo Hollywood that's become a big hit, and the lines to get in are only exacerbated by the abundance of board games inside, including giant Jenga. Those who manage to get a table are quickly charmed by the buzz of the place and the easy-going atmosphere. ⊠ *Honduras 5733, Palermo Hollywood* ☎ *11/4772–0845* ⊕ *www.acabarnet.com.ar* ✛ *2:D3.*

Bar 6. A Palermo Soho institution known for its dangerous happy hour cocktails combo, Bar 6's indifferent waitstaff serve up decent steak sandwiches and an "anti-panic" menu. A central neighborhood meeting point for handsome businessmen and ladies who lunch but not necessarily together thanks to its a stylish bar and comfy armchairs, Bar 6 opens for breakfast at 8 am yet morphs into a cool drinking spot by nightfall. ⊠ *Armenia 1676, Palermo* ☎ *11/4833–6807* ⊕ *www.barseis. com* ☾ *Daily 8 am–2 am* ✛ *3:F3.*

Casa Rica. A low-key cocktail bar, Casa Rica consists of a series of little corners, each with a wooden table and most open to the stars. The atmosphere is relaxed and unpretentious, and patrons tend to arrive early and stay late. It's a good place to go for conversation. ⊠ *Nicaragua 4817, Palermo Soho* ☎ *11/4775–9861* ⊕ *www.casarica.com.ar* ☾ *Daily from 7 pm* ✛ *3:E2.*

Finisterra. With a decent mix of '80s hits to put drinkers in a dancing mood, the unlikely setting of Finisterra, with 1930s posters and ancient coffee machines, attracts a crowd early on looking to nibble on a selection of cured meats and cheeses while taking advantage of the cerveza-o-metro, or a metre of beer. Only the very hardy should give the metre of local tipple Fernet and Coke a go. ⊠ *Honduras 5190, Palermo Viejo* ☎ *11/4832–1240* ⊕ *www.finisterra-bar.com* ✛ *2:D4.*

Isabel. Feel like a star sipping a cocktail under the twinkling ceiling lights, while actually star-spotting if you're up to date with your Argentinian models and polo players. Glamour is the name of Isabel's game, so bling is a must—as is a bottomless wallet. ⊠ *Uriarte 1664, Palermo Soho* ☎ *011/4834–6969* ⊕ *www.isabel.bz* ✛ *2:D4.*

4

Magdalena's Party. The cool kids have taken newbie Magdalena's Party under their wing and rightly so, given that it has all bases covered: great cocktail list, weekend brunch offerings, outdoor terrace, and mood lighting. Pull up a bar stool or a comfy armchair and watch the city's movers and shakers start their nights here. ☒ *Thames 1795, Palermo Viejo* ☎ *011/4833–9127* ⊕ *www.magdalenasparty.com* ✢ *2:E4.*

The Shanghai Dragon. From the folks who brought The Gibraltar and Bangalore to B.A. comes their hatrick establishment, The Shanghai Dragon. Less dark and woody and certainly more spacious than its pub siblings, the Dragon has the air of a modern London watering hole and serves up draught beer as well as a tasty Chinese menu. ☒ *Aráoz 1199, Palermo* ✢ *3:G5.*

Sula. With one of the best terraces on offer, Caracas caters to the city's hip young things with a great selection of rum-based cocktails and the kind of funky vibe you would expect from a Venezuelan night spot. It triples up at times as an art, drinking, and live-music space. Sample the Caribbean bar snacks menu while sipping on a mojito and checking out the DJ's super-smooth sounds. ☒ *Guatemala 4802, Palermo Soho* ☎ *11/4776–8704* ⊕ *www.caracasbar.com* ✢ *3:F2.*

LATE-NIGHT BARS

878. One of the original speakeasies that kicked off a spate of followers over the past few years, 878 remains a leader despite now playing it by the book. A fabulous establishment with an extensive drinks list, armchairs to kick back in, and a super-cool clientele, this bar for cocktail lovers remains a classic. ☒ *Thames 878, Palermo Viejo* ☎ *11/4773–1098* ⊕ *www.878bar.com.ar* ✢ *2:C5.*

★ **Antares.** Originating in Mar del Plata in 1999, Antares is now a successful national brewer making seven of its own ales, which you can taste in shot-size glasses. The bar attracts a cosmopolitan group of drinkers who keep the spacious bar packed from after-office until the small hours. Service is friendly and efficient; the music's feel-good, and the bar snacks tasty. Also check out newer establishment in Las Cañitas at Arévalo 2876. ☒ *Armenia 1447, Palermo Soho* ☎ *11/4833–9611* ⊕ *www.cervezaantares.com* ✢ *3:D5.*

Bangalore. A pub and curry house in Buenos Aires? Well located, the Bangalore has it all—right down to a blazing log fire in winter. There's limited seating both at the bar and in the tiny restaurant upstairs, but somehow there's hardly ever too much of a wait at the bar. Service is friendly, and there's a wide range of draught beers. Revelers spill out onto the street with their pints in summer. ☒ *Humboldt 1416, Palermo Hollywood* ☎ *11/4779–2621* ✢ *2:D4.*

Carnal. Opposite Niceto club, Carnal with its buzzing open terrace is the height of popularity during warmer months and remains busy all night long with fun seekers. The name is completely apt; as the reggaeton blasts and the cocktails flow, many customers aren't shy about getting to know each other a bit better. ☒ *Niceto Vega 5511, Palermo Hollywood* ☎ *11/4772–7582* ⊕ *www.carnalbar.com.ar* ✢ *2:C4.*

★ **Congo.** Beautiful people—in faded fitted jeans, hipster sneakers, and leather jackets—frequent this hangout post-dinner and pre-club. The

FOR THE SPORTS NUTS

Locos x El Futbol. *Porteños* love sports—and sports, for them, means *fútbol* (soccer). Although Argentine teams also excel at basketball, hockey, rugby, and especially polo, it's *fútbol* that evokes the most passion, with fans attending even the smallest scrimmages; most games play on wall-mounted TVs in regular cafés and restaurants. But perhaps it's the ubiquity of soccer that means there aren't the really atmospheric screenings in bars that many visitors hope to find: to get the real buzz, you have to go to the stadium. Your second-best option is definitely Locos x El Futbol. Just try to count the number of TVs here, and you'll realize the extent of their passion for the beautiful game—the *x* stands for *por*, which makes this place "crazy for soccer." Key games require a reservation, but otherwise just turn up for big screens and bigger servings of burgers, fries, and beer. ⊠ *Vicente Lopez 2098, Recoleta* ☎ *11/4807–3777* ⊕ *www.locosxelfutbol.com* 🍽 *Minimum consumption for big matches* ⊙ *Sun.–Thurs. 9–2, Fri. and Sat. 9–4 or 5.*

back garden is large enough and fun enough to easily convince many would-be clubbers to stick around for another drink or three. Offers up a great cocktail list worth browsing at the lengthy bar. ⊠ *Honduras 5329, Palermo Soho* ☎ *11/4833–5857* ✛ *3:C2.*

Frank's Bar. While other bars of its ilk have gone legit, Frank's Bar takes open pride in its reputation as a speakeasy. Simply knowing the address isn't enough—you also need a number for the phone booth which leads the way into an understated yet sophisticated two-floor setting complete with bar staff dressed the old school way in suspenders. Don't forget to browse Frank's rather classy erotica shop on your way out. ⊠ *Arévalo 1445, Palermo Hollywood* ☎ *11/4777–6541* ⊕ *www.franks-bar.com* ➹ *Yes* ⊙ *Closed Sun.–Wed.* ✛ *2:C3.*

Me Leva Brasil. A small and understated *boteco* (Brazilian-style pub) close to busy Plaza Armenia, this is a good place to stop in for an after-dinner caipirinha; it stays open until around 3 am. The music is always upbeat and irresistible, and the atmosphere friendly and welcoming; if you have a weakness for things Brazilian, you'll be happy here. ⊠ *Costa Rica 4488, Palermo Soho* ☎ *11/4832–4290* ⊕ *www.melevabrasil.com. ar* ✛ *3:G4.*

Mundo Bizarro. They've been building their faithful late-night crowd and perfecting cocktails here since 1997, so they've got a magic ingredient or two in terms of B.A. night life longevity. Red lights, kitsch artwork, rock-and-roll, and even a pole for dancing provide the backdrop; the rest gets improvised afresh every evening. ⊠ *Serrano 1222, Palermo Soho* ☎ *11/4773–1967* ⊕ *www.mundobizarrobar.com* ✛ *2:D5.*

Puerta Uno. This speakeasy aone block from Chinatown is modern glamour personified. It's a fun bar with an Asian touch attracting beautiful *porteños* in the know. Grab a spot at the bar for a piece of the main action or throw some shapes on the back room dance floor to some of the best DJs in town. ⊠ *Juramento 1667, Belgrano* ☎ *11/4706–1522* ⊕ *www.puertauno.com* ✛ *2:C1.*

Río Café. Invariably hip, Río Café recently burst onto the scene and is here to stay thanks to its impossibly cool atmosphere. Pick a front table or booth to watch the world bustle through to the back garden, or simply pitch up outside. Wednesdays are throbbing in summer thanks to great cocktails and DJs whipping up some '80s throwback mashups. ✉ *Honduras 4772, Palermo Viejo* ⊕ *www.riocafe.com.ar* ✛ *3:E4.*

Sugar Bar. If cumbia and salsa are becoming a bitter pill to swallow, a trip to Sugar will sweeten up an evening. With an extensive happy hour or three until midnight, this Palermo fixture is run by three expats and attracts a fun-loving crowd of Argentines and foreigners alike looking for good times and big-game matches under the flattering red lighting. ✉ *Costa Rica 4619, Palermo Viejo* ☎ *11/4831–3276* ⊕ *www.sugarbuenosaires.com* ✛ *3:F3.*

Único. There's nothing really special about this corner bar-restaurant *except* for its location at the epicenter of Palermo Hollywood, close to TV studios and an array of great restaurants. A funky mix of rock, rap, and electronic music pumps up the hard-core clubbers who stop to whet their whistles on large Heineken drafts before a night of debauchery. This place is always packed so get there early for a seat. ✉ *Honduras 5604, Palermo Hollywood* ☎ *11/4775–6693* ⊕ *www.unicobar.com.ar* ✛ *2:D4.*

DANCE CLUBS

Club Aráoz. It may be intimate, but Club Aráoz attracts a serious party crowd. Thursday is block-rocking hip-hop night; Friday and Saturday see DJs spinning rock music and electronic dance music for a relatively laid-back bunch of Buenos Aires youth. ✉ *Aráoz 2424, Palermo* ☎ *11/4833–7775* ⊕ *www.clubaraoz.com.ar* ✛ *2:F4.*

Crobar. With frequent visits from "superstar DJs" and a dependable lineup of local party starters and summertime outdoor specials, this is the Buenos Aires base of the international Crobar club brand. There's lots of space plus the obligatory VIP lounges, and the proximity to the transvestite zone means leaving the club in the morning can get as interesting as the time inside. Friday's Masterplan night sees cutting-edge international artists drop in for a spin. ✉ *Avenida del Libertador 3883, Palermo* ☎ *11/4778–1500* ⊕ *www.crobar.com.ar* ⊗ *Fri. and Sat. from midnight* ✛ *2:F2.*

★ **Kika.** Right in the heart of Palermo and next door to Congo bar, Kika is much bigger than you'd guess from the outside. Thanks to its funky musical orientation, its two dance floors fill up quickly. The back room sometimes hosts live bands while Tuesdays are all about Hype, an all-in-one electro, hip-hop, indie, and dubstep night that gets students moving till dawn. ✉ *Honduras 5339, Palermo Soho* ☎ *11/4137–5311* ⊕ *www.kikaclub.com.ar* ✛ *3:C2.*

Fodor'sChoice **Niceto.** One of the city's best venues features everything from demure
★ indie rock to the outrageous and legendary Club 69 on Thursdays (think under-dressed cross-dressers). Check out live bands and dancing in the main room, while something contrasting and chill simultaneously takes

place in the back room. ⊠ *Cnel. Niceto Vega 5510, Palermo Hollywood* ☎ *11/4779–9396* ⊕ *www.nicetoclub.com* ✛ *2:C4.*

Podestá Super Club de Copas. Located slap bang in the middle of Palermo Soho, it's a good mix of locals and students; occasional Dakar Rally drivers keep the atmosphere light and cool. The dark ground-floor bar plays rock and serves stiff drinks and a happy hour from 9 pm to 1 am. Upstairs in the disco, dance-friendly music is pumped into the psychedelic setting: wear white to be especially eye-catching under the neon lights. ⊠ *Armenia 1740, Palermo Soho* ☎ *11/4832–2776* ⊕ *www. podestafotos.com* ✛ *3:F3.*

Voodoo Motel. The self-styled club and music warehouse offers up a large dancefloor and plenty of European beats as well as Britpop, indie nights, and digitial cumbia. Located on the cool northern edge of Palermo Hollywood, Voodoo aims to strike a balance between sushi, trendy cocktails, and rock music. Check out their alternating music cycles. ⊠ *Dorrego 1735, Palermo Hollywood* ☎ *11/4139–7499* ⊕ *www. voodoomotel.com* ✛ *2:C3.*

GAY AND LESBIAN SPOTS

Amerika. This enormous gay disco has three floors of high-energy action and shows. Friday and Saturday are fun and frivolous verging on hectic thanks to its one-fee, drink-all-you-can entry. Thursday and Sunday are quieter, with greater emphasis on the music. Amerika remains the city's gay club to check out, and be checked out in, at least once. ⊠ *Gascon 1040, Palermo* ☎ *11/4865–4416* ⊕ *www.ameri-k.com.ar* ✛ *2:E6.*

MUSIC

JAZZ

★ **Thelonious Bar.** The best *porteño* jazz bands (and occasional foreign imports) play at this intimate, upscale spot. Arrive early for a good seat, as it's a long, narrow bar and not all tables have good views; on weekends there are usually two shows per night. ⊠ *Salguero 1884, Palermo* ☎ *11/4829–1562* ⊕ *www.theloniousclub.com.ar* ✛ *2:G5.*

★ **Virasoro Bar.** This is an intimate art deco venue for local jazz maestros and appreciative audiences. Although the names on the program are only familiar to those on the local circuit, it's a great space and you can get up close and personal with musicians, who draw from a deep well of talent and cover a lot of ground, from improv to standards and experimental. ⊠ *Guatemala 4328, Palermo* ☎ *11/4831–8918* ⊕ *www. virasorobar.com.ar* Ⓜ *D to Scalabrini Ortiz* ✛ *3:H5.*

FOLK MUSIC

La Paila. A little piece of Catamarca transplanted to the middle of Palermo, this place has live folk music most nights from around 10:30. To get in the mood, have some of La Paila's great corn, llama, or potato-and-goat's cheese dishes, plus something from the long list of northwest wines. ⊠ *Costa Rica 4848, Palermo Soho* ☎ *11/4833–3599* ⊕ *www. lapaila-restaurante.com.ar* ✛ *3:E3.*

Club Niceto has some of the city's best club nights, including hip-hop.

★ **La Peña del Colorado.** There's nothing pretentious about this place: laid-back groups gather to enjoy traditional Argentine folk music and hand-held foods like empanadas and tamales. The exposed-brick walls are adorned with rustic memorabilia, including guitars that you're welcome to play if so inspired. ✉ *Guemes 3657, Palermo* ☎ *11/4822–1038* ⊕ *www.delcolorado.com.ar* ✛ *2:G5.*

Los Cardones. Named after the tall cactus plants that typify the northwest, Los Cardones is the place to go for a beer around a big table with strangers you'll get to know by the end of the night. Spontaneous dancing at this *peña folklorica* isn't unheard of; to prepare, ask ahead about their folk-dancing classes. ✉ *Jorge Luis Borges 2180, Palermo Soho* ☎ *11/4777–1112* ⊕ *www.cardones.com.ar* ✛ *3:G1.*

ROCK

No Avestruz. A barely marked door and a narrow passageway open into a world far removed from the flashy bars and restaurants surrounding this music venue. The eclectic programming includes a wide range of folk, tango, jazz, classical, and improvised music as well as some politically charged theatrical performances. Grab the sofa if you can for maximum comfort. ✉ *Humboldt 1857, Palermo Hollywood* ☎ *11/4777–6956* ⊕ *www.noavestruz.com.ar* ✛ *2:D4.*

TANGO

MILONGAS

La Glorieta de Barrancas de Belgrano. For tango alfresco, drop by the bandstand of this Belgrano park Saturday and Sunday evenings year-round. Classes run from 4:30 to 6:30, then the milonga proper starts at 7. Expect lots of old-timers dancing low-key steps. The milonga is canceled only during heavy rain; call ahead if you're unsure. ⊠ *11 de Septiembre at Echeverría, Belgrano* ☎ *11/4674–1026* ⊕ *www.glorietadebelgrano. com.ar* ✛ *2:C1.*

La Viruta. Milongas Wednesday through Sunday make this the place for a very long weekend. Classes at different levels precede them. The vibe on the floor is friendly and rather chaotic, and dancing standards are low, so it's a good place for beginners to get in some practice. DJs mix tango with rock, salsa, and cumbia. ⊠ *Armenia 1366, Palermo Viejo* ☎ *11/4774–6357* ⊕ *www.lavirutatango.com* ✛ *3:C5.*

Fodor's Choice
★ **Salón Canning.** Several milongas call this large dance hall home. The coolest is Parakultural (☎ *11/15–5738–3850* ⊕ *www.parakultural.com. ar*), which takes place late on Monday, Tuesday, and Friday. Reservations are essential on Friday—the dance floor is totally packed by midnight, so get here early, too. Originally an alternative, "underground" milonga, it now attracts large numbers of locals, including longtime expats. ⊠ *Av. Scalabrini Ortíz 1331, Palermo* ☎ *11/4832–6753* ✛ *3:E6.*

COSTANERA

Formerly the place to go for upscale dining, this stretch of riverfront found a new lease on life as the home of the country's most famed and fabulous dance clubs. Most are within a mile of each other along the Río de la Plata, underneath the buzz of the nearby domestic airport.

DANCE CLUBS

★ **Clubland.** The club formally known as Pachá is still a multilevel, riverside behemoth, and remains part of the Buenos Aires dance-music scene mecca pulling in big names and crowds. It can be hot and crowded, but total sensory overload is the name of the game. Watch the sun ease its way up from the river from one of the best vantage points in the city in summer. ⊠ *Av. Costanera Rafael Obligado 5151 at La Pampa, Costanera* ☎ *11/4788–4280* ⊕ *www.clublandba.com* ✛ *2:G1.*

★ **Jet.** When the most beautiful of people feel like dancing with a bottle of champagne at 4 am, they come here. Things get even more glamorous a few hours later, when the dawn breaks through the river and the yacht club is revealed. Only for the super-swanky. ⊠ *Av. Costanera Rafael Obligado 4801, Costanera* ☎ *11/4782–5599* ✛ *2:G1.*

Rumi. Thanks to its strategic location on the main road to the wealthy northern suburbs (close to the River Plate stadium), Rumi packs out with rich socialites and fashion models. All come for the electronica and pop music and for a scene that's less intense than at clubs on the Costanera proper. Two large bars surround the dance floor, and elevated

THE ARTS AFTER DARK

MALBA. Most galleries have opening nights worth casually sauntering into, and MALBA blows out all the stops. Pick up a program for details on their free literary events and talks as well as impressive movie seasons. Its excellent restaurant has an equally impressive wine list for thirsty art critics. ✉ *Figueroa Alcorta 3415, Palermo* ☏ *11/4808–6500* ⊕ *www.malba.org.ar* ✛ *2:H3.*

Ciudad Cultural Konex. Ciudad Cultural Konex offers a mixed bag of fringe theater, dance, music from rock-and-roll through folk and percussion and digitial cumbia, film screenings, wild parties, and *Pecha Kucha* (sort of like a poetry slam but with performance art). ✉ *Sarmiento 3131, Abasto* ☏ *11/4864–3200* ⊕ *www.ciudadculturalkonex.org* ✛ *1:A4.*

4

booths encourage that most Argentine of pastimes: checking people out from Monday to Sunday. ✉ *Av. Figueroa Alcorta 6442, Núñez* ☏ *11/4782–1307* ⊕ *www.rumiba.com.ar* ✛ *2:G1.*

LAS CAÑITAS

The cluster of bars and restaurants along Calle Báez, as well as Arce and Arguibel, has turned Las Cañitas from a nondescript residential neighborhood into a buzzing center that stays busy until dawn.

BARS

COCKTAIL BARS

Arguibel. You can sip Syrah and soak up the art—and the attitude—at this wine bar / art gallery / restaurant. Arguibel is porteño pretentiousness to the max. The service and food are fair, but the building is impressive: a three-story converted warehouse with an industrial, Chelsea-loft feel. ✉ *Arguibel 2826, Las Cañitas* ☏ *11/4899–0070* ✛ *2:E2.*

LATE-NIGHT BARS

The Office Bar & Grill. A compact two-floor bar with a great terrace, The Office is popular with 20-something American expats keen for a taste of home. The Office takes pride in their burger menu and, love it or hate it, it's one of the few foreign-owned bars to offer karaoke. ✉ *Arévalo 3031, Las Cañitas* ☏ *011/2050–3942* ✛ *2:E2.*

Soul Café. One of the neighborhood's first nightspots has some of the city's sexiest female bartenders as well as its tastiest caipirinhas. A sleek red room lined with tables on one side leads to a large back room, where rock and hip-hop tunes fire up the crowd for a long night of partying. ✉ *Báez 246, Las Cañitas* ☏ *11/4778–3115* ✛ *2:E2.*

Van Konig. This cosy, busy Dutch pub has an excellent selection of northern European and Japanese beers, both bottled and on tap. You can snap a pic with Van Gogh's statue or with Argentina's very own Dutch princess Máxima while you decide what to knock back. ✉ *Báez 325, Las Cañitas* ☏ *011/4772–9909* ⊕ *www.vankoning.com* ✛ *2:E2.*

Where to Eat

WORD OF MOUTH

"If you are foodies, I would recommend [the restaurants] Tomo I or La Bourgogne. For steak, El Mirasol de la Recova is hard to beat for a celebration. I have never been to Pura Tierra but have heard good things about it. "

—drdawaggy

Updated by
Dan Perlman

Visitors may flock to Buenos Aires for the steak and Malbec wine, but the food scene goes far beyond those two attractions. Awakening from decades of political repression, the city over the last dozen or so years has burst onto the international food scene with gusto.

There's a demand for more and more creative food. Here three things have come together to create a truly modern cuisine: diverse cultural influences, high culinary aspirations, and a relentless devotion to aesthetics, from plate garnishes to room decor. Tradition dictates late dining, and the majority of restaurants don't open until 8 or 9 pm for dinner and don't get busy until after 10. Dinner is a leisurely affair and the sobremesa, or after-dinner chat over coffee or digestifs, is near obligatory. Rushing from the table is frowned on—anyway, where would you go? Bars and clubs often don't open until after midnight.

The core of the population is of Italian and Spanish heritage, and pizza, pasta, *puchero* (beef boil), and paella are as common as the *parrilla* (steakhouse). Argentines have taken the classics and made them their own with different techniques and ingredients, but they're still recognizable to the international traveler. Pizzas and empanadas are the favored local snack food, the former piled high with cheese, the latter typically filled with steak or chicken. And while steak is indisputably king in this town, it's got fierce competition in tender Patagonian lamb, game meats, fish, and shellfish. In contrast to that of much of Latin America, Argentine cuisine is not known for its spice, and *picante* dishes are not common.

Cafés, too, are an important part of the culture, and locals will stop in at their favorite for a *cafecito* at least once a day, not only to knock back a little caffeine, but also to see friends and catch up on the latest news and gossip.

PLANNING

DRESS

Porteños dress to impress. Looking good is as important as feeling good in Buenos Aires. The finest restaurants in the city employ an "elegant sport" rule, but few require men to wear a tie and jacket. A sport coat and slacks will suffice. Jeans are fine just about anywhere, provided they are paired with a smart shirt or blouse.

RESERVATIONS

Getting a reservation in most Buenos Aires restaurants is easy. Most porteños make dinner reservations a day or two ahead of time instead of weeks in advance.

SMOKING

Smoking is no longer allowed in any indoor public spaces in Buenos Aires. If you're a smoker, be prepared to head outside for a cigarette.

TIPPING

In most restaurants in Buenos Aires a 10% tip is the norm. If the service was superb, 15% is appreciated. In bars you can tip a peso or two per drink, but it's not expected. Bills for parties of six or more sometimes include the tip; look at the check. Many restaurants also charge a *servicio de mesa* (table service) or *cubierto*, which is usually around 6–10 pesos per person, and covers the cost of "breakage and replacement"; it is the source of much local contention—those who don't charge it often make it a selling point. If there is a table charge, many locals tip less, though it should be noted that the *cubierto* does not go to the waiters but to the restaurant's owner.

USING THE MAPS

Throughout the chapter, you'll see mapping symbols and coordinates (✠ 2:D5) after property reviews. To locate the property on the map, turn to the Buenos Aires Dining and Lodging Atlas at the end of the Where to Eat chapter. The first number after the ✠ symbol indicates the map number. Following that is the property's coordinate on the map.

WHAT IT COSTS

Credit cards are widely accepted, but some restaurants accept cash only. If you plan to use a card, it's a good idea to check whether it is accepted when making reservations.

WHAT IT COSTS IN ARGENTINE PESOS			
	$	$$	$$$	$$$$
Restaurants	40 pesos and under	41 pesos–64 pesos	65 pesos–75 pesos	over 75 pesos

Prices are per person for a median main course or equivalent combination of smaller dishes at dinner

5

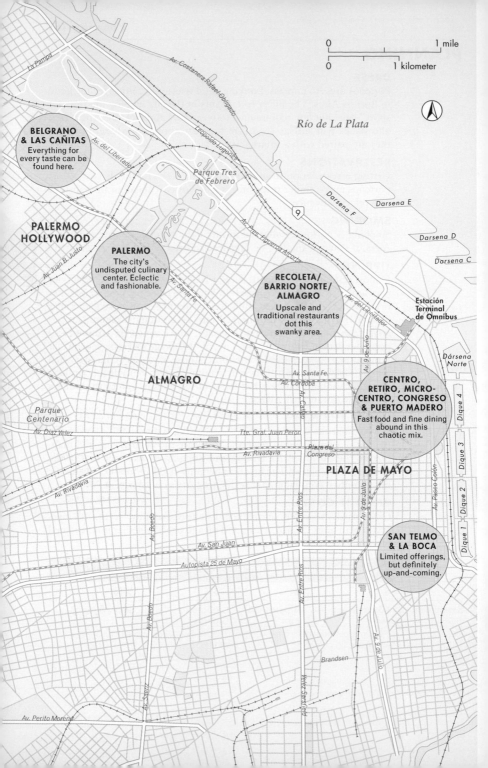

BELGRANO & LAS CAÑITAS
Everything for every taste can be found here.

PALERMO HOLLYWOOD

PALERMO
The city's undisputed culinary center. Eclectic and fashionable.

RECOLETA/ BARRIO NORTE/ ALMAGRO
Upscale and traditional restaurants dot this swanky area.

ALMAGRO

CENTRO, RETIRO, MICRO-CENTRO, CONGRESO & PUERTO MADERO
Fast food and fine dining abound in this chaotic mix.

PLAZA DE MAYO

SAN TELMO & LA BOCA
Limited offerings, but definitely up-and-coming.

Río de La Plata

0   1 mile

0   1 kilometer

Parque Tres de Febrero

9

Darsena F

Darsena E

Darsena D

Darsena C

Estación Terminal de Omnibus

Dársena Norte

Dique 4

Dique 3

Dique 2

Dique 1

Parque Centenario

Av. Díaz Velez

Tte. Graf. Juan Peron

Av. Rivadavia

Plaza del Congreso

Av. Rivadavia

Av. San Juan

Autopista 25 de Mayo

Brandsen

Av. Perito Moreno

La Pampa

Av. Costanera Rafael Obligado

Leopoldo Lugones

Av. del Libertador

Av. Pres. Figueroa Alcorta

Av. Juan B. Justo

Av. Santa Fe

Av. del Libertador

Av. Santa Fe

Av. Córdoba

Av. 9 de Julio

Av. Callao

Av. Entre Ríos

Av. 9 de Julio

Av. Paseo Colón

Av. Boedo

Av. Sáenz

Autopista Frondizi

Av. 9 de Julio

BEST BETS FOR BUENOS AIRES DINING

With thousands of restaurants to choose from, how will you decide where to eat? Fodor's writers and editors have selected their favorite restaurants by price, cuisine, and experience in the Best Bets lists below. In the first column, Fodor's Choice properties represent the "best of the best" in every price category. You can also search by neighborhood for excellent eats—just peruse the following pages. Or find specific details about a restaurant in the full reviews, listed alphabetically within neighborhoods.

Fodor's Choice★

Do Dá, p. 201
Duhau Restaurante & Vinoteca, p. 206
El Sanjuanino, p. 206
Don Julio, p. 213
Francesco, p. 213
Gran Bar Danzón, p. 202
La Bourgogne, p. 207
La Cabrera, p. 215
Las Pizarras Bistró, p. 215
Osaka, p. 217
Oviedo, p. 208
Pura Tierra, p. 220
Rio Alba, p. 217
Tegui, p. 219

Best By Price

$

Bangalore, p. 211
Bar Dorrego, p. 204
Club Eros, p. 212
El Cuartito, p. 198
El Sanjvanino, p. 206
Juana M, p. 206

$$

Don Julio, p. 213
Do Dá, p. 201
El Pobre Luis, p. 220
Filo, p. 202
Gran Bar Danzón, p. 202
Las Pizarras Bistró, p. 215

$$$

Bruni, p. 219
La Cabrera, p. 215
Pura Tierra, p. 220
Rio Alba, p. 217

$$$$

Duhau Restaurante & Vinoteca, p. 206
Francesco, p. 213

La Bourgogne, p. 207
Osaka, p. 217
Oviedo, p. 208
Tegui, p. 219

Best by Cuisine

ARGENTINE

Casa Coupage, p. 212
Dominga, p. 213
Duhau Restaurante & Vinoteca, p. 206
El Sanjuanino, p. 206
Pura Tierra, p. 220
Tegui, p. 219

FRENCH

Brasserie Petanque, p. 204
La Bourgogne, p. 207
Le Sud, p. 202

ITALIAN

Bella Italia, p. 211
Bruni, p. 219
La Baita, p. 215

JAPANESE

Jardín Japonés, p. 214
Osaka, p. 217
Yuki, p. 200

STEAK

Cabaña Las Lilas, p. 201
Don Julio, p. 213
El Estanciero, p. 221
La Cabrera, p. 215
Rio Alba, p. 217

Best by Experience

MOST ROMANTIC

Duhau Restaurante & Vinoteca, p. 206
Le Sud, p. 202
Pura Tierra, p. 220

HOT SPOTS

Osaka, p. 217
Pura Tierra, p. 220
Tegui, p. 219

HOTEL DINING

La Bourgogne, p. 207
Le Sud, p. 202
Tomo I, p. 200

5

CENTRO AND ENVIRONS

Combining the downtown financial district and the relatively new waterfront Puerto Madero, Centro and environs has something for everyone here, from traditional to trendy.

At lunchtime, it is not surprisingly the place where business deals are negotiated over leisurely lunches of steak, potatoes, salad, and wine. Recently there's been a surge of new quick-and-easy take-out joints and lunch counters feeding local office workers on a short break. In the evening the area can get deserted, except for the new pedestrian dining strip along Reconquista, jammed with bars and restaurants catering to those staying in downtown hotels.

Puerto Madero is the center for touristy dining, with large restaurants serving up everything from steaks to Asian specialties at prices that would make restaurant owners in other parts of the city blush with shame. It's a beautiful zone to take a walk in and get a couple of postcard shots with your camera, but unless you're on an expense account, food is generally far better, far more interesting, and far less expensive elsewhere.

COFFEE, OPEN SKY, AND A SEAL

One of the most unusual places to stop and have a coffee or a small bite for lunch in the Centro area is the former rooftop apartment of Daniel Ruffilli, who rented the place more than three decades ago as a teen. **Momentos en el Infinito** is located atop the posh Galeria Güemes (⊠ *San Martín 170, 6th floor*) and features a maze of hallways and small rooms as well as a terrace, where you can sip a properly brewed espresso or tuck into an inexpensive milanesa. And "the Seal"? The apartment used to belong to *Little Prince* author Antoine de Saint-Exupéry, who had a bathtub-dwelling pet seal.

CAFÉ LINGO 101

Coffee is taken seriously in Argentina. A 9 am and 6 pm caffeine jolt is what gets many porteños through their long days and nights. Here's how to order it:

Café: Same as an American espresso.

Cortado: A café topped or "cut" with hot foamy milk.

Filtro: Brewed coffee.

Lagrima: Hot foamy milk with a "drop" of coffee.

Submarino: A tall glass of hot milk served with a chocolate bar submerged into the milk (aka hot chocolate).

Ristretto: A small, very strong shot of espresso.

Café con leche: Half coffee and half milk, served in a larger cup.

Unless you specify otherwise, your café will be served in a short espresso glass. If you want a larger coffee, order a *jarrito,* or medium. If you want an American-size coffee, order a *doble,* or double espresso.

EATING AND ARTING

Buenos Aires is blessed with both wonderful restaurants and talented artists, and in many spots in the city you can combine cuisine and culture.

A free, open-air, year-round art gallery sits outside two popular restaurants in Retiro: the fancy **Piegari** (✉ *Posadas 1042* ⊹ *2:C1*), a favorite of TV talk-show queen Susana Gimenez, and **El Mirasol** (✉ *Posadas 1032* ⊹ *2:C1*), a landmark *parrilla* that's been serving up succulent steaks for four decades.

DOWNTOWN BA'S BEST CAFÉS

Centro is packed with cafés that are an integral part of Buenos Aires' past and present. Jump into café culture at these top spots:

Café Tortoni (✉ *Av. de Mayo 829* ⊹ *2:D4*) is the most famous Buenos Aires café of all, serving coffee to political, literary, and entertainment legends since 1858.

Richmond (✉ *Florida 468* ⊹ *2:D3*), one of the city's oldest and most venerable cafés, is conveniently located on the pedestrian shopping mall of Florida Street.

La Giralda (✉ *Av. Corrientes 1453* ⊹ *2:B4*), a favorite spot for the literary set, is famous for having invented the submarino, BA's answer to hot chocolate, and for its churros.

Nearby, the **Sofitel Buenos Aires** (✉ *Arroyo 841* ⊹ *2:D2*) holds rotating exhibitions of Argentine and French artists in its café and restaurant and is also the perfect jumping off point to enjoy "Gallery Nights," a monthly gathering held at 7 pm on the last Friday of each month, when art galleries, museums, cafés, and restaurants in Retiro and beyond open their doors for art gawking, champagne sipping, and hors d'oeuvre devouring.

(top) Un café, the equivalent of an Americam espresso; (bottom) the historic Café Tortoni.

LA BOCA AND SAN TELMO

To truly step back into the history of Buenos Aires, you need to visit *La Grand Aldea*, or The Grand Village, as the neighborhoods of La Boca and San Telmo were once called. Of course, that was back in the 1800s, when the city had just been founded.

San Telmo was originally home to some of the most elaborate mansions in the city, before the 1871 yellow fever epidemic, when those who could afford to up and moved to what was then the countryside, now the areas bordering Avenida Rivadavia. San Telmo quickly became a barrio of *conventillos*, or rooming houses. These days it's a bit of a Bohemian, artsy neighborhood. Most dining spots are on the cheap, there's plenty of pizza, though here and there you'll find a gem.

La Boca was the dock and warehouse district, and much of that is still in evidence, and much of the area is a bit dicey to wander through. At the same time, it is home to Buenos Aires' emblematic picture-postcard tourist site, *El Caminito*, with its bright-colored buildings, street tango demos, and overpriced, poor-quality pasta shops.

Bar Dorrego is great spot for both eating and people-watching.

DRINKING ON DEFENSA

Hitting the countless antiques shops, art galleries, and fashion stores can be tiring work, so to relax hit one of many old-school bars. Plaza Dorrego is considered the central point of the neighborhood, and the main drag is Calle Defensa, which is lined with places that offer outdoor seating. Check out the historic **Bar Dorrego** (⊠ *Defensa 1098* ✛ *2:E6*) for prime people-watching on the plaza, or wander up to the end of the lane to Parque Lezama and take a seat at the classic Bar Britanico or Bar Hipopotamo (both at ⊠ *Defensa & Brasil* ✛ *2:D6*).

CULINARY Q & A

With Ernesto Oldenburg and Marlano Braga

Ernesto Oldenburg is a former restaurant chef who still continues to cook on a part-time basis. He's been writing about food in Buenos Aires for the last decade, and has a regular column in *Bacanal* magazine. Mariano Braga is one of the new voices on the food scene, with five years of restaurant critiques under his belt; he has been writing about the local wine scene for longer.

Q: What have you seen happen on the food scene over the last few years here in Buenos Aires?

E.O.: Southeast Asian cuisine and a new boom in Peruvian restaurants top the list, along with a surge in molecular cooking. The whole closed-door restaurant movement has developed, and there's also been a return to looking at older, traditional Argentine cooking.

M.B.: Buenos Aires is a constantly changing gastronomic scene, and recently even more so. Some of the newest things have been the rise of "self-service"–style restaurants where you can pick from an array of ingredients to design your own meal, the now ubiquitous sushi bar, the number of which seems to quintuple every time you look, and, of course, the rise in Peruvian cuisine as is happening all over the world.

Q: What do you think is coming down the road in the next few years?

E.O.: What we call *cocina de la vanguardia*—or cutting-edge cooking. I think we'll see a real separation between those who are truly cutting edge and the "fake modern cooking"—the gratuitous usage of molecular techniques in every little restaurant. There will also be a continued resurgence of traditional dishes, updated for today, as well as more emphasis on healthy eating: less fat, and more organic and natural ingredients.

M.B.: I think the *"de autor"* small restaurants where the chef cooks whatever he or she wants with a regularly changing menu are the new hot thing coming along, it's already starting. Also, the next cuisines to arrive will be Malaysian food and Australian food.

PORTEÑO GRUB

Milanesa a la Maryland is a breaded veal or chicken cutlet served with creamed corn, fried bananas, peas, ham, and potatoes.

Eating *ñoquis de papas* (potato dumplings) on the 29th of every month is a local tradition, the day that *ñoquis* (slang for civil servants in patronage jobs) pick up their monthly check.

Revuelta Gramajo is a local classic with a good story behind it to boot. Named after government administrator Artemio Gramajo (friend of then-president Julio Roca), an amateur chef who "designed" a dish of scrambled eggs, fried potatoes, ham, and peas to be served to soldiers in the battlefield. Some of the best spots to find these dishes are in local haunts like **Manolo** (✉ *Bolivar 1299* ✛ *2:D6*), **Bar El Federal** (✉ *Carlos Calvo 599* ✛ *2:D2*), and **Don Carlos** (✉ *Brandsen 699* ✛ *2:F6*).

5

Un mozo (waiter) carrying un chop (glass of beer) and some maníes (peanuts).

RECOLETA, BARRIO NORTE, AND ALMAGRO

Arguably Buenos Aires' poshest neighborhood, Recoleta is the epicenter for high-end shopping, museum-going, and white-tablecloth dining. It's home to most of the swankier hotels, and many of them house excellent restaurants, but it's also home to a good number of classic spots that have been serving up high-quality fare for decades.

At the same time, there's something for everyone, and the somewhat touristy Village Recoleta strip along Junín and R.M. Ortíz has a mix of old-time cafés like La Biela and Munich nestled side by side with family-friendly steak and pasta houses; the city's first microbrewery, Buller; and even a few nightclubs for those who want a little late night fun.

EL SANJUANINO

Once the steak and Malbec fix is sated, it's time to try some of Argentina's varied regional cuisine. And one of the best spots to do that is just a block off the glitzy shopping strip of Avenida Alvear. **El Sanjuanino** (✉ *Posadas 1515* ✛ *2:C1*) packs them in day and night for some of the city's best empanadas and regional stews like *locro* (white corn, squash, and mixed meats), *carbonada* (dried peaches and veal), *lentejas* (lentils), and *mondongo* (tripe), as well as a smattering of classic game dishes. A perennial favorite is the matambre *rescoldo*, a pastry crust packed with ham, eggs, cheese, and peppers, all slow roasted in the embers of the wood-fired oven.

A top-notch steakhouse, La Cabaña's presentation is bar-none.

TAKING TEA

Along Avenida Alvear are some of the best-known names of the fashion world—Hermès, Louis Vuitton, Eremenegildo Zegna, Ralph Lauren, Cartier—and it's no surprise that some of the city's finest hotels are located in the same area.

For a true old-world experience, with white-gloved waiters and silver service, find your way to **L'Orangerie** (✉ *Av. Alvear 1891* ✦ *2:B1*) in the Alvear Palace Hotel, where wave after wave of finger sandwiches and pastries accompany specially blended teas from the **Tealosophy** shop in the hotel's shopping gallery—a world-class tea shop.

More modern, but just as classy, the afternoon teas at the **Palacio Duhau** (✉ *Av. Alvear 1661*) and the **Caesar Park** (✉ *Posadas 1232*) or the **Four Seasons** (✉ *Posadas 1086*) are perfect for devotees of the beverage.

If your tastes run to something simpler, a new chain of great teashops has opened up in the city, **Tea Connection**, with two Recoleta locations (✉ *Arenales 2102 and Uriburu 1597*).

A TEMPLE TO WINE AND CHEESE

In addition to housing two great restaurants, the **Palacio Duhau** (✉ *Av. Alvear 1661*) also has what must be the city's first Cheese Room, offering more than 45 Argentine cheeses produced in the provinces of Buenos Aires, Cordoba, and Santa Fe. You can try goat, blue, Reblochon, Brie, and other types, artfully paired with smoked meats and wine. The hotel's wine list offers more than 500 varieties and 3,500 bottles. Naturally, the selection is dominated by select smoky Malbecs and Cabernets from Argentina, but it also offers hard-to-find Italian, French, and American vintages.

"CLOSED-DOOR" RESTAURANTS

Among the most innovative trends to emerge from the recent culinary renaissance in Buenos Aires is the re-imagining of classic *casas de comida* into trendy dining at *"puertas cerradas"* or "closed door" restaurants. Here proprietors open the doors of their homes to small groups for intimate meals. **Casa Saltshaker** (⊕ *www. casasaltshaker.com*) is run by American chef and sommelier Dan Perlman from his apartment in Recoleta. Another excellent spot is **Casa Felix** (⊕ www.colectivofelix. com), operated by chef Diego Felix. At **TreintaSillas** (⊕ *www.treintasillas. com*) chef Ezequiel Gallardo serves up his self-described "ghetto gourmet" creations. Other top "closed-door" restaurants in Buenos Aires include: **La Cocina Discreta** (⊕ *www. lacocinadiscreta.com*), **Tipo Casa** (⊕ *www.tipo-casa. com.ar*), **Cocina Sunae** (⊕ www.cocinasunae. com), and **Paladar Buenos Aires** (⊕ www. paladarbuenosaires.com.ar).

PALERMO

The city's largest neighborhood, Palermo offers something for every taste, style, and budget. It's the city's undisputed culinary hot spot, with enclaves that have their own distinct style and vibe.

Dried gourds are vessels for maté, that most Argentine of beverages. (top right) Palermo is a good bet for vegetarian, like flavorful tofu soups; (bottom right) great drinking spots abound.

If you want the tastiest, most cutting-edge, most traditional, most ethnic, most daring, and most fashionable food in Buenos Aires, then you head to Palermo. It's that simple. The sprawling neighborhood is home to the hip areas of Palermo Soho and Hollywood as well as the quieter pockets of Palermo Botanico and Chico.

Soho's main landmark is the artsy Plaza Serrano. But steer clear of the restaurants that line the plaza; they uniformly serve bland and overpriced food. Instead, wander a few blocks in any direction, and you're bound to come across a worthwhile dining spot.

Across the train tracks and Avenida Juan B. Justo lies Palermo Hollywood, which does an admirable job of mixing old and new cuisines in a cool setting of TV production houses and studios.

PASS THE MATÉ, MAN

Maté (pronounced MAH-tay) is the unofficial national drink. The bright green herb is packed into a gourd, infused with hot water, and then sucked through a metal straw. Its bitter flavor packs a punch. Drinking mate is a true ritual in Argentina. The custom is a true social event, and there are some places in the city like **La Pena del Colorado** (⊠ Guemes 3657, Palermo ✛ 1:G5 ⊕ www.delcolorado. com.ar) that offer it.

PALERMO PARRILLAS

The most cutting-edge cuisine can be found in Palermo, but it's also home to a high concentration of top-notch parrillas.

La Cabrera (✉ *Cabrera 5099* ⊹ *1:E4*) is always packed to the brim with tourists, and in addition to its fantastic cuts of beef it's well known for its cold and hot side salads.

La Dorita (✉ *Humboldt and Costa Rica* ⊹ *1:E4*) is so popular that it occupies two corners of the same street. Actors, activists, and musicians gather here; ask for a table outside to soak in the scene.

Miranda (✉ *Costa Rica 5602* ⊹ *1:E3*) is perhaps the most fashionable parrilla in all Palermo. It's brimming with beautiful people, and the food is excellent, especially the *ojo de bife*.

COCKTAIL CRAZE

Buenos Aires is undergoing a cocktail craze. These days many porteños are no longer content drinking straight beer or booze, and are now demanding well-mixed libations for their nights out on the town.

In Palermo Soho, **Mundo Bizarro** (✉ *Serrano 1222* ⊹ *1:E5*) has been leading the charge, with scores of original concoctions. The place is decorated in kitschy fluorescent colors, yet it feels like a biker bar—but without the bikers.

Nearby, **Ocho7Ocho** (✉ *Thames 878* ⊹ *1:D5*) was once a hush-hush spot for a quiet cocktail among friends, but the secret's out now. Regardless, it's still worth a visit to take in its speakeasy atmosphere.

Casa Cruz (✉ *Uriarte 1658* ⊹ *1:E4*) is known for its cutting-edge cuisine, but it also has a small bar where the grande dame of the Argentine bartending scene, Inés de los Santos, mixes up delightful drinks like the "Sol V. 2.0" (vodka, grappa, passion fruit, syrup, and Malbec).

VEGETARIAN SPOTS

Bio (✉ *Humboldt 2199* ⊹ *1:E3*), BA's first organic restaurant, continues to wow with creations like quinoa risotto with vegetables and goat cheese, and mustard tofu with yamani rice. **Arevalito** (✉ *Arevalo 1478* ⊹ *1:C4*) has a quirky and colorful decor and serves great salads and vegetable quiches. **Los Sabios** (✉ *Av. Corrientes 3733* ⊹ *1:G6*) is a well-priced buffet-style spot with tasty soups and loads of dishes made with fresh ingredients. **Kensho** (✉ *Zarraga 3799* ⊹ *1:A2*) is run by well-known local organic chef Maximo Cabrera, who has prepared food for visiting rock stars and also gives private cooking classes. New on the scene are **Buenos Aires Verde** (✉ *Gorriti 5657* ⊹ *1:D4*), offering up a mix of raw and cooked vegan dishes, and **Meraviglia** (✉ *Gorriti 5796* ⊹ *1:D4*), with a selection of creatively spiced vegetarian dishes and a wildly popular pastry shop.

5

BELGRANO AND LAS CAÑITAS

Belgrano is filled with family-friendly spots and a few gems, while über-cool Las Cañitas rocks seven nights a week with a vast array of culinary options.

Despite its reputation as a snooty upper-class enclave, Belgrano is in fact one of the city's most diverse food neighborhoods. Indeed, there are million-dollar mansions and embassies, but there are also sections filled with Asian immigrants, traditional English- and Irish-style homes and cafés, a big university, and a chaotic shopping street, Avenida Cabildo.

Until a few years ago a strictly residential neighborhood, the Las Cañitas enclave has become the city's hot-spot "restaurant row," with everything from steak houses, pizza, and pasta to a new influx of Mexican, North American, Middle Eastern, and German spots. It's particularly popular with the expat community, but there are plenty of locals who frequent the area as well.

BARRIO CHINO

Buenos Aires' "Barrio Chino" is a mishmash of Chinese, Korean, and Japanese citizens and cultures. Compared to those of many other big cities, BA's Chinatown is relatively small, occupying just a few blocks on and around Calle Arribenos, near the Belgrano C train station. There you can find a smattering of supermarkets, shops, and restaurants. Among the best are **Lai Lai** (⊠ *Arribenos 2168* ✛ *1:C1*), **Palitos** (⊠ *Arribenos 2243* ✛ *1:C1*), and the fabulous **BuddhaBA** (⊠ *Arribenos 2288* ✛ *1:C1*), which serves excellent pan-Asian fare.

One of Barrio Chino's gems is Todos Contentos, a popular spot for Chinese food.

HEAVENLY HELADO

Buenos Aires has some of the best ice cream in the world. Porteños take their *helado* (ice cream) seriously, and shops can be found on nearly every other corner around the city. The neighborhood with the most *heladerías* is Belgrano, where fantastic mom-and-pop operations and chain shops abound. At many *heladerías* you'll find an entire section of the menu devoted to caramel-y dulce de leche combinations. We recommend:

Cabaña Tuyu (✉ *José Hernández 2275* ✛ *1:C1*) for dozens of selections, including the buttery, wine-infused sabayon.

Freddo (✉ *Av. Libertador 5200* ✛ *1:C1*) for its juicy sorbets and refreshing fruit flavors (try banana).

Persicco (✉ *Vuelta de Obligado 2092 and Migueletes 886* ✛ *1:E1*), a local chain, for its delectable *dulce de leche* combinations.

Un Altra Volta (✉ *Echeverria 2302* ✛ *1:C1*) for its gorgeous chocolates and sculptural ice cream desserts, which taste as good as they look.

TAKE A BREAK FROM STEAK

While steak is listed up there with the top attractions of Buenos Aires, sometimes you want something a little lighter. There's a local saying in the restaurant world these days that if you want to attract customers, offer sushi, and way too many places do. But thankfully, some of them get it right:

Bokoto (✉ *Huergo 261* ✛ *1:E2*), a sushi-roll specialist, for its stylish, relaxed setting and creative presentations.

Moshi Moshi (✉ *Ortega y Gasset 1707* ✛ *1:E2*) for its swanky rooftop sake bar and stellar sushi. Try the sake-ebi roll, with salmon, shrimp, and avocado topped with caviar.

Mikado (✉ *Arevalo 2870* ✛ *1:E2*), one of the area's more elegant spots for truly creative sushi rolls.

KITCHEN MAESTRO

Martín Molteni is Belgrano's rock-star chef, turning out some of the most creative food using indigenous Argentine ingredients at **Pura Tierra** (✉ *3 de Febrero 1167* ✛ *1:C1*). He's living the chef's dream: cooking what he's passionate about in an intimate converted home. He shares that passion with guests and students through series of classes and trips throughout the country, and more widely spread on his own local television show. Molteni developed his passion for food at an early age in his family's kitchen, and was off traveling the world, working, learning, and cooking in Australia, back to Argentina, to France, and back again, at an age when most of his friends were trying to figure out what came after the prom. He's won multiple awards for his cooking style, he's competed in the famed Bocuse d'Or, and at the end of the day, there's nothing he likes better than teaching someone about his native land's food.

5

(top) Ice cream, helado…this stuff is delicious in any language; (bottom) Sushi Club in Las Cañitas.

RESTAURANT REVIEWS

Listed alphabetically within neighborhood. Use the coordinate (✛ 2:D2) at the end of each listing to locate a site on the corresponding map.

CENTRO AND ENVIRONS

CENTRO

$ ✕ **Confitería La Ideal.** Part of the charm of this spacious 1912 coffee
CAFÉ shop–milonga is its sense of nostalgia: think fleur-de-lis motifs, time-worn European furnishings, and stained glass. No wonder they chose to film the 1998 movie *The Tango Lesson* here. La Ideal is famous for its *palmeritas* (glazed cookies) and tea service and for the scores of locals and foreigners who attend the milongas here. Tango lessons are offered Monday through Saturday at varying times throughout the day and night; evening concerts take place every night except Tuesday and Thursday. Its informality is its best trait; just show up at any hour and chances are you'll hear and see some great tango. ⊠ *Suipacha 380, at Av. Corrientes, Centro, Buenos Aires, Buenos Aires* ☎ *11/5265–8069* ⊕ *www.confiteriaideal.com* ⊟ *No credit cards* Ⓜ *C to C. Pellegrini, D to 9 de Julio* ✛ *2:D4.*

$ ✕ **El Cuartito.** For nearly 80 years this icon of *porteño* pizza has been
PIZZA tugging at the heartstrings of locals, who get misty-eyed when they think about the fresh tomato sauce and the mile-high pile of oozing mozzarella on these classics. You'll spot the occasional fellow tourist, but the vast majority of seats will be filled with locals who've been coming here for years. Every square inch of wall space is dedicated to posters, photos, and memorabilia of sports legends, musicians, tango dancers, and actors, and every local has his or her cherished spot in the dining room. The best pizza? A classic *mitad-mitad*, or half and half, one side a straightforward tomato sauce and cheese, the other simply festooned with sauce and anchovies. Don't pass on dessert, with the classic flan leading the pack. ⊠ *Talcahuano 937, Centro, Buenos Aires, Buenos Aires* ☎ *11/4816–4331* ⊟ *No credit cards* Ⓜ *D to Tribunales* ✛ *2:C3.*

$$ ✕ **El Globo.** Much like the neighborhood in which it resides, El Globo is
SPANISH touristy but good. Hearty *pucheros* (mixed boiled meat dinners), roast suckling pig, squid, and other Spanish-Argentine fare are served in a large dining area, as they have been since the restaurant opened in 1908. The *cazuela de mariscos* (seafood stew) is another specialty. ⊠ *Hipólito Yrigoyen 1199, Centro, Buenos Aires, Buenos Aires* ☎ *11/4381–3926* Ⓜ *C to Av. de Mayo, A to Lima* ✛ *2:C5.*

$$ ✕ **El Imparcial.** Founded in 1860, the oldest restaurant in town owes its
SPANISH name (meaning "impartial") to its neutrality in the face of the warring political factions of Buenos Aires' Spanish immigrants. Hand-painted tiles, heavy wooden furniture, and paintings of Spain are all strong reminders of the restaurant's origins, as are the polite, elderly waiters, many of whom are from the old country. Talking politics is no longer banned within, good news for today's Argentines, who keep coming to El Imparcial for the renowned puchero as well as seafood specialties like paella. ⊠ *Hipólito Yrigoyen 1201, Centro, Buenos Aires, Buenos*

Aires ☎ *11/4383–2919* ⊕ *www.elimparcial.com.ar* Ⓜ *C to Av. de Mayo, A to Lima* ✛ *2:C5.*

$ ✕**El Palacio de la Papa Frita.** This longtime standby is popular for its fan-
ARGENTINE ciful Old World atmosphere and hearty traditional meals—steaks, pastas, and salads. The *papas soufflé* (inflated french fries) reign supreme;
try them *à la provençal* (sprinkled with garlic and parsley) along with
the classic *bife a medio caballo* (steak topped with a fried egg). You
don't come here strictly for the service or the food, you come here to
soak in the porteño lifestyle. ✉ *Lavalle 735, Centro, Buenos Aires,
Buenos Aires* ☎ *11/4393–4849* Ⓜ *C to Lavalle* ✛ *2:B4.*

$ ✕**Gran Café Tortoni.** You'll never again find this much local art, Tiffany
CAFÉ lamps, and art nouveau touches in one room. And while you may have
to wait in a line outside, depending on the time of day and how the
tourist season is doing, it'll be worth it to knock back an espresso or
sip a *submarino*, the local version of hot chocolate. Nibble on one of
the dozens of sandwich varieties or fork in one of the exquisite pastries
and contemplate that you may well be sitting in the same seat that a
former president, a tango singer, or a famed artist or writer sat in many
a time before. It's a place and time out of the past, and thankfully well
preserved. Reservations are a must during the dinner-hour tango show.
✉ *Av. de Mayo 825, Centro, Buenos Aires, Buenos Aires* ☎ *11/4342–
4328* ⊕ *www.cafetortoni.com.ar* Ⓜ *A to Perú* ✛ *2:D4.*

$ ✕**Las Cuartetas.** Not known for its decor, this spot is packed with locals
PIZZA who come here for the coal-fired deep-dish pizza—a style not common
☾ to this city. Even less common, but in this spot not unusual: older men
and/or women dining alone at the rickety Formica tables that fill the
room. Not to be missed is their spinach and white-sauce pizza, and
for the meat eaters the *española*, layered with longaniza sausage, BA's
answer to pepperoni. Service is spotty, and it can take a while to get
anyone's attention, and friendliness is not the first order of the day, but
the wait and the attitude won't matter once you sink your fork into one
of their slices. ✉ *Corrientes 838, Centro, Buenos Aires, Buenos Aires*
☎ *11/4326–0171* ▭ *No credit cards* ☾ *No lunch Sun.* Ⓜ *B to C. Pellegrini, C to Diagonal Norte, D to Estación 9 de Julio* ✛ *2:D4.*

$$$ ✕**Matías Downtown.** In the heart of the downtown business district,
ARGENTINE Matías is the flagship of a group of Victorianesque pseudo-Irish pubs.
Drop in at lunchtime for a simple steak with mushroom sauce, a well-
prepared piece of fish, or even just a simple sandwich. Pints of ale on
tap and plenty of noise, particularly at dinnertime, are the order of the
day. Weekday evenings there's an early happy hour followed by live
music, generally local rock groups, which can make dinner conversation
a challenge. At their other locations outside of downtown, the ambience
is a bit more laid-back, and prices are a touch lower. ✉ *Reconquista
701, Centro, Buenos Aires, Buenos Aires* ☎ *11/4311–0327* ⊕ *www.
matiaspub.com.ar* ☾ *Closed Sun.* Ⓜ *C to San Martín* ✛ *2:E3.*

$ ✕**Pippo.** Historic Pippo, open since 1942, is a porteño classic known for
ARGENTINE its simplicity and down-to-earth cooking. Pastas like *tallarines* and ravi-
oli are the most popular choices, but also try the *estofado* (beef stew)
or *lomo* (sirloin) with fries. For dessert, flan is topped off with cream
or dulce de leche. It's in the heart of the Corrientes theater district;

accordingly, don't expect particularly attentive service, but it's perfect for a pre- or post-show meal. The old wooden tables and tiled floors are tired, but for many they only add to the no-nonsense charm of the place. ✉ *Paraná 356, Centro, Buenos Aires, Buenos Aires* ☎ *11/4374–6365* Ⓜ *B to Uruguay* ✛ *2:B4.*

$$ ✕ **Restó.** After training with two of the world's most renowned chefs—
ARGENTINE Spain's Ferran Adriá and France's Michel Bras—chef-owner María Barrutia came back to Buenos Aires and made a very big splash in this very small space, hidden deep inside the Society of Architects. Her menu is short, sweet, and reasonably priced. Three set-price menus pair ingredients like *codorniz* (quail) with Argentina's more traditional foods like *zapallo* (squash). They're all honored with classic European treatments, including expertly reduced sauces. The molten chocolate cake, adapted from Bras, is unforgettable. ✉ *Montevideo 938, Centro, Buenos Aires, Buenos Aires* ☎ *11/4816–6711* ⚄ *Reservations essential* ▭ *No credit cards* ◷ *Closed weekends. No dinner Mon.–Wed.* Ⓜ *D to Callao* ✛ *2:B3.*

$$$ ✕ **Sabot.** Likely you'll be the only tourist amid scores of older busi-
ARGENTINE nessmen who've been making this landmark a classic for more than 40 years. Day in and day out, this is the spot where behind-the-scenes negotiations take place over French-influenced local fare. The *centolla* (king crab) or *langostino* (prawn) salad is a throwback to another age, but it's perfectly prepared. Tuck into properly prepared pastas and a house specialty, semolina gnocchi, or slice into a delicious steak—the *entrecote* is king here. Add to the food some of the friendliest and most efficient service you'll find in town, and it's a don't-miss downtown lunch. ✉ *25 de Mayo 756, between Cordoba and Viamonte, Centro, Buenos Aires, Buenos Aires* ☎ *11/4313–6587* ⚄ *Reservations essential* ◷ *Closed weekends. No dinner* Ⓜ *B to L.N. Alem* ✛ *2:E3.*

$$$$ ✕ **Tomo I.** For a truly sublime dining experience, visit the recently reno-
ARGENTINE vated Tomo I, the consistently superb restaurant that's been run by the Concaro sisters since 1971. The inviting beige burlap walls lead to a back-lighted bar fronted by a gorgeous wood table made from an Algarrobo tree. The two dining rooms can be both romantic and functional; perfect for closing a business deal or celebrating an anniversary. The food is extraordinary: chilled carrot soup with orange and ginger, fresh Spanish octopus in pesto and garlic, and mouth-watering suckled pig are all top choices. This is food you won't soon forget. Reservations are recommended. ✉ *Carlos Pellegrini 521, Centro, Buenos Aires, Buenos Aires* ☎ *11/4326–6695* ⊕ *www.tomo1.com.ar* ◷ *Closed Sun. No lunch Sat.* Ⓜ *B to Carlos Pellegrini, D to 9 de Julio* ✛ *2:C3.*

$$$$ ✕ **Yuki.** Getting in requires a reservation, but once you're through the
JAPANESE unmarked facade, you'll find yourself in the closest thing Buenos Aires has to a sushi temple. Japanese businessmen are quietly making deals in semi-hidden salons with tatami mats, while local aficionados are deftly wielding chopsticks at the small tables, or, if they're lucky, seated at the sushi bar in front of sushi-master Kazuo-san. The fish is pristinely fresh and changes daily based on availability, but always goes far beyond the BA standard of salmon and cream cheese (the latter thankfully not offered). For a special experience, order the *omakase* (chef's choice)

menu and let the chef do his thing while you knock back a sake or two from the impressive selection. ✉ *Pasco 740, between Independencia and Chile, Congreso, Buenos Aires, Buenos Aires* ☎ *11/4942–7510* 🍴 *Reservations essential* Ⓜ *E to Pichincha* ✛ *2:A6.*

PUERTO MADERO

$$$$
STEAKHOUSE

✗ **Cabaña Las Lilas.** This place is a tourist trap, but a good one. It's probably the most famous steak house in all of Argentina, and has become wildly popular with foreigners. Although you'll hear lots of English, German, and French spoken here, if you look around, it's also populated with lots of locals, at least the ones who can afford it. Las Lilas is best known for its beef that comes directly from its own estancia in the Pampas. The best cuts are the rib eye and *bife de lomo*. Salads and desserts are fantastic, too. Bottom line: if you're pressed for time, and can't leave Puerto Madero, this is your place for steak, even though you'll pay dearly for it. Otherwise, venture out to some better, and cheaper, places outside downtown. ✉ *A. M. de Justo 516, Puerto Madero, Buenos Aires, Buenos Aires* ☎ *11/4313–1336* ⊕ *www.laslilas.com* ✛ *2:E3.*

RETIRO

$$$
ITALIAN

✗ **Bengal.** Stepping into the wood-paneled room, with tables draped in white cloths and a ceiling tented with a large Indian-print carpet, you may feel like you've entered a British officers' club from the late 1800s. During the day the clientele seem to be mostly embassy and foreign-service workers, which just adds to that atmosphere. At night it changes over to a mix of neighbors and tourists dining their way through the offbeat menu that's half Italian and half Indian. For those in the mood for spice, a half-dozen curries are on offer (the fish and prawn curries are the stars). For something milder, pasta is the thing, and the excellent lasagnas are the house specialty. The waitstaff are trained to sell, and can sometimes seem a little pushy. ✉ *Arenales 837, Retiro, Buenos Aires, Buenos Aires* ☎ *11/4314–2926* ☾ *Closed Sun. No lunch Sat.* Ⓜ *C to San Martín* ✛ *2:D2.*

$$
ARGENTINE
Fodor's Choice
★

✗ **DaDá.** Poster-art kitsch is the decor in this foodie favorite. With a short but creative menu, this spot serves up some of the most interesting food to be found in the district. Don't miss out on the house specialties: phyllo-wrapped Morbier cheese salad as a starter and the perfectly cooked *ojo de bife* (rib-eye steak). The kitchen also deftly turns out perfectly cooked pastas, particularly those with seafood. Relax, enjoy a glass of wine, read the paper, sit at the bar and chat, and eat well. Hours can be as eclectic as their food, and they may or may not open at posted times, though likely they won't be too far off. ✉ *San Martín 941, Retiro, Buenos Aires, Buenos Aires* ☎ *11/4314–4787* ☾ *Closed Sun.* Ⓜ *C to San Martín* ✛ *2:D3.*

$$
ARGENTINE

✗ **El Federal.** An homage to the rugged terrain of the Argentine wilds, from the *pampas* to Patagonia, every surface in this downtown eatery seems to be rough wood or tanned leather. Chef Paula Comparatore turns out modern twists on classic regional dishes, often making use of rarely seen indigenous ingredients. Her *tehuelches*, a type of Patagonian empanada named after a near-extinct southern tribe are among the best empanadas in the city, and her classic slow braises of lamb, goat, and beef are simply divine. For those with something lighter in mind, there are indigenous fish preparations and even a vegetarian dish or two. A small offshoot of the restaurant is located in Puerto Madero, primarily for takeout and delivery to local offices. ⊠ *San Martín 1015, Retiro, Buenos Aires, Buenos Aires* 🕾 *11/4313–1324* ⊕ *www. elfederalrestaurante.com* ⊗ *Closed Sun. No dinner Sat.* Ⓜ *C to San Martín* ⊹ *2:D3.*

$$ ✕ **Filo.** Crowded and lively, particularly at lunch, this is the hot spot
ITALIAN for pizza and pasta in the downtown area. True Neapolitan-style pizzas with smoky, charred crusts direct from the wood-fired oven are among the best in the city. For a real treat, order the *Filo*, a wheel of a pizza with each slice a different topping according to the pizzero's whims. Pastas are served perfectly *al dente*, a rarity in town, and come with both classic and creative sauces. If you're dining solo, the bar is a great spot to grab a stool and dine, and the pizzas are available in individual sizes. One note, no photos allowed: "some of our guests may be dining with someone that they'd prefer their spouse doesn't see." Check out the ever-changing art gallery in the basement. ⊠ *San Martín 975, between Alvear and Paraguay, Retiro, Buenos Aires, Buenos Aires* 🕾 *11/4311– 1871* ⊕ *www.filo-ristorante.com* Ⓜ *C to San Martín* ⊹ *2:D3.*

$$ ✕ **Gran Bar Danzón.** It's a two-story climb up the steep stairs to BA's best
SUSHI wine bar. Go early in the evening, and it's your worst nightmare of a
Fodor's Choice dimly lit lounge with hard-drinking middle-aged businessmen. Wait
★ until dinner hour—after 8—and the crowd changes to the local yuppie and wine-geek set wolfing down some of the best lounge food in town, including great sushi (don't miss the crispy prawn rolls), eclectic appetizers and main courses, and a selection of wines by the glass that can't be beat. It's not too bad on the wallet either, particularly for the neighborhood and quality. Wednesday nights there's live jazz early. ⊠ *Libertad 1161, 2nd floor, Retiro, Buenos Aires, Buenos Aires* 🕾 *11/4811–1108* ⊕ *www.granbardanzon.com.ar* ⌀ *Reservations essential* ⊗ *No lunch* Ⓜ *C to San Martín* ⊹ *2:C2.*

$$$$ ✕ **Le Sud.** This French restaurant inside the fancy Sofitel Hotel is one of
FRENCH the nicest in the city. Smart, warm service coupled with an elegant and refined atmosphere make for a truly enjoyable dining experience. Start off with a duck pâté with plum chutney or prawns sautéed in tequila and honey. A top entrée is the *merluza negra* (black hake) with ginger butter, citrus, and a white wine reduction, or Patagonian lamb loins with mashed potatoes and white truffles. If you order the tender *ojo de bife*, you're made to feel like royalty by choosing your own ornate stainless-steel knife with handles made of deer hoofs and horns, one of the many small touches that make this restaurant so special. ⊠ *Hotel Sofitel, Arroyo 841, Retiro, Buenos Aires, Buenos Aires* 🕾 *11/4131– 0131* ⌀ *Reservations essential* Ⓜ *C to San Martín* ⊹ *2:D2.*

$ ✕ **Piola.** The first Piola opened in Treviso, Italy, in 1986; this outpost
PIZZA is the second. Although there are now replicas in Brazil, Chile, Miami,
☾ and New York, this branch has become a well-loved landmark, and for good reason: beneath the trendy, funky veneer—modern art, modern music, and a palm-shaded garden—the imposing oven turns out some of the best pizza in town. Crusts are perfectly seared, and sauce

and toppings are judiciously applied for an uncanny replica of the real Italian thing. Don't miss the pizza with *muzzarella di bufala* (buffalo-milk mozzarella), which must be the most authentic in South America. ⊠ *Libertad 1078, Retiro, Buenos Aires, Buenos Aires* ☎ *11/4812–0690* ⊘ *No lunch Sat.–Sun.* Ⓜ *C to San Martín* ✛ *2:C2.*

$$$$
FRENCH
✗**Plaza Grill.** Wrought-iron lamps and fans hang from the high ceilings, and Delft tiles decorate the walls at this favorite spot of executives and politicians. Visiting dignitaries and local playmakers have been dining here since the turn of the 20th century. The feeling, as you might expect, is formal. The wine list is extensive, and the Europe-centric menu includes excellent steak, salmon with basil and red wine, and pheasant with foie gras. ⊠ *Marriott Plaza Hotel, Florida 1005, Retiro, Buenos Aires, Buenos Aires* ☎ *11/4318–3074* Ⓜ *C to San Martín* ✛ *2:D2.*

$$
SPANISH
✗**Tancat.** Who would have thought that this unassuming Catalan tapas restaurant in a calm part of downtown could be such a showstopper? Tancat's romantic, warmly lighted room has a mellow vibe, just the right balance of bustle, music, and noise. The food couldn't be more authentic if this were Barcelona. Begin with *pan con tomate* (grilled bread rubbed with garlic, olive oil, and tomato) paired with buttery Spanish ham. A rich stew of *callos* (tripe) and *gambas al ajillo* (garlic shrimp) enjoys equal success. Even the price is right. ⊠ *Paraguay 645, Retiro, Buenos Aires, Buenos Aires* ☎ *11/4312–5442* ⊘ *Closed Sun.* Ⓜ *C to San Martín* ✛ *2:D3.*

LA BOCA AND SAN TELMO

LA BOCA

$$
STEAKHOUSE
✗**El Obrero.** You'll half expect sawdust on the floor and a saloon fight to break out when you walk into this old-time steak house just off the docks of La Boca. While the place is filled with locals, it's also a spot for in-the-know tourists, and a regular stop for touring rock stars who seem to have chosen it as "the" spot to go when in town for a perfor-mance. Big, juicy steaks, cooked right, massive side dishes, and more ambience than you can shake a stick at, El Obrero is a movie director's dream of an Argentine steak house come to life. The neighborhood is a little iffy, particularly at night, and it's down a little side street—take a taxi to and from (they'll call one for you). ⊠ *Augustin R. Caffarena 64, La Boca, Buenos Aires, Buenos Aires* ☎ *11/4362–9912* ⊟ *No credit cards* ⊘ *Closed Sun.* ✛ *2:F6.*

$$$$
ARGENTINE
✗**Patagonia Sur.** Located just off the picture-postcard tourist trap of El Caminito in La Boca, this was once Francis Mallman's flagship restau-rant. Arguably the country's most beloved chef, he's moved most of his attention to his newer ventures in Uruguay. Fame, particularly television fame, have had their price—mostly in raising them. Patagonia Sur is likely the most expensive restaurant in the country, particularly since it serves up rustic steak-house fare, with a flare to be sure, but nothing extraordinary. These days, the only option at either lunch or dinner is a three-course prix fixe at a price that would make a London or New York chef blush with embarrasment. ⊠ *Rocha 801, La Boca, Buenos Aires, Buenos Aires* ☎ *11/4303–5917* ⊕ *www.restaurantepatagoniasur. com* ⊘ *Closed Sun.–Mon.* ✛ *2:F6.*

5

SAN TELMO

$ ✗ **Bar Dorrego.** Not a place to take a table if you plan to eat a meal, there
CAFÉ are far better options pretty much anywhere. But, Bar Dorrego has the
unquestioned best view of Plaza Dorrego. Have a coffee, sip a cocktail,
order a beer, and get a dish of peanuts. Then sit back and people-watch.
It's a place filled with local businessmen grabbing a sandwich or pastry on weekdays, and no one but tourists on the weekends. Given the
century-old decor and grime, the nose-in-the-air attitude of the waiters
is far misplaced. ⊠ *Defensa 1098, at Humberto I, on Plaza Dorrego,
San Telmo, Buenos Aires, Buenos Aires* ☎ *11/4361–0141* ▭ *No credit
cards* Ⓜ *C or E to Independencia* ✚ *2:E6.*

$$ ✗ **Brasserie Petanque.** Upon entering this classic French brasserie, you're
FRENCH greeted by a long and imposing bar, bookended by white pillars and
backed by shelf after enticing shelf of liquor and wine. This festive
San Telmo locale has scores of small white-linen tables where you can
enjoy great onion soup and local interpretations of French classics,
like steak tartare and beef bourguignonne. Surprisingly, the wine list
is quite small, with only a few French wines, but they make up for it
with an ample spirits selection and friendly bartenders. Get a table by
the window to check out the people cruising by outside. Reservations
are recommended. ⊠ *Defensa 596, San Telmo, Buenos Aires, Buenos
Aires* ☎ *11/4342–7930* ⊕ *www.brasseriepetanque.com* ☉ *Closed Mon.*
✚ *2:D5.*

$$ ✗ **La Brigada.** Amid elaborate decor, including scores of soccer memen-
STEAKHOUSE tos, a courtly staff will treat you to unimpeachable *mollejas* (sweet-
breads) and *chinchulines de chivito* (kid intestines), plus a brilliant array
of grilled steaks. The baby beef is tender enough to cut with a spoon,
which the waiters insist on doing, to much fanfare. This place is definitely on the tourist map, so be prepared pay a bit more and listen to
several different languages at a time. Reservations are recommended.
⊠ *Estados Unidos 465, between Bolívar and Defensa, San Telmo, Buenos Aires, Buenos Aires* ☎ *11/4361–5557* ☉ *Closed Mon.* Ⓜ *C or E to
Independencia* ✚ *2:D6.*

$$$$ ✗ **La Vineria de Gualterio Bolivar.** The pioneer of molecular cooking spots
ARGENTINE in Buenos Aires, chef Alejandro Digilio deserves all credit for bringing
this style of cooking with foams, gels, and powders to the dining scene in
Buenos Aires. Over the last couple of years, however, the restaurant has
started to rest on its laurels a bit, with repetitve menus and less attention to detail than in its early days. It's still an eye-opening experience,
but one that can now be had at any of a dozen other spots in town, and
often a lower price. Still, it's a charming room, impeccable service, and
an opportunity to try something different from the pizzerias and steak
houses that surround it in San Telmo. No à la carte menu available, just
a multi-course tasting menu. ⊠ *Bolivar 865, San Telmo, Buenos Aires,
Buenos Aires* ☎ *11/4361–4709* ⊕ *www.lavineriadegualteriobolivar.com*
☉ *Closed Mon.* ✚ *2:D6.*

$$ ✗ **Martiño.** You know wine is going to be important here when you
WINE BAR step in and see the gleaming glass wine cave that dominates the back
wall, and that's what owner Marcelo Soto intends. A regularly chang-
ing selection of some of Argentina's best wines, many available by the

La Vineria de Gualterio Bolivar

glass, are paired up with some of the best Spanish tapas in the city. Don't miss his grandmother's rendition of a *tortilla española* or, if you're feeling adventurous, the sampler plate of delicious offal preparations. Share multiple small plates or order from the equally good dinner menu. ⊠ *Bolívar 933, San Telmo, Buenos Aires, Buenos Aires* ☎ *11/4300–6897* ⊕ *www.martinio.com.ar* ⊘ *No lunch weekdays* Ⓜ *C or E to Independencia* ✢ *2:D6.*

$$ ✕**Taberna Baska.** Old-world decor and efficient service are hallmarks of

SPANISH this busy, no-nonsense Spanish restaurant whose loyal clientele keeps coming back year after year. Try typical dishes such as *chiripones en su tinta* (a variety of squid in ink) or *fideua de chipirones* (a saffron dish with baby squid that's like a noodle version of paella). Meals come served with four different Basque sauces. ⊠ *Chile 980, San Telmo, Buenos Aires, Buenos Aires* ☎ *11/4334–0903* ⊘ *Closed Mon. No dinner Sun. No lunch Fri. and Sat.* Ⓜ *C to Independencia* ✢ *2:C5.*

RECOLETA, BARRIO NORTE, AND ALMAGRO

RECOLETA

$$ ✕**Buller Brewing Company.** Smack in the middle of the touristy Village

AMERICAN Recoleta strip, a respite from one steak house after another, Buller (English pronounciation) is the city's first microbrewery. Turning out an impressive seven different styles of beer (don't miss the Oktoberfest or the Porter), they also offer up a sampler tasting of the whole range that's worth a try. Great sandwiches and one of the better burgers in the neighborhood are even more reason to drop in. Service can seem a bit slow, at least until you get your first beer in hand, but it's worth the wait. ✉ *R. M. Ortíz 1827, Recoleta, Buenos Aires, Buenos Aires* ☎ *11/4808–9061* ✛ *2:B1.*

$$
MIDDLE EASTERN

✕**Club Sirio.** This is where local foodies in the know come for Syrian food. Walk up a curved, marble staircase to the lobby bar of this breathtaking second-floor Syrian restaurant. Expect hummus, stuffed grape leaves, and lamb in the superb Middle Eastern buffet. Belly dancers entertain Wednesday through Saturday, and coffee-ground readers predict fortunes. You can order a *narguilah* (large water-filtered tobacco pipe) to finish things off in Syrian style. The place lacks charm and is a bit tired, but the intriguing (by BA standards, at least) cuisine makes it worth a visit. ✉ *Syrian Cultural Club, Ayacucho 1496, at Pacheco de Melo, Recoleta, Buenos Aires, Buenos Aires* ☎ *11/4806–5764* ☉ No lunch ✛ *2:A2.*

$$$$
MODERN
ARGENTINE
Fodor's Choice
★

✕**Duhau Restaurante & Vinoteca.** An oasis of elegance and grace in the heart of old, wealthy Recoleta, the Duhau is not only a grand hotel, but it also serves up some of the best food of any hotel in the city. While French technique may be the base, the ingredients are pure South America. Particularly favored by the chef are the seafood and meats of Patagonia. Standout dishes include butter-soft Angus tenderloin, crispy sweetbreads, and a decadent molten chocolate cake. If the weather is nice, grab a table on the terrace overlooking the courtyard gardens. Don't miss a pre- or post-dinner visit to the wine and cheese bar with a fantastic array of each, by glass, bottle, and small plate, respectively, and then take an after-meal walk through the hotel's underground art gallery. ✉ *Av. Alvear 1661, Recoleta, Buenos Aires, Buenos Aires* ☎ *11/5171–1340* ⊕ *www.buenosaires.park.hyatt.com* ☉ No lunch weekends ✛ *2:C1.*

$
ARGENTINE
☾
Fodor's Choice
★

✕**El Sanjuanino.** Mostly tourists from the nearby hotels flock to this Northern Argentine regional spot, but you'll spot some longtime locals, particularly at lunchtime. It's cramped, crowded, and kitschy, and in hot weather the roaring wood-fired ovens can make the main floor a bit too toasty (head downstairs, where it's cooler), but it's worth it for great empanadas, the city's best *locro* (corn, squash, and meat stew), and, if you're feeling adventurous, one of their iconic game dishes. Don't bother with the wine list, the house wine served in pitchers is just as good at half the price. The waiters have fun with the crowd, and generally speak at least basic conversational phrases in a half-dozen or more languages. ✉ *Posadas 1515, at Callao, Recoleta, Buenos Aires, Buenos Aires* ☎ *11/4804–2909* ☉ *Closed Mon.* ✛ *2:C1.*

$
STEAKHOUSE

✕**Juana M.** The minimalist chic decor of this hip basement restaurant stands in stark contrast to the menu: down-to-earth parrilla fare at good prices. Catch a glimpse of meats sizzling on the grill behind the bar, check out the impressive artwork on the walls, and then head to your table to devour your steak and *chorizo* (fat, spicy sausage). This place has the best salad bar in the city, hands down. The homemade pastas aren't bad, either. The staff is young and friendly. It's wildly popular with a lunchtime work crowd during the week and for birthday parties at night. ✉ *Carlos Pellegrini 1535, Recoleta, Buenos Aires, Buenos Aires* ☎ *11/4326–0462* Ⓜ *C to San Martín* ✛ *2:D2.*

$ ✕ **La Biela.** Porteños linger at this quintessential sidewalk café oppo-
CAFÉ site the Recoleta Cemetery, sipping espressos, discussing politics, and
people-watching—all of which are best done at a table beneath the
shade of an ancient rubber tree. Service can be spotty, but if you're just
there for a coffee, who cares. Keep your eyes open for actor and tango
enthusiast Robert Duvall, who is a regular here. ✉ *Quintana 596, at
Junín, Recoleta, Buenos Aires, Buenos Aires* ☎ *11/4804–0449* ✛ *2:B1.*

$$$$ ✕ **La Bourgogne.** White tablecloths, fresh roses, and slick red-leather
FRENCH chairs emphasize the restaurant's innate elegance, and it is consistently
Fodor's Choice considered to be one of the city's very best restaurants. A sophisticated
★ waitstaff brings you complimentary hors d'oeuvres as you choose from
chef Jean-Paul Bondoux's creations, which include foie gras, rabbit,
lamb, chateaubriand, *côte de veau* (veal steak), and black hake. The
loquacious chef is known to stroll through the vast room and sit down
for a chat with patrons. The fixed-price tasting menu is more affordable
and more adventurous than à la carte selections and features a different
wine with each plate. Arrange to be seated in the mysterious wine cel-
lar for a more intimate experience. The wine list reads like a book, and
offers the very best blends from France, Italy, and Argentina. ✉ *Alvear
Palace Hotel, Ayacucho 2027, Recoleta, Buenos Aires, Buenos Aires*
☎ *11/4805–3857, 11/4808–2100* ⌚ *Reservations essential* ☾ *Closed
Sun. No lunch Sat.* ✛ *2:B1.*

$$ ✕ **La Parolaccia.** Right off the main shopping strip on Santa Fé, this place
ITALIAN feels like a warm, family-run and family-friendly Italian restaurant you
☽ could find in any big city. Given the corporate ownership, they serve up
surprisingly excellent homemade pastas with a wide variety of sauces
and styles at each of their nine locations in town. Particularly good are
their hand-rolled *fusilli;* don't overlook the three-course lunch specials.
They're happy to make half portions of pasta for your kids as well.
You'll be greeted at your table with a complimentary cocktail and sent
off with a digestif of limoncello at the end of your meal. ✉ *Riobamba
1046, Recoleta, Buenos Aires, Buenos Aires* ☎ *11/4783–0200* ⊕ *www.
laparolaccia.com* Ⓜ *C to Congreso, B to Callao* ✛ *2:B4.*

$$$$ ✕ **Le Mistral.** The superb dining room at the Four Seasons is warm, invit-
MEDITERRANEAN ing, and, well, Mediterranean—without any of the bright, antiseptic, or
stuffy qualities of competing hotel restaurants. Lobster is treated with
loving care, and the flavors on the menu may be refreshingly subtle and
delicate or bold. The restaurant pays particular care to Middle Eastern
and Spanish cuisine, offering marinated lamb kebabs and tapas, like
fried crab with a green-apple purée. Reservations are recommended.
✉ *Four Seasons Hotel, Posadas 1086, Recoleta, Buenos Aires, Buenos
Aires* ☎ *11/4321–1730* ☾ *No lunch Sat.–Sun.* ✛ *2:C1.*

$$ ✕ **Munich Recoleta.** Jam-packed Munich Recoleta has been a favorite
ARGENTINE gathering spot for high-brow locals for half a century, and the menu
has barely changed since its 1956 opening. Premium cuts of meat, milanesas, creamed spinach, shoestring potatoes, and *chucrut* (cabbage) are
served quickly and in generous portions. The reasonably priced wine
list is enormous but well chosen. The lively atmosphere attracts young
and old alike, despite the often cantankerous waiters. You might see
a local politician, television journalist, or fashion model in here—you

5

never know. Arrive early to avoid a wait. Reservations are not accepted after 9 pm. ⊠ *R. M. Ortíz 1871, Recoleta, Buenos Aires, Buenos Aires* ☎ *11/4804–3981* ✧ *2:B1.*

$$$$
FRENCH

✕ **Nectarine.** Both elegant and quaint, the second-floor dining room of this modern French temple to haute cuisine is a spot for the wealthy, both local and visiting. The regularly changing menu is set up as a one- to five-course prix-fixe (with some supplements) of like-sized courses—nothing is specifically appetizer or entrée, it's entirely up to you to design your dinner. The place generates mixed sentiments from diners, who find some dishes to be exquisite and others overwrought. At lunch it's quiet; at dinner reservations are a must. Expect to shell out a fair amount for a meal, even by international standards. ⊠ *Pasaje del Correo, Vicente López 1661, Recoleta, Buenos Aires, Buenos Aires* ☎ *11/4813–6993* ⌇ *Reservations essential* ⊘ *Closed Sun. No lunch Sat.* ✧ *2:B2.*

$$$$
SPANISH
Fodor's Choice
★

✕ **Oviedo.** Soft lighting, white tablecloths, tranquil ambience, and sea-themed artwork adorning the walls will greet you in this elegant Spanish-style establishment in the heart of Recoleta. In a meat-centric city like Buenos Aires, beautifully cooked seafood is a welcome change, and Oviedo is the best in the city. From classics to modern creative, the kitchen turns out beautifully plated fillets of fish—don't miss their daily catch with pickled baby vegetables and the pristine shellfish. They're no slouches in the meat department either. Top it all off with one of the better wine lists in the area, and you're in for a memorable lunch or dinner. ⊠ *Beruti 2602, at Ecuador, Recoleta, Buenos Aires, Buenos Aires* ☎ *11/4821–3741* ⊕ *www.oviedoresto.com.ar* ⊘ *Closed Sun.* Ⓜ *D to Pueyrredón* ✧ *2:A2.*

$$$$
ITALIAN

✕ **San Babila.** This trattoria is known for its excellent handmade pastas and classic Italian dishes created from the century-old recipes of the chef's grandmother. *Cappelletti di formaggio* (cheese-filled round pasta) and *risotto alla milanese* (risotto and veal cutlet) are good bets. Prices are high and blatantly geared towards tourists, but there are fixed-price menus to choose from and a friendly English-speaking staff. The outdoor terrace is a treat. ⊠ *R. M. Ortíz 1815, Recoleta, Buenos Aires, Buenos Aires* ☎ *11/4804–1214* ⊕ *www.sanbabilaristorante.com. ar* ⊘ *No lunch Mon.* ✧ *2:B1.*

BARRIO NORTE

$$
ECLECTIC

✕ **Due Resto Café.** It may look like a little neighborhood coffee shop, and it may even look, at first glance, like folks are just sitting, sipping a coffee, and reading the paper. But check it out at lunch or dinner time, when the kitchen turns out some of the best pasta and fish dishes in the barrio. The menu changes daily, depending on the chef's whims, but you can count on the best dishes are virtually always the ravioli which show up in a stunning variety of styles, and also the excellent stir-fries. ⊠ *Juncal 2391, Barrio Norte, Buenos Aires, Buenos Aires* ☎ *11/4829–9400* ⊕ *www.duerestocafe.blogspot.com* ⊘ *Closed Sun. No lunch Sat.* Ⓜ *D to Pueyreddón* ✧ *1:H6.*

A simple, seasonal dessert at Duhau

$$ | **✕ Tandoor.** An excellent choice for Indian food in Barrio Norte, Tan-
INDIAN | door occupies a corner space in a beautiful French-style building dat-
ing back to the early 19th century. The rich red walls, simple white
linens, and big windows make for a relaxing dining experience, and
the food is tops, too. A variety of meat, chicken, and vegetable kebabs
(cooked in the tandoor) and curries are spiced to taste; the lamb plates
are also highly recommended, as is the naan. It's somewhat pricey, but
because of the lack of Indian offerings in Buenos Aires, they can get
away with it. ⊠ *Laprida 1293, Barrio Norte, Buenos Aires, Buenos
Aires* ☎ *11/4821–3676* ⊕ *www.tandoor.com.ar* ☾ *Closed Sun.* ✛ *1:H5.*

ALMAGRO

$$ | **✕ Katmandú.** Despite many shortcomings, this remains the most popular
INDIAN | Indian restaurant in the city. It fills up every night with locals and expats
looking for some spice. Chefs create tasty vindaloos and curries in full
view. Consider sharing the tandoori or Indian sampling platter for two;
then indulge in creamy and milky desserts. The food is consistently
good, but pricey by local standards. The waitstaff is always arrogant
and one step behind, and the ambience is a bit dreary. And yet—reservations are recommended. ⊠ *Córdoba 3547, Almagro, Buenos Aires,
Buenos Aires* ☎ *11/4963–1122* ⊕ *www.katmandu.restaurant.com.ar*
☾ *Closed Sun. No lunch* ✛ *1:G6.*

$ | **✕ Cantina La Maroma.** The specials in this chaotic *bodegón* (tavern-style
ARGENTINE | restaurant) are erratically scrawled on bits of paper stuck on the walls
under hams hanging from the ceiling, strings of garlic, and demijohns
of wine. The homemade pastas are excellent, especially the lasagna,
and so are the *milanesas*. Portions are large—don't be surprised if you

Dining at the Alvear Hotel's La Bourgogne is nothing short of elegant.

can't finish your order. Loyal customers keep coming back year after year. This is a true Buenos Aires original. ✉ *Mario Bravo 584, at Humahuaca, Almagro, Buenos Aires, Buenos Aires* ☎ *11/4862–9308* Ⓜ *B to Carlos Gardel* ✢ *1:D6.*

$$ ✕ **Malevo.** Named for the villain of the tango, Malevo was the first eat-
ARGENTINE ery to bring sleek modern dining to the city's classic tango district. The old corner building has large plate-glass windows and an intimate slate-and-aubergine interior where lights are low and white linen abounds. The house's excellent wine selection is on display behind a polished wooden bar—savor a bottle with your *Rebelión en la Granja* (pork with braised fennel and tapenade) or homemade goat-cheese ravioli with sun-dried tomatoes and almonds. ✉ *Mario Bravo 908, at Tucumán, Almagro, Buenos Aires, Buenos Aires* ☎ *11/4861–1008* ☉ *Closed Sun. No lunch Sat.* Ⓜ *B to Carlos Gardel* ✢ *1:G6.*

PALERMO

$$$$ ✕ **Astrid & Gaston.** Its opening in early 2009 was marked by much hype
PERUVIAN by BA foodies, who had longed for famed Peruvian chef Gaston Acurio's cuisine in their city. As a whole, the food and atmosphere inside the beautifully recycled Palermo home is spirited, but in many cases style trumps service. The waitstaff look great in black suits and ties, but they don't offer consistent service, and non-Spanish speakers may have a hard time communicating with them. That said, the food is deli-cious and imaginative: marinated boneless pork with sweet potatoes and red onions; white salmon with peas and scallop risotto; *arroz con mariscos* (rice and shellfish), and *aji de gallina* (chili chicken) are all

top choices. Most of the food lacks the spice normally found in many Peruvian dishes, a regrettable trend that most ethnic restaurants in BA adhere to in order to cater to Porteños' weak palates. ✉ *Lafinur 3222, Palermo, Buenos Aires, Buenos Aires* ☎ *11/4802–2991* ⚑ *Reservations essential* ◔ *Closed Sun.* ✛ *1:H3.*

$ ✕ **Bangalore.** This eatery does an admirable job of re-creating the atmo-
INDIAN sphere of a typical London pub, which probably explains its roaring popularity with Buenos Aires' booming expat population. Come here for fantastically spicy curries, microbrews, and the rowdy atmosphere. Seating is upstairs in a dark alcove. You won't be able to ignore the noise from the drinkers below, but who cares, you're not here for romance. This is a place for a quick Indian meal and jovial conversation. It's per-fect for cheap food and a good beer before heading out to the many hot spots nearby. ✉ *Humboldt 1416, Palermo Hollywood, Buenos Aires, Buenos Aires* ☎ *11/4779–2621* ▭ *No credit cards* ✛ *1:D4.*

$$ ✕ **Bardot.** Peruvian fusion is all the rage in Buenos Aires these days,
PERUVIAN   and one of the best is this slinky, loungy spot under the direction of chef Dennys Yupanqui. Dine at table or go for a more relaxed seat on one of the comfy bar couches. Either way you're in for a treat. Don't miss the excellent *ceviche*, nor the strangely named "pizza" of shell-fish and smoked potatoes, which isn't a pizza, but is stunningly good. Great drinks from the bar plus friendly and efficient service all add up to a great night out without the pretensions of some of the more well-publicized *nueva peruana* spots. ✉ *Honduras 5237, Palermo Soho, Buenos Aires, Buenos Aires* ☎ *11/4831–1112* ⊕ *www.restobardot.com* ▭ *No credit cards* ◔ *Closed Mon.* Ⓜ *D to Palermo* ✛ *1:E4.*

$$ ✕ **Bar 6.** The seasonally changing menu is ambitious—sometimes too
ARGENTINE   ambitious—cycling through a universe of ingredients and preparations, from Asian stir-fry to polenta to grilled seafood. Past highlights have included marinated salmon with cilantro, and goat-cheese ice cream with candied tomatoes. The waiters are usually too busy being beauti-ful to attend to you in a hurry. Even if the service lags and the kitchen can be inconsistent, it's worth stopping by to admire this dramatic stone, wood, and glass space—simultaneously modern and down to earth. This place is wildly popular for its well-priced lunch specials. There's an impressive cocktail menu as well. ✉ *Armenia 1676, Palermo Soho, Buenos Aires, Buenos Aires* ☎ *11/4833–6807* ⊕ *www.barseis. com* ◔ *Closed Sun.* ✛ *1:E5.*

$$$ ✕ **Bella Italia.** The best veal chop in the city can be found here; it's
ITALIAN   sprinkled with rosemary, is served with salty potatoes, and is enough to feed two people. The lemon ravioli with salmon is fantastic, too, as is the bruschetta. In addition to the delicious food, Bella Italia wins points for its cozy, romantic atmosphere, extensive wine list, and friendly, although sometimes overworked, servers. It's in a quaint section of Palermo near the zoo and close to good shopping. The owners also run an Italian-style café a block away, another restaurant in another part of Palermo and one in Belgrano, and a sister branch of the restaurant in Fort Worth, Texas. ✉ *Republica Arabe Siria 3285, Palermo, Buenos Aires, Buenos Aires* ☎ *11/4802–4253* ⊕ *www.bellaitalia-gourmet.com. ar* ◔ *Closed Sun. No lunch* ✛ *1:H3.*

Hip meets cozy at Casa Cruz's bar and lounge.

$$$$
ARGENTINE

✕ **Casa Coupage.** Casa Coupage is consistently cited by local foodies and critics alike as serving some of the best food in the city. It's worth a visit to taste the fantastic modern Argentine dishes prepared by Chef Martin Lukesch: rabbit confit with a carrot and citrus salad; white salmon with smoked bacon and Brussels sprouts; veal cutlet with garlic mashed potatoes and mushroom dust. Owner/sommelier Santiago Mymicopulo picks perfect wine pairings with each course and once a week hosts wine tastings and classes. ✉ *Soler 5518, Palermo, Buenos Aires, Buenos Aires* 🕿 *11/4777–9295* ⊕ *www.casacoupage.com* 🍴 *Reservations essential* 🕙 *Dinner only Thurs. and Fri.* ✛ *1:E3.*

$$$$
ARGENTINE

✕ **Casa Cruz.** Trendsetters come and go, but there are few whose food is truly sublime. With its imposing bronze-doored entrance, dim lighting, expanses of mahogany, and cozy banquettes, you'd have to be a bumbling fool not to impress your date here. And yet it's chef Germán Martitegui's kitchen that will really blow your mind, working rabbit medallions into a state of melting tenderness, and pairing delicately crisped *morcilla* (blood sausage) with jammy fruit. The wine list is huge, and wildly overpriced. The cocktails served up by resident bar maiden Inés de los Santos are the best in the city. This is a place you won't soon forget. ✉ *Uriarte 1658, Palermo Soho, Buenos Aires, Buenos Aires* 🕿 *11/4833–1112* ⊕ *www.casacruz-restaurant.com* 🍴 *Reservations essential* 🕙 *Closed Sun. No lunch* ✛ *1:E4.*

$
ARGENTINE

✕ **Club Eros.** A basic dining room attached to an old soccer club, Club Eros has developed a cult following for its downscale charm. The excellent fare at rock-bottom prices have begun to draw young Palermo trendies as well as older customers who have been loyal to the club for decades. There's no menu, but you can confidently order a crispy *milanesa* (breaded meat cutlet), or, if available, a *bife de chorizo* and fries. Pasta sauces fall flat, but the *flan con dulce de leche* is one of the best (and biggest) in town. ⊠ *Uriarte 1609, Palermo Soho, Buenos Aires, Buenos Aires* ☏ *11/4832–1313* ⊟ *No credit cards* ✛ *1:E4*.

$$$
ARGENTINE

✕ **Dominga.** This Palermo Hollywood locale is one of the most consistent choices in this neighborhood, where new restaurants come and go all the time. It's also well located near hot-spot bars and clubs. The white wood floors and white walls are contrasted with shiny black tables and a softly illuminated wall that creates an intimate, if sometimes overly snug, environment. The menu is small, but each dish is well prepared, including a tasty *entrana* (skirt steak) as well as colorful sushi platters made to order at the bar in the back. Expect a hip crowd of varying ages; if you're coming with a large group, ask for a table in the covered garden patio. ⊠ *Honduras 5618, Palermo, Buenos Aires, Buenos Aires* ☏ *11/4771–4443* ☉ *No lunch Closed Sun.* ✛ *1:D4*.

$$
STEAKHOUSE
Fodor's Choice
★

✕ **Don Julio.** Behind an unassuming facade, and amid rows and rows of empty wine bottles that festoon every available surface, one of Palermo's best steak houses awaits you. A mixed local and expat crowd packs the place at lunch and dinner, dining on the fantastic *ojo de bife* (rib eye) and *cuadril* (rump steak), plus great chorizo sausages, and pretty much anything else you might want off a grill. One of the city's better curated wine lists adds to the fun—ask for Pablo, the owner, who knows the ins and outs of every bottle on his list. ⊠ *Guatemala 4691, at Gurruchaga, Palermo Soho, Buenos Aires, Buenos Aires* ☏ *11/4831–9564* ✛ *1:F4*.

$$$
STEAKHOUSE

✕ **El Trapiche.** It's hard to believe this bare, unadorned space was "refurbished" a few years ago. Luckily the lack of design aesthetic doesn't translate to the plates, which, while not fancy, serve up hearty portions of Argentine grilled and fried dishes and a smattering of Spanish specialties. At lunch it's packed with Palermo office workers, at dinner with a mix of locals and tourists, all tucking into the well-seasoned and properly cooked steaks and chops. Don't miss the *boquerones* as an appetizer; the *entraña*, or hanger steak, particularly accompanied by the excellent *papas a la crema*, are a don't-miss main course to share for two. Note: while it may look slightly pricey at first glance, most of the steak portions easily serve more than one person. There are also good combinations on the well-priced prix-fixe lunch options. ⊠ *Paraguay 5099, at Humboldt, Palermo Hollywood, Buenos Aires, Buenos Aires* ☏ *11/4772–7343* Ⓜ *D to Estación Palermo* ✛ *1:E3*.

$$$$
PERUVIAN
Fodor's Choice
★

✕ **Francesco.** With a privileged elevated view of a quiet residential street in Palermo, Francesco serves the city's finest Peruvian cuisine. Start your evening with what must be the tastiest, frothiest pisco sour in town, then move on to one of the many fresh fish appetizers. Naturally, this restaurant does wonderful *ceviche* dishes that perfectly blend citrus juices with subtly spicy flavors. The main courses run the gamut from fish to pasta to meat. A highlight is the *piqueo criollo*, a salmon and shrimp platter with fresh tomatoes, onions, and peppers. For dessert, try the *suspiro de limena*, a delicious custard-like dessert topped with merengue and cinnamon. The owners operate two similar namesake restaurants in Lima and Miami, and know how to satisfy an international

5

clientele, which shows in the modern, but welcoming dining room and in the top-notch service. ⊠ *Sinclair 3096, Palermo, Buenos Aires, Buenos Aires* ☎ *11/5291–1597* ⊕ *www.francesco.com.pe* ☉ *No lunch Sat. Closed Sun.* ⊹ *1:F2.*

$$$
ARGENTINE

✗**Freud y Fahler.** Red walls, colorful glass screens, and vintage chandeliers give warmth to this glassed-in corner restaurant along a peaceful cobblestone street. The menu is short but imaginative; try the braised lamb, if available, perhaps followed by spiced white-chocolate cake with plum ice cream and orange sauce. The young, well-informed staff gives friendly advice on food and wine. The lunch menus, which are more vegetable-oriented, are an excellent value. It's also a popular stop for an afternoon drink or a coffee. ⊠ *Cabrera 5300, Palermo Soho, Buenos Aires, Buenos Aires* ☎ *11/4833–2153* ☉ *Closed Sun.* ⊹ *1:D4.*

$$$
VIETNAMESE

✗**Green Bamboo.** At this Vietnamese restaurant (BA's first), the walls are black, the waiters slick, and the olive-green vinyl chairs are usually occupied by thirtysomething actors and producers. And those chairs are usually *all* occupied. The food is reasonably authentic; take your time over it and then move on to one of the fantastic *maracuyá* (passion fruit) daiquiris. Belgian-born bartender Peter Van Den Bossche mixes up some wildly creative drinks. ⊠ *Costa Rica 5802, Palermo Hollywood, Buenos Aires, Buenos Aires* ☎ *11/4775–7050* ⊕ *www.green-bamboo. com.ar* ☉ *No lunch* ⊹ *1:D3.*

$$
ITALIAN

✗**Guido Restaurant.** This Italian eatery near the zoo in Palermo attracts an in-the-know crowd ranging from local journalists to businessmen. It's the sister location of Guido's Bar, a more informal spot a block away that's been serving family-style Italian grub for three decades. The restaurant has an old-style bodega feel, with exposed brick walls covered with Italian mementos and black-and-white photos of celebrities. The small front bar serves cocktails made with classics like Campari, Negroni, and Fernet. The menu is somewhat limited, but does offer decent interpretations of pizza, pasta, and fish. The desserts are where they shine, though: delicious tiramisu is the perfect end to a quiet night in this cozy locale. ⊠ *Cervino 3943, Palermo, Buenos Aires, Buenos Aires* ☎ *11/4802–1262* ☉ *Closed Mon. Lunch Sun. only* ⊹ *1:G3.*

$$$
ECLECTIC

✗**Hernán Gipponi Restaurant.** The long, narrow, cream-colored room leading to the hotel's garden patio may not seem like the "in-spot" for creative cooking, but don't let appearances fool you. The chef is turning out some of the most creative food in Palermo, with a skill honed by years of working in top kitchens in Spain. While you can order from the *a la carte* menu, local foodies are packing in for the daily changing 9-course chef's tasting menu. Gipponi is particularly deft with his fish dishes. Backing up the kitchen is one of the better wine lists in the city, managed by a team of top sommeliers, and an excellent cocktail selection from the bar. ⊠ *Fierro Hotel Boutique, Soler 5862, Palermo, Buenos Aires, Buenos Aires* ☎ *11/3220–6820* ⊕ *www.fierrohotel.com* ⌛ *Reservations essential* ☉ *No dinner Sun. and Mon.* Ⓜ *D to Ministro Carranza* ⊹ *1:D3.*

$$$
JAPANESE

✗**Jardín Japonés.** Easily the most impressive setting for sushi in Buenos Aires is inside the Japanese Garden on the northern edge of Palermo. Come for lunch, before or after touring the garden, or come for a romantic dinner. The sushi and sashimi are fresh, especially the salmon, but the hot dishes, such as pork with mushrooms, won't necessarily blow you away. ✉ *Jardín Japonés, Av. Casares 2966, Bosques de Palermo, Buenos Aires, Buenos Aires* ☎ *11/4800–1322* ⊕ *www.jardinjapones.org.ar* ✆ *Closed Tues. dinner* ✢ *1:G4.*

$$　✕ **Kansas.** If you absolutely need to eat American cuisine during your
AMERICAN　time in Buenos Aires, Kansas is your spot. Boisterous groups come here for barbecued pork ribs, chicken, burgers, and beers. This place offers the best Caesar salad in town; the fries and bread are great, too. Its sprawling open dining area has comfy booths and dim lighting, but it's anything but romantic. It does offer a view of the horse track next door. Expect to get your food fast, and you are encouraged to eat quickly. The rowdy bar has good drinks and is popular with forty-something singles on the prowl. ✉ *Av. Libertador 4625, Palermo, Buenos Aires, Buenos Aires* ☎ *11/4776–4100* ✢ *1:E1.*

$$　✕ **La Baita.** In a city filled with first- and second-generation Italians, it
ITALIAN　can be surprisingly hard to find a good Italian meal. Look no further than La Baita, a cozy corner spot in the heart of Palermo Soho that attracts highbrow porteños and Europeans looking for some Mediterranean cuisine. They do fantastic fresh pastas and nice meat dishes, including rabbit and lamb. The main dining room is quaint, and some of the tables are too close together, but the romantic atmosphere, live music, and friendly service make up for it. ✉ *Thames 1603, Palermo Soho, Buenos Aires, Buenos Aires* ☎ *11/4832–7234* ⊕ *www.labaita-restaurante.com.ar* ✆ *No lunch Mon.* ✢ *1:E4.*

$$$　✕ **La Cabrera.** Palermo's best parrilla is on the quiet corner of Cabrera
STEAKHOUSE　and Thames. Fun paraphernalia hangs everywhere, giving the feel of
Fodor's Choice　an old grocery store. La Cabrera is particularly known for its excellent
★　*provoleta de queso de cabra* (grilled goat cheese) and its *chinchulines de cordero* (small lamb intestines). Try also the *cuadril vuelta y vuelta* (rare rump steak) and the *mollejas* (sweetbreads), which are also top-notch. The servings are abundant, as is the noise. What really sets it apart from other parrillas are the complimentary side dishes like pumpkin purée, eggplant salad, and others. ✉ *Cabrera 5099, Palermo Soho, Buenos Aires, Buenos Aires* ☎ *11/4831–7002* ⊕ *www.parrillalacabrera.com* ⚑ *Reservations essential* ✢ *1:E5.*

$$　✕ **Las Pizarras Bistró.** Quirky and kitschy, this 40-seat hole-in-the-wall
ECLECTIC　looks like any of hundreds of other neighorhood hangouts throughout
Fodor's Choice　the city. But stop for a moment and take a look at the chalkboard-
★　covered walls *(las pizarras)* and you'll know instantly this isn't your typical spot for cheap steaks and *milanesas.* Chef Rodrigo Castillo is one of the most unsung chefs in the city. He turns out a constantly changing, market-driven menu of a dozen plates of some of the most interesting, eclectic food you'll find in the area, and the local food *cognoscenti* line up to get in. There's an equally creative wine list spread out on other boards along one wall. Pricing is civil, portions are huge, service can be a trifle slow, but it's worth the wait. ✉ *Thames 2296, at Charcas, Palermo, Buenos Aires, Buenos Aires* ☎ *11/4775–0625* ⚑ *Reservations essential* ✆ *Closed Mon. No lunch* Ⓜ *D to Plaza Italia* ✢ *1:F4.*

$$$
ECLECTIC

✕ **Lelé de Troya.** This is one of the most spectacularly unusual spaces in the city. Each room of this converted old house is drenched in a different color—from the walls to the chairs to the plates—and the food is just as bold. The kitchen can be viewed from the vine-covered lemon-yellow patio, and you can watch as loaf after loaf of the restaurant's homemade bread is drawn from the clay oven. Follow dishes like salmon ravioli or mollejas in cognac with one of Lelé's many Middle Eastern and Italian desserts. The restaurant holds tango classes on Monday nights and has an art space. ✉ *Costa Rica 4901, Palermo Soho, Buenos Aires, Buenos Aires* ☎ *11/4832–2726* ⊕ *www.leledetroya.com* ✛ *1:E4.*

$$
MEXICAN

✕ **María Félix.** Housed in a beautifully restored three-story home in Palermo Soho, María Félix serves some of the best Mexican food in the city. The rooms are decorated with Mexican artwork and artifacts; venture all the way to the roof garden if you want to dine alfresco. The large menu covers all the Mexican basics; the enchiladas and mole are delicious, as are the quasi-authentic margaritas, about the best you're going to get in a city some 6,400 km (4,000 mi) from the Mexican border. Mariachi bands play Thursday through Saturday evenings and holidays. ✉ *Guatemala 5200, Palermo Soho, Buenos Aires, Buenos Aires* ☎ *11/4775–0380* ⊕ *www.mariafelix.com.ar* ✛ *1:F4.*

$
AMERICAN
☺

✕ **Mark's Deli & Coffee House.** The first deli to arrive in Palermo Viejo, Mark's has been steadily drawing crowds for all-day munching (it's open 8:30 am–9:30 pm) with big sandwiches and salads. It's also become something of a scene for twentysomethings with New York fetishes—and perhaps unsurprisingly, also a top choice for brunch. Ingredients are top quality, combinations inventive, and the large variety of breads—the house specialty—is baked on premise. Tastefully mismatched tables, chairs, and sofas are available if you want to eat in; there's also a small patio if you want some sun. The cheesecake in itself is an excuse for a visit. Be warned though: service is always slow. ✉ *El Salvador 4701, Palermo Soho, Buenos Aires, Buenos Aires* ☎ *11/4832–6244* ⊕ *www.markspalermo.com* ▭ *No credit cards* ✛ *1:F5.*

$
ARGENTINE

✕ **Ña Serapia.** Ña Serapia, across from Parque Las Heras, is well known for its hearty authentic northern Argentine food. Creamy steamed *humitas,* made from cornmeal and fresh corn, are excellent, as are cheese-and-onion empanadas. Carafes of wine, like everything else, are a bargain. This is strictly no-frills—it's nothing but a basic room with a few little tables—but the food is consistently good. Don't miss the quirky wall art, which includes a portrait of the owner stabbed in the heart. ✉ *Av. Las Heras 3357, Palermo, Buenos Aires, Buenos Aires* ☎ *11/4801–5307* ▭ *No credit cards* ✛ *1:F4.*

$$$
SCANDINAVIAN

✕ **Ølsen.** Ølsen is a showcase for Nordic flavors *and* contemporary Scandinavian design. Past the walled sculpture garden and white lounge chairs is a cavern of exposed-brick walls. Lime-green furniture and cowhide barstools lend a '70s feel. Best are the *smørrebrød* (open sandwiches) with different vodka shots (the vodka selection is impressive here); other starters like gravlax and *rösti* (crispy sautéed potatoes) are better than the often dry and underseasoned meat entrées. This is *the* place for Sunday brunch, where expats flock for scrambled eggs and bagels. ⊠ *Gorriti 5870, Palermo Hollywood, Buenos Aires, Buenos Aires* ☎ *11/4776–7677* ▭ *No credit cards* ⊘ *Closed Mon.* ✛ *1:D4.*

$$$$ ✕ **Osaka.** Osaka blends tradition with innovation, fusing Peruvian and
JAPANESE Asian cuisines for lofty results, making it one of the most exciting res-
FUSION taurants in the city. However, it does attract a pretentious crowd: there
Fodor's Choice are too many people trying too hard to look too cool, but the food all
★ but makes up for it. The snug downstairs dining area has both a sushi
bar and a cocktail bar, surrounded by tables of varying sizes. Upstairs,
you can dine outside in a more relaxed patio setting. *Ceviche* is your best
bet for starters, followed by rounds of fresh, delicious, and imaginative
(by local standards, anyway) sushi. Don't miss spot-on interpretations
of Peruvian recipes that were imported directly from the chain's Lima
location, like the *Misoudado*, an amazing red-curry grouper. ⊠ *Soler
5608, Palermo, Buenos Aires, Buenos Aires* ☎ *11/4775–6964* ⊕ *www.
osaka.com.pe* ⊘ *Closed Sun.* ✛ *1:E3.*

$$ ✕ **Quimbombó.** In a beautiful, tri-level, sunlit space overlooking Plaza
VEGETARIAN Armenia, chef Daniel López Martitegui serves up the most creative food
on the plaza—do your best to get a table looking out one of the high
windows. In general, the fare here is lighter, healthy options, with a
good number of vegetarian dishes. The food is delightfully spiced with
blends from Asia, India, and wherever the chef's mind wanders. Cocktails and teas are tasty, but tend to be made on the sweet side unless
you ask for them otherwise. The vegetable carpaccio salad and various
wraps are the best dishes on the menu. ⊠ *Costa Rica 4562, on Plaza
Armenia, Palermo Soho, Buenos Aires, Buenos Aires* ☎ *11/4831–5556*
Ⓜ *D to Scalabrini Ortíz* ✛ *1:F5.*

$$$ ✕ **Rio Alba.** In terms of quality, price, and charm, this is the best parrilla
STEAKHOUSE in Buenos Aires. Period. It consistently serves the tastiest and tenderest
Fodor's Choice cuts of beef. The *asado de tira* is particularly good, as is the flavorful
★ *entrana.* Ask for a minigrill at your table to keep your meat warm;
you're going to need time to finish the enormous servings. The old-
school waiters wear vests and bow ties and refuse to write anything
down, but they always get the order right. This place is packed every
night of the week with businesspeople and families. If you arrive after
9:30 pm, expect to wait for a table. ⊠ *Cervino 4499, Palermo, Buenos
Aires, Buenos Aires* ☎ *11/4773–5748* ✛ *1:G3.*

$ ✕ **Sarkis.** Filled with cane tables and chairs, this chaotic family-style
MIDDLE EASTERN restaurant produces great Middle Eastern food. You could easily fill up
☺ on several dishes from the large selection of mezes, which are the res-
taurant's best work. Be sure to leave room for baklava and other drip-
ping, nut-filled pastries. The place is technically in Villa Crespo, but it's
only about a block from Palermo Soho, across Avenida Córdoba. Most
nights there are belly dancers and palm readers wandering through the
restaurant. Arrive early or expect to wait for a table. ⊠ *Thames 1101,
at Jufré, Palermo, Buenos Aires, Buenos Aires* ☎ *11/4772–4911* ▭ *No
credit cards* ✛ *1:D5.*

$$ ✕ **Siamo nel Forno.** Every country has its own style of pizza and in
PIZZA Argentina it's piled high with cheese. It's not for everyone, and *pizzero*
Nestor Gattorna took another route, spending a year studying tradi-
tional techniques in Naples. He even imported a wood-burning oven,

Japanese style meets Peruvian panache at Osaka.

and brings in specially milled flour and olive oil, all to reproduce the best of Neapolitan-style pizza in the heart of Palermo. Italophiles jam into the place for a bite of one of his smoky, perfectly charred pies and equally good *calzones*. Try a delicious specialty like his potato pizza or end the meal with a "white pie" chockful of nutella. ⊠ *Costa Rica 5886, Palermo, Buenos Aires, Buenos Aires* ☎ *11/5290–9529* ⊘ *No lunch except Sun.* Ⓜ *D to Ministro Carranza* ✛ *1:D3.*

$$ ✕ **Social Paraíso.** Simple, airy, friendly, elegant—this Med-Argentine bis-
ARGENTINE tro has just the vibe for a lunch or dinner stop after a round of shopping. Pastas such as ravioli are best. Vegetarians will also be happy here, with inventive entrées that feature meaty vegetables like eggplant. Social Paraíso has kept its prices low even as its fame has grown, and the two-course lunch is always a steal. It gets crowded and loud in here, but that adds to the charm. You can practically sit inside the kitchen and watch the young cooks work their magic. A small open-air patio fits a few tables; if the weather and mood are right, ask to sit outside. ⊠ *Hondu-ras 5182, Palermo Soho, Buenos Aires, Buenos Aires* ☎ *11/4831–4556* ⊘ *Closed Mon. No dinner Sun.* ✛ *1:E4.*

$$$$ ✕ **Te Mataré, Ramírez.** Te Mataré Ramírez, which translates as "I Will
ECLECTIC Kill You, Ramirez," is as unusual as it sounds. This self-styled "erotic restaurant" seduces with dishes such as "You Surrender to My Inti-mate Perversions" (roast lamb with fennel, celery, quinoa, and cream hummus) and desserts like "Do What I'm Doing to You" (a four-layer *alfajor,* with cocoa, peanut butter, and red tart sauce). Tuesday through Thursday the temperature rises with a tastefully done "erotic theater" show, and Monday night brings live jazz and bossa nova. From behind

the bar come all variety of cocktails to sip as you peruse the illustrated menu or gaze at the restaurant's erotic art collection. ⊠ *Gorriti 5054, Palermo Soho, Buenos Aires, Buenos Aires* ☎ *11/4831–9156* ⊕ *www. tematareramirez.com* ⊟ *No credit cards* ⊗ *No lunch* Ⓜ *D to Plaza Italia* ✛ *1:E4.*

$$$$ ✕ **Tegui.** Local culinary hotshot German Martitegui has enjoyed tre-
ECLECTIC mendous success with his two other BA endeavors, Ølsen and Casa
Fodor's Choice Cruz, and in 2009 opened Tegui, a slick spot that gets high marks for
★ its high-concept cuisine but disastrous grades for its snide service. An unassuming, unmarked entrance leads to a long, thin room decorated in black and white, with leather benches and stylish upholstered chairs. A garden allows for alfresco dining, and an 8-seat private dining room gives a sneak peak into the open-aired kitchen. The menu is fixed-price, offering four choices each for starters, entrées, and desserts. The cow-brain pie with prosciutto and shallot cream sauce is divine, as are the rabbit-stuffed ravioli with truffle sauce and peaches. The wine list is extensive but outrageously priced. Regardless, the food is inspiring, and worth a visit. ⊠ *Costa Rica 5852, Palermo, Buenos Aires, Buenos Aires* ☎ *11/5291–3333* ⊕ *www.tegui.com.ar* ⊗ *Closed Sun.–Mon.* ✛ *1:D3.*

$ ✕ **Xalapa.** You can guess what you're in for when the entry vista is
MEXICAN dominated by frozen margarita machines and bags of supermarket corn chips. Clueless service is the order of the day. But wait: this place serves up some of the best Mexican food in town—more Tex-Mex than traditional, but one of the few places that will make things truly spicy on request and actually serves up some reasonably authentic fare. Then again, they have little competition. Don't expect to be wowed, but an ice-cold beer or margarita with a plate or two of *quesadillas* or the delicious *tacos al pastor* may just hit the spot. ⊠ *El Salvador 4800, Palermo Soho, Buenos Aires, Buenos Aires* ☎ *11/4833–6102* ⊟ *No credit cards* ⊗ *No lunch weekdays* ✛ *1:E5.*

BELGRANO AND LAS CAÑITAS

BELGRANO

$$$ ✕ **Bruni.** This Italian restaurant has helped reinvigorate what was a
ITALIAN staid culinary enclave on Sucre Street in Bajo Belgrano. The corner spot is owned by two rock stars of the Argentine gastronomy scene: restaurateur and musician Fabian "Zorro" Von Quintiero and Donato De Santis, a native of Italy who is one of Argentina's most recognizable chefs. The duo hits the mark with Bruni, offering up fresh and authentic Italian dishes in a lively and lovely environment. The pastas are made fresh on-site with a machine imported from Italy. Don't miss the mouth-watering *burratta* with prosciutto or the rucula risotto served with Patagonian ribs. Finish things off with *affogato*, a smorgasbord of gelato, chocolate, sambuca, amaretto, and espresso that is truly to die for. ⊠ *Sucre 696, Belgrano, Buenos Aires, Buenos Aires* ☎ *11/4783–6267* ⊗ *No lunch* ✛ *1:E1.*

$$$ ✕ **BuddhaBA.** An oasis of calm and haute cuisine in the heart of BA's
ASIAN Chinatown, BuddhaBA is one part pan-Asian restaurant, one part tea garden, and one part art gallery. Service is understated, but always gracious, and the food is a pleasure to both look at and eat. The best dish

on the menu is the *Pâté Imperial*, a unique twist on the classic Vietnamese *banh mi* sandwich, reinterpreted as a pair of long, delicate, crispy spring rolls. The Chinese sweet-and-sour dishes are always delicious, if sometimes erring a trifle on the sweet side. Finish up with a pot of tea, perhaps out in the garden during nice weather. ⊠ *Arribeños 2288, at Olazabal, Retiro, Buenos Aires, Buenos Aires* ☎ *11/4706–2382* ⊕ *www.buddhaba.com.ar* ⊙ *Closed Mon.* Ⓜ *D to Juramento* ✛ *1:C1.*

$$
STEAKHOUSE
✕ **El Pobre Luis.** It's worth a visit to this Belgrano parrilla just to see the impressive collection of sports memorabilia, especially soccer jerseys autographed by some of the sport's legends. Fortunately, the food is fantastic, too. Jovial owner Luis Acuna ("Poor Luis") is from Uruguay, and serves some of that country's signature dishes, like *pamplona:* grilled meat, vegetables, cheese, and spices rolled into a wrap. This place packs in a raucous clientele, and the service suffers as a result. But the good food and fun atmosphere make it well worth the trip. ⊠ *Arribenos 2393, Belgrano, Buenos Aires, Buenos Aires* ☎ *11/4780–5847* ⊙ *Closed Sun.* ✛ *1:C1.*

$$$
THAI
✕ **Lotus Neo Thai.** Like the proverbial tortoise, Buenos Aires' first Thai restaurant has kept a slow, steady pace and outlasted all other Southeast Asian comers, while at the same time moving locations one by one to its most recent incarnation in the city's Chinatown on the north side. Huge glowing flowers dominate the decor, and there's perhaps a bit too much incense filling the air. While by international standards the food here won't amaze anyone, in a city with few Thai options it's a change of pace, primarily for expats missing the cuisine or locals looking to try something different. The options are fresh and tasty, particularly the curries, though if you want any heat, don't forget to tell them you really do want it *picante*. Portions can be a bit skimpy, given the prices, though there are lunch prix-fixe options that are more wallet friendly. ⊠ *Arribeños 2265, Belgrano, Buenos Aires, Buenos Aires* ☎ *11/4783–7993* ⊕ *www.lotusneothai.com* ⊙ *No lunch Mon.* Ⓜ *D to Juramento* ✛ *1:C1.*

$$$
ARGENTINE
Fodor's Choice
★
✕ **Pura Tierra.** Set in a charming, converted Belgrano home, chef Martín Molteni's creative dining room offers up a tribute to the lesser known products of Argentina. Specializing in unusual meats—llama, wild boar, rabbit, and quail are regular offerings—as well as fresh fish, unusual grains and vegetables, and hand-crafted cheeses, he brings his overseas training in France and Australia to bear on his Argentine heritage. The menu changes completely every 2–3 months to reflect the freshest in seasonal ingredients. While the menu doesn't list vegetarian options, give advance notice when you reserve, and the kitchen will turn out equally stunning vegetable plates. A chef's tasting menu is also available. ⊠ *3 de Febrero 1167, Belgrano, Buenos Aires, Buenos Aires* ☎ *11/4899–2007* ⊕ *www.puratierra.com.ar* ⊙ *Closed Sun.* ✛ *1:C1.*

$$$
ARGENTINE
✕ **Sucre.** "Cavernous" is the first thought that comes to mind upon entering this near-three-story concrete and metal space with a backlit bar taking up one entire wall, an open kitchen dominating the rear, and a hulking concrete-and-glass wine cave smack in the center of the dining area. Sucre was and is the cutting edge of cuisine in Bajo Belgrano, and though it's way off the beaten path, it is well worth the trip. Enjoy the delicious and creative appetizers, but save room for a main course

Staying Up with the Porteños

Buenos Aires is a 24-hour city, and you *can* find places that serve food around the clock, but most of these are downtown and tend to fall into the fast-food and pizza categories. Although much is made about porteños' late eating habits, the truth is the ideal and the most popular dining time is 9–9:30 pm (though you can easily show up for dinner at midnight and no one will blink an eye). Most restaurants open at 8 pm for dinner

and will serve until 1 or 2 am. You can find more late-night *confiterias* (confectioneries) and cafés in the Centro area; most other neighborhoods have scarce late-night offerings.

You can find breakfast—coffee and pastries—anywhere, at any time. Lunch is served from noon to 4 pm, 1–2 pm being the rush hour, especially downtown, which is packed with office workers.

5

straight off the wood-fired grill: spit-roasted *bondiola* (pork shoulder) and melt-in-your-mouth Patagonian lamb are among the stars, but any meat or fish coming off the *parrilla* is going to be a winner and be accompanied by something far more creative than the ubiquitous french fry *guarnición*. Locals and tourists alike fill the room, and with no soft surfaces it can get loud. ⊠ *Sucre 676, Belgrano, Buenos Aires, Buenos Aires* ☎ *11/4782–9082* ⊕ *www.sucrerestaurant.com.ar* ✛ *1:C1.*

LAS CAÑITAS

$$ ✕ **El Estanciero.** It perfectly captures the vibrancy of Las Cañitas: even on
STEAKHOUSE weekdays you can see groups casually ambling in to dine at El Estanciero as late as midnight. They come for the juicy steaks and *achuras* (innards), all of which are grilled over an open fire in full view. Grab one of the tables on the open second floor and you'll get an even better view of the parrilla and the action outside. Ask for your steak *vuelta y vuelta* (rare) for best results. ⊠ *Báez 202, at Argüibel, Las Cañitas, Buenos Aires, Buenos Aires* ☎ *11/4899–0951* Ⓜ *D to Ministro Carranza* ✛ *1:E2.*

$ ✕ **Morelia.** The typical style of pizza that visitors and locals have come
PIZZA to expect in Argentina is with medium crust, little sauce, and mounds of melted cheese. But long before the grilled pizza became commonplace in northern climes it was already part of local tradition, where pizza dough was tossed on the grill, cooked quickly like a flatbread and then topped with favored ingredients. The best for this style in town is Morelia, with this branch on the trendy restaurant row of Báez, and another in Palermo at Humboldt and Nicaragua. Choose your favorite topping combination, though a perennial favorite is the *Montecattini* with prosciutto and arugula. In nice weather grab a seat on the rooftop terrace, one of the best spots to eat pizza in town. ⊠ *Báez 260, Las Cañitas, Buenos Aires, Buenos Aires* ☎ *11/4772–0329* ▭ *No credit cards* ☽ *No lunch* Ⓜ *D to Ministro Carranza* ✛ *1:E2.*

$$ ✕ **Novecento.** Originally founded in New York and Florida, these bistro-
ARGENTINE style spots were a successful attempt to bring Argentine food to the States. Doing the same back home in Argentina didn't make sense, so

the trend was reversed and the theme is North American specialties like burgers, sandwiches, salads, and some more interesting plates—the grilled salmon is a winner. Novecento is known in the expat community for serving up one of the best *norteamericano* brunches around town; on weekends crowds flock in looking for a taste of home, mixing it up with neighborhood families checking out the fare. ✉ *Báez 199, Las Cañitas, Buenos Aires, Buenos Aires* ☎ *11/4778–1900* ⊕ *www. novecento.com* Ⓜ *D to Ministro Carranza* ⚓ *1:E2.*

Buenos Aires Dining and Lodging

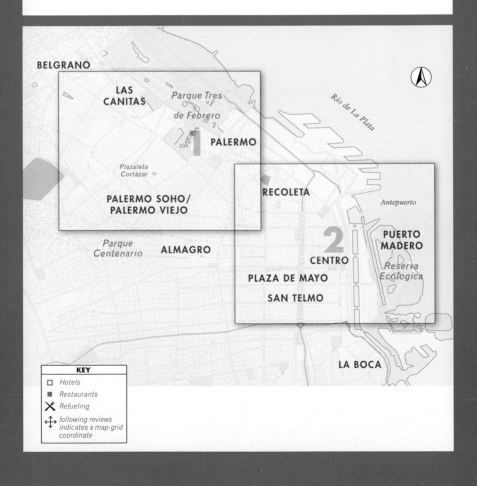

BELGRANO

LAS CANITAS

Parque Tres de Febrero

PALERMO

Plazaleta Cortázar

PALERMO SOHO/ PALERMO VIEJO

RECOLETA

Río de La Plata

Antepuerto

PUERTO MADERO

Reserva Ecológica

Parque Centenario

ALMAGRO

2 CENTRO

PLAZA DE MAYO

SAN TELMO

LA BOCA

KEY

□ Hotels
■ Restaurants
✕ Refueling
⟷ following reviews indicates a map-grid coordinate

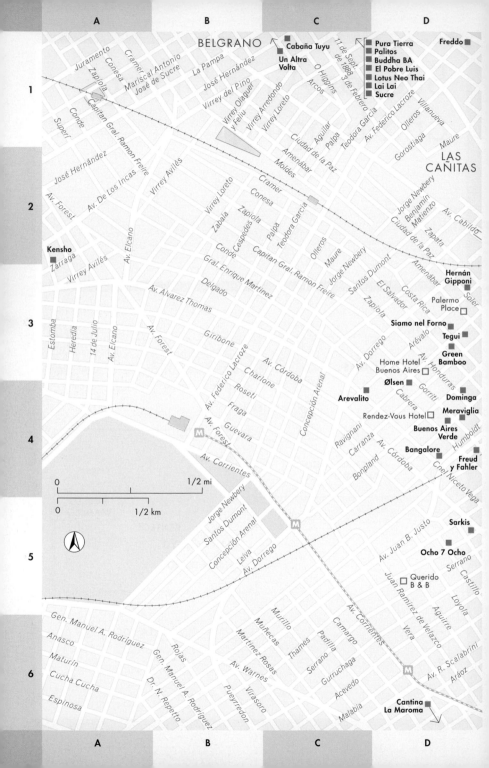

BELGRANO

Cabaña Tuyu
Un Altra Volta

Pura Tierra
Palitos
Buddha BA
El Pobre Luis
Lotus Neo Thai
Lai Lai
Sucre

Freddo

LAS CAÑITAS

Kensho

Hernán Gipponi

Palermo Place

Siamo nel Forno
Tegui
Green Bamboo

Home Hotel Buenos Aires

Ølsen
Dominga

Arevalito

Meraviglia
Rendez-Vous Hotel

Buenos Aires Verde

Bangalore
Freud y Fahler

Sarkis

Ocho 7 Ocho

Querido B & B

Cantina La Maroma

0 ——————— 1/2 mi

0 ——————— 1/2 km

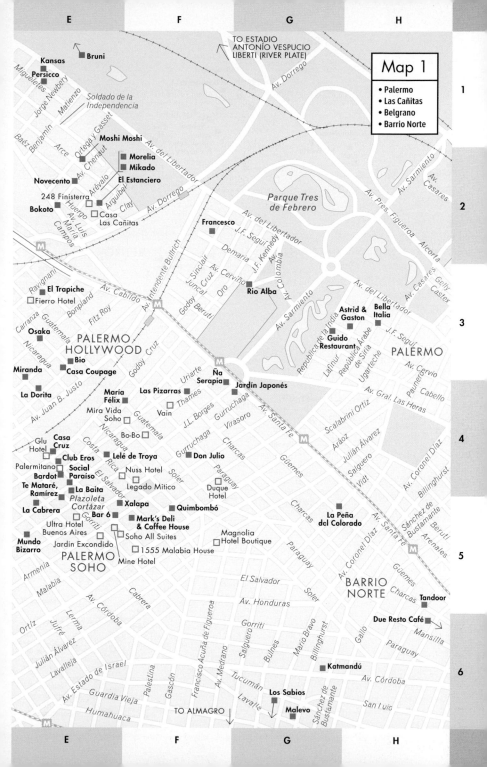

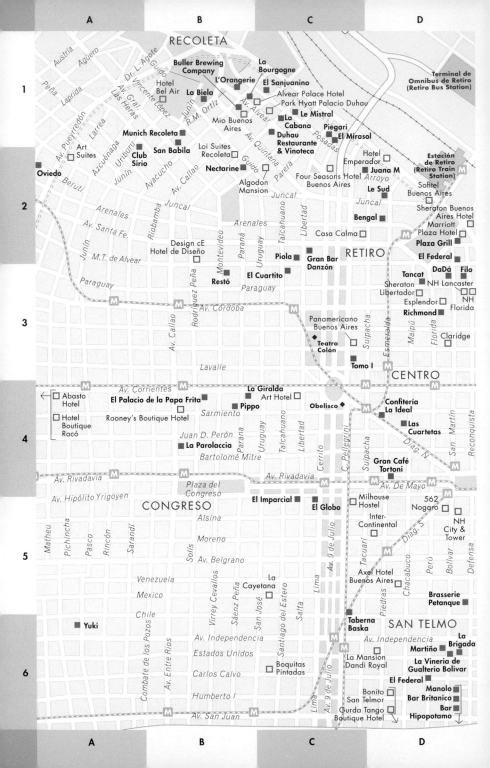

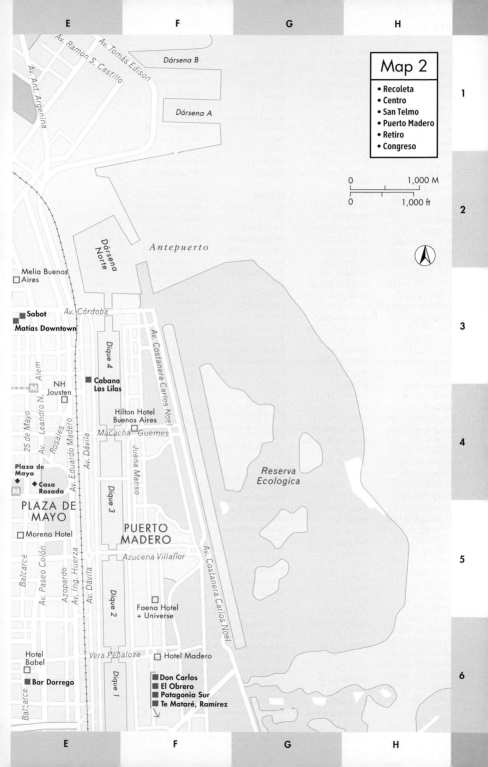

Where to Stay

WORD OF MOUTH

"Well, I wouldn't rule out Palermo as a good neighborhood—especially Palermo Botanico and Palermo Soho. You might want to check some of the boutique hotels there. We feel quite safe in these parts of Palermo, and not far from so many lovely parks. However, I absolutely love Recoleta."

—MarnieWDC

By Karina
Martinez-Carter

In Buenos Aires, European elegance collides with Latin American style, with creative, animated, and ever-morphing results. The neighborhoods of Buenos Aires each have their own energy and spirit, and hotels tend to both mimic the identity of their neighborhood and help to shape it.

The lodging options in Buenos Aires are some of the most impressive of any international, cosmopolitan locale. From luxurious, majestic hotels (many with recognizable chain names) to boutique hotels operating a handful of rooms and injected with local flair, one thing is certain: you're bound to encounter plenty of attractive lodging options. Though prices have climbed in Argentina in recent years, the city is still highly affordable for international visitors on the dollar, euro, and real, and people continue to flock here. Many visitors, having discovered the intoxicating energy of the city, return again and again. Hotel owners and staff are some of the key players in helping people to fall in love with the city or lure them back, as hotels are constantly opening, renovating, and amplifying their offerings.

Downtown—in the Centro and Puerto Madero—you'll find sleek, soaring hotel properties; inch toward Recoleta and you can choose from some of the ritziest hotels in town, especially around Avenida Alvear and the Recoleta Cemetery. Boutique hotels are where Buenos Aires' options really shine, and while intimate, stylish spots dot most of the city's neighborhoods, they are found in greatest concentration in the vast, hip barrio of Palermo, as well as in nearby Las Cañitas. San Telmo is one of the city's oldest neighborhoods, steeped in porteño history. Almagro, Villa Crespo, and Abasto are more working-class neighborhoods, and a stay in one will bring you close to the everyday life of Buenos Aires residents. Each neighborhood offers visitors the chance to experience one facet of the buzzing, intriguing city of Buenos Aires.

PLANNING

Buenos Aires has chain hotels, boutique hotels, apart-hotels (short-term rental apartments), bed-and-breakfasts, hostels—you name it. World-class facilities include the majestic Alvear Palace Hotel, the ultrahip Faena Hotel + Universe, and the luxurious Four Seasons—all celebrity favorites. High season includes the summer months of mid-December through February and the winter holidays that fall in July. (Keep in mind that seasons in the Southern Hemisphere are opposite those in the Northern Hemisphere.) Most hotels try to have at least one English-speaking employee on call at a given time.

RESERVATIONS

Buenos Aires has steadily climbed as a popular tourist destination, a trend that shows little signs of slowing. As a result, many hotels are at full capacity year-round, not just in the October–March high season. It is always best to make a reservation as early as possible. Most hotels in the city have Web sites equipped with online reservation services. Some require a credit card.

FACILITIES

In general, hotels have bidets and high-speed Internet, but not, say, ice makers or vending machines. Although Internet access is available in nearly every hotel in the city, the kind of access varies. The majority of hotels offer Wi-Fi in rooms, though some charge guests extra for the service. Cable television is a near sure bet in your room as well, and many favorite U.S. television programs play around the clock in Argentina, often subtitled. English-language news channels will be harder to find, though.

CHECK-IN/OUT

As a rule, check-in is after 3 pm, and check-out is before noon; smaller hotels tend to be more flexible.

MEAL PLANS

Most hotel rates include breakfast, although with the exception of the most expensive hotels this generally means a Continental breakfast with Argentine fare, such as pastries, fruit, meats, cheese, and perhaps eggs. If you are looking for a heartier breakfast, be sure to inquire what breakfast includes when making a reservation. Remember, though, that most Argentineans eat small, simple breakfasts. Still, some properties take the extra step to shine in the morning and offer a more varied spread.

FAMILY TRAVEL

International chain hotels are always the most family-friendly, often ready with booster seats, changing tables, roll-away beds, or other family lodging necessities. Most smaller, trendy boutique hotels do not often accommodate families with children, though some are more than prepared and happy to do so. It is best to ask ahead exactly what your stay may be like with children in tow. In the listings, look for the ☾, which indicates a property that we recommend for when you're traveling with little ones.

6

USING THE MAPS

Throughout the chapter, you'll see mapping symbols and coordinates (⊕ 2:D5) after property reviews. To locate the property on the map, turn to the Buenos Aires Dining and Lodging Atlas at the end of the Where to Eat chapter. The first number after the ⊕ symbol indicates the map number. Following that is the property's coordinate on the map.

PARKING

Driving in Buenos Aires is more trouble than it's worth for a tourist. The city streets are clogged and chaotic, and parking is scarce. Renting a car for your stay will prove to be a hassle, especially considering that the public transportation system (buses and the subte) and taxis can get you anywhere you want to go. If you do have a car, some hotels provide parking, but it is usually off-site, and they will probably charge a fee, likely a minimum of 50–100 pesos per day.

PRICES

Though some small Argentinean-owned hotels advertise their rates in pesos, most places cite them in dollars. That said, always confirm which currency is being quoted. Unless there is a clearly advertised special for Argentine citizens, prices are the same for all visitors, regardless of nationality. There may be a discount if you're paying for your stay in cash. That said, some properties, especially cheaper hostel properties, only accept cash. Be sure to ask when booking. The lodging tax is 21%; this may or may not be included in a rate, so always ask about it up front.

WHAT IT COSTS IN ARGENTINE PESOS			
$	**$$**	**$$$**	**$$$$**
Hotels	under 450 pesos	451 pesos–700 pesos	701 pesos–1,000 pesos	over 1,000 pesos

Hotel prices are for two people in a standard double room in high season.

HOTEL REVIEWS

Listed alphabetically within neighborhoods. Use the coordinate (⊕ 2:D5) at the end of each listing to locate a site on the corresponding map.

For expanded hotel reviews, visit Fodors.com.

CENTRO AND ENVIRONS

CENTRO

$$ ▣ **562 Nogaro.** The gigantic red neon sign outside may need a face-lift, but the rest of this downtown hotel—open since 1936—is in decent shape. **Pros:** breakfast includes an omelet bar, a rarity in Buenos Aires. **Cons:** rooms and bathrooms are small by modern standards. ✉ *Av. Julio A. Roca 562, Centro* ☎ *11/4331–0091* ⊕ *www.562nogarohotel. com* ⇄ *134 rooms* ⌂ *In-room: safe, Wi-Fi. In-hotel: bar, gym, parking* ¶⊙¶ *Breakfast* Ⓜ *E to Bolivar* ⊕ *2:D5.*

WHERE SHOULD I STAY?

NEIGHBORHOOD	VIBE	PROS	CONS
CENTRO and ENVIRONS	The center of it all; you have a little bit of everything here, from history (Retiro and Congreso) to modernity (Puerto Madero). It buzzes by day, but is quiet at night.	Close to all major city sights; good transportation options to other parts of the city. If you're only in town briefly, this is your place.	Certain areas are loud, chaotic, dirty, and deserted at night, which can make them dangerous. Don't walk around alone.
LA BOCA and SAN TELMO	The oldest barrios in the city; you can get a real feel of how Buenos Aires has operated for the past 100-plus years.	Old-world charm: cobblestone streets, corner cafés, tango music. You're sure to meet some interesting characters in this area.	Streets are dark and not well policed. Limited public transportation options. Locals have been known to target tourists.
RECOLETA/BARRIO NORTE	The most upscale area of the city, home to Argentina's high society. Certain enclaves will convince you you're in Paris.	Proximity to sights in Centro. It's safe, friendly, and chic. Great eating options; high-end stores and art galleries abound.	Prices are sometimes inflated for foreigners. Streets and sights are often crowded with tourists.
PALERMO	The biggest neighborhood in the city; it's a mix of old family homes, soaring new towers, and renovated warehouses.	It's the undisputed hot spot of Buenos Aires' gastronomic scene. The city's biggest park, polo field, horse track, and casino are also here.	The über-cool attitude of some locals can be a turn-off. Quality-of-life issues like clean sidewalks and quiet streets have been ignored in recent property developments.
ALMAGRO/BELGRANO/LAS CAÑITAS	Quiet, leafy, family neighborhoods home to schools, and universities. Las Cañitas is more of a Palermo vibe, whereas Belgrano and Almagro are more no-frills, working class.	Fantastic restaurants and bars in Las Cañitas. Stately, unique homes in Belgrano. In certain areas it's easy to forget you're in a mega-metropolis.	In other areas, the main thoroughfares are packed with noisy city buses and reckless messengers on motorcycles. You're far from downtown action.

$$ 🖼 **Design cE Hotel de Diseño.** This hotel drips with coolness; rooms feel like pimped-out Tribeca lofts, with rotating flat-screen TVs that let you watch from bed or from one of the leather recliners. The lobby's glass floor looks down to a small pool, just one example of the transparency theme that runs throughout. **Pros:** supermodern and spacious suites; great location; breakfast is served 24 hours a day. **Cons:** common areas are on the small side. ⊠ *Marcelo T. Alvear 1695, Centro* ☎ *11/5237–3100* ⊕ *www.designce.com* ⤴ *20 rooms, 8 suites* ⚷ *In-room: a/c, safe, kitchen, Internet, Wi-Fi. In-hotel: bar, pool, gym* Ⓜ *D to Callao* ✛ *2:B2.*

$$$ 🖼 **Casa Calma.** This boutique property and "wellness hotel" in the heart of downtown Buenos Aires has taken the concept of in-house spa to a new level, equipping each of its 17 rooms with a Jacuzzi, and the six

Fodor's Choice
★

BEST BETS FOR
FOR BUENOS AIRES LODGING

Fodor's offers a selective listing of quality lodging experiences at every price range, from the city's best budget stay to its most sophisticated luxury hotel. Here we've compiled our top recommendations by price and experience. The very best properties—in other words, those that provide a particularly remarkable experience in their price range—are designated in the listings with the Fodor's Choice logo.

Fodor'sChoice★

1555 Malabia House, p. 244

Algodon Mansion, p. 242

Alvear Palace Hotel, p. 242

Casa Calma, p. 233

Faena Hotel + Universe, p. 238

Fierro Hotel, p. 244

Hotel Babel, p. 239

Hotel Boutique Racó, p. 244

Magnolia Hotel Boutique, p. 245

Moreno Hotel, p. 239

Rooney's Boutique Hotel, p. 237

Park Hyatt Palacio Duhau, p. 243

Sofitel Buenos Aires, p. 237

BY PRICE

$

Gurda Tango Boutique Hotel, p. 239

Hotel Babel, p. 239

Hotel Bel Air, p. 243

Hotel Boutique Racó, p. 244

$$

1555 Malabia House, p. 244

Home Hotel Buenos Aires, p. 245

Moreno Hotel, p. 239

NH City & Tower, p. 236

Rooney's Boutique Hotel, p. 237

$$$

Casa Calma, p. 233

Fierro Hotel, p. 244

The Glu Hotel, p. 245

InterContinental, p. 235

Magnolia Hotel Boutique, p. 245

Mira Vida Soho, p. 246

$$$$

Algodon Mansion, p. 242

Alvear Palace Hotel, p. 242

Faena Hotel + Universe, p. 238

Legado Mitico, p. 245

Sofitel Buenos Aires, p. 237

BY EXPERIENCE

BEST RESTAURANT

Alvear Palace Hotel, La Bourgogne and L'Orangerie, p. 242

Algodon Mansion, Chez Nous at Algodon Mansion, p. 242

BoBo, p. 244

Fierro Hotel, Hernan Gipponi, p. 244

Sofitel Buenos Aires, Le Sud, p. 237

BEST VIEWS

Hilton Hotel Buenos Aires, p. 238

Hotel Emperador, p. 235

NH City & Tower, p. 236

Soho All Suites, p. 248

BEST TO FEEL LIKE A LOCAL

Art Hotel, p. 242

Hotel Boutique Racó, p. 244

Querido B&B, p. 246

BEST PLACE FOR TANGO JUNKIES

Abasto Hotel, p. 243

Gurda Tango Boutique Hotel, p. 239

La Cayetana, p. 239

Rooney's Boutique Hotel, p. 237

BEST DESIGN

Axel Hotel Buenos Aires, p. 238

Mio Buenos Aires, p. 243

Moreno Hotel, p. 239

Palermitano, p. 246

BEST FOR ROMANCE

Alvear Palace Hotel, p. 242

Four Seasons Hotel Buenos Aires, p. 242

Legado Mitico, p. 245

Mio Buenos Aires, p. 243

Rooney's Boutique Hotel, p. 237

deluxe rooms also with saunas. **Pros:** the "honesty bar" allows guests to help themselves to juice, wine, and sweets, and counts on them to pay the tab. **Cons:** situated on a chaotic city street; during the day the movement outside can be suffocating and at night can attract some sketchy characters. ⊠ *Suipacha 1015, Centro* ☎ *11/5199–2800* ⊕ *www. casacalma.com.ar* ⇡ *17 rooms* ᴖ *In-room: safe, Wi-Fi. In-hotel: restaurant, bar, spa, laundry facilities* ✢ *2:C2.*

$$$ ⛨ **Claridge.** Tall white columns front the entrance, beyond which is the high-ceilinged lobby and a traditional British café and piano bar that draws a steady stream of politicians and businessmen. **Pros:** just blocks from shopping on Florida Street; lobby bar serves up superb, stiff cocktails. **Cons:** clientele is homogeneous—almost all retirement age; bathrooms are small. ⊠ *Tucumán 535, Centro* ☎ *11/4314–2020, 800/223–5652 in U.S., 34/902–932424 international* ⊕ *www.claridge. com.ar* ⇡ *146 rooms, 6 suites* ᴖ *In-room: safe, Internet, Wi-Fi. In-hotel: restaurant, bar, pool, gym, spa* ⵏ⵿ⵏ *Breakfast* Ⓜ *C to San Martín* ✢ *2:D3.*

$$$ ⛨ **Esplendor Buenos Aires.** This iconic building is home to downtown's brashest hotel: The Esplendor calls upon Argentine icons—Eva Perón, Che Guevara, Jorge Luis Borges, among others—to remind you just where you are; their enormous portraits line the walls of the lobby and art gallery. **Pros:** roomy suites have comfy chaise longues and the three VIP suites have in-room Jacuzzis; hotel is steps from Galerias Pacifico shopping mall. **Cons:** open-air hallways have a corporate feel; weekday traffic nearby is disconcerting. ⊠ *San Martin 780, Centro* ☎ *11/5217–5777* ⊕ *www.esplendorbuenosaires.com* ⇡ *23 rooms, 28 suites* ᴖ *In-room: safe, Internet, Wi-Fi. In-hotel: restaurant, bar, business center, parking* Ⓜ *C to San Martin* ✢ *2:D3.*

$$$ ⛨ **Hotel Emperador.** The first thing that strikes you upon entering is the magnificently ornate lobby, replete with beautiful marble floors, plush sofas, and gurgling fountains. **Pros:** fantastic location near both the business district and shopping and sights; huge, classically decorated rooms. **Cons:** hotel still charges extra for Wi-Fi service; a popular spot for corporate events, so the common areas can get chaotic. ⊠ *Av. del Libertador 420, Centro* ☎ *11/4131–4000* ⊕ *www.hotel-emperador. com.ar* ⇡ *214 rooms, 51 suites* ᴖ *In-room: safe, Wi-Fi. In-hotel: restaurant, bar, pool, gym, spa, parking* ✢ *2:D2.*

$$$ ⛨ **InterContinental.** The hotel is lovely, but the location is lousy; inside, rooms are modern, spacious, and equipped with sleeper chairs. **Pros:** modern, spacious rooms; good bar; smart staff knows how to handle expectations of foreign visitors. **Cons:** lower floors have limited views; surrounding area can be dangerous at night. ⊠ *Moreno 809, Centro* ☎ *11/4340–7100, 800/444–0022* ⊕ *www.ichotelsgroup.com/ intercontinental* ⇡ *309 rooms, 10 suites* ᴖ *In-room: safe, Internet. In-hotel: restaurant, bar, pool, gym, business center, parking* ⵏ⵿ⵏ *Breakfast* Ⓜ *E to Belgrano* ✢ *2:D5.*

$$$ ⛨ **Marriott Plaza Hotel.** This Buenos Aires landmark brims with old-school style; built in 1909 and renovated in 2003, the hotel sits at the top of pedestrian-only Florida Street and overlooks the leafy Plaza San Martín. **Pros:** elegant lobby; clean rooms; every area of the building

6

offers a unique and fascinating view of the city. **Cons:** the main lobby is small and often gets crowded; check-in can be a lengthy process, especially now that it has become a popular stop for cruise-ship passengers; rooms aren't huge. ⊠ *Florida 1005, Centro* ☎ *11/4318–3000, 800/228–9290 in U.S.* ⊕ *www.marriott.com* ↝ *270 rooms, 48 suites* ⌂ *In-room: safe, Internet. In-hotel: restaurant, bar, pool, gym* ⊺⊙⊦ *Breakfast* Ⓜ *C to San Martín* ✛ *2:D2.*

$$$ ⊞ **Meliá Buenos Aires.** In the heart of the financial district and on a pedestrian-only thoroughfare, this efficient Spanish-owned hotel is a good option for business travelers and cruise-ship visitors. **Pros:** for those looking for a night out or nightcap, the nearby pubs are hopping at night. **Cons:** the aforementioned proximity to these watering holes often means dodging inebriated office workers and backpackers on your way inside. ⊠ *Reconquista 945, Centro* ☎ *11/4891–3800* ⊕ *www. solmelia.com* ↝ *187 rooms, 22 suites* ⌂ *In-room: safe, Wi-Fi. In-hotel: restaurant, bar, pool, gym, spa, parking* ✛ *2:E3.*

$ ⊞ **Milhouse Hostel.** This lovely and lively hostel goes the extra mile to make backpackers feel welcome, with pool tables, televisions, and concierge services. **Pros:** fun and funky place; it's ideal for meeting travelers from around the world; close to all of San Telmo's nighttime offerings; there's a sister location nearby at Avenida de Mayo 1245. **Cons:** hygiene standards are sometimes below par; no a/c. ⊠ *Hipólito Yrigoyen 959, Centro* ☎ *11/4345–9604, 11/4343–5038* ⊕ *www.milhousehostel.com* ↝ *13 private rooms, 150 beds total* ⌂ *In-room: Internet, Wi-Fi. In-hotel: restaurant, bar, laundry facilities, parking* ▬ *No credit cards* ⊺⊙⊦ *Breakfast* Ⓜ *A to Piedras, C to Av. de Mayo* ✛ *2:C5.*

$$ ⊞ **NH City & Tower.** This enormous art deco hotel is a throwback to an earlier era; the contemporary rooms have dark-wood floors and color schemes that include bold oranges, reds, and black. **Pros:** old-school feel brings you back to another period in Buenos Aires' history; amazing views from the roof. **Cons:** despite its downtown location, feels isolated from other attractions; area can be sketchy at night. ⊠ *Bolívar 160, Centro* ☎ *11/4121–6464* ⊕ *www.nh-hotels.com* ↝ *369 rooms* ⌂ *In-room: safe, Internet, Wi-Fi. In-hotel: restaurant, bar, pool, gym* ⊺⊙⊦ *Breakfast* Ⓜ *A to Perú, E to Bolívar* ✛ *2:D5.*

$$ ⊞ **NH Florida.** Shiny parquet floors, extra fluffy pillows, and smiling young staffers are among the reasons to stay here. **Pros:** a block from busy Florida street; well priced. **Cons:** room views are lacking; the surrounding area is dead on weekends. ⊠ *San Martin 839, Centro* ☎ *11/4321–9850* ⊕ *www.nh-hoteles.com* ↝ *139 rooms, 21 suites* ⌂ *In-room: safe, Internet, Wi-Fi. In-hotel: restaurant, bar, parking* ⊺⊙⊦ *Breakfast* Ⓜ *C to San Martín* ✛ *2:D3.*

$$ ⊞ **NH Jousten.** The historic Jousten Building on crazy Avenida Corrientes has some of the most luxurious rooms in the NH chain, and has hosted the likes of Evita Perón over the years. **Pros:** classic charm and service make this a great choice for history buffs. **Cons:** the building dates back a century, and some of the spaces are sized to another era. ⊠ *Corrientes 280, Centro* ☎ *11/4321–6750* ⊕ *www.nh-hoteles.com* ↝ *80 rooms, 5 suites* ⌂ *In-room: safe, Internet, Wi-Fi. In-hotel: restaurant, bar* ⊺⊙⊦ *Breakfast* Ⓜ *B to L.N. Alem* ✛ *2:E4.*

$$ ⊡ **NH Lancaster.** This historic hotel got a face-lift when it was purchased and rehabbed by Spanish group NH Hotels. **Pros:** ideal for corporate types for its meeting rooms and services, as well as its proximity to the financial district. **Cons:** Avenida Cordoba is crowded and loud 24/7. ⊠ *Av. Córdoba 405, Centro* ☎ *11/4131–6464* ⊕ *www.nh-hotels.com* ⌁ *72 rooms, 18 suites* ⚬ *In-room: safe, Wi-Fi. In-hotel: restaurant, bar* ⏋◯⏉ *Breakfast* Ⓜ *C to San Martín* ✛ *2:D3.*

$$$ ⊡ **Panamericano Buenos Aires.** The popular, upscale Panamericano is
↻ near the famed Teatro Colón and the landmark Obelisco; the lobby's checked-marble floors lead to large salons, a snazzy café, and myriad conference rooms that are popular with local politicians for meetings and rallies. **Pros:** in the heart of the downtown action; amazing views of the city; spacious rooms. **Cons:** located on a busy, noisy avenue; at night sketchy characters frequent nearby bars. ⊠ *Carlos Pellegrini 551, Centro* ☎ *11/4348–5000* ⊕ *www.panamericano.us* ⌁ *267 rooms, 95 suites* ⚬ *In-room: safe, Internet, Wi-Fi. In-hotel: restaurant, bar, pool, gym, parking* Ⓜ *B to C. Pellegrini* ✛ *2:C3.*

$$ ⊡ **Rooney's Boutique Hotel.** The former boarding house on the third floor
Fodor's Choice of a century-old building is evocative of French elegance, such that one
★ would expect to find Marie Antoinette herself lolling about in the teal living area or in one of the guest rooms, all outfitted in unique pieces of antique, refurbished furniture. **Pros:** the hotel clears out one of the parlors for complimentary, nightly tango lessons. **Cons:** the location smack in the Centro near historic sites means forgoing a relaxed, neighborhood feel. ⊠ *Sarmiento 1775, Centro* ☎ *11/5252–5060* ⊕ *www. rooneysboutiquehotel.com* ⌁ *14* ⚬ *In-room: a/c, safe, Wi-Fi. In-hotel: bar* ⏋◯⏉ *Breakfast* Ⓜ *B to Callao* ✛ *2:B4.*

$$ ⊡ **Sheraton Buenos Aires Hotel.** What it lacks in intimate charm, it makes
↻ up for in practicality, professionalism, and energy. **Pros:** provides all the creature comforts you expect at home; well located; well priced. **Cons:** for some, perhaps overwhelmingly big; rooms could use a sprucing up. ⊠ *San Martín 1225, Centro* ☎ *11/4318–9000, 800/325–3535 in U.S.* ⊕ *www.sheraton.com/buenosaires* ⌁ *711 rooms, 29 suites* ⚬ *In-room: safe, Internet. In-hotel: restaurant, bar, pool, tennis court, gym, parking* ⏋◯⏉ *Breakfast* Ⓜ *C to Retiro* ✛ *2:D2.*

$$$ ⊡ **Sheraton Libertador.** It's on chaotic Avenida Córdoba, so you're better off choosing it if you're here in town on business or if you're looking for American-style service and nothing more. **Pros:** professional, no-nonsense staff; centrally located. **Cons:** on a noisy avenue; lacks charm. ⊠ *Av. Córdoba 690, Centro* ☎ *11/4321–0000* ⊕ *www.sheraton.com* ⌁ *193 rooms, 4 suites* ⚬ *In-room: safe, kitchen, Internet. In-hotel: restaurant, bar, pool, gym* ⏋◯⏉ *Breakfast* Ⓜ *C to Lavalle* ✛ *2:D3.*

$$$$ ⊡ **Sofitel Buenos Aires.** Built in 1929 by a Yugoslavian shipping magnate,
Fodor's Choice the tower was the tallest building in the city for some years; left to disre-
★ pair, it was restored and renovated by Sofitel in 2003, and is now one of the classiest hotels in Buenos Aires, known for its understated elegance with French flair. **Pros:** on a quiet, swanky street lined with art galleries; lovely beds and amenities. **Cons:** the lobby can get crowded and noisy during receptions and art-gallery exhibition openings. ⊠ *Arroyo 841, Centro* ☎ *11/4131–0000* ⊕ *www.sofitelbuenosaires.com.ar* ⌁ *115*

6

rooms, 28 suites ⚐ *In-room: safe, Internet, Wi-Fi. In-hotel: restaurant, bar, pool, gym, spa, parking* Ⓜ *C to San Martin* ✢ *2:D2.*

PUERTO MADERO

$$$$ 🖭 **Faena Hotel + Universe.** Argentine fashion impresario Alan Faena and
Fodor's Choice famed French architect Philippe Starck set out to create a "universe"
★ unto itself, and they have succeeded in spades: Rooms are feng-shui
perfect, with rich reds and crisp whites, sporting velvet curtains and
Venetian blinds opening electronically to river and city views. **Pros:**
quite simply, one of the most dramatic hotels on the planet; luxury
abounds; feng shui galore. **Cons:** an "are you cool enough?" vibe is
ever-present. ✉ *Martha Salotti 445, Puerto Madero* 🕾 *11/4010–9000*
⊕ *www.faenahotelanduniverse.com* ⤳ *110 rooms, 16 suites* ⚐ *In-
room: safe, Internet, Wi-Fi. In-hotel: restaurant, bar, pool, gym, parking* ⏐◉⏐ *Breakfast* ✢ *2:G5.*

$$$ 🖭 **Hilton Hotel Buenos Aires.** This massive glass-and-steel structure puts
ↁ you close to downtown *and* the restaurants and fresh air of Puerto
Madero. **Pros:** well priced, well run, and well located. **Cons:** popular
with conventioneers and cruise-ship groups, which often means lots
of people try to check in and out at the same time; no subte service
nearby. ✉ *Macacha Guemes 351, Puerto Madero* 🕾 *11/4891–0000,
800/774–1500 in U.S.* ⊕ *www.hilton.com* ⤳ *418 rooms, 13 suites*
⚐ *In-room: safe, Internet. In-hotel: restaurant, bar, pool, gym, parking*
⏐◉⏐ *Breakfast* ✢ *2:F4.*

$$ 🖭 **Hotel Madero.** This slick hotel is within walking distance of downtown as well as the riverside ecological reserve, and is a favorite for
visiting British rock stars and fashion photographers. **Pros:** the lobby
bar attracts a cool after-office crowd, and has some of the most original cocktails in the city. **Cons:** the gym and pool are in cramped quarters; extra fee for Internet service; no subte service nearby. ✉ *Rosario
Vera Peñaloza 360, Dique 2, Puerto Madero* 🕾 *11/5776–7777* ⊕ *www.
hotelmadero.com* ⤳ *169 rooms, 28 suites* ⚐ *In-room: safe, Internet,
Wi-Fi. In-hotel: restaurant, bar, pool, gym* ⏐◉⏐ *Breakfast* ✢ *2:F6.*

LA BOCA AND SAN TELMO

$$ 🖭 **Axel Hotel Buenos Aires.** Billed as Latin America's first gay hotel, the
Axel Hotel Buenos Aires is modeled after the successful original hotel
in Barcelona. **Pros:** gigantic outside pool, bar, and deck area offer an
upbeat and festive environment, a respite from the chaotic city streets.
Cons: rooms are small and very close together; the doors and balco-
nies practically sit on top of each other, so privacy is at a minimum.
✉ *Venezuela 649, San Telmo* 🕾 *11/4136–9393* ⊕ *www.axelhotels.com*
⤳ *48 rooms* ⚐ *In-room: safe, Wi-Fi. In-hotel: restaurant, bar, pool,
gym, parking* Ⓜ *E to Belgrano* ✢ *2:D5.*

$ 🖭 **Bonito San Telmo.** Formerly the Cocker, Bonito is in an art nouveau
mansion on a bustling avenue in San Telmo. **Pros:** a rooftop garden
offers a wonderful cityscape, and is filled with plants and flowers; hum-
mingbirds and butterflies stop by often. **Cons:** the metal spiral staircase
(there is no elevator) connecting the rooms with the common areas
can cause vertigo in the faint of heart. ✉ *Av. Juan de Garay 458, San*

Telmo ☎ *11/4362–8451* ⊕ *www.bonitobuenosaires.com* ⤐ *7 rooms* ⚴ *In-room: Wi-Fi* ⵀ❘ *Breakfast* Ⓜ *C to San Juan* ✣ *2:D6.*

$ ⊞ **Boquitas Pintadas.** The whimsically named "Little Painted Mouths" (a tribute to Manuel Puig's novel of the same name) is a self-proclaimed "pop hotel," and the German owner, Heike Thelen, goes out of her way to keep things weird and wild. **Pros:** a delightfully unique place that makes for an unforgettable stay. **Cons:** use caution at night: the surrounding area is dodgy. ✉ *Estados Unidos 1393, Constitución* ☎ *11/4381– 6064* ⊕ *www.boquitas-pntadas.com.ar* ⤐ *5 rooms* ⚴ *In-room: Wi-Fi. In-hotel: restaurant, bar* ⊟ *No credit cards* Ⓜ *E to San José* ✣ *2:C6.*

$ ⊞ **Gurda Tango Boutique Hotel.** In the heart of San Telmo, the Gurda will give you a glimpse of what life was like at the turn of the 19th century. **Pros:** the young, friendly staff can organize wine tastings with local sommeliers and tango lessons. **Cons:** the entrance is right on a busy street full of buses; the restaurant and bar are noisy. ✉ *Defensa 1521, San Telmo* ☎ *11/4307–0646* ⊕ *www.gurdahotel.com* ⤐ *7 rooms* ⚴ *In-room: safe, Wi-Fi. In-hotel: restaurant, bar, parking* ⵀ❘ *Breakfast* Ⓜ *C to Constitucion* ✣ *2:D6.*

$ ⊞ **Hotel Babel.** This 200-year-old former home of late Argentine president Juan Manuel de Rosas sits on one of the city's most historic streets, exactly nine blocks from the Casa Rosada, in the heart of San Telmo. **Pros:** beautiful and welcoming lobby; only nine rooms, all lovely; guests are greeted with a complimentary glass of Argentine wine upon arrival; local artists display their works throughout the hotel and hold monthly openings. **Cons:** it's an old house: rooms are close together and the open-air patio can mean noise—and sometimes rainwater—outside your door. ✉ *Balcarce 946, San Telmo* ☎ *11/4300–8300* ⊕ *www. hotelbabel.com.ar* ⤐ *9 rooms* ⚴ *In-room: safe, Wi-Fi. In-hotel: bar* ⵀ❘ *Breakfast* ✣ *2:E6.*

Fodor'sChoice ★

$$ ⊞ **La Cayetana.** This reformed *casa chorizo*—named such because the connected rooms resemble the links of a chorizo sausage—dates back to 1820, a fact that won't escape you as you enter the long, open-air entrance with plants and fountains on the left and rooms on the right. **Pros:** a cozy common area and well-stocked library are perfect for relaxing and reading; a *parrilla* (grill) is available if you feel like trying your hand at an Argentine *asado* (barbecue). **Cons:** a bit off the beaten path; the neighborhood can be dodgy at night, so take a taxi. ✉ *Mexico 1330, San Telmo* ☎ *11/4383–2230* ⊕ *www.lacayetanahotel.com.ar* ⤐ *11 rooms* ⚴ *In-room: safe, Wi-Fi. In-hotel: parking* ⵀ❘ *Breakfast* ✣ *2:C5.*

$$ ⊞ **La Mansión Dandi Royal.** For a glimpse of early-20th-century high society, look no further than this hotel, where 20 exquisite rooms are decorated with classic wood furnishings and period murals. **Pros:** a tango junkie's heaven; stunning interiors. **Cons:** the surrounding streets are often populated with unsavory characters. ✉ *Piedras 922/936, San Telmo* ☎ *11/4361–3537* ⊕ *www.mansiondandiroyal.com* ⤐ *20 rooms* ⚴ *In-room: safe, Internet, Wi-Fi. In-hotel: bar, pool, gym, spa, parking* Ⓜ *C to San Juan* ✣ *2:D6.*

$$ ⊞ **Moreno Hotel.** A gorgeous art deco building dating back to 1929, Fodor'sChoice the Moreno's architects were posed with the challenge of restoring the ★ 80-year-old site without disturbing its original elements, like mosaic

6

Faena Hotel + Universe

Algodon Mansion

Alvear Palace Hotel

Park Hyatt Palacio Duhau

Sofitel Buenos Aires

Casa Calma

tiling and stained-glassed windows; the seven-floor hotel has spacious and sexy rooms, each decorated in a color motif complete with chaise longues, Argentine cowhide rugs, and big fluffy beds. **Pros:** there's a top-notch restaurant and 130-seat theater on-site. **Cons:** some rooms are just steps away from the main lobby and elevator. ⊠ *Moreno 376, San Telmo* ☎ *11/6091–2003* ⊕ *www.morenobuenosaires.com* 🖙 *39 rooms* ☖ *In-room: safe, Internet, Wi-Fi. In-hotel: restaurant, bar, gym, parking* ❤ *Breakfast* Ⓜ *A to Plaza de Mayo* ✛ *2:E5.*

RECOLETA, BARRIO NORTE, AND ALMAGRO

RECOLETA

$$$$ 🖩 **Algodon Mansion.** It is clear every detail of this hotel, one of the ritzi-
Fodor's Choice est properties in the city, that a guest's stay was considered through and
★ through: Private concierge services contact each guest ahead of time to begin preparing an itinerary, and, once they arrive, guests are welcomed with a drink, have a butler tend to them throughout their stay, and can request whatever they desire for breakfast. **Pros:** the Algodon brand also operates a vineyard in Mendoza, and each room comes with a compli-mentary bottle of wine. **Cons:** the draw of the hotel's bars and restau-rant means a number of non-guests are in and out. ⊠ *Montevideo 1647, Recoleta* ☎ *11/3535–1367* ⊕ *www.algodonmansion.com* 🖙 *10 suites* ☖ *In-hotel: restaurant, bar, pool* ❤ *Breakfast* Ⓜ *D to Callao* ✛ *2:C2.*

$$$$ 🖩 **Alvear Palace Hotel.** The Alvear Palace has been the standard-bearer
Fodor's Choice for upscale sophistication since 1932, and is undoubtedly the shining
★ star of Buenos Aires' hotel offerings; scores of dignitaries, celebrities, and VIPs have passed through its doors over the years, and they keep coming back for the world-class service and atmosphere. **Pros:** gor-geously appointed rooms; the beautiful spa features therapeutic wave pools, a sauna, and steam rooms. **Cons:** bathrooms are on the small side, owing to the building's age; one of the country's most expensive hotels. ⊠ *Av. Alvear 1891, Recoleta* ☎ *11/4808–2100, 11/4804–7777, 800/448–8355 in U.S.* ⊕ *www.alvearpalace.com* 🖙 *97 rooms, 100 suites* ☖ *In-room: safe, Internet, Wi-Fi. In-hotel: restaurant, bar, pool, gym, spa, business center* ❤ *Breakfast* ✛ *2:C1.*

$ 🖩 **Art Hotel.** The aptly named Art Hotel has an impressive ground-floor gallery where exhibits of paintings, photographs, and sculptures by acclaimed Argentine artists change monthly. **Pros:** its bohemian vibe will make you feel like you've joined an artists' colony. **Cons:** rooms are dark and somewhat antiquated. ⊠ *Azcuenaga 1268, Recoleta* ☎ *11/4821–4744* ⊕ *www.arthotel.com.ar* 🖙 *35 rooms* ☖ *In-room: safe, Internet. In-hotel: bar, pool* ❤ *Breakfast* Ⓜ *D to Pueyrredón* ✛ *2:C4.*

$$ 🖩 **Art Suites.** Perfect for businesspeople on extended stays or couples
ⓒ looking for some stretching room, this hotel's 15 suites are bright, roomy, and pleasant. **Pros:** fantastic price; friendly service. **Cons:** Wi-Fi is unreliable above the second floor. ⊠ *Azcuenaga 1465, Recoleta* ☎ *11/4821–6800* ⊕ *www.artsuites.com.ar* 🖙 *15 suites* ☖ *In-room: safe, Internet. In-hotel: parking* ❤ *Breakfast* Ⓜ *D to Pueyrredon* ✛ *2:A2.*

$$$$ 🖩 **Four Seasons Hotel Buenos Aires.** This exquisite hotel envelops you in a pampering atmosphere that screams turn-of-the-19th-century Paris. **Pros:** classic elegance; good location. **Cons:** pandemonium breaks out when rock stars stay here. ⊠ *Posadas 1086, Recoleta* ☎ *11/4321–1200* ⊕ *www.fourseasons.com/buenosaires* ↻ *116 rooms, 49 suites* ♿ *In-room: a/c, safe, Internet, Wi-Fi. In-hotel: restaurant, bar, pool, gym, spa, parking* ⓘⓞⓘ *Breakfast* ✛ *2:C2.*

$$ ⊡ **Hotel Bel Air.** Given the fancy French-style facade, you could mistake the Bel Air for a neighborhood hotel somewhere in Paris. **Pros:** great price and great location on one of the city's poshest streets. **Cons:** the staff is easily distracted; hallways and common areas are cramped. ⊠ *Arenales 1462, Recoleta* ☎ *11/4021–4000* ⊕ *www.hotelbelair.com. ar* ↻ *77 rooms* ♿ *In-room: safe, Wi-Fi. In-hotel: restaurant, bar, gym* ⓘⓞⓘ *Breakfast* Ⓜ *D to Tribunales* ✛ *2:B1.*

$$$ ⊡ **Loi Suites Recoleta.** A white-marble lobby leads to a garden area where you can enjoy a poolside breakfast or an afternoon drink. **Pros:** in the heart of swanky Recoleta, close to historic sites, museums, art fairs, and restaurants. **Cons:** despite its clean, white appearance, the place seems dated and lacks charm. ⊠ *Vicente López 1955, Recoleta* ☎ *11/5777–8950* ⊕ *www.loisuites.com.ar* ↻ *88 rooms, 24 suites* ♿ *In-room: safe, Internet. In-hotel: restaurant, bar, pool, gym, parking* ⓘⓞⓘ *Breakfast* ✛ *2:B2.*

$$$$ ⊡ **Mio Buenos Aires.** This vineyard-themed hotel juxtaposes wood pieces including hand-crafted bathtubs in rooms and wine-barrel wood doors with metals and marble to mix modern and classic styles. **Pros:** some suites include in-room saunas, others private rooftop Jacuzzis; gym, pool, and spa open 24 hours. **Cons:** with the dominance of dark colors, the business area, library, and ground floor common area feel elegant but somewhat somber. ⊠ *Avenida Quintana 465, Recoleta* ☎ *11/5295–8500* ⊕ *miobuenosaires.com* ↻ *30 rooms, 12 suites* ♿ *In-room: a/c, safe, Wi-Fi. In-hotel: restaurant, bar, pool, gym, spa, business center* ⓘⓞⓘ *Breakfast* Ⓜ *Linea D to Callao* ✛ *2:B1.*

$$$$ ⊡ **Park Hyatt Palacio Duhau.** This gorgeous hotel has upped the ante for
Fodor's Choice elegance in Buenos Aires: Its two buildings, a restored 1930s-era man-
★ sion (the palace) and a 17-story tower, are connected by an underground art gallery and a leafy garden, and the rooms are decorated in rich hues of wood, marble, and Argentine leather. **Pros:** understated elegance; great restaurant; the 3,500 bottle Wine Library and "Cheese Room" are unique attractions. **Cons:** a long walk from one side of the hotel to the other; although elegantly decorated, some of the common areas lack warmth. ⊠ *Av. Alvear 1661, Recoleta* ☎ *11/5171–1234* ⊕ *www. buenosaires.park.hyatt.com* ↻ *126 rooms, 39 suites* ♿ *In-room: a/c, safe, Internet, Wi-Fi. In-hotel: restaurant, bar, pool, gym, spa* ✛ *2:C1.*

ALMAGRO

$$ ⊡ **Abasto Hotel.** This place is *all* about the tango: Suites each have their own dance floor for private lessons, or you can join other guests for nightly tango lessons and a live show. **Pros:** if you're in Buenos Aires to tango, this is your place; large rooms. **Cons:** tango overload is a very real possibility; the furnishings and bedding are a bit tired. ⊠ *Av. Corrientes 3190, Almagro* ☎ *11/6311–4466* ⊕ *www.abastohotel.com* ↻ *120 rooms, 6 suites* ♿ *In-room: Internet, Wi-Fi. In-hotel: restaurant, bar, pool, gym* ⓘⓞⓘ *Breakfast* Ⓜ *B to Carlos Gardel* ✛ *2:A4.*

6

$
Fodor's Choice
★
Hotel Boutique Racó. Occupying a former home identical in style to the old-money mansions of San Telmo, this hotel's rooms open to the central patio, where many guests, often couples, choose to take their breakfast. **Pros:** the working-class neighborhood of Almagro where the owner was born and raised is a taste of "real" Buenos Aires and a short distance from many main attractions. **Cons:** the downstairs common area feels somewhat hodgepodge and functions as a gallery, breakfast space, bar, and wine-tasting room. ⊠ *Yapeyu 271, Almagro* ☎ *11/3530–6075* ⊕ *www.racodebuenosaires.com.ar* ⇆ *13 rooms* ⏃ *In-room: a/c, safe, Wi-Fi. In-hotel: bar* ⦿⦿ *Breakfast* Ⓜ *Linea A to Castro Barros* ✛ *2:A4.*

PALERMO

$$
Fodor's Choice
★
1555 Malabia House. Behind the unassuming white facade of this 100-year-old Palermo Soho town house and former convent is what the proprietors have dubbed Argentina's "first designer B&B." **Pros:** you can walk home from daytime shopping and nighttime carousing; a complimentary afternoon "picada" (Argentine snack tray) daily. **Cons:** it can be noisy; at the end of the day, it's still a house that was built more than a century ago. ⊠ *Malabia 1555, Palermo Soho* ☎ *11/4832–3345, 11/4833–2410* ⊕ *www.malabiahouse.com.ar* ⇆ *11 rooms, 4 suites* ⏃ *In-room: safe, Wi-Fi. In-hotel: bar, parking* ⦿⦿ *Breakfast* Ⓜ *D to Scalabrini Ortíz* ✛ *1:F5.*

$$
BoBo. Comfortable, quirky BoBo shrewdly combines the bourgeois with the bohemian. **Pros:** first-rate and friendly staff go out of their way to help you out. **Cons:** some rooms are on the small side. ⊠ *Guatemala 4870, Palermo Soho* ☎ *11/4774–0505* ⊕ *www.bobohotel.com* ⇆ *15 rooms* ⏃ *In-room: safe, Internet, Wi-Fi. In-hotel: restaurant, bar, parking* ⦿⦿ *Breakfast* Ⓜ *D to Plaza Italia* ✛ *1:F4.*

$$
Duque Hotel Boutique & Spa. This 1920s French-style hotel is fit for a duke, as the name suggests, or even a president, as the mansion is a late Argentine president's former home. **Pros:** shared common area is spacious and inviting; a dining room, business center, enclosed patio, spa, and outdoor terrace with a pool mean guests often just use rooms for sleeping. **Cons:** some rooms are on the small side. ⊠ *Guatemala 4364, Palermo Soho* ☎ *11/4832–0312* ⊕ *www.duquehotel.com* ⇆ *14 rooms* ⏃ *In-room: a/c, safe, Wi-Fi. In-hotel: restaurant, pool, spa, business center* ⦿⦿ *Breakfast* ✛ *1:F4.*

$$$
Fodor's Choice
★
Fierro Hotel. "The hotel for the gourmand" opened in late 2010 has quickly become choice lodging for visiting executives, film production teams, and all those looking for a five-star stay in a boutique package. **Pros:** the hotel's rooftop pool, heated in winter months, has skyline views of Palermo and neighboring barrios; iPads for rent at the front desk. **Cons:** while rooms are much larger (at least 42 meters) than the

city's average hotel rooms, common areas are small. ⊠ *Soler 5862, Palermo Hollywood* ☎ *11/3220–6800* ⊕ *www.fierrohotel.com* ⟿ *27 rooms* ⟳ *In-room: a/c, Wi-Fi. In-hotel: restaurant, bar, pool, gym, spa* ⍾◎⍾ *Breakfast* ✧ *1:E3.*

$$$ ⚏ **The Glu Hotel.** Run with love by the Glusman Family, this boutique hotel has 11 spacious rooms, all stylishly equipped with wood furnishings, bright wooden floors, and a small bar. **Pros:** the sauna and Scottish shower, which is a shower that alternates hot and cold water for a therapeutic effect in the small spa, are welcome treats after a long day on Palermo's cobblestone streets. **Cons:** on a busy thoroughfare with traffic and a soccer field across the street. ⊠ *Godoy Cruz 1733, Palermo* ☎ *11/4831–4646* ⊕ *www.theglu hotel.com* ⟿ *11 rooms* ⟳ *In-room: safe, Wi-Fi. In-hotel: restaurant, bar, spa* ✧ *1:E4.*

$$ ⚏ **Home Hotel Buenos Aires.** Run by Argentinean Patricia O'Shea and her British husband, Tom Rixton, a well-known music producer, Home Hotel oozes coolness and class. **Pros:** impossibly hip and fun; always interesting people staying here. **Cons:** lots of nonguests come here to hang out, reducing the intimacy factor. ⊠ *Honduras 5860, Palermo Hollywood* ☎ *11/4778–1008* ⊕ *www.homebuenosaires.com* ⟿ *14 rooms, 4 suites, 2 apartments* ⟳ *In-room: safe, Internet, Wi-Fi. In-hotel: restaurant, bar, pool, spa* ⍾◎⍾ *Breakfast* Ⓜ *D to Ministro Carranza* ✧ *1:D3.*

$$$$ ⚏ **Jardin Escondido.** This is the personal home of director Francis Ford Coppola, who lived here while filming *Tetro* in 2008 and still visits regularly. **Pros:** 24-hour concierge service; on-call sommelier and parrillero (barbecue master); a chance to mingle with creative minds from around the world. **Cons:** vibe can be pretentious and bit too Hollywood for some tastes. ⊠ *Gorriti 4746, Palermo* ☎ *800/746–3743, 501/824–4085* ⊕ *www.coppolajardinescondido.com* ⟿ *6 rooms* ⟳ *In-room: Wi-Fi. In-hotel: bar* ✧ *1:E5.*

$$$$ ⚏ **Legado Mitico.** Blessed with city's most gorgeous sitting room, the Legado Mitico transforms guests to another era by evoking the legacy of Argentine icons, after whom the hotel's 11 rooms are named. **Pros:** large, exquisitely decorated rooms provide an authentic and unique Argentine experience; on-site security guard. **Cons:** common areas and hallways are very dark, and the upstairs terrace disappoints for a property of this quality. ⊠ *Gurruchaga 1848, Palermo* ☎ *11/4833–1300* ⊕ *www.legadomitico.com* ⟿ *11 rooms* ⟳ *In-room: safe, Wi-Fi. In-hotel: bar, pool, laundry facilities* ⍾◎⍾ *Breakfast* ✧ *1:F4.*

$$$ ⚏ **Magnolia Hotel Boutique.** Magnolia Hotel feels like home—that is if
Fodor's Choice home were a high-ceilinged Palermo town house from the 1890s, com-
★ plete with wrapped staircase. **Pros:** an airy, top-floor terrace with large, plush outdoor couches and a grill; homemade baked goods at breakfast. **Cons:** some rooms require walking outdoors. ⊠ *Julián Álvarez 1746, Palermo Soho* ☎ *11/4867–4900* ⊕ *www.magnoliahotel.com.ar* ⟿ *8* ⟳ *In-room: a/c, safe, Wi-Fi* ⍾◎⍾ *Breakfast* ✧ *1:F5.*

$$$ ⚏ **Mine Hotel.** A modernist and minimalist property built of concrete and exposed stones, this boutique hotel comes complete with a cool common area, youthful staff, and a full bar and restaurant. **Pros:** a large pool surrounded by grass and a waterfall is the perfect spot to

laze away the day or usher in the night. **Cons:** rooms are on the small side, and many are very close to the outside pool area; pricey compared to other similar properties. ✉ *Gorriti 4770, Palermo* ☏ *11/4832–1100* ⊕ *www.minehotel.com* ↪ *20 rooms* ⚛ *In-room: safe, Wi-Fi. In-hotel: restaurant, bar, pool, business center* ⦿ *Breakfast* ✛ *1:E5.*

$$ 🖳 **Mira Vida Soho.** This dreamy boutique hotel is owned and operated by two German expats, and smartly combines the Old World charm of the 1930s-era building with modern touches. **Pros:** quaint, ground-floor patio is great for cocktails; the upstairs terrace has unique views of the neighborhood. **Cons:** the property is fronted by a small plaza frequented by vagrants and vandals. ✉ *Darregueyra 2050, Palermo* ☏ *11/4774–6433* ⊕ *www.miravidasoho.com* ↪ *6 rooms* ⚛ *In-room: safe, Wi-Fi. In-hotel: bar, parking* ⦿ *Breakfast* Ⓜ *D to Palermo* ✛ *1:F4.*

$$$$ 🖳 **Nuss Hotel.** Housed in a former convent on one of Palermo's most happening corners, the Nuss is a great option for those who want to be in the heart of the barrio's action. **Pros:** large, sunny lobby bar perfect for business meetings or lunch; small gym and spa perfect for working up a sweat. **Cons:** extremely small bathrooms. ✉ *El Salvador 4916, Palermo Soho* ☏ *11/4833–8100* ⊕ *www.nusshotel.com* ↪ *22 rooms* ⚛ *In-room: a/c, safe, Internet, Wi-Fi. In-hotel: restaurant, bar, pool, gym* ✛ *1:E4.*

$$ 🖳 **Palermitano.** Palermitano occupies a spot on one of the chicest strips in Palermo Soho, more than holding its own against neighboring see-and-be-seen Isabel Bar & Restaurant and upscale eateries Casa Cruz and Sipan Restaurant, which Palermitano actually houses within its own building and which guests use for breakfasts. **Pros:** spacious outdoor areas; proximity to some of the best spots in Palermo Soho. **Cons:** virtually no indoor common space, especially on the ground floor, which is evenly split between Sipan and Palermitano. ✉ *Uriarte 1648, Palermo Soho* ☏ *11/4897–2100* ⊕ *www.palermitano.biz* ↪ *14 rooms, 2 suites* ⚛ *In-room: a/c, safe, Wi-Fi. In-hotel: restaurant, bar, pool* ⦿ *Breakfast* Ⓜ *D to Plaza Italia* ✛ *1:E4.*

$$$$ 🖳 **Palermo Place.** It is all about the little touches at Palermo Place: the slippers set out by the bed, the Argentine *alfajore* cookies waiting in the fridge, the complimentary bottle of Argentine wine, and fresh fruit basket. **Pros:** a full kitchen with burners, a microwave, and dishes, which few hotels in the city can claim. **Cons:** the bathroom sink area is a tight squeeze; spotty Wi-Fi. ✉ *Nicaragua 5865, Palermo Hollywood* ☏ *11/3220–9600, 800/281–5951 U.S. and Canada only* ⊕ *www.palermoplace.com* ↪ *26 rooms* ⚛ *In-room: a/c, safe, kitchen, Wi-Fi. In-hotel: gym* Ⓜ *D to Ministro Carranza* ✛ *1:D3.*

$$ 🖳 **Querido B&B.** The biggest draw to staying at this sunny B&B is its location, the very cool yet relaxed up-and-coming neighborhood of Villa Crespo, a 10-minute walk from Palermo. **Pros:** the B&B was built from scratch on the lot, so walls are thick and things like plumbing work well; discounts for paying in cash. **Cons:** televisions are small; tall white walls surrounding the patio make it feel confining. ✉ *Juan Ramírez del Velazco 934, Villa Crespo* ☏ *11/4854–6297* ⊕ *www.queridobuenosaires.com/english* ↪ *6 rooms* ⚛ *In-room: a/c, safe, Wi-Fi* ⦿ *Breakfast* Ⓜ *B to Malabia* ✛ *1:D5.*

CLOSE UP

Homes Away From Home

Buenos Aires is bursting with an array of hotel options, but if you are looking to save money, or if you want a more independent experience, consider renting an apartment.

The options for renting in Buenos Aires run the gamut from simple and sparsely decorated apartments to enormous, luxurious homes.

The city is an exciting hodgepodge of architectural styles, so it's not unusual to see a 150-year-old home next to a gleaming 25-story apartment complex. As a result, some amenities or services are available in some properties but not in others. Make sure you ask in advance what the price includes, such as utilities, cleaning, and Internet fees.

AGENCIES

There are many apartment-rental agencies in the city, and all have Web sites where you can view photos, see a list of each apartment's amenities, and make a reservation. Many of these agencies also provide concierge service and can help you arrange an airport pick-up.

We recommend the following apartment rental agencies: ⊕ www.oasiscollections.com/buenosaires; www.takeoverba.com; www.domumbarental.com; www.spareroomsba.com; www.apartmentsba.com; www.bytargentina.com; www.alojargentina.com; www.buenosaireshabitat.com; www.waytobaway.com.

LOCATION, LOCATION

The best way to decide in which neighborhood to rent is to consider the types of activities you plan to indulge in during your stay.

Centro has fewer options than most other neighborhoods because the downtown area, for the most part, is a commercial district housing offices and government buildings. Many one- and two-bedroom apartments, however, around Plaza San Martín are good options if you prefer to be close to downtown.

In San Telmo the past is the present. With a few exceptions, most apartments in this area are two- or three-story homes that lack modern conveniences. If you're a tango junkie, then this is the barrio for you. La Boca is one of the city's dodgiest neighborhoods, and many direct tourists toward lodgings in other barrios.

In Recoleta the options are varied. The prime location and upper-crust inhabitants mean that this is likely the most expensive neighborhood in which to rent.

In Palermo fancy new apartment towers abound, matched with private homes and lofts that owners have rehabbed in ever-so-cool ways. Because Palermo is the city's largest barrio and home to the best restaurants and shopping, it is ideal for visitors who want a more residential feel and want to steer clear of tourist traps downtown.

Belgrano and Las Cañitas offer much the same choices as Palermo, but at cheaper rates. Many stately homes dot this area, and some are available for short- and long-term rentals.

6

$$ ⊡ **Rendez-Vous Hotel.** The fresh, white exterior of this French Petit Hotel pops on the streets of Palermo Hollywood, while the warm oranges, creams, and dark browns decorating the ground floor lure guests inside. **Pros:** an inviting ground floor setup, including a bar, for breakfast, drinks, reading (peruse the ample magazine offerings set out), and relaxing. **Cons:** the daily wine-tasting sessions from Anuva Wines, run by American expats, do come at an extra cost. ✉ *Bonpland 1484, Palermo Hollywood* ☎ *11/3964–5222* ⊕ *www.rendezvoushotel.com.ar* ⤢ *11 rooms* ♿ *In-room: a/c, safe, Wi-Fi. In-hotel: bar* ⦿ *Breakfast* Ⓜ *D to Ministro Carranza* ✛ *1:D4.*

$$$ ⊡ **Soho All Suites.** In the heart of Palermo Soho, this smart hotel offers
☯ sneak peaks into the backyards of the neighborhood's many private homes, where some of Argentina's coolest artists reside. **Pros:** massage parlor on-site for those urgent post-shopping sores. **Cons:** not well maintained: walls need painting and wood floors need polishing. ✉ *Honduras 4762, Palermo Soho* ☎ *11/4832–3000* ⊕ *www. sohoallsuites.com* ⤢ *21 suites* ♿ *In-room: a/c, safe, kitchen, Wi-Fi. In-hotel: bar, gym, parking* ⦿ *Breakfast* Ⓜ *D to Plaza Italia* ✛ *1:E5.*

$$$ ⊡ **Ultra Hotel Buenos Aires.** An eye-catching outdoor clock welcomes guests to this intriguing property in the heart of Palermo Soho. **Pros:** great location; attracts an in-the-know international clientele. **Cons:** a slow elevator, dirty hallways, and tired terrace and pool sap its potential. ✉ *Gorriti 4929, Palermo* ☎ *11/4833–9200* ⊕ *www.hotelultra.com* ⤢ *20 rooms* ♿ *In-room: safe, Wi-Fi. In-hotel: restaurant, bar, pool* ⦿ *Breakfast* ✛ *1:E5.*

$$ ⊡ **Vain.** This Palermo Soho spot encourages guests to "unleash" their vanity and indulge in its offerings of modern luxury and minimalist design. **Pros:** the upstairs terrace is a great place for morning breakfast, which can be made to order. **Cons:** it can be noisy: buses pass right in front, and a nearby school means the sounds of kids every afternoon. ✉ *Thames 2226, Palermo Soho* ☎ *11/4776–8246* ⊕ *www.vainuniverse. com* ⤢ *9 rooms, 6 suites* ♿ *In-room: safe, Internet, Wi-Fi. In-hotel: bar, parking* ⦿ *Breakfast* Ⓜ *D to Plaza Italia* ✛ *1:F4.*

LAS CAÑITAS

$$ ⊡ **248 Finisterra.** A mix of modern and vintage designs characterizes this boutique hotel located on the main drag of trendy Las Cañitas, where gastronomic and fashion offerings continue to grow by leaps and bounds. **Pros:** close proximity to a dozen restaurants and bars. **Cons:** tiny bathrooms and even tinier showers. ✉ *Báez 248, Las Cañitas* ☎ *11/4773–0901* ⊕ *www.248finisterra.com* ⤢ *10 rooms, 1 suite* ♿ *In-room: safe, Internet, Wi-Fi. In-hotel: bar, gym, parking* ⦿ *Breakfast* Ⓜ *D to Ministro Carranza* ✛ *1:E2.*

$ ⊡ **Casa Las Cañitas.** As its name suggests, this place feels like a home. **Pros:** good rates; perfect for those who partake in the famous "noche porteño." **Cons:** common area is small and a bit disheveled. ✉ *Huergo 283, Las Cañitas* ☎ *11/4771–3878* ⊕ *www.casalascanitas.com* ⤢ *9 rooms* ♿ *In-room: safe, Wi-Fi. In-hotel: bar, parking* Ⓜ *D to Ministro Carranza* ✛ *1:E2.*

Side Trips

TRIPS TO URUGUAY, BUENOS AIRES PROVINCE, THE COAST, AND IGUAZÚ FALLS

WORD OF MOUTH

"The zodiac plows right into the falls and we became totally drenched. It was over 100 degrees, so it felt great. This ride made the 'Maid of the Mist' at Niagara Falls seem like child's play. "

—jstoll

WELCOME TO BUENOS AIRES' ENVIRONS

TOP REASONS TO GO

★ **The Wall of Water:** Nothing can prepare you for the roaring, thunderous Cataratas del Iguazú (Iguazú Falls). We think you'll agree.

★ **Cowboy Culture:** No visit to the *pampas* (grasslands) is complete without a stay at an *estancia,* a stately ranch house, like those around San Antonio de Areco. Sleep in an old-fashioned bedroom and share meals with the owners for a true taste of the lifestyle.

★ **Colonial Days:** Gorgeous 18th- and 19th-century stone buildings line Colonia del Sacramento's cobbled streets. Many now contain the stylish bed-and-breakfasts favored by porteños looking to escape the big city.

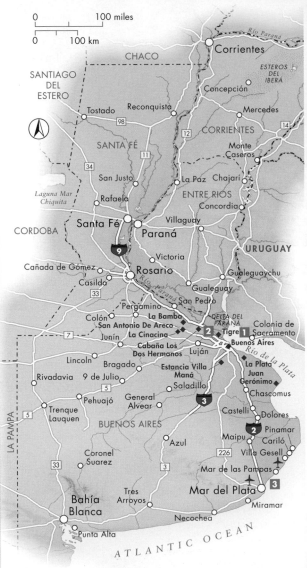

3 The Atlantic Coast.
Rolling dunes and coastal pine woods make windy Atlantic beaches peaceful places for some sea air in the low season; in summer, though, they're among Argentina's top party spots. Although they're a good escape from the city's stifle, don't expect sugary sand or crystal-clear waters.

4 Iguazú Falls (Cataratas del Iguazú). The grandeur of this vast sheet of white water cascading in constant cymbal-banging cacophony makes Niagara Falls and Victoria Falls seem sedate. Allow at least two full days to take in this magnificent sight.

1 Colonia del Sacramento, Uruguay. It's hard not to fall in love with Colonia. The picturesque town has a six-by-six-block old city with wonderfully preserved architecture, rough cobblestone streets, and a sleepy grace. Tranquility reigns here—bicycles and golf carts outnumber cars.

2 Buenos Aires Province. An hour's drive from Buenos Aires leads to varied sights. The gaucho town of San Antonio de Areco lies northwest of other sites such as the semitropical delta of the Paraná River, near the town of Tigre, and the provincial capital La Plata.

GETTING ORIENTED

Argentina's famous pampas begin in Buenos Aires Province—an unending sea of crops and cattle-studded grass that occupies nearly one-quarter of the country's landscapes. Here are the region's most traditional towns, including San Antonio de Areco. In southern Buenos Aires Province the pampas stretch to the Atlantic coast, which is dotted with resort towns that spring to life in summer. From Buenos Aires ferries cross the massive Río de la Plata (River Plate) estuary to the small Uruguayan town of Colonia del Sacramento. Suburban trains connect Buenos Aires to Tigre, close to the labyrinthine waterways of the Paraná Delta, explorable only by boat. The delta feeds the Esteros del Iberá, an immense wetland reserve hundreds of kilometers north, in Corrientes Province. On Argentina's northeastern tip, readily accessible by plane, are the jaw-dropping Cataratas del Iguazú.

7

Updated
by Victoria
Patience and
Jessica Pollack

To hear *porteños* (inhabitants of Buenos Aires) talk of their city, you'd think Argentina stops where Buenos Aires ends. Not far beyond it, however, the skies open up and the pampas—Argentina's huge flat grasslands—begin. Pampean traditions are alive and well in farming communities that still dot the plains that make up Buenos Aires Province.

The best-known is San Antonio de Areco, a well-preserved provincial town that's making a name for itself as gaucho central. You can ride across the pampas and get a taste of country life (and lots of grass-fed beef) by visiting—or staying at—a traditional estancia (ranch).

If you like your natural wonders supersized, take a short flight or a long bus-ride to Iguazú Falls, northeast of Buenos Aires in semitropical Misiones Province. Here, straddling the border between Argentina and Brazil, two natural parks contain and protect hundreds of roaring falls and a delicate jungle ecosystem. The spectacle caused Eleanor Roosevelt to exclaim "Poor Niagara!", but most people are simply left speechless by the sheer size and force of the Garganta del Diablo, the grandest falls of them all.

The sand and sea of the Atlantic coast begin just a few hours south from the capital. It might not be the Caribbean, but there's something charmingly retro about resorts like Mar del Plata. In the summer months, when temperatures in Buenos Aires soar, hordes of porteños seek relief here, and the capital's music and theater scene decamps with them, making these *the* places to see and be seen.

One of South America's most beautiful towns, Colonia del Sacramento, Uruguay, juts out on a small peninsula into the Río de la Plata and is only an hour from Buenos Aires. Here sleepy cobbled streets and colonial buildings are a reminder of days gone by.

PLANNING

WHEN TO GO

Temperatures in Buenos Aires Province rarely reach extremes. Note that some hotels and restaurants in areas popular with local tourists open *only* on weekends outside of peak season—this coincides with school holidays in summer (January and February), winter (July), and the Easter weekend. You'll get great discounts at those that open mid-week in winter.

Early November's a good time to visit San Antonio de Areco, which holds its annual gaucho festival then. Like Buenos Aires, it feels curiously empty in January, when everyone decamps to the coast. December through March is peak seaside season, and beach-town establishments are usually booked up; make advance reservations. Beaches get cold and windy in winter (June–September).

Though the falls are thrilling year-round, seasonal rainfall and upstream Brazilian barrages (minidams) can affect the falls' water volume. If you visit between November and March, booking a hotel with air-conditioning and a swimming pool is as essential as taking mosquito repellent.

BORDER CROSSINGS

U.S., Canadian, and British citizens need only a valid passport for stays of up to 90 days in Uruguay. Crossing into Brazil at Iguazú is a thorny issue. In theory, *all* U.S. citizens need a visa to enter Brazil. Visas are issued in about three hours from the Brazilian consulate in Puerto Iguazú (as opposed to the three days they take in Buenos Aires) and cost the peso equivalent of $140. The Buenos Aires consulate also has a reputation for refusing visas to travelers who don't have onward tickets from Brazil.

If you stay in Foz do Iguaçu, travel on to other Brazilian cities, or do a day trip to Brazil by public bus or through an Argentinean company, you'll need a visa. There have been reports of getting around this by using a Brazilian travel agent or by using local taxis (both Argentine and Brazilian) that have "arrangements" with border control. Though the practice is well established (most hotels and travel agents in Puerto Iguazú have deals with Brazilian companies and can arrange a visa-less visit), it *is* illegal. Enforcement of the law is generally lax, but sudden crackdowns and on-the-spot fines of hundreds of dollars have been reported.

BRAZILIAN CONSULATES

In Buenos Aires. ⊠ *Carlos Pellegrini 1363, 5th fl.* ☎ *11/4515–6500* ⊕ *www.conbrasil.org.ar.*

In Puerto Iguazú. ⊠ *Av. Córdoba 264, Puerto Iguazú* ☎ *3757/421–348.*

CAR TRAVEL

Driving is the most convenient—though rarely the cheapest—option for getting around the province. Avis, Alamo, and Hertz have branches in many large towns and cities. At this writing, gas—known as *nafta*—costs around 5.20 pesos a liter, and if you plan to drive extensively, it's worth looking into renting a vehicle running on diesel, which will reduce fuel costs significantly. There are plenty of gas stations in cities and on major highways, but they can be few and far between on rural roads. A useful Web site when planning road trips is ⊕ *www.ruta0. com*, which calculates distances and tolls between two places and offers several route options.

Be careful on the road. Argentina has one of the world's worst records for traffic accidents, and the busy highways of Buenos Aires Province are often where they happen. January and February are the worst times, when drivers anxious to get to and from their holiday destination speed, tailgate, and exercise illegal maneuvers even more alarmingly than usual. If you're driving, do so very defensively and avoid traveling on Friday and Sunday, when traffic is worst.

Expressways and interprovincial routes tend to be atrociously sign-posted, so take a map. Getting a GPS-equipped rental car costs an extra 35 pesos or so per day: devices usually work well in cities, but the calibration is often a couple of hundred yards off in rural areas. Major routes are usually privately owned, which means frequent tolls. There are sometimes alternative roads to use, but they're generally smaller, slower, and in poor condition. On main roads the speed limit is 80 kph (50 mph), while on highways it's 130 kph (80 mph), though Argentinean drivers rarely pay heed to this.

SAFETY

Provincial towns like San Antonio de Areco and Colonia del Sacramento in Uruguay are usually extremely safe, and the areas visited by tourists are well patrolled.

Puerto Iguazú is fairly quiet in itself, but mugging and theft are common in nearby Foz do Iguaçu in Brazil, especially at night, when its streets are deserted. Worse yet is neighboring Ciudad del Este in Paraguay, where gun crime is a problem. Avoid the area near the border.

Taxi drivers are usually honest, and are less likely to rip you off than the transport services arranged by top hotels. All the same, locals recommend that unaccompanied women phone for taxis late at night rather than hailing them on the street. The police in the provinces have an iffy reputation: at worst, horribly corrupt, and at best, rather inefficient. Don't count on support, sympathy, or much else from them if you're the victim of a crime.

Argentina Emergency Services Ambulance ☎ *107.* **Fire** ☎ *100.* **Police** ☎ *101.*

Brazil Emergency Services General Emergencies ☎ *199.* **Ambulance** ☎ *192.* **Fire** ☎ *193.* **Police** ☎ *194.*

Uruguay Emergency Services General Emergencies ☎ *911.* **Ambulance** ☎ *105.* **Fire** ☎ *104.* **Police** ☎ *109.* **Policía Caminera (Highway Patrol)** ☎ *108.*

MONEY MATTERS

Argentine currency is accepted everywhere in Colonia, Uruguay—have an idea of the exchange rate to avoid overcharging. Not changing money? Use Argentine pesos for small transactions; hotels give better rates for dollars. Avoid exchanging at the ferry terminal, as the commission's often high.

Uruguayan bills come in denominations of 20, 50, 100, 200, 500, 1,000, and 2,000 pesos uruguayos. Coins are available in 1, 2, 5, and 10 pesos. At this writing, there are 4.50 Uruguayan pesos to the Argentine peso, and 19.50 Uruguayan pesos to the U.S. dollar.

Brazil's currency is the real (R$; plural: *reais* or *reals*). One real is 100 centavos. There are 1, 5, 10, 20, 50, and 100 real notes and 1, 5, 10, 25, and 50 centavo and 1 real coins. At this writing, there are 0.41 reais to the Argentine peso, and 1.75 reais to the U.S. dollar.

HOTEL AND RESTAURANT COSTS
Hotels and restaurants in Colonia list prices in U.S. dollars.

PRICE CATEGORIES IN U.S.DOLLARS				
	$	$$	$$$	$$$$
Restaurants	$8 and under	$9–$12	$13–$16	over $16
Hotels	$80 and under	$81–$130	$131–$200	over $200

Restaurant prices are based on the median main course price at dinner. Hotel prices are for two people in a standard double room in high season.

COLONIA DEL SACRAMENTO, URUGUAY

7

The peaceful cobbled streets of Colonia are just over the Río de la Plata from Buenos Aires, but they seem a world away. Founded in 1680, the city was subject to a long series of wars and pacts between Spain and Portugal, which eventually gave up its claim. Its many tiny museums are dedicated to the story of its tumultuous history.

The best activity in Colonia, however, is walking through its *Barrio Histórico* (Old Town), a UNESCO World Heritage Site. Porteños come to Colonia for romantic getaways or a break from the city. If you like to keep busy on your travels, a late-morning arrival and early-evening departure gives you plenty of time to see the sights and wander at will. To really relax or see the city at its own pace, consider spending the night in one of its many colonial-style bed-and-breakfasts: this offsets travel costs and time and makes a visit here far more rewarding.

GETTING HERE AND AROUND
Hydrofoils and ferries cross the Río de la Plata between Buenos Aires and Uruguay several times a day. Boats often sell out, particularly on summer weekends, so book tickets at least a few days ahead. The two competing companies that operate services—Buquebus and Colonia Express—often wage a reduced rates war in the low season.

Buquebus provides two kinds of service for passengers and cars: the quickest crossing takes an hour by hydrofoil (190 pesos one-way, three daily services in each direction), and the slower ferry takes around three hours (130 pesos, two daily services). The Buquebus terminal is at the northern end of Puerto Madero at the intersection of Avenida Alicia M. de Justo and Avenida Córdoba (which changes its name here to Bulevar

Cobblestones abound in the Old Town section of Colonia del Sacramento, Uruguay.

Cecilia Grierson). It's accessible by taxi or by walking seven blocks from Leandro N. Alem subte station along Trinidad Guevara.

Colonia Express operates the cheapest and fastest services to Colonia but has only three daily services in each direction. The 50-minute catamaran trip costs 173 pesos one-way or 268 pesos for a same-day return, but there are often huge discounts if you buy tickets in advance. The Colonia Express terminal is south of Puerto Madero on Avenida Pedro de Mendoza, the extension of Avenida Huergo. It's best reached by taxi, but Bus 130 from Avenidas Libertador and L.M. Alem also stops outside it.

The shortest way to the Barrio Histórico is to turn left out of the port parking lot onto Florida—it's a six-block walk. Walking is the perfect way to get around this part of town; equally practical—and lots of fun—are golf carts and sand buggies that you can rent from Thrifty.

ESSENTIALS

Bank Banco República ⊠ *Av. Gral. Flores 151.*

Ferry Contacts Buquebus ⊠ *Av. Antartida Argentina 821, Puerto Madero* ☎ *11/4316–6500* ⊕ *www.buquebus.com* ⊠ *Av. Córdoba 867, Centro.* **Colonia Express** ⊠ *Av. Pedro de Mendoza 330, La Boca* ☎ *11/4317–4100 in Buenos Aires, 52/29676 in Colonia* ⊕ *www.coloniaexpress.com* ⊠ *Av. Córdoba 753, Centro.*

Medical Assistance Hospital de Colonia ⊠ *18 de Julio 462* ☎ *52/22994.*

Rental Cars Thrifty ⊠ *Av. Gral. Flores 172* ☎ *52/22939* ⊕ *www.thrifty.com.uy.*

Taxi Taxis Colonia ☎ *52/22920.*

Visitor Info Colonia del Sacramento Tourist Board ✉ *General Flores and Rivera* ☎ *52/23700* ⊕ *www.coloniaturismo.com* ⊙ *Daily 9 am–7 pm* ✉ *Manuel Lobo between Ituzaingó and Paseo San Antonio.*

EXPLORING

Begin your tour at the reconstructed Portón de Campo or city gate, where remnants of the old bastion walls lead to the river. A block farther is Calle de los Suspiros, the aptly named Street of Sighs, a cobblestone stretch of one-story colonials that can rival any street in Latin America for sheer romantic effect. It runs between a lookout point on the river, called the Bastión de San Miguel, and the Plaza Mayor, a lovely square filled with Spanish moss, palms, and spiky, flowering *palo borracho* trees. The many cafés around the square are ideal places to take it all in. Clusters of bougainvillea flow over the walls here and in the other quiet streets of the Barrio Histórico, many of which are lined with art galleries and antiques shops.

Another great place to watch daily life is the Plaza de Armas Manoel Lobo, where you can find the Iglesia Matriz, the oldest church in Uruguay. The square itself is crisscrossed with wooden catwalks over the ruins of a house dating to the founding of the town. The tables from the square's small eateries spill from the sidewalk right onto the cobblestones: they're all rather touristy, but give you an excellent view of the drum-toting *candombe* (a style of music from Uruguay) squads that beat their way around the Old Town each afternoon.

You can visit all of Colonia's museums with the same ticket, which you buy from the Museo Portugués or the Museo Municipal for about $2.50. Most take only a few minutes to visit, but you can use the ticket on two consecutive days.

Casa Nacarello. A colonial Portuguese residence has been lovingly re-created inside this 17th-century structure. The simple bedroom and kitchen furnishings are period pieces, but the real attraction is the house itself, with its thick whitewashed walls and low ceilings. ✉ *Plaza Mayor at Henríquez de la Peña* ⊙ *Closed Thurs.*

Faro. Towering above the Plaza Mayor is the lighthouse, which was built in 1857 on top of a tower that was part of the ruined San Xavier convent. The whole structure was engulfed in flames in 1873 after a lighthouse keeper had an accident with the oil used in the lamp at the time. Your reward for climbing it are great views over the Barrio Histórico and the River Plate. ✉ *Plaza Mayor* ⊙ *Weekdays 1 pm–sunset; weekends 11 am–sunset.*

Museo del Azulejo. A small collection of the beautiful handmade French majolica tiles that adorn fountains all over Colonia are on display at the tile museum, housed in a small 18th-century building near the river. ✉ *Misiones de los Tapies at Paseo San Gabriel* ⊙ *Fri.–Wed. 11:15–4:45.*

Museo Municipal. A sundry collection of objects related to the city's history is housed here. ✉ *Plaza Mayor at Misiones de los Tapies* ⊙ *Closed Tues.*

7

Museo Portugués. The museum that's most worth a visit is this one, which documents the city's ties to Portugal. It's most notable for its collection of old map reproductions based on Portuguese naval expeditions. A small selection of period furnishings, clothes, and jewelry from Colonia's days as a Portuguese colony complete the offerings. Exhibits are well labeled, but in Spanish only. ✉ *Plaza Mayor between Calle de los Suspiros and De Solís* ⊙ *Thurs.–Tues 11:15–4:45.*

WHERE TO EAT

In Colonia prices are displayed in dollars at all hotels and many restaurants. Uruguayan food is as beef-based as Argentine fare, and also has a notable Italian influence. The standout national dish is *chivito*, a well-stuffed steak sandwich that typically contains bacon, fried egg, cheese, onion, salad, olives, and anything else you care to throw into it, heavily laced with ketchup and mayonnaise.

$$ ✕ **El Mesón de la Plaza.** Simple dishes—many steak-based—made with
SOUTH   good-quality ingredients have made this traditional restaurant a favorite
AMERICAN   with porteño visitors to Colonia. The comprehensive wine list showcases Uruguayan vineyards hard to sample anywhere outside the country. Try to get one of the outside tables that sit right on the peaceful Plaza de Armas. ✉ *Vasconcellos 153* ☎ *52/24807* ⊙ *No dinner Mon.*

$$ ✕ **La Bodeguita.** This hip restaurant serves incredibly delicious, crispy
PIZZA   pizza, sliced into bite-size rectangles. The backyard tables overlook the river, and inside is cozy, with warm walls. ✉ *Calle del Comercio 167* ☎ *52/25329* ▭ *No credit cards* ⊙ *Closed Mon., no lunch Tues.–Fri.*

$$$$ ✕ **La Florida.** The black-and-white photos, lace tablecloths, and quaint
ECLECTIC   knickknacks that clutter this long, low house belie the fact that it was once a brothel. It still has private rooms, but it's dining that politicians and the occasional celeb rent them for these days. You, too, can ask to be seated in one, but consider the airy back dining room, which has views over the river. It's hard to say if it's the flamboyant French-Argentine owner's tall tales that keep regulars returning, or his excellent cooking. Specialties include kingfish, sole, and salmon cooked to order: you can suggest sauces of your own or go with house suggestions like orange-infused cream. ✉ *Florida 215* ☎ *94/293–036* ▭ *No credit cards* ⊙ *Closed Wed., Apr.–Nov. dinner by reservation only.*

WHERE TO STAY

For expanded hotel reviews, visit Fodors.com.

$$ ⊡ **Four Seasons Carmelo.** Serenity pervades this harmoniously decorated
★   resort an hour west of Colonia del Sacramento, reachable by car, boat, or a 25-minute flight from Buenos Aires. **Pros:** all rooms are spacious bungalows; fabulous, personalized service; on-site activities compensate for distance to sights and restaurants. **Cons:** despite copious netting and bug spray, the mosquitoes can get out of hand; food quality is erratic; noisy families can infringe on romantic getaways. ✉ *Ruta 21, Km 262, Carmelo* ☎ *54/29000* ⊕ *www.fourseasons.com/carmelo* ⤴ *20*

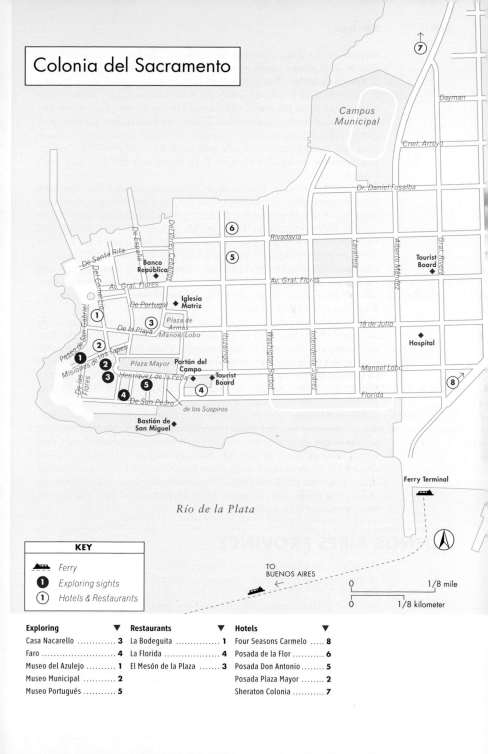

Colonia del Sacramento

KEY

🚢 Ferry
❶ Exploring sights
① Hotels & Restaurants

Campus Municipal

Río de la Plata

TO BUENOS AIRES

Ferry Terminal

| 0 | 1/8 mile |
| 0 | 1/8 kilometer |

bungalows, 24 duplex suites ⑤ In-room: safe. In-hotel: restaurant, golf course, pool, tennis court, gym, spa, children's programs ⓄⅠBreakfast.

$ ⊞ **Posada de la Flor.** This colonial-style hotel is on a quiet street leading
★ to the river and is arranged around a sunny courtyard. **Pros:** peaceful location near river and the Barrio Histórico; gorgeous breakfast area and roof terrace; great value. **Cons:** standard rooms are cramped; damp spots on some ceilings; ground-floor rooms open onto the courtyard and can be noisy. ⊠ *Calle Ituzaingó 268* ☎ *52/30794* ⊕ *www. posada-delaflor.com* ⇌ *14 rooms ⑤ In-room: safe ▭ No credit cards* ⓄⅠ *Breakfast.*

$ ⊞ **Posada Don Antonio.** Rooms open onto long galleries that overlook an enormous split-level courtyard at Posada Don Antonio, the latest incarnation of a large, elegant building which has housed one hotel or another for over a century. **Pros:** sparkling turquoise pool, surrounded by loungers; two blocks from the Barrio Histórico; rates are low but there are proper hotel perks like poolside snacks. **Cons:** staff are sometimes indifferent; plain, characterless rooms; ill-fitting doors let in courtyard noise. ⊠ *Ituzaingó 232* ☎ *52/25344* ⊕ *www.posadadonantonio. com* ⇌ *38 rooms ⑤ In-room: Wi-Fi. In-hotel: pool, laundry facilities, business center* ⓄⅠ *Breakfast.*

$ ⊞ **Posada Plaza Mayor.** A faint scent of jasmine fills the air at this lovely old hotel. **Pros:** beautiful green spaces; on a quiet street of the Barrio Histórico; cheerful, accommodating staff. **Cons:** cramped bathrooms; the three cheapest rooms are small and lack the atmosphere of the regular standard rooms; high price of deluxe rooms isn't justified by the amenities. ⊠ *Calle del Comercio 111* ☎ *52/23193* ⊕ *www. posadaplazamayor.com* ⇌ *14 rooms ⑤ In-room: Wi-Fi* ⓄⅠ *Breakfast.*

$$$$ ⊞ **Sheraton Colonia.** This riverside hotel and spa is a favorite with porte-
★ ños on weekend escapes. **Pros:** peaceful location with river views from many rooms; great spa; rooms are often discounted mid-week. **Cons:** it's a 15-minute drive or taxi ride north of the Barrio Histórico; lots of noisy kids on weekends; staff sometimes unhelpful. ⊠ *Cont. Rambla de las Américas s/n* ☎ *54/29000* ⊕ *www.sheraton.com* ⇌ *88 rooms, 4 suites ⑤ In-room: safe, Internet. In-hotel: restaurant, bar, golf course, pool, gym, spa* ⓄⅠ *Breakfast.*

BUENOS AIRES PROVINCE

Plains fan out where the city of Buenos Aires ends: this is the beginning of the pampas, which derive their name from the native Quechua word for "flat field." All over this fertile earth are signs of active ranch life, from the grazing cattle to the modern-day gauchos. The region is also noted for its crops, although these days the traditional alfalfa, sunflowers, wheat, and corn have largely been replaced by soy.

While Argentina was still a Spanish colony, settlers gradually began to force indigenous tribes away from the pampas near Buenos Aires, making extensive agriculture and cattle breeding possible. (In 1880, during the bloody Campaign of the Desert, the southern pampas were also "cleared" of indigenous tribes.) By the latter half of the 19th century the region had become known as the grain supplier for the world. From

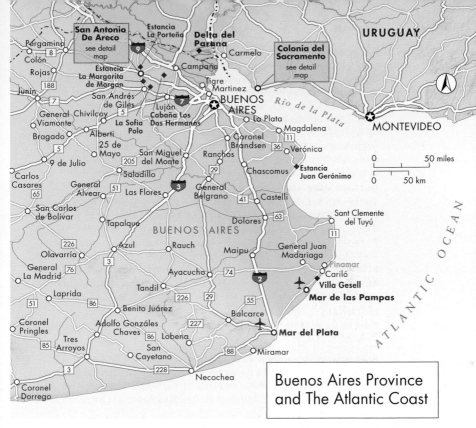

Buenos Aires Province and The Atlantic Coast

1850 to 1950 more than 400 important estancias were built in Buenos Aires Province alone. Some of these have been modified for use as guest ranches and provide the best glimpse of the fabled Pampean lifestyle.

SAN ANTONIO DE ARECO

110 km (68 mi) west of Buenos Aires.

There's no better place to experience traditional provincial life in the pampas than this well-to-do farming town off RN 8. Grand *estancias* (ranches) dot the land in and around San Antonio. Many of the families that own them, which form a sort of local aristocracy, mix lucrative soy farming with estancia tourism. The gauchos who were once ranch hands now cook up huge *asados* (barbecues) and lead horseback expeditions for the ever-growing numbers of foreign tourists. You can visit one for a day—*un día de campo*—or immerse yourself with an overnight visit.

Porteño visitors tend to base themselves in the town itself, which is becoming known for its B&Bs. The fiercely conservative inhabitants have done a good job of preserving the turn-of-the-20th-century Italianate buildings that fill the sleepy *casco histórico* (historic center). Many contain bars and general stores, which maintain their original fittings; others are the workshops of some of the best craftspeople in the country.

In summer the banks of the Río Areco (Areco River), which runs through town, are teeming with picnickers—especially near the center of town, at the Puente Viejo (Old Bridge), which is overlooked by the open-air tables of various riverside parrillas. Nearby is the Museo Gauchesco y Parque Criollo Ricardo Güiraldes, which celebrates historical gaucho life. During the week surrounding November 10, the *Día de la Tradición* (Day of Tradition) celebrates the gaucho with shows, community barbecues, riding competitions, and a huge crafts fair. It's more fun to visit San Antonio on weekends, as many restaurants are closed Monday–Thursday.

GETTING HERE AND AROUND

To drive to San Antonio de Areco, leave Buenos Aires on RN 9, crossing to RN 8 when it intersects at Km 35 (total tolls of 15.6 pesos). There are more than 20 daily buses from Buenos Aires' Retiro Station to San Antonio; most are run by Nueva Chevallier, and some by Pullman General Belgrano. Each company operates from its own bus stop in San Antonio. Once you've arrived, the best way to get around is on foot, but you'll need a *remis* (radio taxi) to get to most estancias, though some have their own shuttle service.

ESSENTIALS

Bank Banco de la Nación Argentina ⊠ *Alsina 250, at San Martín, San Antonio de Areco* ☎ *2326/452150* ⊕ *www.bna.com.ar.*

Bus Contacts Chevallier ☎ *2326/453–904 in San Antonio de Areco, 11/4311–0033 in Buenos Aires* ⊕ *www.nuevachevallier.com.* **Pullman General Belgrano** ☎ *2326/454–059 in San Antonio de Areco, 11/4315–6522 in Buenos Aires* ⊕ *www.gralbelgrano.com.ar.* **Terminal de Ómnibus Retiro** ☎ *11/4310–0700* ⊕ *www.tebasa.com.ar.*

Medical Assistance Farmacia Risolino ⊠ *Arellano at San Martín, San Antonio de Areco* ☎ *2326/455–200.* **Hospital Emilio Zerboni** ⊠ *Moreno at Lavalle, San Antonio de Areco* ☎ *2326/452–759.*

Taxi Remis Centro ☎ *2326/456–225.*

Visitor Info San Antonio de Areco Tourist Board ⊠ *Bul. Zerboni at Arellano, San Antonio de Areco* ☎ *2326/453–165* ⊕ *www.pagosdeareco.com.ar* ⊙ *Weekdays 8–7, weekends 8–8.*

EXPLORING

Museo Gauchesco y Parque Criollo Ricardo Güiraldes. Gaucho life of the past is celebrated—and idealized—at this quiet museum on a small estate just outside town. Start at the 150-year-old *pulpería* (the gaucho version of the saloon), complete with dressed-up wax figures ready for a drink. Then head for the museum proper, an early-20th-century replica of a stately 18th-century *casco de estancia* (estancia house). Here, polished wooden cases contain a collection of traditional gaucho gear: matés, elaborately decorated knives, ponchos, and all manner of elaborate saddlery and bridlery. The museum is named for local writer Ricardo Güiraldes (1886–1927), whose romantic gaucho novels captured the imagination of the Argentinean people. Several rooms document his life in San Antonio de Areco and the real-life gauchos who

San Antonio de Areco

inspired his work. ⊠ *Camino Ricardo Güiraldes, San Antonio de Areco* ☎ *2326/455–839* ☉ *Wed.–Mon. 11–5.*

Museo Las Lilas de Areco. Although iconic Argentinean painter Florencio Molina Campos was not from San Antonio de Areco, the foundation behind this museum felt that this was the most appropriate home for his humorous paintings of traditional pampas life. The works usually depict red-nosed, pigeon-toed gauchos astride comical steeds, staggering drunkenly outside pulperías (taverns), engaged in cockfighting or folk dancing, and taming bucking broncos. The collection is fun and beautifully set out but too small to justify the unreasonably high entrance price, which seems more to reflect the no-expenses-spared renovation of the traditional house that contains the museum. Still, your ticket includes coffee and croissants in the jarringly modern café, which also does great empanadas and sandwiches. Behind its curtained walls lie huge theme park–style 3D recreations of three paintings, periodically revealed. The lively and insightful voice-over explaining them is in Spanish only. ⊠ *Moreno 279, San Antonio de Areco* ☎ *2326/456–425* ⊕ *www.museolaslilas.org* ⊠ *20 pesos* ☉ *June–Sept., Fri.–Sun. 10–6; Oct.–May, Fri.–Sun. 10–8.*

Museo Taller Draghi. San Antonio is famed for its silversmiths, and the late Juan José Draghi was the best in town. This small museum adjoining his workshop showcases the emergence and evolution of the Argentine silver-work style known as *platería criolla*. The pieces are mostly ornate takes on gaucho-related items: spurs, belt buckles, knives, stirrups, and the ubiquitous matés, some dating from the 18th century. Also on display is the incredibly ornate work of Juan José Draghi himself; you can buy original pieces in the shop. His son and a host of disciples keep the family business alive—they're often at work shaping new pieces at the back of the museum. ⊠ *Lavalle 387, San Antonio de Areco* ☎ *2326/454–219* ⊕ *www.draghiplaterosorfebres.com* ☉ *Daily 9–1 and 4–8.*

WHERE TO EAT

$$
ARGENTINE

✕ **Almacen de Ramos Generales.** This old general store is airy and charming, and its classic Argentine fare is consistently good. You can snack on *picadas* of salami, prosciutto, cheeses, olives, and eggplant "*en escabeche*" (pickled). The *bife de chorizo* (sirloin steak), meanwhile, is perfectly juicy, tender, and flavorful, all the more so when accompanied by wondrous french fries with basil. The atmosphere, too, is just right: it's country-store-meets-elegant-restaurant. No wonder locals and visiting porteños alike vie for tables—on weekends, reservations are essential. ⊠ *Zapiola 143, between Lavalle and Sdo. Sombra, San Antonio de Areco* ☎ *2326/456–376* ⊕ *www.ramosgeneralesareco.com.ar* ☉ *Open daily for lunch and dinner.*

$$
CONTEMPORARY

✕ **Café de las Artes.** The charismatic owner of this intimate restaurant clearly gets a kick out of breaking the rules. Instead of the country style most San Antonio eateries go for, the walls here are painted bordello red and are cluttered with art, crafts, photos, and souvenirs from all over the world. Pasta dishes are the specialty: expect unusual combinations like duck ravioli in a saffron and walnut sauce or tenderloin and carrot ravioli in spiced tomato. Only the wine list comes up short—literally so—though the few options on it are very reasonably priced, as is the food. ⊠ *Bolívar 70, San Antonio de Areco* ☎ *2326/456–398* ⊟ *No credit cards* ☉ *Closed Mon.–Thurs.*

$$
CONTEMPORARY
★

✕ **Don Cleofe.** Three things set Don Cleofe apart: a peaceful location just outside of town; a setting inside a century-old adobe house with buttercup-yellow walls hung with weavings and pottery from northwestern Argentina, where the chef is from; and the food. Forget about asado and *milanesas:* here the stars are *lomo* (tenderloin) in a Malbec reduction and rabbit stew with *papines* (small potatoes native to the Andes). Locals make the 10-block trek here on weekend nights, but consider coming at lunch for the fabulous views over surrounding fields. Note that this restaurant is officially only open Friday through Sunday, but as it's in a hotel (that's always open), the management has been known to open during off-hours (even for only two people); just call ahead. ⊠ *Guido s/n, west of town over old train tracks, San Antonio de Areco* ☎ *2326/455–858* ⊕ *www.doncleofe.com* ▭ *No credit cards* ⊘ *Closed Mon.–Thurs. except by reservation.*

$$ ✕ **Puesto La Lechuza.** Your first difficult decision is where to sit: the breezy
ARGENTINE outside tables overlook the river, and the rustic yellow-painted interior is hung with historic pictures of gauchos. Let gaucho-diet principles guide your order—go for the asado or *vacío* (beef on and off the bone, respectively), slow-cooked over hot coals. The little stage where folky guitar players perform in the evenings might look touristy, but locals love the sing-song here as much as visitors. Weekend reservations are essential. ⊠ *Arrellano (at the river), San Antonio de Areco* ☎ *2326/452–351.*

WHERE TO STAY

For expanded hotel reviews, visit Fodors.com.

$ ▦ **Don Cleofe.** Rolling farmland spreads out before this family-run establishment, which is a bit out of town but feels a million miles from everywhere. **Pros:** fabulous home cooking; fresh air and serious peace and quiet within walking distance of the main drag; friendly but nonintrusive owners. **Cons:** small rooms; only the best room has views of the fields; cold in winter. ⊠ *Guido s/n, west of town over old train tracks, San Antonio de Areco* ☎ *2326/455–858* ⊕ *www.doncleofe.com* ⇌ *7 rooms* & *In-room: no a/c, no TV. In-hotel: restaurant* ▭ *No credit cards* ▮⊙▮ *Breakfast.*

$$$ ▦ **El Patio de Moreno.** You might be in gauchoville, but that doesn't
★ mean you have to renounce creature comforts or slick design: hip hotel chain New Age has turned this 1910 town house into the coolest digs in town. **Pros:** two blocks from main street; beautifully designed rooms and lobby; most bathrooms have double sinks and shower heads. **Cons:** rooms overlooking street can be noisy; kids might be uncomfortable with very adult vibe; service is professional but not personal. ⊠ *Moreno 251, at San Martín, San Antonio de Areco* ☎ *2326/455–197* ⊕ *www.patiodemoreno.com* ⇌ *11 rooms* & *In-room: safe, no TV, Wi-Fi. In-hotel: bar, pool, business center* ▮⊙▮ *Breakfast.*

$$ ▦ **La Antigua Casona.** The dusky pink walls, brass bedsteads, antique wardrobes, and embroidered linens of this small B&B make you feel like you're staying in a Merchant-Ivory film. **Pros:** vintage furnishings; sunny, sheltered patio; two blocks from the main square. **Cons:** high ceilings make some rooms drafty in winter; getting to the bathroom of one room involves crossing the (admittedly pretty) kitchen. ⊠ *Segundo Sombra 495, at Bolívar, San Antonio de Areco* ☎ *2326/456–600* ⊕ *www.antiguacasona.com* ⇌ *5 rooms* & *In-room: no TV* ▭ *No credit cards* ▮⊙▮ *Breakfast.*

Continued on page 273

THE COWBOYS at WORLD'S END

by Victoria Patience

Along a country road, you may come across riders herding cattle. Dressed in baggy pants and shirts, a knife stuck in the back of their belts, these are the descendants of the gauchos, Argentina's cowboys. These men of few words symbolize honor, honesty, and courage— so much so that a favor or good deed is known locally as a *gauchada*.

WHAT'S IN A NAME?

No one can agree on where the word "gaucho" comes from. Some say it's derived from the native Quechua-language word *guachu*, meaning "orphan" or "outcast"; others attribute similar meanings to the French word *gauche*, another suggested source. Yet another theory traces it (via Andalusian Spanish) to the Arabic word *chaouche*, a kind of whip for herding cattle.

Gauchos were the cattle-herding settlers of the pampas (grasslands), renowned for their prowess as horsemen. Most were criollos (Argentina-born descendants of Spanish immigrants) or mestizos (of mixed Spanish and native Argentine descent). They lived in villages but spent much of their time riding the plains, much like North American cowboys.

With the establishment of big estancias (ranches) in the early- and mid-19th century, landowners began taking on gauchos as hired hands. The sheer size of these ranches meant that the gaucho's nomadic lifestyle remained largely unchanged, however.

In the 1860s Argentina's president Domingo Faustino Sarmiento encouraged massive settlement of the pampas, and branded gauchos as barbaric, potentially criminal elements. (Despite being of humble origins, Sarmiento as a snob about anything he saw as uncivilized.) Laws requiring travelers to carry passes ended the gaucho's right to roam. Many more than ever signed on as permanent ranch hands; others were drafted into military service, at times becoming deserters and outlaws.

Vindication came in the late-19th and early-20th century, when a wave of literary works like José Hernández's Martín Fierro and Ricardo Güiraldes's Don Segundo Sombra captured the national imagination with their dramatic, romantic descriptions of gauchos and their nomadic lifestyle. The gaucho—proud, brave, and melancholy—has been a national icon ever since.

Gaucho on an estancia near
El Calafate, Patagonia, Argentina

GAUCHO GEAR

SOMBRERO
Although a sombrero (flat-crowned, wide-brimmed hat) is the most typical style, conical felt hats (shown), berets, flat caps, and even top hats are also worn.

CAMISA
Traditionally smocked shirt with baggy sleeves. Modern gauchos wear regular long-sleeved cotton shirts.

BOMBACHA
Baggy pants cinched at the ankle; the story goes that after the Crimean War, surplus Turkish-style army pants were sold to Argentina by Britain and France. The fashion caught on: no gaucho is seen without these.

BOTAS
Early gauchos wore rough, rawhide boots with open toes or a flip-flop-style thong. Today, gauchos in colder parts of Argentina wear flat-soled, tapered boots, usually with a baggy pirate-style leg.

PAÑUELO
Large, brightly colored kerchief, worn knotted around the neck; some gauchos drape them under their hats to protect their necks from the sun or cold.

CHAQUETA
Jacket; often kept for special occasions, and usually worn short and unbuttoned, to better display the shirt and waistcoat underneath.

CHIRIPÁ
Before bombachas arrived, gauchos used to wind a large swathe of woven fabric (like an oversize loincloth) over thin, long underpants.

FAJA
A long strip of colorful woven fabric once worn to hold the pants up, now mainly decorative and often replaced by a leather belt. Either way, gauchos stick their knives in the back.

ESPUELAS
Spurs; most gauchos favor those with spiked wheel-like designs.

Gaucho traditionally dressed

SUPER GAUCHOS

REBENQUE
A short rawhide crop, often with a decorative metal handle.

PONCHO

Woven from sheep's or llama's wool, usually long and often vertically striped. Some colors denote certain provinces.

ALPARGATAS

Spanish immigrants in the 18th century popularized flat, rope-soled espadrilles in warmer parts of Argentina. Today, rubber-soled versions are more common.

BOLEADORAS

Gauchos adopted this native Argentinian device for catching animals. It's made of two or three stones wrapped in cowhide and mounted at the end of a cowhide cord. You whirl the boleadora then release it at the animal's legs.

LAZO
A braided rawhide lasso used for roping cattle.

CUCHILLO OR FACÓN

No gaucho leaves home without his knife. Indeed, most Argentine men have one to use at barbecues (early gauchos used theirs for fighting, too). Handles are made of wood or horn, blades are triangular.

Unsigned mural of Gauchito Gil, a saint-like character in popular Argentine belief (supposedly a Robin Hood-type outlaw called Antonio Mamerto Gil Núñez).

EL GAUCHITO GIL: legend has it that this gaucho from Corrientes Province was hunted down by a sheriff over a woman. He was hung by his feet from a tree but, just before his throat was cut, he predicted that the sheriff would find his son at home mortally ill and only able to recover if the sheriff prayed to Gil. The prediction came true, and the repentant sheriff spread the word. Today, roadsides all over Argentina are dotted with red-painted shrines to this folk saint. Superstitious locals leave offerings, hoping for help with their problems.

MARTÍN FIERRO: the fictional hero of an eponymous 19th-century epic poem written by José Hernández. Fierro is a poor but noble gaucho who's drafted into the army. He deserts and becomes an outlaw. His pride, independence, and love of the land embody the national ideal of what a man should be. Writer Jorge Luis Borges so loved the poem that he started a literary magazine with the same name.

JUAN MOREIRA: a real-life gaucho who married the daughter of a wealthy landowner, provoking the wrath of a jealous local judge. Wrongly accused of various crimes, Moreira became a fugitive and a famed knife-fighter, killing 16 men before eventually dying in a police ambush in 1874 in the town of Lobos in Buenos Aires Province. A 1973 biographical film by arty local director Leonardo Favio was a box-office smash.

7

IN FOCUS THE COWBOYS AT WORLD'S END

UN DIA DE CAMPO

In the late 19th century, well-to-do European families bought huge blocks of pampas land on which to build estancias, often with luxurious houses reminiscent of the old country. The advent of industrial agriculture has led many estancias to turn to tourism for income; others combine tourism with small-scale farming.

The gauchos who once herded cows now have a new sideline shepherding visitors, putting on riding shows or preparing large-scale *asados* (barbecues). You can visit an estancia for a *día de campo* (day in the country) or to stay overnight or for a weekend. There are estancias for most budgets: some are ultraluxurious bed-and-breakfasts, others are homey, family-run farms.

A day at an estancia typically involves a late breakfast; horseback riding or a long walk; a full-blown asado accompanied by Argentine red wine; and afternoon tea. Longer stays at upscale establishments might also include golf or other sports; at working farms you can feed

Gaucho on an estancia near El Calafate, Patagonia, Argentina

animals or help with the milking. Estancia accommodation generally includes all meals, and although some estancias are close to towns, it's rare to leave the grounds during a stay.

HORSEMANSHIP

During a visit to an estancia, you may see gauchos demonstrating traditional skills and games such as:

Zapateo Criollo: a complicated, rhythmic, foot-stomping dance.

Jineteada or Doma: rodeo, gaucho-style.

La Carrera de Sortija: riders gallop under a bar from which metal rings are hung, trying to spear a ring on a stick as they pass.

Carrera Cuadrera: a short horseback sprint that riders start from a standstill.

Boleadas and Pialadas: catching an animal using boleadoras or a lasso, respectively.

La Maroma: participants hang from a bar or rope and jump onto a horse that gallops beneath them.

GAUCHO GRUB

When gauchos were out on the pampas for weeks, even months, at a time, their diet revolved around one food—beef—and one drink—mate (a type of tea). Times may have changed, but most Argentinians still consume a lot of both.

MAKING THE MOST OF AN ASADO

Whether you're just at someone's home or out on an estancia, a traditional Argentinian asado is a drawn-out affair. All sorts of meats go on the grill initially, including chorizo sausage, black pudding, and sweetbreads. These are grilled and served before the larger cuts. You'll probably also be served a picada (cheese, salami, and other snacks). Follow the local example and go easy on these starters: there's lots more to come.

The main event is, of course, the beef. Huge, grass-fed chunks of it, roasted for at least two hours over hot coals and flavored with little more than salt. While the asador (barbecuer) does his stuff, it's traditional to admire his or her skills; interfering (criticism, touching the meat, or the like) is not part of this tradition. The first meat to be served is often thick-cut ribs, accompanied simply by a mixed salad and bread. Then there will be a pause for digestion, and the asador will serve the choicest cuts: flank or tenderloin, usually. All this is washed down with a robust red wine and, not surprisingly, followed by a siesta.

Gaucho *asado* (barbecue), Argentina

MATE FOR BEGINNERS

Mate (mah-tay) is a strong tea made from the dried leaves of *Ilex paraguariensis*, known as yerba. It's drunk from a gourd (also called a mate) through a metal straw with a filter on the end (the *bombilla*).

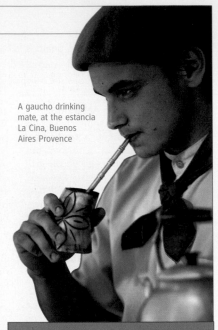

A gaucho drinking mate, at the estancia La Cina, Buenos Aires Provence

Mate has long been a traditional drink for the Guaraní people native to Argentina's northeast. They introduced it to Jesuit missionaries, who learned to cultivate it, and today, most yerba mate is still grown in Misiones and Corrientes provinces. The drink eventually became popular throughout Argentina, Uruguay, and southern Brazil.

Much like tea in England, mate serves as the basis of social interaction: people drink it at any hour of the day. Several drinkers share the same gourd, which is refilled and passed round the group. It's often extended to strangers as a welcoming gesture. If you're shown this hospitality be sure to wait your turn, drink all the mate in the gourd fairly quickly, and hand the gourd directly back to the *cebador* (server). Don't pour yourself a mate if someone else is the cebador, and avoid wiping or wiggling the straw around. Also, you don't say "gracias" until you've had your fill.

WHAT'S IN A MATE?

Caffeine: 30 mg per 8-oz serving (versus 47 mg in tea and 100 mg in coffee)

Vitamins:
A, C, E, B1, B2, B3, B5, B complex

Minerals:
Calcium, manganese, iron, selenium, potassium, magnesium, phosphorus, zinc

Antioxidant properties:
similar to green tea

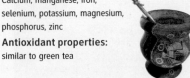

SERVING MATE

1) Heat a kettle of water to just before boiling (176°F/80°C)—boiling water ruins yerba.

2) Fill ⅔ of the gourd with yerba.

3) Without the bombilla in place, cover the gourd with your hand, and turn it quickly upside down (to get rid of any fine yerba dust that can block the bombilla).

4) For some reason, yerba never sits flat in the gourd; pour some hot water in the empty space left by the slightly slanting yerba leaves. Let the yerba swell a little, cover the top of the bombilla with your thumb, and drive it firmly into the leaves.

5) Finish filling the gourd with water, pouring it in slowly near the bombilla's base. (Some people also add sugar at this point.)

6) Drink all the mate in the gourd (the cebador traditionally drinks first, so the mate isn't so bitter when brewed for others) and repeat Step 5, passing the gourd to the next drinker—and so on—until the yerba mate loses its flavor.

THE ATLANTIC COAST

Southern Buenos Aires Province is synonymous with one thing—*la playa* (the beach). Every summer Argentines flock to resort towns along the coast, many of which were originally large estates. Now they all hinge around a long *peatonal* (a pedestrians-only street) or central avenue. It can be hard to see the sand in the summer months. However, by walking (or driving) a little farther, you can get some beach action in more agreeable surroundings even in peak season. Locals prefer to be in the thick of things by renting a canvas tent at a *balneario* or *paraje* (beach club); weekly rents are extortionate, but include access to toilets and showers, otherwise nonexistent on Argentine beaches. Happily, buying a drink at their snack bars earns you the same privilege.

Although the weather is usually hot and sunny December through February, the sea is usually bracing, and temperatures drop in the evenings, when the wind picks up. Off-peak, the beaches tend to be deserted, and luxury accommodations are half price or cheaper. Though the weather can get chilly, walks along the windswept sands—when followed by an evening in front of a warm log fire—can be very romantic. Bear in mind, though, that many hotels and restaurants open only on weekends April through November.

GETTING HERE AND AROUND

Comfortable long-distance buses connect Buenos Aires with the Atlantic Coast. Although extra buses are added in January and February, tickets sell out fast. The best service to Mar del Plata is with Flechabus and Nueva Chevallier; there are 10–20 daily departures, and the five-hour trip costs 145–180 pesos. There are numerous daily services to Villa Gesell, the closest town to Mar de las Pampas, with Expreso Alberino and Nueva Chevallier; the five-hour trip costs 125–150 pesos. Local company El Último Querandí runs buses every hour from Villa Gesell to Mar de las Pampas.

Ferrobaires runs comfortable daily trains between Buenos Aires' Estación Constitución and Mar del Plata (150–200 pesos; six hours). Services leave Buenos Aires at 8 am and Mar del Plata at 4 pm, and have three classes: primera, pullman, and super-pullman (the most luxurious).

The Aeropuerto Internacional Mar del Plata (Km 398 on AU 2, about five minutes outside the city) is the beach region's main airport. There are two daily flights (around 500 pesos one-way) year-round to and from Buenos Aires on Aerolíneas Argentinas. Note that this is a coveted route in summer, so make reservations early.

Having your own wheels is a great boon on the coast. You can rent cars locally, or drive from Buenos Aires via Autopista La Plata and AU 2, a two-lane highway that continues straight to Mar del Plata (tolls of 18 pesos). The four- to five-hour drive is just one long straight highway, though that highway does get very busy in summer. To reach the northern coast, come off AU 2 at Dolores, continue 30 km (20 mi) on RP 63 to Esquina de Crotto, then turn onto RP 56. This takes you the 110 km (70 mi) to Pinamar. The Pinamar turn-off also intersects with

7

RP 11, also known as the Interbalnearia, a two-lane coast road that connects Pinamar with Mar de las Pampas.

ESSENTIALS

Airline Contact Aerolíneas Argentinas ☎ *0810/2228–6527* ⊕ *www. aerolineas.com.ar.*

Bus Contacts El Rápido Argentino ☎ *0800/333–1970* ⊕ *www.rapido-argentino.com.* **Expreso Alberino** ☎ *11/4576–7940* ⊕ *www.expresoalberino. com.* **Flechabus** ☎ *11/4000–5200* ⊕ *www.flechabus.com.ar.* **Nueva Cheval-lier** ☎ *11/4000–5255 in Buenos Aires* ⊕ *www.nuevachevallier.com.* **Plusmar** ☎ *0810/999–1111* ⊕ *www.plusmar.com.ar.* **Montemar** ☎ *2254/404–501.* **Ter-minal de Ómnibus de Retiro** ☎ *11/4310–0700* ⊕ *www.tebasa.com.ar.*

Train Contact Ferrobaires ☎ *0810/666–8736* ⊕ *www.ferrobaires.gba.gov.ar.*

MAR DE LAS PAMPAS

21 km (13 mi) south of Pinamar on RN 11.

The secret is out: this tiny town, once known only to campers and backpackers, has suddenly become the most sought-after vacation spot on the northern coast. Those willing to fork out the immense summer rents are generally rich, nature-loving porteños. They come for the quiet sandy streets, heavily wooded lots, and stylish stone-and-wood cabins that have become Mar de las Pampas's trademark. Most of these are really glorified hotels and include breakfast and maid service.

Huge dunes separate the town from the beach, and despite the fleets of new four-wheel drives that pack the few blocks around Avenida Cruz del Sur and El Lucero, the commercial center, the sands are wide and peaceful. Two smaller towns, Las Gaviotas and Mar Azul, lie south of Mar de las Pampas and maintain an equally peaceful—if less-exclusive—back-to-nature vibe.

GETTING HERE AND AROUND

The nearest long-distance bus station to Mar de las Pampas is in Villa Gesell, a crowded, unattractive resort town 6 km (4 mi) north of Mar de las Pampas. Taxis depart from an official stand in the Villa Gesell terminal and cost around 35 pesos to Mar de las Pampas. Local bus company El Ultimo Querandí also connects the two: their groaning, sand-filled buses leave Avenida 3 in Villa Gesell every hour on the half hour, and return from Mar de las Pampas's main square on the hour.

As Mar de las Pampas has no supermarket or bank (only an ATM), a car is useful for stays of more than a day or two. If you don't fancy the drive from Buenos Aires, you can rent a car in Pinamar or Villa Gesell, then continue along RN 11 until you reach the clearly labeled left-hand turnoff to Mar de las Pampas.

ESSENTIALS

Bank (ATM only) Red Link ✉ *Miguel Cané, between Av. Lucero y El Ceibo, Mar de las Pampas* ⊕ *www.redlink.com.ar.*

Medical Assistance Farmacia Pujol ✉ *In Paseo Sendas del Encuentro shop-ping center, Santa María between El Lucero and El Ceibo, Mar de las Pampas*

☎ 2255/451–827. **Hospital General de Agudos** ⊠ *Av. 8 at Paseo 124, Villa Gesell* ☎ 2255/462–618.

Taxi Remises Sol ⊠ *Villa Gesell* ☎ 2255/464–377.

Visitor Info Mar de las Pampas Tourist Board ⊠ *Av. Antonio Vazquez at Av. Del Plata, Mar de las Pampas* ☎ 2255/470–324 ⊕ *www.mardelaspampas.info* ⊙ *Dec.–Mar., daily 10–8.*

WHERE TO EAT AND STAY

Mar de las Pampas has several campsites, which the tourist office can direct you to. Be warned that in summer they're often packed to bursting with noisy teenagers. Most other accommodations here are cabins and apart-hotels (a cross between a furnished apartment and a hotel—breakfast is usually offered, as is maid service, and each room has a private kitchen and living room). In January and February, the minimum stay is often one week.

For expanded hotel reviews, visit Fodors.com.

$$ ✗ **Amorinda.** Mom and dad are in the kitchen, and their grown-up
ITALIAN daughters wait tables, but the real secret to this family-run restaurant are the killer pasta recipes grandma brought with her from Italy. The creamy whiskey-and-tomato sauce packs a punch, but it's not just flavors that knock you over here. Portions of pancetta-and-broccoli or ricotta ravioli easily serve two, while the mammoth lasagna, scattered with tiny meatballs, might fill even more. Their dense tiramisu might be too much to contemplate; the trembling panna cotta in marmalade sauce is easier to deal with. ⊠ *Av. Lucero at Cerchunoff, Mar de las Pampas* ☎ 2255/479–750 ⚑ *Reservations essential* ▭ *No credit cards* ⊙ *Closed Mon.–Thurs., no dinner Sun. Apr.–June and Aug.–Nov.*

$ ✗ **Viejos Tiempos.** Teahouses abound in this area, but none have more
CAFÉ tranquil surroundings than this one, which sits in a beautifully kept garden. In summer hummingbirds hover over the flowers, while tea and cakes are served at heavy wooden tables set with floral-patterned china. Inside, the chintz-and-lace drapes and cloying red cloths look like something your great-grandma would love, but at least the open fireplace keeps things toasty in winter. After years of making some of the best cakes in town, Viejos Tiempos has added (bizarrely) Mexican dishes to the menu, but it's the sweets that remain the main draw here. ⊠ *Leoncio Paiva at Cruz del Sur, Mar de las Pampas* ☎ 2255/479–524 ▭ *No credit cards* ⊙ *Closed weekdays Apr.–Oct.*

$$$ ⚇ **Abedul.** Solid stone walls, oak fixtures, and handwoven drapes make the split-level cabins at Abedul very earthy. **Pros:** close to the beach and even closer to restaurants in the town center; lovely wooded grounds; low-key and laid-back but staff still try hard to please. **Cons:** in summer, four-wheel drives roar up and down the road outside; limited nearby grocery stores make the kitchen redundant; beds are on the hard side. ⊠ *Santa María between El Lucero and El Ceibo, Mar de las Pampas* ☎ 2255/455–819 ⊕ *www.abedulmardelaspampas.com* ⤳ *7 cabins* ⚒ *In-room: no a/c, kitchen, Wi-Fi. In-hotel: pool* ▭ *No credit cards* ⊙ *Closed weekdays Apr.–June and Aug.–Nov.* ⊙❘ *Breakfast.*

7

Mar del Plata isn't just surf and sand; explore some of the unique architecture.

$$$ ☑ **Heiwa.** The sea breezes that ruffle the cotton drapes at this beachfront
★ hotel are almost as calming as the owners' Zenned-out approach. **Pros:**
any closer to the sea and you're in it; breakfast is served on the beach;
incredible sushi restaurant by the same name and beach bar on-site.
Cons: far from other restaurants and the center of Mar de las Pampas;
dead zone after midnight, aside from the in-house bar; tiny bedrooms.
⊠ *Calle 34 at beachfront, Las Gaviotas* ✢ *3 km (2 mi) from Mar de
las Pampas* 🕾 *2255/453–674* ⊕ *www.heiwa.com.ar* ⟳ *5 apartments*
⚲ *In-room: no a/c, kitchen. In-hotel: restaurant, bar, beach* ⊟ *No credit
cards* ⊘ *No lunch, closed weekdays Apr.–June and Aug.–Nov.* ⦿ *Mul-
tiple meal plans.*

MAR DEL PLATA

400 km (248 mi) south of Buenos Aires via AU2.

Come summer, Argentina becomes obsessed with Mar del Plata. The
city of 600,000 residents is the country's most popular beach resort—
and at least five times as big as any runners-up. Dull gray sand and chilly
water may not make for the best beach experience, but in Mar del Plata
activities like people-watching, eating, shopping, and clubbing are just
as important. The sands are comically crowded in January and Febru-
ary, when there's a carnival-like atmosphere day and night.

The tourist infrastructure hums, with more than 700 hotels and count-
less eateries. Off-season can get a bit lonely, though the windy sands and
almost deserted boulevards feel cinematic. The city becomes literally

cinematic each November, when it hosts the Festival Internacional de Cine de Mar del Plata, Argentina's biggest film festival.

Although most hotels are within walking distance of a beach, and the city center is navigable on foot, you'll need a taxi or bus to get to other parts of town, like the port. There are several downtown-area beaches; the summertime action revolves around Playa Bristol. The trendiest strip of sand is south of the lighthouse, but you need a car to get here comfortably.

ESSENTIALS

Bank Banco de la Nación Argentina ⊠ *San Martin 2594, Mar del Plata* ☎ *223/491–5477* ⊕ *www.bna.com.ar.*

Medical Assistance Hospital Español de Mar del Plata ⊠ *San Luis 2562, Mar del Plata* ☎ *223/410–8810.*

Taxi Tele Taxi Mar del Plata ☎ *223/475–8888.*

Visitor Info Mar del Plata Tourist Board ⊠ *Blvd. Marítimo P. Peralta Ramos 2270, Local 51, Mar del Plata* ☎ *223/495–1777* ⊕ *www.turismomardelplata.gov. ar* ⊙ *Jan.–Mar., daily 8 am–10 pm; Apr.–Nov., Mon.–Sat. 8–8, Sun. 10–5.*

EXPLORING

🐾 **Aquarium Mar del Plata.** More of a sea-theme amusement park than a true aquarium, this slick set-up has performing dolphins and sea lions, waterskiing shows, and a 3-D movie theater. Penguins, crocodiles, tortoises, and, yes, some fish, are also present. The place also has its own beach (open December through March) with beach chairs, umbrellas, and a bar. ⊠ *Av. Martínez de Hoz 5600, Mar del Plata* ☎ *223/467–0000* ⊕ *www.mdpaquarium.com.ar* 🎫 *85 pesos* ⊙ *Check "horarios" on Web site before your visit.*

🐾 **El Puerto.** Beaches aside, Mar del Plata's tourist action hinges around the port area, 7 km (4 mi) south of the city center. A cluster of tacky but fun seafood restaurants form the **Complejo Comercial Puerto.** A half-mile walk toward the sea along 12 de Octubre brings you to a stretch of souvenir shops and fishmongers, beyond which lies the **Barranca de Lobos.** This is the port proper, home to hundreds of brightly painted fishing vessels and a colony of lobos marinos (sea lions)—their powerful stench announces their presence well before you sight them. The huge creatures often haul themselves out of the water to sun themselves on the breakwater as happy crowds of holiday makers snap photos. ⊠ *Av. Martínez de Hoz at 12 de Octubre, Mar del Plata.*

🐾 **Museo del Mar.** More than 30,000 seashells are the main exhibit at this attractive, modern museum. The four-story complex has numerous sea-related exhibits, including a petting pool and explanations of marine life and rock formations. You can also check out the café, library, movie theater, and gift shop. The rooftop lookout provides panoramic city views. Puppet shows and kiddie-oriented theater are common during school vacations. ⊠ *Av. Colón 1114, Mar del Plata* ☎ *223/451–9779* ⊕ *www.museodelmar.com* 🎫 *18 pesos* ⊙ *Jan.–Mar., daily 10–9; Apr.–June and Aug.–Nov., Tues.–Thurs. 10–8, Fri.–Sun. 10–9; July and Dec., daily 10–8.*

7

WHERE TO EAT AND STAY

For expanded hotel reviews, visit Fodors.com.

$
SEAFOOD

✗**Chichilo.** Fancy, it ain't: you line up cafeteria style to be served, then elbow your way to a Formica table, scattering the seagulls that peck at scraps from the floor. But the plates are piled with calamari and fries, and the huge portions of hake and sole are cooked on griddles as you watch. This friendly seafood joint has been a local favorite for more than 40 years. ✉ *Complejo Comercial del Puerto Local 17, Av. Martínez de Hoz at 12 de Octubre, Mar del Plata* ☎ *223/489–6317* ⊟ *No credit cards* ⊘ *Closed weekdays Apr.–June and Aug.–Nov.*

$$$
CONTEMPORARY

✗**Sarasanegro.** The menu and portions might be small, but each dish is packed with enough flavor—and enough ingredients—to make variety moot. Mar del Plata staples like fried prawns and sole come in a lettuce sauce or bathed in clam juice. The *mollejas* (sweetbreads) are crisply caramelized in sherry. The two young chefs behind the restaurant are so intent on the food that they've left the restaurant rather bare. Still, by the time you're through your scallops with tomato couscous and are on to the apple millefeuille, you probably won't care. The eight-course tasting menu is a great way to sample everything. ✉ *San Martín 3458, Mar del Plata* ☎ *223/473–0808* ⊕ *www.sarasanegro.com.ar* ⊟ *No credit cards* ⊘ *No lunch. Closed Mon. and Sun. Apr.–Nov.*

$$$
SEAFOOD

✗**Viento en Popa.** Word of mouth is the only advertising this restaurant seems to need: it doesn't even have a sign outside yet its tables are always full. Owner Ñeco Gioffi is a pioneer of so-called south Atlantic cuisine, aiming to show off the quality of ultra-fresh local fish and seafood, rather than bathe them in sauces. Dishes such as the *burriqueta en oliva* (burriqueta fish in olive oil and tarragon) or *lenguado con alcaparras* (sole with capers) are testament to the success of his formula. ✉ *Av. Martínez de Hoz 257, Mar del Plata* ☎ *223/489–0220* ⌁ *Reservations essential* ⊟ *No credit cards* ⊘ *Closed Mon.*

$$$$

🏨 **Hotel Costa Galana.** This may be Argentina's most popular seaside resort, but the look at Costa Galana is anything but beachy: rooms are richly decorated with thick wool carpets, mahogany furniture, and heavy drapes. **Pros:** large pool protected from the wind, direct access to a (relatively) quiet beach through a small underpass, great service. **Cons:** far from the center of town; despite high prices, they charge for extras like Internet; standard rooms are a bit small. ✉ *Blvd. Marítimo P. Peralta Ramos 5725, Mar del Plata* ☎ *223/410–5000* ⊕ *www.hotelcostagalana.com* ⌁ *186 rooms* ⌂ *In-room: safe, Internet. In-hotel: restaurant, bar, pool, gym, spa, beach* ⊙*Breakfast.*

IGUAZÚ FALLS

1,358 km (843 mi) north of Buenos Aires; 637 km (396 mi) west of Curitiba, 544 (338 mi) west of Vila Velha.

Iguazú consists of some 275 separate waterfalls—in the rainy season there are as many as 350—that plunge more than 200 feet onto the rocks below. They cascade in a deafening roar at a bend in the Iguazú River (Río Iguazú/Rio Iguaçu) where the borders of Argentina, Brazil, and Paraguay meet. Dense, lush jungle surrounds the falls: here the tropical sun and the omnipresent moisture produce a towering pine tree in two decades instead of the seven it takes in, say, Scandinavia. By the falls and along the roadside, rainbows and butterflies are set off against vast walls of red earth, which is so ubiquitous that eventually even paper currency in the area turns red from exposure to the stuff.

> **DOOR-TO-DOOR**
>
> Argentinean travel agency **Sol Iguazú Turismo** (☎ 3757/421–008 ⊕ www.soliguazu.com.ar) organizes door-to-door transport to both sides of the falls, and can reserve places on the Iguazú Jungle Explorer trips. It also runs day trips to the Jesuit ruins in San Ignacio, the Itaipú Dam, and to other areas of Misiones Province.

The falls and the lands around them are protected by Argentina's Parque Nacional Iguazú (where the falls are referred to by their Spanish name, the Cataratas de Iguazú) and by Brazil's Parque Nacional do Iguaçu (where the falls go by the Portuguese name of Cataratas do Iguaçu). The Argentine town of Puerto Iguazú and the Brazilian city of Foz do Iguaçu are the hubs for exploring the falls (the Paraguayan city of Ciudad del Este is also nearby).

GETTING HERE AND AROUND

ARGENTINA INFO

Aerolíneas Argentinas flies four to five times daily between Aeroparque Jorge Newbery in Buenos Aires and the Aeropuerto Internacional de Puerto Iguazú (20 km/12 mi southeast of Puerto Iguazú); the trip takes 1¾ hours. LAN does the same trip two or three times daily. Normal rates start at about 800 pesos each way. Four Tourist Travel runs shuttle buses from the airport to hotels in Puerto Iguazú. They leave after every flight lands and cost 25 pesos. Taxis to Puerto Iguazú cost 100 pesos.

Vía Bariloche operates several daily buses between the Retiro bus station in Buenos Aires and the Puerto Iguazú Terminal de Omnibus in the center of town. The trip takes 16–18 hours, so it's worth paying the little extra for *coche cama* (sleeper) or *cama ejecutivo* (deluxe sleeper) services, which cost about 470 pesos one-way (regular semi-cama services cost around 410 pesos). You can travel direct to Rio de Janeiro (22 hours) and São Paolo (15 hours) with Crucero del Norte; the trips cost 545 and 476 pesos, respectively.

From Puerto Iguazú to the falls or the hotels along RN 12, take El Práctico from the terminal or along Avenida Victoria Aguirre. Buses leave every 15 minutes 7–7 and cost 20 pesos round-trip.

There's little point in renting a car around Puerto Iguazú: daily rentals start at 260–300 pesos, more than twice what you pay for a taxi between the town and the falls. A hire car is useful for visiting the Jesuit ruins at San Ignacio, 256 km (165 mi) south of Puerto Iguazú on RN 12, a two-lane highway in excellent condition.

ARGENTINA ESSENTIALS

Airline Contacts Aerolíneas Argentinas ☎ 0810/2228–6527 ⊕ www.aerolineas.com.ar. **LAN** ☎ 0810/999–9526 ⊕ www.lan.com.

Foz do Iguaçu

Banks and Currency Exchange Argencam ⊠ *Av. Victoria Aguirre 1162, Puerto Iguazú, Misiones.* **Banco de la Nación** ⊠ *Av. Victoria Aguirre 179, Puerto Iguazú, Misiones* ⊕ *www.bna.com.ar.*

Bus Contacts Crucero del Norte ☎ *11/4315–1652 in Buenos Aires, 3757/421–916 in Puerto Iguazú* ⊕ *www.crucerodelnorte.com.ar.* **Four Tourist Travel** ☎ *3757/422–962 at airport, 3757/420–681 in Puerto Iguazú.* **Vía Bariloche** ☎ *0810/333–7575 in Buenos Aires, 3757/420–854 in Puerto Iguazú* ⊕ *www.viabariloche.com.ar.*

Internet Telecentro ⊠ *Av. Victoria Aguirre Norte 294, Puerto Iguazú, Misiones* ☎ *3757/422–454.*

Medical Assistance Farmacia Bravo ⊠ *Av. Victoria Aguirre 423, Puerto Iguazú, Misiones* ☎ *3757/420–479.* **Hospital Samic** ⊠ *Av. Victoria Aguirre 131, Puerto Iguazú* ☎ *3757/420–288.*

Taxis Remises Iguazú ⊠ *Puerto Iguazú* ☎ *3757/422–008.*

Visitor Info Cataratas del Iguazú Visitors Center ⊠ *Park entrance, Puerto Iguazú, Misiones* ☎ *3757/420–180* ⊕ *www.iguazuargentina.com* ☉ *Mar.–Aug., daily 8 am–6 pm; Sept.–Feb., daily 8 am–8 pm.* **Puerto Iguazú Tourist Office** ⊠ *Av. Victoria Aguirre 311, Puerto Iguazú* ☎ *3757/420–800* ☉ *Daily 7–1 and 2–9.*

BRAZIL INFO

There are direct flights between Foz do Iguaçu and São Paulo (1½ hours; $230), Rio de Janeiro (2 hours; $260), and Curitiba (1 hour; $280) on TAM, which also has connecting flights to Salvador, Recife, Brasilia, other Brazilian cities, and Buenos Aires. Low-cost airline GOL operates slightly cheaper direct flights on the same three routes.

The Aeroporto Internacional Foz do Iguaçu is 13 km (8 mi) southeast of downtown Foz. The 20-minute taxi ride should cost R$40–50; the 45-minute regular bus ride about R$2.60. Note that several major hotels are on the highway to downtown, so a cab ride from the airport to these may be less than R$30. A cab ride from downtown hotels directly to the Parque Nacional in Brazil costs about R$70.

Via bus, the trip between São Paolo and Foz do Iguaçu takes 15 hours (R$153). The Terminal Rodoviário in Foz do Iguaçu is 5 km (3 mi) northeast of downtown. There are regular buses into town; they stop at the Terminal de Transportes Urbano (local bus station, often shortened to TTU) at Avenida Juscelino Kubitschek and Rua Mem de Sá. From platform 2, Bus 120 (labeled "Parque Nacional") also departs every 15 minutes (7–7) to the visitor center at the park entrance; the fare is R$2.60. The buses run along Avenida Juscelino Kubitschek and Avenida Jorge Schimmelpfeng, where you can also flag them down.

There's no real reason to rent a car in Foz do Iguaçu: it's cheaper and easier to use taxis or local tour companies to visit the falls, especially as you can't cross the border in a rental car. There are taxi stands (*pontos de taxi*) at intersections all over town, each with its own phone number. Hotels and restaurants can call you a cab, but you can also hail them on the street.

CROSS-BORDER BUS

Crucero del Norte. This company runs an hourly cross-border public bus service (8 pesos) between the bus stations of Puerto Iguazú and Foz do Iguaçu. Locals don't have to get on and off for immigration, but be sure you do so. To reach the Argentine falls, change to local minibus service El Práctico at the intersection with RN 12 on the Argentine side. For the Brazilian park, change to a local bus at the Avenida Cataratas roundabout. ☎ *3757/421–916 in Puerto Iguazú* ⊕ *www.crucerodelnorte.com.ar.*

BRAZIL ESSENTIALS

Airline Contacts GOL ☎ *300/115–2121 toll-free, 45/3521–4230 in Foz do Iguaçu* ⊕ *www.voegol.com.br.* **TAM** ☎ *800/570–5700 toll-free, 45/3521–7500 in Foz do Iguaçu* ⊕ *www.tam.com.br.*

Bus Contacts Pluma ☎ *0800/646–0300 toll-free, 045/3522–2515 in Foz do Iguaçu* ⊕ *www.pluma.com.br.*

Banks and Currency Exchange Banco do Brasil ✉ *Av. Brasil 1377, Foz do Iguaçu* ⊕ *www.bb.com.br.*

Medical Assistance FarmaRede (pharmacy) ✉ *Av. Brasil 46, Foz do Iguaçu* ☎ *45/3572–1363.* **Hospital Ministro Costa Cavalcanti** ✉ *Av. Gramado 580, Foz do Iguaçu* ☎ *45/3576–8000.*

Taxis Ponto de Taxi 20 ☎ *45/3523–4625.*

Visitor Info Foz do Iguaçu Tourist Office ⊠ *Praça Getúlio Vargas 69, Foz do Iguaçu* ☎ *45/3521–1455* ⊕ *www.iguassu.tur.br* ⊙ *8 am–6 pm.*

WHERE TO EAT

Booming tourism is kindling the restaurant scenes of Puerto Iguazú and Foz do Iguaçu, and each has enough reasonably priced, reliable choices to get most people through the two or three days they spend there. Neither border town has much of a culinary tradition to speak of, though most restaurants at least advertise some form of the local specialty *surubí* (a kind of catfish), although it's frequently out of stock. Instead, parrillas or churrascarias abound, as do pizza and pasta joints.

PUERTO IGUAZÚ

$$$$
SEAFOOD

✗ **Aqva.** Locals are thrilled: finally, a date-night restaurant in Puerto Iguazú (reservations are essential on weekends). Although the high-ceilinged split-level cabin seats too many to be truly intimate, they make up for it with well-spaced tables, discreet service, and low lighting. Softly gleaming timber from different local trees lines the walls, roof, and floor. Local river fish like *surubí* and *dorado* are the specialty: have them panfried, or, more unusually, as pasta fillings. Forget being romantic at dessert time: the chef's signature dessert, fresh mango and pineapple with a *torrontés* sabayon, is definitely worth keeping to yourself. ⊠ *Av. Córdoba at Carlos Thays, Puerto Iguazú, Misiones, Argentina* ☎ *3757/422–064.*

$$$$
ARGENTINE

✗ **La Rueda.** This parrilla is so popular with visitors that they start serving dinner as early as 7:30 pm—teatime by Argentine standards. The local beef isn't quite up to Buenos Aires standards, but La Rueda's *bife de chorizo* is one of the best in town. Surubí is another house specialty, but skip the traditional Roquefort sauce, which overwhelms the fish's flavor. The surroundings stay true to the restaurant's rustic roots: hefty tree trunks hold up the bamboo-lined roof, and the walls are adorned by a curious wooden frieze carved by a local artist. ⊠ *Av. Córdoba 28, Puerto Iguazú, Misiones, Argentina* ☎ *3757/422–531* ⚑ *Reservations essential* ⊙ *No lunch Mon.–Tues.*

FOZ DO IGUAÇU

$$$$
BRAZILIAN

✗ **Búfalo Branco.** The city's finest and largest churrascaria does a killer *rodizio* (all-you-can-eat meat buffet). The *picanha* stands out from the 25 meat choices, but pork, lamb, chicken, and even—yum—bull testicles find their way onto the metal skewers they use to grill the meat. The salad bar is well stocked, a boon for vegetarians. ⊠ *Av. Rebouças 530, Foz do Iguaçu* ☎ *45/3523–9744.*

$$$$
SEAFOOD

✗ **Tempero da Bahia.** If you're not going as far as Bahia on your trip, you can at least check out its flavors at this busy tangerine-painted restaurant. It specializes in northeastern fare like *moquecas* (a rich seafood stew made with coconut milk and palm oil); their delicious versions are unusual for mixing prawns with local river fish. Spicy panfried sole and salmon are lighter options. The flavors aren't quite so subtle at the all-out seafood (and river food) buffets they hold several times a week, but at R$40 for all you can eat, they certainly pull in crowds. ⊠ *Rua*

Continued on page 290

By Victoria Patience

IGUAZÚ FALLS

Big water. That's what *y-guasu*—the name given to the falls by the indigenous Guaraní people—means. As you approach, a thundering fills the air and steam rises above the trees. Then the jungle parts. Spray-soaked and speechless, you face the Devil's Throat, and it's clear that "big" doesn't come close to describing this wall of water.

Taller than Niagara, wider than Victoria, Iguazú's raging, monumental beauty is one of nature's most awe-inspiring sights. The Iguazú River, on the border between Argentina and Brazil, plummets 200 feet to form the Cataratas de Iguazú (as the falls are known in Spanish) or Foz do Iguaçu (their Portuguese name). Considered to be one waterfall, Iguazú is actually made up of around 275 individual drops, that stretch along 2.7 km (1.7 mi) of cliff-face. Ranging from picturesque cascades to immense cataracts, this incredible variety is what makes Iguazú so special. National parks in Brazil and Argentina protect the falls and the flora and fauna that surround them. Exploring their jungle-fringed trails can take two or three days: you get right alongside some falls, gaze down dizzily into others, and can take in the whole spectacle from afar. You're sure to come across lizards, emerald- and sapphire-colored hummingbirds, clouds of butterflies, and scavenging raccoonlike coatis. You'll also glimpse monkeys and toucans, if you're lucky.

GEOLOGY 101

Over 100 million years ago, lava surged up through cracks in the earth's crust near Iguazú. It spread out over the surrounding area, forming three layers of basalt (a dark, fine-grained rock) tens of meters high. The Iguazú River, which starts 1,200 km (745 mi) east, flowed over this. Later, the movement of tectonic plates raised parts of the surface, which became stepped. As the river flowed over these steps it eroded the rock surface it fell on even more, and over the next few million years, the waters carved out what are now the falls.

WHEN TO GO

Time of year	Advantages	Disadvantages
Nov.—Feb.	High rainfall in December and January, so expect lots of water.	Hot and sticky. December and January are popular with local visitors. High water levels stop Zodiac rides.
Mar.—Jun.	Increasingly cooler weather. Fewer local tourists. Water levels are usually good.	Too cold for some people, especially when you get wet. Occasional freak water shortages.
Jul.—Oct.	Cool weather.	Low rainfall in July and August—water levels can be low. July is peak season for local visitors.

WHERE TO GO: ARGENTINA VS. BRAZIL

Argentines and Brazilians can fight all day about who has the best angle on the falls. But the two sides are so different that comparisons are academic. To really say you've done Iguazú (or Iguaçu), you need to visit both. If you twist our arm, we'll say the Argentine side is a better experience with lots more to do, but (and this is a big "but") the Brazilian side gives you a tick in the box and the best been-there-done-that photos. It's also got more non-falls-related activities (but you have to pay extra for them).

	ARGENTINA	BRAZIL
Park Name	Parque Nacional Iguazú	Parque Nacional do Iguaçu
The experience	Up close and personal (you're going to get wet).	What a view!
The falls	Two-thirds are in Argentina including Garganta del Diablo, the star attraction.	The fabulous panoramic perspective of the Garganta do Diablo is what people really come for.
Timing	One day to blitz the main attractions. Two days to explore fully.	Half a day to see the falls; all day if you do other activities.
Other activities	Extensive self-guided hiking and Zodiac rides.	Organized hikes, Zodiac rides, boat rides, helicopter rides, rafting, abseiling.
Park size	67,620 hectares (167,092 acres)	182,262 hectares (450,379 acres)
Animal species	80 mammals/450 birds	50 mammals/200 birds

VITAL STATISTICS

Number of falls: 160—275*	Total length: 2.7 km (1.7 mi)	Average Flow: 396,258 gallons per second Peak Flow: 1,717,118 gallons per second
Major falls: 19	Height of Garganta del Diablo: 82 m (270 feet)	Age: 120—150 million years

*Depending on water levels

IGUAZÚ ITINERARIES

LIGHTNING VISIT. If you only have one day, limit your visit to the Argentine park. Arrive when it opens, and get your first look at the falls aboard one of Iguazú Jungle Explorer's Zodiacs. The rides finish at the Circuito Inferior: take a couple of hours to explore this. (Longer summer opening hours give you time to squeeze in the **Isla San Martín**.) Grab a quick lunch at the Dos Hermanas snack bar, then blitz the shorter Circuito Superior. You've kept the best

Tren Ecologico de la Selva

for last: catch the train from **Estación Cataratas** to **Estación Garganta del Diablo,** where the trail to the viewing platform starts (allow at least two hours for this).

BEST OF BOTH SIDES. Two days gives you enough time to see both sides of the falls. Visit the Brazilian park on your second day to get the panoramic take on what you've experienced up-close in Argentina. If you arrive at 9 AM, you've got time to walk the entire trail, take photos, have lunch in the Porto Canoas service area, and be back at the park entrance by 1 PM. You could spend the afternoon doing excursions and activities from Macuco Safari and Ma-

KEY

♿	Wheelchair-accessible
🍴	Restaurant
🔱	Scenic Viewpoint
- - -	Walking/Hiking Trails
🚢	Ferry Lines
┼┼┼	Rail Lines

Estación Garganta del Diablo

Garganta del Diablo

Garganta del Diablo

ARGENTINA

Parque Nacional do Iguaçu

BRAZIL

Isla San Martín

Río Iguazú

Walkway view at Garganta del Diablo

cuco EcoAventura, or visiting the Itaipú dam. Alternatively, you could keep the visit to Brazil for the afternoon of the second day, and start off with a lightning return visit to the Argentine park and see the **Garganta del Diablo** (left) with the sun rising behind it.

SEE IT ALL. With three days you can explore both parks at a leisurely pace. Follow the one-day itinerary, then return to the Argentine park on your second day. Make a beeline for the Gar-

ganta del Diablo, which looks different in the mornings, then spend the afternoon exploring the **Sendero Macuco** (and Isla San Martín, if you didn't have time on the first day). You'll also have time to visit Güira Oga bird sanctuary or La Aripuca (both on RN 12) afterwards. You could spend all of your third day in the Brazilian park, or just the morning, giving you time to catch an afternoon flight or bus.

Estación Central

Estación Cataratas

Circuito Superior

Parque Nacional Iguazú

Circuito Inferior

Dos Hermanas

VISITING THE PARKS

Visitors gaze at the falls in Parque Nacional Iguazú.

Argentina's side of the falls is in the **Parque Nacional Iguazú,** which was founded in 1934 and declared a World Heritage Site in 1984. The park is divided into two areas, each of which is organized around a train station: Estación Cataratas or the Estación Garganta del Diablo. (A third, Estación Central, is near the park entrance.)

Paved walkways lead from the main entrance past the **Visitor Center,** called *Yvyrá Retá*—"country of the trees" in Guaraní (☎ 3757/49-1469 ⊕ www.iguazuargentina. com ✉ 60 pesos ☉ Mar.–Aug. 8–6; Sept.–Feb. 8–8). Colorful visual displays provide a good explanation of the region's ecology and human history. To reach the park proper, you cross through a small plaza containing a food court, gift shops, and ATM. From the nearby Estación Central, the gas-propelled Tren de la Selva (Jungle Train) departs every 20 minutes.

In Brazil, the falls can be seen from the **Parque Nacional Foz do Iguaçu** (☎ 45/3521–4400 ⊕ www.cataratasdoiguacu.com.br ✉ R$21.15 ☉ Apr.–Sep 9–5; Oct.–Mar. 9–6). Much of the park is protected rain forest—off-limits to visitors and home to the last viable populations of panthers as well as rare flora. Buses and taxis drop you off at a vast, plaza alongside the park entrance building. As well as ticket booths, there's an ATM, a snack bar, gift shop, and information and currency exchange. Next to the entrance turnstiles is the small **Visitor Center,** where helpful geological models explain how the falls were formed. Double-decker buses run every 15 minutes between the entrance and the trailhead to the falls, 11 km (7 mi) away; the buses stop at the entrances to excursions run by private operators Macuco Safari and Macuco Ecoaventura (these aren't included in your ticket). The trail ends in the **Porto Canoas** service area. There's a posh linen-service restaurant with river views, and two fast-food counters the with tables overlooking the rapids leading to the falls.

VISAS

U.S. citizens don't need a visa to visit Argentina as tourists, but the situation is more complicated in Brazil. ⇨ See the planning section at the beginning of the chapter.

EXCURSIONS IN AND AROUND THE PARKS

A Zodiac trip to the falls.

Iguazú Jungle Explorer (☎ 3757/42–1696 ⊕ www.iguazujungleexplorer.com) runs trips within the Argentine park. Their standard trip, the Gran Aventura, costs 150 pesos and includes a truck ride through the forest and a Zodiac ride to San Martín, Bossetti, and the Salto Tres Mosqueteros (be ready to get soaked). The truck carries so many people that most animals are scared away: you're better off buying the 75-peso boat trip—Aventura Nautica—separately.

You can take to the water on the Brazilian side with **Macuco Safari** (☎ 045/3574–4244 ⊕ www.macucosafari.com.br). Their signature trip is a Zodiac ride around (and under) the Salto Tres Mosqueteros. You get a more sedate ride on the Iguaçu Explorer, a 3½ hour trip up the river.

It's all about adrenaline with **Iguazú Forest** (☎ 3757/42–1140 ⊕ www.iguazuforest.com). Their full day expedition involves kayaking, abseiling, waterfall-climbing, mountain-biking, and canopying all within the Argentine park.

In Brazil, **Cânion Iguaçu** (☎ 045/3529–6040 ⊕ www.campodedesafios.com.br) offers rafting and canopying, as well as abseiling over the river from the Salto San Martín. They also offer wheelchair-compatible equipment.

Argentine park ranger Daniel Somay organizes two-hour Jeep tours with an ecological focus through his Puerto Iguazú–based **Explorador Expediciones** (☎ 3757/42–1632 ⊕ www.rainforestevt.com.ar). The tours cost 120 pesos and include detailed explanations of the Iguazú ecosystem and lots of photo ops. A specialist leads the birdwatching trips, which cost US$100 and include the use of binoculars and hotel pick-up and drop-off.

Macuco Ecoaventura (☎ 045/3529–6927 ⊕ www.macucoecoaventura.com.br) is one of the official tour operators within the Brazilian park. Their Trilha do Pozo Negro combines a 9-km guided hike or bike ride with a scary boat trip along the upper river (the bit before the falls). The aptly-named Floating trip is more leisurely; shorter jungle hikes are also offered.

ON THE CATWALK

You spend most of your visit to the falls walking the many trails and catwalks, so be sure to wear comfortable shoes.

Marechal Deodoro 1228, Foz do Iguaçu ☎ *45/3025–1144* ⊙ *Mon.–Sat. open from 6, Sun. from noon* ⊙ *No dinner Sun.*

$$$$ ✕ **Zaragoza.** On a tree-lined street in a quiet neighborhood, this tradi-
SPANISH tional restaurant's Spanish owner is an expert at matching Iguaçu's fresh river fish to authentic Spanish seafood recipes. Brazilian ingredients sneak into some dishes—the *surubi à Goya* (catfish in a tomato-and-coconut-milk sauce) definitely merits a try. ⊠ *Rua Quintino Bocaiúva 882, Foz do Iguaçu* ☎ *45/3028–8084.*

WHERE TO STAY

Once you've decided which country to base yourself in, the next big decision is whether to stay in town or at the five-star hotel inside each park. If you're on a lightning one-night visit and you only want to see one side of the falls, the convenience of staying inside the park might offset the otherwise unreasonably high prices for mediocre levels of luxury. Otherwise, you get much better value for money at the establishments in town or on highways BR 489 (Rodavia das Cataratas) in Brazil or RN 12 in Argentina. During the day you're a 20-minute bus ride from the falls and the border, and at night you're closer to restaurants and nightlife (buses stop running to the park after 7 or 8; after that, it's a 100-peso taxi ride into town from the park).

Hotels in Argentina are generally cheaper than in Brazil. During low season (late September–early November and February–May, excluding Easter) rooms are often heavily discounted. ⚠ Staying on the Brazilian side (apart from at the Hotel das Cataratas in the park) is not recommended. It's dangerous, especially after dark, more expensive, and the hotels are worse.

PUERTO IGUAZÚ

For expanded hotel reviews, visit Fodors.com.

$$$ 🏨 **Hostel-Inn Iguazú.** An enormous turquoise pool surrounded by classy wooden loungers and well-kept gardens lets you know this hostel is far from typical. **Pros:** beautiful pool area; rooms are simple but clean and well designed; location between town and the falls gives you the best of both worlds. **Cons:** impersonal service from indifferent staff; lounge and kitchen are run-down; very basic breakfast. ⊠ *Ruta 12, Km 5, Puerto Iguazú, Misiones, Argentina* ☎ *3757/421–823* ⊕ *www.hostel-inn.com* 🛏 *52 rooms* ⚬ *In-room: Wi-Fi. In-hotel: restaurant, bar, pool* ▭ *No credit cards* ⊠ *Breakfast.*

$$$$ 🏨 **Panoramic Hotel Iguazú.** The falls aren't the only good views in Iguazú:
★ half the rooms of this chic hotel look onto the churning, jungle-framed waters of the Iguazú and Paraná rivers. **Pros:** river views; great attention to detail in the beautifully designed rooms; the gorgeous pool. **Cons:** the in-house casino can make the lobby noisy; indifferent staff aren't up to the price tag; it's a short taxi ride to the town center, and in-house transport is overpriced. ⊠ *Paraguay 372, Puerto Iguazú, Misiones, Argentina* ☎ *3757/498–100, 3757/498–050* ⊕ *www.panoramic-hoteliguazu.com* 🛏 *91 rooms* ⚬ *In-room: safe, Wi-Fi. In-hotel: restaurant, bar, pool* ⊠ *Breakfast.*

$$$ ★ ⊞ **Río Tropic.** Friendly owners Rémy and Romina give you a warm welcome at this rootsy B&B, which is surrounded by a lush garden. **Pros:** the wonderfully helpful and attentive owners; peaceful surroundings; abundant homemade breakfasts served on a terrace in the garden. **Cons:** too far from the town center to walk to; low on luxury. ⊠ *Montecarlo s/n, at Km 5, RN 12, Puerto Iguazú, Misiones, Argentina* ☎ *5493757/571–403* ⊕ *www.riotropic.com.ar* ↝ *10 rooms* ⅏ *In-room: no TV, Wi-Fi. In-hotel: bar, pool* ⊟ *No credit cards* ☉ *Breakfast.*

$$ ⊞ **Secret Garden Iguazú.** Dense tropical vegetation overhangs the wooden walkway that leads to this tiny guesthouse's three rooms, tucked away in a pale-blue clapboard house. **Pros:** wooden deck overlooking the back-to-nature garden; knowledgeable owner John's charm and expert mixology; home-away-from-home vibe. **Cons:** the three rooms book up fast; no pool; comfortable but not luxurious. ⊠ *Los Lapachos 623, Puerto Iguazú, Misiones, Argentina* ☎ *3757/423–099* ⊕ *www. secretgardeniguazu.com* ↝ *3 rooms* ⅏ *In-room: no TV, Wi-Fi* ⊟ *No credit cards* ☉ *Breakfast.*

$$$$ ⊞ **Sheraton International Iguazú.** That thundering you can hear in the distance lets you know how close this hotel is to the falls. **Pros:** the falls are on your doorstep; great buffet breakfasts; well-designed spa. **Cons:** rooms are in need of a complete makeover; mediocre food and service at dinner; other restaurants are an expensive taxi-ride away. ⊠ *Parque Nacional Iguazú, Argentina* ☎ *3757/491–800* ⊕ *www.sheraton.com* ↝ *176 rooms, 4 suites* ⅏ *In-room: safe, Internet. In-hotel: restaurant, bar, pool, tennis court, gym, spa* ☉ *Breakfast.*

FOZ DO IGUAÇU

$$$$ ★ ⊞ **Hotel das Cataratas.** Not only is this stately hotel *in* the national park, with views of the smaller falls from the front-side suites, but it also provides the traditional comforts of a colonial-style establishment: large rooms, terraces, vintage furniture, and hammocks. **Pros:** right inside the park, a short walk from the falls; serious colonial-style charm; friendly, helpful staff. **Cons:** rooms aren't as luxurious as the price promises; far from Foz do Iguaçu so you're limited to the on-site restaurants; only the most-expensive suites have views of the falls. ⊠ *Km 28, Rodovia das Cataratas, Foz do Iguaçu* ☎ *045/2102–7000, 0800/726–4545* ⊕ *www.hoteldascataratas.com.br* ↝ *198 rooms, 5 suites* ⅏ *In-room: safe, Wi-Fi. In-hotel: restaurant, pool, tennis court, gym, business center* ☉ *Breakfast.*

7

UNDERSTANDING BUENOS AIRES

SPANISH VOCABULARY

MENU GUIDE

SPANISH VOCABULARY

	ENGLISH	SPANISH	PRONUNCIATION
BASICS			
	Yes/no	Sí/no	see/noh
	Please	Por favor	por fah-vor
	Thank you (very much)	(Muchas) gracias	(**moo**-chas) **grah**-see-ass
	You're welcome	De nada	deh **nah**-da
	Excuse me	Con permiso	con pehr-**mee**-so
	Pardon me	¿Perdón?	pehr-**don**
	Could you tell me...?	¿Podría decirme...?	po-**dree**-ah deh-**seer**-me
	I'm sorry	Lo siento/Perdón	lo see-**en**-to/pehr-**don**
	Hello!/Hi!	¡Hola!	**o**-la
	Good morning!	¡Buen día!	bwen **dee**-a
	Good afternoon!	¡Buenas tardes!	**bwen**-as **tar**-des
	Good evening/Good night!	¡Buenas noches!	**bwen**-as **no**-ches
	Goodbye!	¡Chau!/¡Adiós!	chow/a-dee-**os**
NUMBERS			
	0	Cero	seh-ro
	1	Un, uno	oon, **oo**-no
	2	Dos	doss
	3	Tres	tress
	4	Cuatro	**kwah**-troh
	5	Cinco	**sin**-koh
	6	Seis	**say**-iss
	7	Siete	see-**yet**-eh
	8	Ocho	och-oh
	9	Nueve	nweh-veh
	10	Diez	dee-**ess**
DAYS OF THE WEEK			
	Sunday	domingo	doh-**ming**-oh
	Monday	lunes	**loo**-ness

ENGLISH	SPANISH	PRONUNCIATION
Tuesday	martes	**mar**-tess
Wednesday	miércoles	mee-**er**-koh-less
Thursday	jueves	**hweh**-vess
Friday	viernes	vee-**er**-ness
Saturday	sábado	**sah**-bad-oh

USEFUL PHRASES

Do you speak English?	¿Habla usted inglés? / ¿Hablás inglés?	**ab**-la oo-**sted** ing-**less** / **ab**-las ing-**less**
I don't speak Spanish	No hablo castellano	No **ab**-loh cas-**teh**-sha-no
I don't understand	No entiendo	No en-tee-**en**-doh
I understand	Entiendo	en-tee-**en**-doh
I don't know	No sé	No seh
What's your name?	¿Cómo se llama usted? / ¿Cómo te llamás?	ko-mo seh **shah**-mah oo-**sted** / ko-mo teh **shah**-mass
My name is...	Me llamo...	meh **shah**-moh...
What time is it?	¿Qué hora es?	keh **o**-rah ess
It's one o'clock	Es la una	ess la **oo**-na
It's two/three/four... o'clock	Son las dos/tres/ cuatro	son lass doss/tress/ **kwah**-troh
Yes, please/	Si, gracias.	see, **grah**-see-ass
No, thank you	No, gracias.	noh, **grah**-see-ass
How?	¿Cómo?	**ko**-mo
When?	¿Cuándo?	kwan-doh
Tonight	Esta noche	**ess**-tah **noch**-eh
What?	¿Qué?	Keh
What is this?	¿Qué es esto?	keh ess **ess**-toh
Why?	¿Por qué?	por keh
Who?	¿Quién?	kee-**yen**
Telephone	teléfono	tel-**eff**-on-oh
I am ill	Estoy enfermo(a)	ess-**toy** en-**fer**-moh(mah)

ENGLISH	SPANISH	PRONUNCIATION
Please call a doctor	Por favor, llame a un médico	Por fah-**vor, shah**-meh a oon **meh**-dik-oh
Help!	¡Auxilio!	owk-**see**-lee-oh
Fire!	¡Incendio!	in-**sen**-dee-oh
Look out!	¡Cuidado!	kwee-**dah**-doh

OUT AND ABOUT

Where is...?	¿Dónde está...?	**don**-deh ess-**tah**...
the train station	la estación de tren	la ess-tah-see-**on** deh tren
the subway station	la estación de subte	la ess-tah-see-**on** deh **soob**-teh
the bus stop	la parada del colectivo	la pah-**rah**-dah del col-ek-**tee**-voh
the post office	el correo	el cor-**reh**-yoh
the bank	el banco	el **ban**-koh
the hotel	el hotel	el oh-**tel**
the museum	el museo	el moo-**seh**-yoh
the hospital	el hospital	el oss-pee-**tal**
the elevator	el ascensor	el ass-**en**-sor
the bathroom	el baño	el **ban**-yoh
Left/right	izquierda/derecha	iss-kee-**er**-dah/ deh-**rech**-ah
Straight ahead	derecho	deh-**rech**-oh
Avenue	avenida	av-en-**ee**-dah
City street	calle	**cah**-sheh
Highway	carretera/ruta	cah-ret-**eh**-rah
Restaurant	restaurante/restorán	rest-ow-**ran**-teh/ rest-oh-**ran**
Main square	plaza principal	**plass**-ah prin-see-**pal**
Market	mercado	mer-**kah**-do
Neighborhood	barrio	**bah**-ree-oh

MENU GUIDE

With so much meat on the menu, you'll need to know how to order it: *jugoso* (juicy) means medium rare, *vuelta y vuelta* (flipped back and forth) means rare, and *vivo por adentro* (alive inside) is barely warm in the middle. Argentineans like their meat *bien cocido* (well cooked).

aceite de olivo: olive oil

alfajores: Argentine cookies, usually made with dulce de leche and often covered with chocolate, though there are hundreds of varieties

arroz: rice

bife de lomo: filet mignon

bife de chorizo: like a New York strip steak, but double the size (not to be confused with *chorizo*, which is a type of sausage)

budín de pan: Argentine version of bread pudding

cabrito: roasted kid

cafecito: espresso

café con leche: coffee with milk

centolla: King crab, a Patagonian specialty

chimichurri: a sauce of oil, garlic, and salt, served with meat

chinchulines: small intestines

chorizo: thick, spicy pork-and-beef sausages, usually served with bread (*choripan*)

churros: baton-shaped donuts for dipping in hot chocolate

ciervo: venison

chivito: kid

cordero: lamb

cortado: coffee "cut" with a drop of milk

dulce de leche: a sweet caramel concoction made from milk and served on pancakes, in pastries, on cookies, and on ice cream

empanadas: pockets stuffed with meat—usually beef—chicken, or cheese

ensalada de fruta: fruit salad (sometimes fresh, sometimes canned)

estofado: beef stew

facturas: small pastries

huevos: eggs

humitas: steamed cornhusks wrapped around cornmeal and cheese

jamón: ham

lechón: roast suckling pig

lengua: tongue

licuado: milk shake

locro: local stew, usually made with hominy and beans, that's cooked slowly with meat and vegetables; common in northern Argentina

medialuna: croissant

mejillones: mussels

merluza: hake

milanesa: breaded meat cutlet, usually veal, pounded thin and fried; served as a main course or in a sandwich with lettuce, tomato, ham, cheese, and egg

milanesa a la napolitana: a breaded veal cutlet with melted mozzarella cheese and tomato sauce

mollejas: sweetbreads; the thymus glands, usually of the cow but also can be of the lamb or the goat

morcilla: blood sausage

pejerrey: a kind of mackerel

pollo: chicken

provoleta: grilled provolone cheese sprinkled with olive oil and oregano

puchero: boiled meat and vegetables; like pot-au-feu

queso: cheese

salchichas: long, thin sausages

sambayon: an alcohol-infused custard

tamales: ground corn stuffed with meat, cheese, or other fillings and tied up in a corn husk

tenedor libre: all-you-can-eat meat and salad bar

tinto: red wine

trucha: trout

Travel Smart
Buenos Aires

WORD OF MOUTH

"Keep your small change if you decide to travel around in urban bus. Buenos Aires has a coin [shortage], and . . . bus tickets are paid in machines that only [take] coins."

—quilmes

"Consider renting an apartment. It's much cheaper than a hotel, and you feel like a real *porteño*. . . . You can't go wrong with food and wine in BA. Meat and steak are religions there!"

—jasha7

www.fodors.com/community

GETTING HERE AND AROUND

Argentina measures around 3,650 km (2,268 mi) from tip to tail, and many of its attractions are hundreds of miles apart. Carefully planning how get around on your trip will help you save lots of time and money.

Buenos Aires lies about two-thirds of the way up Argentina's eastern side, on the banks of the Río de la Plata. It's the country's capital and main transport hub.

Three of the country's main draws are around 1,000 km (621 mi) from Buenos Aires, as the crow flies: Puerto Iguazú, the base for exploring Iguazú Falls, in northeastern Misiones Province; Salta, the gateway to the Andean Northwest; and Mendoza, in the wine region, near the Chilean border. Slightly farther, this time southwest of Buenos Aires, is Bariloche, the hub for the Lakes District of northern Patagonia. The hub of southern Patagonia is El Calafate, close to the Perito Moreno glacier, a whopping 2,068 km (1,285 mi) southwest of Buenos Aires.

TRAVEL TIMES FROM BUENOS AIRES		
	· BY AIR	BY BUS
San Antonio de Areco	n/a	2 hours
Atlantic Coast	1 hour	5–6 hours
Córdoba	1¼ hours	9–11 hours
Mendoza	1¾ hours	12–14 hours
Puerto Iguazú	1¾ hours	16–19 hours
Salta	2¼ hours	18–21 hours
Bariloche	2¼ hours	21–23 hours
El Calafate	3¼ hours	40 hours

Most domestic flights operate from Buenos Aires, so to fly from the extreme south of the country to the extreme north you often have to change planes here. Flying within the country makes sense given these huge distances. That said, domestic flights are expensive, so many visitors opt for the overnight sleeper buses for trips of up to 1,000 km (621 mi; around 12 hours). A well-developed network of long-distance buses connects Buenos Aires with cities all over Argentina; buses also operate between many cities without passing through Buenos Aires.

▌ AIR TRAVEL

TO ARGENTINA

There are direct daily services between Buenos Aires and several North American cities, with New York and Miami as primary departure points. Many airlines fly to Buenos Aires via Santiago de Chile or São Paulo in Brazil, which only adds a little to your trip time.

Aerolíneas Argentinas, the flagship airline, operates direct flights between Buenos Aires and Miami. Since being renationalized in 2008, Aerolíneas's reputation for chronic delays has improved vastly.

Chilean airline LAN is Aerolíneas's biggest local competition. LAN flies direct from Buenos Aires to Miami, and via Santiago de Chile, São Paulo, or Lima to JFK, Dallas, San Francisco, and Los Angeles. LAN also allows you to bypass Buenos Aires on routes into Mendoza and Córdoba from JFK and Miami, via Santiago de Chile.

There are direct flights from Atlanta on Delta. American also has nonstop service from JFK, Miami, and Dallas. United flies from JFK via Washington, D.C. Continental connects Buenos Aires nonstop with Houston and Washington, D.C.

Flying times to Buenos Aires are: 11–12 hours from New York, 9 hours from Miami, 10½ hours from Dallas or Houston, and 13–14 hours from Los Angeles via Santiago de Chile.

WITHIN ARGENTINA

Aerolíneas Argentinas and its subsidiary Austral operate flights from Buenos Aires to more Argentine cities than any other airline, including daily services (often more than one) to Puerto Iguazú, Salta, Mendoza, Córdoba, Bariloche, Ushuaia, and El Calafate. LAN also flies to these cities. Andes Líneas Aéreas operates flights between Buenos Aires and Salta, Jujuy, Córdoba, Puerto Madryn, and Bariloche, and sometimes runs direct services between Puerto Iguazú and Salta and Córdoba.

Airline Contacts Aerolíneas Argentinas
⊕ *www.aerolineas.com.ar.* **American Airlines** ⊕ *www.aa.com.* **Andes Líneas Aéreas** ⊕ *www.andesonline.com.* **Continental Airlines** ⊕ *www.continental.com.* **Delta Airlines** ⊕ *www.delta.com.* **LAN** ⊕ *www.LAN.com.* **United Airlines** ⊕ *www.united.com.*

AIR PASSES

Aerolíneas Argentinas runs two coupon-based air passes. Although you do not need to fly in and out of the continent with Aerolíneas to be eligible for either, you must purchase your pass before you arrive.

The South American Pass allows you to visit Argentina and at least two of the other countries Aerolíneas flies to in the region (Brazil, Chile, Colombia, Paraguay, Peru, Uruguay, and Venezuela). With the Visit Argentina Pass you can travel to between three and twelve destinations within Argentina. With both passes you use one coupon for each flight you take, but the catch is that many routes only operate from Buenos Aires, so you often have to return there. If you want to visit El Calafate and Iguazú with the Visit Argentina Pass, for example, you would need to buy four coupons.

Three coupons (the minimum purchase) cost $579 before tax for either pass, though this is reduced to $479 on the Visit Argentina pass if you fly in and out of the continent on Aerolíneas. Tax varies according to the destination.

If you plan to take at least three flights within Argentina or South America in general, you might save money with the Visit South America pass run by the

AEROLÍNEAS ARGENTINAS

Ongoing industrial disputes and internal changes were taking place at Aerolíneas Argentinas when this book went to press. Be sure to check the carrier's flights and offerings in advance, as they are subject to change.

OneWorld Alliance, which LAN is part of. Flights are categorized by mileage; segments (both domestic and international) start at $200.

Airlines and Airports Airline and Airport Links.com ⊕ *www.airlineandairportlinks.com.*

Airline Security Issues Transportation Security Administration ⊕ *www.tsa.gov.*

Air Passes South American Pass
☎ 800/333-0276 Aerolíneas Argentinas ⊕ *www.aerolineas.com.ar.* **Visit Argentina Pass** ☎ 800/333-0276 Aerolíneas Argentinas. **Visit South America Pass** ☎ 866/435-9526 LAN, OneWorld Alliance ⊕ *www.oneworld.com.*

AIRPORTS

Buenos Aires' Aeropuerto Internacional de Ezeiza Ministro Pistarini (EZE)—known simply as Ezeiza—is 35 km (22 mi) southwest of and a 45-minute drive from the city center.

Aerolíneas Argentinas and its partner Austral operate out of the older Terminal B. All other airlines are based at Terminal A, a pleasant, glass-sided building. A covered walkway connects the two terminals. Each has a few small snack bars, a small range of shops—including a pharmacy—a public phone center with Internet services, and a visitor information booth.

The ATM, 24-hour luggage storage, and car-rental agencies are in Terminal A. ■**TIP→** By far the best currency exchange rates are at the small Banco de la Nación in the Terminal A arrivals area; it's open around the clock.

Most domestic flights operate out of Aeroparque Jorge Newbery (AEP). It's next to the Río de la Plata in northeast

Palermo, about 8 km (5 mi) north of the city center.

Security at Argentine airports isn't as stringent as it is in the States—computers stay in cases, shoes stay on your feet, and there are no random searches. Air travel is expensive for Argentines, so airports are more likely to be crowded with foreigners than locals.

Airport Information Aeropuertos Argentinos 2000 ⊕ *www.aa2000.com.ar.* **Aeroparque Jorge Newbery** ☏ *11/4576–5300* ⊕ *www. aa2000.com.ar.* **Aeropuerto Internacional de Ezeiza Ministro Pistarini** ☏ *11/5480–2500* ⊕ *www.aa2000.com.ar.*

GROUND TRANSPORTATION

From Ezeiza, the quickest way of getting into town is by taxi. The cheapest and safest option is to use a fixed-rate service such as Manuel Tienda León or Taxi Ezeiza, which have booths just after customs and in the arrivals hall, respectively. You can also book with both companies online or by phone. The trip into town costs between 150 and 200 pesos and takes 45–60 minutes. Avoid the black-and-yellow city taxis that you can get at booths or on the curb outside either terminal: their metered price tends to be much more expensive, and overcharging (either by rigging the meter or by taking circuitous routes) is commonplace.

Manuel Tienda León also operates private shuttle buses that are nearly as fast as taxis and much cheaper. Services to and from its terminal in the Retiro district leave roughly every half hour; some include free drop-off at downtown hotels. You can buy the 55-peso one-way ticket at booths in the arrival halls of both terminals and in the walkway connecting the two.

The only public transport that connects Buenos Aires and Ezeiza is Bus 8, recorrido (branch) A. It leaves from a shelter in the parking area opposite the Aeropuertos Argentinos 2000 building (turn left out of Terminal B). You need change for the 2-peso ticket and patience for the two to

three hours it takes to reach San Telmo and Plaza de Mayo (it runs along Avenida Paseo Colón).

The highway connecting Ezeiza with the city is the Autopista Ricchieri, which is best reached by taking Autopista 25 de Mayo out of the city. ■**TIP**➔ Note that most flights to the United States depart from Buenos Aires in the evening, so plan to offset afternoon traffic snarls by allowing at least an hour of travel time to Ezeiza.

Aeroparque Jorge Newbery is actually inside Buenos Aires, on the Costanera Norte in northeast Palermo. There are several routes to Aeroparque from downtown—about a 15-minute trip. The easiest way is to take Avenida Libertador north to Avenida Sarmiento, and then take a right and follow it until Costanera Rafael Obligado. Note that traffic is usually heavy between 5 and 8 pm.

A taxi to Microcentro or San Telmo costs 30–40 pesos and takes anything from 15 to 45 minutes, depending on traffic. Manuel Tienda León operates shuttle buses to and from its terminal and downtown hotels, but a ticket costs 20 pesos—not that much less than a taxi, really.

Several city buses run along Avenida Rafael Obligado, outside the airport: the 160 goes to Plaza Italia, as does the 37, which continues to the Microcentro. The 33 and 45 go to Retiro, the Microcentro, and San Telmo. All cost 1.25 pesos.

TRANSFERS BETWEEN AIRPORTS

Taxi Ezeiza and Manuel Tienda León operate reliable taxi services between Ezeiza and Aeroparque. The ride costs 150–200 pesos including tolls and luggage and takes an hour in normal traffic. Manuel Tienda León shuttles make the same trip for 55 pesos per person; there are usually two departures per hour in each direction.

Taxis and Shuttles Manuel Tienda León ☏ *11/4383–4454, 810/888–5366* ⊕ *www. tiendaleon.com.ar.* **Taxi Ezeiza** ☏ *11/5480– 0066* ⊕ *www.taxiezeiza.com.ar.*

▌BOAT TRAVEL

Ferries run frequently across the Río de la Plata between Buenos Aires and the Uruguayan cities of Colonia and Montevideo. The best-value services are the Colonia Express catamarans, which take an hour or less to Colonia and three hours to Montevideo. Full-price round-trip tickets cost 280 and 380 pesos, respectively, but are often reduced to as low as 120 and 170 pesos if you book online. Buquebus operates similar services on high-speed ferries (round-trip tickets cost 398 pesos to Colonia and 649 pesos to Montevideo).

The two companies also sell packages that include bus tickets to La Paloma, Montevideo, and Punta del Este on services direct from Colonia's ferry terminal. You can order tickets by phone or online.

Buquebus leaves from a terminal at the northern end of Puerto Madero. The Colonia Express terminal is south of Puerto Madero on Avenida Pedro de Mendoza (the extension of Avenida Huergo) at 20 de Septiembre. It's best reached by taxi.

Contacts Buquebus ☎ *11/4316–6500* ⊕ *www.buquebus.com.* **Colonia Express** ☎ *11/4317–4100 English operator* ⊕ *www. coloniaexpress.com.*

▌BUS TRAVEL

TO AND FROM BUENOS AIRES

A range of frequent, comfortable, and dependable long-distance bus services connect Buenos Aires with cities all over Argentina as well as neighboring countries. Bus travel is substantially cheaper than flying. Both Argentineans and visitors often choose overnight sleeper services for trips up to 12 hours long.

TERMINAL

Most long-distance buses depart from the Terminal de Omnibus de Retiro, which is often referred to as the Terminal de Retiro or simply Retiro. Ramps and stairs from the street lead to a huge concourse where buses leave from more than 60 numbered platforms. There are restrooms, restaurants, phone and Internet centers, lockers, news kiosks, and a tourism office on this floor.

You buy tickets from the *boleterías* (ticket offices) on the upper level, where there are two ATMs. Each company has its own booth; they're arranged in zones according to the destinations served, which makes price comparisons easy.

The bus terminal's comprehensive Web site (in Spanish) lists bus companies by destination, including their telephone number and ticket-booth location.

TICKETS

Most major companies have online timetables; some allow you to buy tickets online or over the phone. Web sites also list alternative *puntos de venta* (sales offices)—in many cases you can buy tickets from booths in shopping malls or subway stations, though outside peak season you can usually buy them at the terminal right up until departure time.

Arrive early to get a ticket, and be prepared to pay cash. During January, February, and July, buy your ticket as far in advance as possible—a week or more, at least—and arrive at the terminal extra early.

CLASSES

All long-distance buses have toilets, air-conditioning, videos, and snacks like sandwiches or cookies. The most basic service is *semi-cama,* which has minimally reclineable seats and often takes a little longer than more luxurious services. It's worth paying the little extra for *coche cama,* sometimes called *ejecutivo,* where you get large, business-class-style seats and, sometimes, pillows and blankets.

The best rides of all are on the fully reclineable seats of *cama suite* or *suite premium* services, which are often contained in their own little booth. Bus attendants and free drinks are other perks. The more expensive the service, the cleaner and newer the bus.

Contacts Terminal de Ómnibus Retiro ⊠ *Av. Antártida Argentina at Av. Ramos Mejía, Retiro, Buenos Aires* ☎ *11/4310 0700* ⊕ *www.tcbasa. com.ar.*

WITHIN BUENOS AIRES

City buses, called *colectivos*, connect the city's barrios and greater Buenos Aires. Stops are roughly every two to three blocks (approximately 650–1,000 feet apart). Some are at proper shelters with large numbered signposts, others are marked by small, easy-to-miss metal disks or stickers stuck on nearby walls, posts, or even trees. Buses are generally safe, and run 24 hours a day, although service is less frequent at night.

A few routes have smaller, faster *diferencial* buses (indicated by a sign on the front) as well as regular ones; they run less frequently and are more expensive, but you usually get a seat on them.

Hail your bus and tell the driver the value of the ticket you want. Fares within the city are 1.10 pesos for up to 3 km (2 mi) or 1.20 or 1.25 pesos (depending on the bus line) for up to 6 km (4 mi), so say "*uno diez*," "*uno veinte*," or "*uno veinticinco*," respectively); then insert your coins in the machine, which will print your ticket. Fares outside the city are 1.75–2 pesos. Diferenciales cost 3 pesos. There are no daily or weekly discount passes. Exact change isn't necessary, but coins are. This can be a problem, because Buenos Aires suffers from a severe coin shortage. The majority of the city's bus lines also accept payment using SUBE (Sistema Único de Boleto Electrónico), a rechargeable swipe-card system that works on buses, trains, and the subte. Cards are available for free from branches of Correo Argentino (the post office), but you need to fill out a form and show your passport. You can add credit to your card at any subte station and at convenience stores displaying the green and purple SUBE logo.

Once on board, head for the back, which is where you exit. A small button on the grab bar lets you signal for a stop. Don't depend on drivers for much assistance; they're busy navigating traffic. Note that routes follow different streets in each direction—these are detailed in the *Guía T*, an essential route guide that you can

BUENOS AIRES BUS

Buenos Aires Bus, a hop-on, hop-off service run by the city's official tourism body, is an efficient way to tick off all the main tourist spots in the city. The colorful double-decker buses leave two to three times per hour and have bilingual guides aboard who point out landmarks. The 3- to 4-hour circuit takes you from El Centro through San Telmo and La Boca, then through Puerto Madero and on to Retiro, Palermo Chico, Las Cañitas, and Belgrano, before returning through Palermo and Recoleta to Tribunales. Your 70-peso ticket entitles you to get on and off the service as many times as you like during the day.

purchase at any news kiosk, or visit the Spanish-language Los Colectivos Web site for info.

Information Buenos Aires Bus ☎ 11/5239–5160 ⊕ www.buenosairesbus.com. **Los Colectivos** ⊕ www.loscolectivos.com.ar. **SUBE (Sistema Único de Boleto Electrónico)** ☎ 800/777–7823 ⊕ www.sube.gob.ar.

▌ CAR TRAVEL

Having a car in Buenos Aires is really more hassle than it's worth; there are ample taxis and public transportation options. A more convenient option than driving yourself is to have your travel agent or hotel arrange for a *remis* (car and driver), especially for a day's tour of the suburbs (⇨ *Remis Travel, below*). However, a car can be useful for longer excursions to the Atlantic Coast or interior towns of Buenos Aires Province.

ROUTES

Avenida General Paz is Buenos Aires' ring road. If you're driving into the city, you'll know you're in Buenos Aires proper once you cross it. If you're entering from the north, chances are you'll be on the Ruta Panamericana, which has wide lanes and good lighting, but many accidents. The quickest way from downtown to Ezeiza

Airport is Autopista 25 de Mayo to Autopista Ricchieri. Ruta 2 takes you to the Atlantic beach resorts in and around Mar del Plata.

During the week the Microcentro, the bustling commercial district bounded by Carlos Pellegrini, Avenida Córdoba, Avenida Leandro Alem, and Avenida de Mayo, is off-limits to all but public transit vehicles.

HAZARDS

Porteño driving styles range from erratic to downright psychotic, and the road mortality rate is shockingly high. Drive defensively.

City streets are notorious for potholes, uneven surfaces, and poorly marked lanes and turnoffs.

Rush-hour traffic affects the roads into Buenos Aires between 8 and 10 am, and roads out between 6 and 9 pm; the General Paz ring road and the Panamericana are particularly problematic.

■**TIP**➔ Be cautious when approaching or exiting overpasses on General Paz, where there have been incidences of *ladrillazos* (brick throwing): you stop the car to examine your broken windshield, at which point thieves appear.

PARKING

On-street parking is limited. Some neighborhoods, such as San Telmo and Recoleta, have meters: you pay with coins (1.50 pesos per hour for up to four hours), then display the ticket you receive on your dashboard. In meter-free areas, parking is usually only allowed on the right side of the street. In popular areas there's often a self-appointed caretaker who guides you into your spot and watches your car: you pay anything from 2 to 5 pesos when you leave. Most attendants won't do much more than yell at you if you don't, but most locals see not paying as rude.

Car theft is fairly common, so many rental agencies insist you park in a guarded lot—Buenos Aires is full of them. Look for a circular blue sign with a white "E" (for *estacionamiento* [parking]). Downtown,

expect to pay 10–12 pesos per hour, or 36–48 pesos for 12 hours. Illegally parked cars are towed from the Microcentro and San Telmo. Getting your car back is a bureaucratic nightmare and costs around 200 pesos. Most malls have lots, which sometimes give you a reduced rate with a purchase.

RULES OF THE ROAD

Buenos Aires has a one-way system in which parallel streets run in opposite directions: never going the wrong way along a street is one of the few rules that Argentines abide by. Where there are no traffic lights at an intersection, you give way to drivers coming from the right, and have priority over those coming from the left.

Most driving rules in the United States theoretically apply here (although locals flout them shamelessly). However, keep in mind the following: right turns on red are not allowed; never park on the left side of the street, where there's a yellow line on the curb, or alongside a bus stop; and turning left on two-way avenues is prohibited unless there's a left-turn signal or light.

The legal blood-alcohol limit is 500 mg of alcohol per liter of blood, and breathalyzing is becoming more common within the city.

In Buenos Aires a 40-kph (25-mph) speed limit applies on streets, and a 60-kph (37-mph) limit is in effect on avenues. However, locals take speed-limit signs, the ban on driving with cell phones, and drinking and driving lightly, so drive very defensively.

Local police tend to be forgiving of foreigners' driving faults and often waive tickets and fines when they see your passport or driver's license. If you do get a traffic ticket, don't argue. Most aren't payable on the spot, but some police officers offer "reduced" on-the-spot fines in lieu of a ticket: it's out-and-out bribery, and you'd do best to avoid it by insisting on receiving the proper ticket.

CAR RENTALS

Daily rates range from 215 pesos to 450 pesos, depending on the type of car and the distance you plan to travel. This generally includes tax and 200 free km (125 mi) daily. If you plan to do a lot of driving, consider renting with Hertz, the only local agency that offers unlimited mileage. Note that nearly all rental cars in Argentina have manual transmissions, so if you need an automatic, request it in advance.

Reputable firms don't rent to drivers under 21, and renters under 23 often have to pay a daily surcharge. In general, you cannot cross the border in a rental car. Children's car seats aren't compulsory, but are available for about 15 pesos per day. Some agencies charge a 10% surcharge for picking up a car from the airport.

Rental deals usually include roadside assistance. Argentina's automobile association, the Automóvil Club Argentina, also offers free roadside assistance to members of North American clubs and automobile associations. However, bear in mind when you call for assistance that most operators speak only Spanish.

INSURANCE

Collision damage waiver (CDW) is mandatory in Argentina and is included in standard rental prices. However, you may still be responsible for a deductible fee (known locally as a franquicia or deducible)—a maximum amount that you'll have to pay if damage occurs. The amount is generally around 3,000 pesos for a car and can be much higher for a four-wheel-drive vehicle. You can reduce the figure substantially or altogether by paying an insurance premium (anywhere from 30–80 pesos per day, depending on the company and type of vehicle).

Some companies include loss damage waiver (LDW) in the CDW fee, others charge a premium for it (usually 20–50 pesos per day). Car theft is common enough in Argentina for it to make sense to pay.

Many rental companies don't insure you for driving on unpaved roads. Discuss your itinerary carefully with the agent to be certain you're always covered.

Major car-rental agencies with branches in Buenos Aires include Avis, Budget, Hertz, Alamo, Dollar, and local agency Abbey Rent-a-Car. You can rent cars at both airports and through many hotels. If the agency has a branch in another town, arrangements can usually be made for a one-way drop-off, for a hefty surcharge.

Automobile Association Automóvil Club Argentina (ACA) ☎ 11/4808–4000 ⊕ www. aca.org.ar.

Rental Agencies Alamo ☎ 11/4322–3320 in Buenos Aires ⊕ www.alamoargentina.com. ar. **Avis** ☎ 810/9991–2847, 11/4326–5542 in Buenos Aires ⊕ www.avis.com.ar. **Budget** ☎ 810/999–2834, 11/4326–3825 in Buenos Aires ⊕ www.budget.com.ar. **Dollar** ☎ 800/555–3655, 11/4315–1670 in Buenos Aires ⊕ www.dollar.com.ar. **Hertz** ☎ 810/222–43789, 11/4816–8001 in Buenos Aires ⊕ www. milletrentacar.com.ar.

▌ REMIS TRAVEL

An alternative to renting a car is to hire a *remis*, a car with a driver, especially for day outings. Hotels and travel agents can make arrangements for you. You'll have to pay cash, but you'll often spend less than you would on a rental car or hiring cabs for whole days. Remis service costs about 60–100 pesos per hour, depending on the type of car. There is usually a three-hour minimum and an additional charge per kilometer (0.5 mi) if you drive over a certain distance or go outside the city limits. If your driver is helpful and friendly, a 10% tip is appropriate.

Remises Abbey Rent-A-Car ☎ 11/4924–1984 ⊕ www.abbeyrentacar.com.ar. **Annie Millet Transfers** ☎ 11/6777–7777. **Remises Universal** ☎ 11/4105–5555 ⊕ www.universalvans.com. **Vía Remis** ☎ 11/4777–8888.

▮ SUBTE TRAVEL

The *subte* (subway) is one of the quickest ways to get around. Packed trains mean it's not always the most comfortable, though it's generally fairly safe. Most stations are reasonably well patrolled by police and many are decorated with artworks. You'll likely hear musicians and see actors performing on trains and in the stations.

Single-ride tickets to anywhere in the city cost 1.10 pesos; you can buy passes in stations for 1, 2, 5, or 10 trips. Two types of rechargeable contact-free card—called SUBE and Monedero—can be used on the subte, but you need to present your passport and fill in a form to obtain both. The SUBE card also works on most city bus lines and is available at all branches of Correo Argentino. The *Monedero* card is only accepted on a few bus lines, but you can use it to pay for small purchases at many kiosks in the Centro. You sign up for it at the ticket booths in stations Tribunales (Línea D) and Independencia (Línea E). ⇨ *For SUBE card information, see "Bus Travel, Within Buenos Aires," above.*

The subte shuts down between 10:30 and 11 pm and reopens at 5 am.

Línea A travels beneath Avenida Rivadavía from Plaza de Mayo to Carabobo in Flores and is serviced by handsome but rattling antique wooden cars. At this writing two new stations were under construction in Flores.

Línea B begins at Leandro Alem Station, in the financial district, and runs under Avenida Corrientes to Los Incas Station in Parque Chas, and will eventually continue on to Villa Urquiza.

Línea C, under Avenida 9 de Julio, connects the two major train stations, Retiro and Constitución, making stops along the way in the Centro and San Telmo.

Línea D runs from Catedral Station on Plaza de Mayo to Congreso de Tucumán in Belgrano.

Línea E takes you from Bolívar Station, on Plaza de Mayo, to Plaza de los Virreyes, in the neighborhood of Flores. At this writing, three new stations were being built in order to connect Bolívar with Retiro Station.

Línea H, the subte's newest line, is only partially open, and runs from Corrientes through Plaza Miserere in Once to Caseros, crossing lines A and E. It will eventually be extended north to Retiro, crossing lines B and D, and south to Pompeya.

Information Metrovías ☎ 800/555-1616 ⊕ www.metrovias.com.ar. **Monedero Card** ☎ 800/362-6663 ⊕ www.monedero.com.ar.

▮ TAXI TRAVEL

Taxis in Buenos Aires are relatively cheap and plentiful. All are black with yellow tops. An unoccupied one will have a small, red "Libre" sign in its windshield.

Local wisdom has it that the safest taxis to hail on the street are those with a light on the roof that says "radio taxi," which are part of licensed fleets and are in constant contact with dispatchers. If you phone for a taxi, you'll have to wait a few minutes, but you can be sure where it has come from and that it is safe.

Legally, all taxis are supposed to have working seatbelts in the front and back seats, but this isn't always the case.

Meters start at 5.80 pesos and charge 58¢ per 200 meters (650 feet); you'll also end up paying for standing time spent at a light or in a traffic jam. From downtown it will cost you around 15 pesos to Recoleta, 12–16 pesos to San Telmo, 20–26 pesos to Palermo, and 30–35 pesos to Belgrano. Drivers don't expect tips; rounding up to the next peso is sufficient.

Taxi Companies Del Plata ☎ 11/4505-1111 ⊕ www.delplataradiotaxi.com. **Pídalo** ☎ 11/4956-1200 ⊕ www.radiotaxipidalo.com.ar. **Premium** ☎ 11/4374-6666 ⊕ www.taxipremium.com. **Radio Taxi Ciudad** ☎ 11/4923-7007 ⊕ www.radiotaxiciudad.com.ar.

▌ TOURS

Turismo Buenos Aires. The Web site of the city tourist board, Turismo Buenos Aires has lively, downloadable MP3 walking tours in English. Other English-language information on the site is so badly translated it's almost cryptic, however. Information booths at the airports and seven other locations provide maps and have English-speaking staff. Hours can be erratic, but the booth at the intersection of Florida and Marcelo T. de Alvear is usually open during the day. ⊕ *www.bue. gov.ar.*

ORGANIZED TOUR COMPANIES

Ghosts, crimes, and spooky legends are the basis for the Buenos Aires Misteriosa tours by **Ayres Viajes,** which also offers general tours in and around town.

The service—for tours in town and out—you get from Isabel at **Buenos Aires Tours** is almost heroic.

For a local's perspective, contact the **Cicerones de Buenos Aires,** a free service that pairs you with a porteño to show you parts of town you might not see otherwise.

Informed young historians from the University of Buenos Aires lead cultural and historical tours at **Eternautas.** It offers general city tours, themed private outings (e.g., Evita and Peronism, the literary city, Jewish Buenos Aires), and excursions outside town.

With **La Bicicleta Naranja** you can rent a bicycle and gear—delivered to your hotel—to follow one of the routes on their excellent maps or go with a bilingual guide on general or themed trips.

See Buenos Aires from the river on a 2½-hour sailboat tour with **Smile on Sea.**

Look down on the city and its surroundings from a helicopter, hot-air balloon, or glider on one of the aerial tours run by **Buenos Aires Alternativo.**

Large onboard screens make the posh minibuses used by **Opción Sur** part transport and part cinema. Each stop on their tours of the city and the Tigre Delta is introduced by relevant historical footage (e.g., Evita rallying the masses at Plaza de Mayo).

You get serious insight into the Jewish community on day tours run by Deb Miller's company, **Travel Jewish.**

Tick off the major sights and get the lay of the land on the basic three-hour bus tours in English and Spanish run by **Travel Line.**

For tailor-made city tours, contact **Wow! Argentina** well in advance of your arrival in Buenos Aires. Enthusiastic Cintia Stella and her team also arrange excursions all over Argentina.

Tour Companies Ayres Viajes ☎ *11/4383–9188* ⊕ *www.ayresviajes.com.ar.* **Buenos Aires Tours** ☎ *11/4785-2753* ⊕ *www. buenosaires-tours.com.ar.* **Cicerones de Buenos Aires** ☎ *11/4431–9892* ⊕ *www. cicerones.org.ar.* **Eternautas** ☎ *11/5031–9916* ⊕ *www.eternautas.com.* **La Bicicleta Naranja** ☎ *11/4362–1104* ⊕ *www.labicicletanaranja. com.ar.* **Smile on Sea** ⊕ *www.smileonsea. com.* **Buenos Aires Alternativo** ☎ *11/5779–4140* ⊕ *www.bsasalternativo.com.ar.* **Opción Sur** ☎ *11/4777–9029* ⊕ *www.opcionsur. com.ar.* **Travel Jewish** ☎ *877/826–4674 in U.S.* ⊕ *www.traveljewish.com.* **Travel Line** ☎ *11/4393–9000* ⊕ *www.travelline.com.ar.* **Wow! Argentina** ☎ *11/5239–3019* ⊕ *www. wowargentina.com.*

ESSENTIALS

▮ BUSINESS TRAVEL

DOING BUSINESS

Suits are definitely still the norm for Argentinean men in the office. Local businesswomen are usually immaculately groomed, and wear either skirt or pants suits with high heels; they often wear sexier or more revealing clothing than their North American counterparts might.

Arriving late for social occasions may be normal and acceptable among porteños, but arriving late for a business appointment is not, even though proceedings may take a while to get going. Business cards are always appreciated.

Argentinean businesspeople are mostly direct and to the point. Giving someone your word or shaking hands on something doesn't carry the same weight in Argentina as in the United States. If you want something set in stone, get it down on paper and signed.

Most local businesspeople eat lunch out, but meals are often a break from the boardroom, not an extension of it. At a typical business dinner the flow of conversation is much like it is in the United States—discussing common interests such as sports, hobbies, family, travel, and even politics are all part of the ritual of getting to know and trust an individual.

Porteño businesspeople tend to use first names in all but the most formal meetings; some professions use their jobs as titles: *doctor/a* is a catchall used by medical and legal professionals; *ingeniero/a* for engineers; and *arquitecto/a* for architects.

BUSINESS SERVICES

Ámbito Financiero is Argentina's leading financial daily. *BAE* is another local business-oriented newspaper. Both are in Spanish. You can get information on business opportunities in English at Fundación Invertir, which has useful information on investing in Argentina.

Stationery stores (*papelerías*) are easy to find in Buenos Aires—most offer photocopying and binding services. For special printing and document design, ask your hotel to recommend a *gráfica* (print and design company).

AreaTres offers a variety of serviced office, meeting, and conference facilities in Buenos Aires' Palermo neighborhood, including secretarial services. Contact Virtual Assistance Argentina for secretarial services. Speziali Communications offers reliable translation and interpretation services.

Buenos Aires' flagship convention center is enormous La Rural, which has event-organizing services.

Contacts Ambito Financiero ⊕ *www. ambitoweb.com.* **AreaTres** ☎ *11/5353–0333* ⊕ *www.areatresworkplace.com.* **BAE** ⊕ *www. diariobae.com.* **Fundación Invertir** ⊕ *www. invertir.com.* **La Rural** ☎ *11/4777–5500* ⊕ *www.larural.com.ar.* **Speziali Communications** ☎ *11/15–5698–0584* ⊕ *www. spezialicommunications.com.* **Virtual Assistance Argentina** ☎ *11/5353–9851* ⊕ *www. vaargentina.com.*

■ COMMUNICATIONS

INTERNET

Inexpensive Internet access is widely available in Buenos Aires. Top-end hotels tend to have high-speed in-room data ports and Wi-Fi, which may incur a charge, while most lower-budget establishments (including hostels) have free Wi-Fi. Many hotels have a PC in the lobby for guests to use.

If you're traveling without a laptop, look for a *ciber* (Internet café) or *locutorio* (telephone and Internet center). It's hard to walk more than a block without coming across one. Expect to pay between 4 and 6 pesos per hour to surf the Web. Broadband connections are common.

Many bars and restaurants have free Wi-Fi—look out for stickers on their windows. In general, these are open networks and you don't need to ask for a password to use them. You can also find Wi-Fi in many hotel lobbies, libraries, business and event centers, some airports, and in public spaces—piggybacking is common practice.

Contact Cybercafes. Cybercafes lists over 4,000 Internet cafés worldwide. ⊕ *www. cybercafes.com.*

PHONES

The country code for Argentina is 54. To call landlines in Argentina from the United States, dial the international access code (011) followed by the country code (54), the two- to four-digit area code without the initial 0, then the six- to eight-digit phone number. For example, to call the Buenos Aires number (011) 4123–4567, you would dial 011–54–11–4123–4567.

Any number that is prefixed by a 15 is a cell-phone number. To call cell phones from the United States, dial the international access code (011) followed by the country code (54), Argentina's cell-phone code (9), the area code without the initial 0, then the seven- or eight-digit cell phone number without the initial 15. For example, to call the Buenos Aires cell phone (011) 15 5123–4567, you would dial 011–54–9–11–5123–4567.

CALLING WITHIN ARGENTINA

Argentina's phone service is run by the duopoly of Telecom and Telefónica. Telecom does the northern half of Argentina (including the northern half of the city of Buenos Aires) and Telefónica does the south. However, both companies operate public phones and phone centers, called *locutorios* or *telecentros*, throughout the city.

Service is generally efficient, and direct dialing—both long-distance and international—is universal. You can make local and long-distance calls from your hotel (usually with a surcharge) and from any public phone or locutorio. Public phones aren't particularly abundant, and are often broken. All accept coins; some have slots for phone cards.

Locutorios are useful if you need to make lots of calls or don't have coins on you. Ask the receptionist for *una cabina* (a booth), make as many local, long-distance, or international calls as you like (a small LCD display tracks how much you've spent), then pay as you leave. There's no charge if you don't get through.

All of Argentina's area codes are prefixed with a 0, which you need to include when dialing another area within Argentina. You don't need to dial the area code to call a local number. Confusingly, area codes and phone numbers don't all have the same number of digits. The area code for Buenos Aires is 011, and phone numbers have eight digits. Area codes for the rest of the country have three or four digits, and start with 02 (the southern provinces, including Buenos Aires province) or 03 (the northern provinces); phone numbers have six or seven digits.

For local directory assistance (in Spanish), dial 110.

Local calls cost 23¢ for two minutes at peak time (weekdays 8–8 and Saturday 8–1) or four minutes the rest of the time. Long-distance calls cost 57¢ per *ficha* (unit)—the farther the distance, the shorter each unit. For example, 57¢ lasts about two minutes to places less than 55 km (34 mi) away, but only half a minute to somewhere more than 250 km (155 mi) away.

To make international calls from Argentina, dial 00, then the country code, area code, and number. The country code for the United States is 1.

CALLING CARDS

You can use prepaid calling cards (*tarjetas prepagas*) to make local and international calls from public phones, but not locutorios. All cards come with a scratch-off panel, which reveals a pin number. You dial a free access number, the pin number, and the number you wish to call.

Most *kioscos* and small supermarkets sell prepaid cards from different companies: specify it's for *llamadas internacionales* (international calls), and compare each card's per-minute rates to the country you want to call. Many cost as little as 9¢ per minute for calls to the United States.

Telecom and Telefónica also sell prepaid 5-, 10-, and 20-peso calling cards from kioscos and locutorios. They're called Tarjeta Países and Geo Destinos, respectively. Calls to the United States cost 19¢ per minute using both.

Calling card information Telecom ☎ *0800/555–0030* ⊕ *www.telecom.com. ar.* **Telefónica** ☎ *0800/333–4004* ⊕ *www. telefonica.com.ar.*

MOBILE PHONES

Mobile phones are immensely popular; all are GSM 850/1900 Mhz. If you have an unlocked dual-band GSM phone from North America and intend to call local numbers, it makes sense to buy a prepaid Argentinean SIM card on arrival—rates will be cheaper than using your U.S. network or renting a phone. Alternatively, you can buy a basic pay-as-you-go handset and SIM card for around 200 pesos.

All Argentinean cell-phone numbers use a local area code, then the cell phone prefix

(15), then a seven- or eight-digit number. To call a cell phone in the same area as you, dial 15 and the number. To call a cell phone in a different area, dial the area code including the initial 0, then 15, then the number.

Local charges for calling a cell phone from a landline vary depending on factors like the company and time of day, but most cost between 50¢ and 1.50 pesos per minute. You only pay for outgoing calls from cell phones, which cost between 50¢ and 2 pesos a minute. Calls from pay-as-you-go phones are the most expensive and calls to phones from the same company as yours are usually cheaper.

There are three mobile phone companies in Argentina: Movistar, owned by Telefónica; Claro; and Personal. Their prices are similar, but Claro is said to be cheaper, Movistar has the most users and best coverage, and Personal is the least popular service, so cards can be harder to find. All three companies have offices and sales stands all over the country.

You can buy a SIM card (*tarjeta SIM*) from any of the companies' outlets. Top up credit by purchasing pay-as-you-go cards (*tarjetas de celular*) at kioscos, locutorios, supermarkets, and gas stations, or by *carga virtual* (virtual top-ups) at locutorios, where sales clerks can add credit to your line directly. Adding 30 pesos or more often gives you extra credit.

You can rent a cell—including smartphones—at the airport from Phonerental, which also delivers to hotels. A basic handset is free for the first week and 20 pesos weekly thereafter; outgoing local calls cost about 3.50 pesos per minute, but you pay 2.40 pesos per minute to receive both local and international calls. For very short stays, however, renting can be good value.

Contacts Cellular Abroad ☎ *800/287–5072* ⊕ *www.cellularabroad.com.* **Claro** ⊕ *www. claro.com.ar.* **Mobal** ☎ *888/888–9162* ⊕ *www. mobalrental.com.* **Movistar** ⊕ *www.movistar. com.ar.* **Personal** ⊕ *www.personal.com.*

LOCAL DO'S AND TABOOS

CUSTOMS OF THE COUNTRY

Welcoming and helpful, porteños are a pleasure to travel among. Although cultural differences between here and North America are few, they're still palpable.

Porteños are usually fashionably late for all social events—don't be offended if someone keeps you waiting over half an hour for a lunch or dinner date. However, tardiness is frowned upon in the business world.

Political correctness isn't a valued trait, and just about everything and everyone—except mothers—is a target for playful mockery. Locals are often disparaging about their country's shortcomings, but Argentina-bashing is a privilege reserved for Argentineans.

Sadly, the attitudes of many porteños toward foreigners vary greatly according to origin and race. White Europeans and North Americans are held in far greater esteem than, say, Peruvians or Bolivians. Racist reactions—anything from insults or name-calling to giving short shrift—to Asian, black, or Native American people are, unfortunately, not unusual. Although there's little you can do about this in day-to-day dealings, Argentina does have an antidiscrimination body, Institución Nacional contra la Discriminación, la Xenofobia y el Racismo (INADI; ⊕ www.inadi.gov.ar), that you can contact if you're the victim of serious discrimination.

GREETINGS

Porteños have no qualms about getting physical, and the way they greet each other reflects this. One kiss on the right cheek is the customary greeting between both male and female friends. Women also greet strangers in this way, although men—especially older men—often shake hands the first time they meet someone. Other than that, handshaking is seen as very cold and formal.

When you arrive at a party it's normal to kiss and greet absolutely everyone in the room (or, if you're in a restaurant, everyone at your table). When you leave, you say good-bye to everyone and repeat the performance.

Porteños only use the formal "you" form, *usted,* with people much older than they or in very formal situations, and the casual greeting ¡Hola! often replaces *buen día, buenas tardes,* and *buenas noches.* In small towns formal greetings and the use of *usted* are much more widespread.

SIGHTSEEING

You can dress pretty much as you like: skimpy clothing causes no offense. Argentine men almost always encourage women to go through doors and board buses and elevators first, often with exaggerated ceremony. Far from finding this sexist, local women take it as a god-given right. Frustratingly, there's no rule about standing on one side of escalators to allow people to pass you.

Despite bus drivers' best efforts, locals are reluctant to move to the back of buses. Pregnant women, the elderly, and those with disabilities have priority on the front seats of city buses; offer them your seat if these are taken.

Children and adults selling pens, notepads, or sheets of stickers are regular fixtures on urban public transport. Some children also hand out tiny greeting cards in exchange for coins. The standard procedure is to accept the merchandise or cards as the vendor moves up the carriage, then either return them (saying *no, gracias*) or give them money when they return.

Most porteños are hardened jaywalkers, but given how reckless local driving can be, you'd do well to cross at corners, wait for pedestrian lights, and even then keep a close eye on nearby cars.

OUT ON THE TOWN

A firm nod of the head or raised eyebrow usually gets waiters' attention; "*disculpa*" (excuse me) also does the trick. You can ask your waiter for *la cuenta* (the check) or make a signing gesture in the air from afar.

Alcohol—especially wine and beer—is a big part of life in Argentina. Local women generally drink less than their foreign counterparts, but there are no taboos about this. Social events usually end in general tipsiness rather than all-out drunkenness, which is seen as a rather tasteless foreign habit.

Smoking is very common in Argentina, but antismoking legislation introduced in Buenos Aires in 2006 has banned smoking in all but the largest cafés and restaurants (which must have extractor fans and designated smoking areas). Smoking is prohibited on public transport, in government offices, in banks, and in cinemas.

Public displays of affection between heterosexual couples attract little attention in most parts of the country; beyond downtown Buenos Aires, same-sex couples may attract hostile reactions.

All locals tend to make an effort to look nice—though not necessarily formal—for dinner out. Older couples get very dressed up for the theater; younger women usually put on high heels and makeup for clubbing.

If you're invited to someone's home for dinner, a bottle of good Argentine wine is the best gift to take to the hosts.

LANGUAGE

Argentina's official language is Spanish, known locally as *castellano* (rather than *español*). It differs from other varieties of Spanish in its use of *vos* (instead of *tú*) for the informal "you" form. Locals readily understand the use of *tú* but you blend in more with *vos*. You conjugate it by simply replacing the "r" of the infinitive with "s" and placing the stress (and accent) on the last syllable; thus the vos form of *caminar* (to walk) is "*vos caminás*," and of *decir* (to say) is "*vos decís*." The verb *ser* (to be) is irregular: "*vos sos*" (you are) is the local equivalent of "*tú eres*."

There are also lots of small vocabulary differences, especially for everyday things like food. Porteño intonation is rather singsong, and sounds more like Italian than Mexican or peninsular Spanish. And, like Italians, porteños supplement their words with lots and lots of gesturing. Another porteño peculiarity is pronouncing the letters "y" and "ll" as a "sh" sound.

In hotels, restaurants, and shops that cater to visitors, many people speak at least some basic English; in less touristy places, English-speaking staff are rarer. Attempts to speak Spanish are usually appreciated. Basic courtesies like *buen día* (good morning) or *buenas tardes* (good afternoon), and *por favor* (please) and *gracias* (thank you) are a good place to start. Even if your language skills are basic and phrasebook bound, locals generally make an effort to understand you.

Buenos Aires' official tourism body runs a free tourist assistance hotline (☎ *0800/999–2838*) between 9 am and 8 pm with English-speaking operators.

ar. **Phonerental** ☎ *11/4311–2933* ⊕ *www. phonerental.com.ar.* **Planet Fone** ☎ *888/988– 4777* ⊕ *www.planetfone.com.*

■ CUSTOMS AND DUTIES

Customs uses a random inspection system that requires you to push a button at the inspection bay—if a green light comes on, you walk through; if a red light appears, your bags are X-rayed and very occasionally opened. In practice, many officials wave foreigners through without close inspection.

Officially, you can bring up to 2 liters of alcoholic beverages, 400 cigarettes, and 50 cigars into the country duty-free. However, Argentina's international airports have duty-free shops after you land, and customs officials never take alcohol and tobacco purchased there into account. Personal clothing and effects are admitted duty-free, provided they have been used, as are personal jewelry and professional equipment including laptops. Fishing gear and skis present no problems.

Argentina has strict regulations designed to prevent illicit trafficking in antiques, fossils, and other items of cultural and historical importance. For more information, contact the Dirección Nacional de Patrimonio y Museos (National Heritage and Museums Board).

Information in Argentina Dirección Nacional de Patrimonio y Museos ☎ *11/4381– 6656* ⊕ *www.cultura.gov.ar.*

U.S. Information U.S. Customs and Border Protection ⊕ *www.cbp.gov.*

■ ELECTRICITY

The electrical current is 220 volts, 50 cycles alternating current (AC), so most North American appliances can't be used without a converter. Older wall outlets take continental-type plugs, with two round prongs, whereas newer buildings take plugs with three flat, angled prongs or two flat prongs set at a "V" angle.

Electricity is a hit-and-miss thing in Argentina. Brief power outages (and surges when the power comes back) are fairly regular, so it's a good idea to unplug your laptop when leaving your hotel for the day.

■ EMERGENCIES

In a medical emergency, taking a taxi to the nearest hospital—taxi drivers usually know where to go—can sometimes be quicker than waiting for an ambulance. If you do call for an ambulance, it will take you to the nearest hospital—possibly a public one that may well look rundown; don't worry, though, as the medical attention will be excellent. Alternatively, you can call a private hospital directly.

For theft, wallet loss, small road accidents, and minor emergencies, contact the nearest police station. Expect all dealings with the police to be a lengthy, bureaucratic business—it's probably only worth bothering if you need the report for insurance claims.

American Embassy American Embassy ✉ *Av. Colombia 4300, Palermo* ☎ *11/5777– 4354, 11/5777–4873 after hours* ⊕ *argentina. usembassy.gov.*

General Emergency Contacts Ambulance & Medical Emergencies ☎ *107.* **Fire** ☎ *100.* **Police** ☎ *101.* **All Buenos Aires Emergency Services** ☎ *911.*

■ HEALTH

No specific vaccinations are required for travel to Argentina. However, the Centers for Disease Control (CDC) recommend vaccinations against hepatitis A and B and typhoid for all travelers. Yellow fever is also advisable if you're traveling to the Iguazú area. Children traveling to Argentina should have current inoculations against measles, mumps, rubella, and polio.

People in Buenos Aires drink tap water and eat uncooked fruits and vegetables.

However, if you're prone to tummy trouble, stick to bottled water, which costs about 4.50 pesos for 2 liters.

You wouldn't know it from locals' intense love of sunbathing, but the sun is a significant health hazard in Argentina. Stay out of the sun at midday and, regardless of whether you normally burn, wear plenty of good-quality sunblock. A limited selection is available in most supermarkets and pharmacies, but if you use high SPF factors or have sensitive skin, bring your favorite brands with you. A hat and decent sunglasses are also essential.

Health Warnings National Centers for Disease Control & Prevention (⊕ *www.cdc.gov/travel*). **World Health Organization** (WHO ⊕ *www.who.int*).

HEALTH CARE

Argentina has free national health care that also provides foreigners with free outpatient care. Although medical practitioners working at Buenos Aires' *hospitales públicos* (public hospitals) are usually first-rate, the institutions themselves are often underfunded: bed space and basic supplies are at a minimum, and except in emergencies, consider leaving these resources for those who really need them.

Private consultations and treatment at Buenos Aires' best private hospitals are reasonably priced compared to those in North America (so much so that medical tourism is booming). All the same, it's a good idea to have some kind of medical insurance. Doctors at the Hospital Británico and Hospital Alemán generally speak English; indeed, so do staff at many private hospitals.

Hospitals Hospital Británico (*British Hospital*). ✉ *Pedriel 74, Barracas* ☎ *11/4309–6400* ⊕ *www.hospitalbritanico.org.ar.* **Hospital Alemán** (*German Hospital*). ✉ *Av. Pueyrredon 1640, Recoleta* ☎ *11/4827–7000* ⊕ *www.hospitalaleman.com.ar.*

INSURANCE

You might want to consider buying trip insurance with medical-only coverage. Neither Medicare nor some private insurers cover medical expenses anywhere outside the United States. Medical-only policies typically reimburse you for medical care (excluding that related to pre-existing conditions) and hospitalization abroad, and provide for evacuation. You still have to pay the bills and await reimbursement from the insurer, though.

Medical-Only Insurers International Medical Group ☎ *800/628–4664* ⊕ *www. imglobal.com.* **International SOS** ⊕ *www. internationalsos.com.* **Wallach & Company** ☎ *800/237–6615, 540/687–3166* ⊕ *www. wallach.com.*

MEDICAL EVACUATION

Membership in a medical-evacuation assistance company gets you doctor referrals, emergency evacuation or repatriation, 24-hour hotlines for medical consultation, and other assistance. International SOS *(listed above, under "Insurance")* and AirMed International provide evacuation services and medical referrals. MedjetAssist offers medical evacuation.

Medical Assistance Companies AirMed International ⊕ *www.airmed.com.* **Medjet-Assist** ⊕ *www.medjetassist.com.*

OVER-THE-COUNTER REMEDIES

Farmacias (pharmacies) carry painkillers, first-aid supplies, contraceptives, diarrhea treatments, and a range of other over-the-counter treatments, including drugs that would require a prescription in the United States (antibiotics, for example).

Note that acetominophen—or Tylenol—is known as "paracetamol" in Spanish. If you think you'll need to have prescriptions filled while you're in Argentina, be sure to have your doctor write down the generic name of the drug, not just the brand name.

Farmacity is a supermarket-style drugstore chain with stores all over town;

many of its branches are open 24 hours and have a delivery service.

24-Hour Pharmacies Farmacity ✉ *Florida 474, Centro* ☎ *11/4322-7777* ✉ *R. M. Ortíz 1861, Recoleta* ☎ *11/4809-0043* ✉ *Scalabrini Ortíz 3149, Palermo* ☎ *11/4770-9506* ⊕ *www. farmacity.com.*

■ HOLIDAYS

January through March is summer holiday season for Argentineans. Winter holidays fall toward the end of July and beginning of August. Most public holidays are celebrated on their actual date, except August 17, October 12, and November 20, which move to the following Monday. When public holidays fall on a Thursday or Tuesday, the following Friday or preceding Monday, respectively, is also declared a holiday, creating a four-day weekend known as a *feriado puente*.

Año Nuevo (New Year's Day), January 1. **Carnaval** (Carnival), Monday and Tuesday six weeks before Easter. **Día Nacional de la Memoria por la Verdad y la Justicia** (National Memory Day for Truth and Justice; commemoration of the start of the 1976–82 dictatorship), March 24. **Día del Veterano y de los Caídos en la Guerra de Malvinas** (Malvinas Veterans' Day), April 2. **Semana Santa** (Easter Week), March or April. **Día del Trabajador** (Labor Day), May 1. **Primer Gobierno Patrio** (First National Government, Anniversary of the 1810 Revolution), May 25. **Día de la Bandera** (Flag Day), June 20. **Día de la Independencia** (Independence Day), July 9. **Paso a la Inmortalidad del General José de San Martín** (Anniversary of General José de San Martín's Death), August 17. **Día del Respeto a la Diversidad Cultural** (Day of Respect for Cultural Diversity), October 12. **Día de la Soberanía Nacional** (National Sovereignty Day; Anniversary of the Battle of Vuelta de Obligado), November 20. **Inmaculada Concepción de María** (Immaculate Conception), December 8. **Christmas**, December 25.

■ HOURS OF OPERATION

Banks in Buenos Aires are open only weekdays 10–3. Government offices are usually open to the public on weekday mornings from 7:30 to noon or 1. Government offices, banks, and post offices close on all public holidays, but malls and supermarkets generally only close on Christmas, New Year's Day, and Labor Day (May 1).

Private businesses are generally open weekdays 9–7. Malls and clothes and souvenir shops 10–8 or 9; and supermarkets 8:30 am–9 or 10 pm. Shops that aren't part of chains or in malls are often closed Saturday afternoon and Sunday, except in Palermo Viejo, where Monday is often the day they close.

Post offices are open weekdays from 9 to 5 or 6 and Saturday 9–1. Telephone centers generally stay open daily 8–8 or later. Most gas stations are open 24 hours.

Museums usually close one day a week (Tuesday is common), and often shut their doors for a whole month in summer. Restaurants generally don't open for dinner until 8:30 or 9 pm but stay open until midnight or 1 am. Most bars don't get going until midnight, and often open right through the night. There's no official last call.

■ MAIL

Correo Argentino, Argentina's mail service, has an office in most neighborhoods; some *locutorios* (phone centers) serve as collection points and sell stamps. Postboxes are dark blue and yellow, but there are very few that are not directly outside—or even inside—post offices.

Mail delivery is far from dependable: it can take 6–21 days for standard letters and postcards to get to the United States. Regular airmail letters cost 9 pesos for up to 20 grams. If you want to be sure something will arrive, sent it by *correo certificado* (registered mail), which costs 26 pesos for international letters up to 20 grams. Valuable items are best sent with private express services such as DHL, UPS, or FedEx—delivery within one to two days for a 5 kilogram package starts at about 800 pesos.

Argentina's post-code system is based on a four-digit code. Each province is assigned a letter (the city of Buenos Aires is "C," for instance), which goes before the number code, and each city block is identified by three letters afterward (such as ABD). In practice, however, only very big cities use these complete postal codes (which look like C1234ABC), whereas the rest of Argentina uses the basic number code (1234, for example).

Contacts Correo Argentino ✉ *Perón 300, Microcentro* ☎ *11/4891–9191* ⊕ *www. correoargentino.com.ar.* **DHL** ✉ *Corrientes 315, Microcentro* ☎ *0810/1223–345* ⊕ *www.dhl. com.ar.* **Federal Express** ✉ *25 de Mayo 386, Microcentro* ☎ *0810/333–3339* ⊕ *www.fedex. com.* **UPS** ✉ *Pte. Luis Saenz Peña 1351, Constitución* ☎ *0800/22222–877* ⊕ *www.ups.com.*

▌MONEY

Although prices in Argentina have been steadily rising, Buenos Aires is still a reasonable value if you're traveling from a country with a strong currency. Eating out is affordable, as are mid-range hotels. Room rates at first-class hotels approach those in the United States, however.

You can plan your trip around ATMs—cash is king for day-to-day dealings. U.S. dollars can be changed at any bank and are widely accepted as payment. ⚠ There's a perennial shortage of small change in Buenos Aires—so much so that small shops may refuse a sale if you don't have near-correct change. Follow the locals' example and hoard your coins.

Hundred-peso bills can be hard to get rid of, so ask for tens, twenties, and fifties when you change money. Traveler's checks are useful only as a reserve.

You can usually pay by credit card in top-end restaurants, hotels, and stores. Some establishments only accept credit cards for purchases over 50 pesos. Outside big cities, plastic is less widely accepted.

Visa is the most widely accepted credit card, followed closely by MasterCard. American Express is also accepted in hotels and restaurants, but Diners Club and Discover might not even be recognized. If possible, bring more than one credit card, as some establishments accept only one type. You usually have to produce photo ID—preferably a passport, but otherwise a driver's license—when making credit-card purchases. *Note that throughout this guide the following abbreviations are used: AE, American Express; DC, Diners Club; MC, Master-Card; and V, Visa.*

Nonchain stores often display two prices for goods: *precio de lista* (the standard price, valid if you pay by credit card) and a discounted price if you pay in *efectivo* (cash). Many travel services and even some hotels also offer cash discounts—it's always worth asking about.

ITEM	AVERAGE COST
Cup of Coffee and Three Medialunas (croissants)	10–13 pesos
Glass of Wine	18–25 pesos
Liter Bottle of Local Beer	18–24 pesos
Steak and Fries in a Cheap Restaurant	25–30 pesos
One-Mile Taxi Ride in Buenos Aires	3.80 pesos
Museum Admission	Free–15 pesos

Prices throughout this guide are given for adults. Substantially reduced fees are often available for children, students, and senior citizens.

ATMS AND BANKS

There are ATMs, called *cajeros automáticos,* all over Buenos Aires. Most are inside bank lobbies or small cubicles that you have to swipe your card to get into. Make withdrawals from ATMs in daylight, rather than at night.

There are two main systems. Banelco, indicated by a burgundy-color sign with white lettering, is used by BBVA Banco Francés, HSBC, Banco Galicia, Banco Santander Río, and Banco Patagonia, among others. Link, recognizable by a green-and-yellow sign, is the system used by Banco Provincia and Banco de la Nación, among others. Cards on the Cirrus and Plus networks can be used on both systems.

Many banks have daily withdrawal limits of 1,000 pesos or less (calculated by 24-hour period, not from one day to the next). ■TIP➜ Sometimes ATMs will impose unexpectedly low withdrawal limits (say, 300 pesos) on international cards. You can get around this by requesting a further transaction before the machine returns your card. But first check whether your bank back home charges high per-withdrawal fees. Breaking large bills can be tricky, so try to withdraw change (for example, 490 pesos, rather than 500).

ATM Locations Banelco ⊕ *www.banelco.com. ar.* **Link** ⊕ *www.redlink.com.ar.*

CURRENCY AND EXCHANGE

Argentina's currency is the peso, which equals 100 centavos (100¢). Bills come in denominations of 100 (violet), 50 (navy blue), 20 (red), 10 (ocher), 5 (green), and 2 (blue pesos). Coins are in denominations of 1 peso (a heavy bimetallic coin); and 50, 25, 10, and 5 centavos.

U.S. dollars are widely accepted in big-city stores and supermarkets, and at hotels and restaurants (usually at a slightly worse exchange rate than you'd get at a bank; exchange rates are usually clearly displayed). You always receive change in pesos, even when you pay with U.S. dollars. Taxi drivers may accept dollars, but it's not the norm.

At this writing, the exchange rate is 4.10 pesos to the U.S. dollar. You can change dollars at most banks (between 10 am and 3 pm), at a *casa de cambio* (money

changer), or at your hotel. Forex and Cambio America are two reliable downtown exchange services. All currency exchange involves fees, but as a rule, banks charge the least and hotels the most. You need to show your passport to complete the transaction.

Contacts Banco Francés ⊠ *Av. Corrientes 1102, Microcentro* ☎ *11/4382–1405* ⊕ *www.bancofrances.com.ar.* **Banco de la Nación** ⊠ *Bartolomé Mitre 326, Microcentro* ☎ *11/4347–6000* ⊕ *www.bna.com.ar.* **Cambio America** ⊠ *Sarmiento 501, Microcentro* ☎ *11/4393–0081* ⊕ *www.cambioamerica. com.ar.* **Forex Cambio** ⊠ *M. T. de Alvear 540, Microcentro* ☎ *11/4010–2000* ⊕ *www.forexar. com.ar.* **HSBC** ⊠ *Florida 201, Microcentro* ☎ *11/4320–2800.*

Exchange-Rate Information Oanda.com ⊕ *www.oanda.com.* **XE.com** ⊕ *www.xe.com.* **Visa Center** ⊕ *www.visacenter.com.*

▋ PASSPORTS AND VISAS

As a U.S. citizen, you only need a passport valid for at least six months to enter Argentina for visits of up to 90 days. Argentina operates a reciprocal entry fee scheme for citizens of countries that charge Argentineans for visas, which includes U.S. citizens. However, at this writing, the $140 fee was only being charged to passengers arriving on international flights at Ezeiza and Jorge Newbery airports. The fee is valid for multiple entries over 10 years; you pay in cash or by credit card at booths near immigration, after which you receive a tourist visa stamp on your passport. Check the Visa Center Web site for up-to-date information about visa requirements.

In Argentina you should carry a copy of your passport or other photo ID with you at all times: you need it to make credit-card purchases, change money, and send parcels, as well as in the unlikely event that the police stop you. If you need to stay in Argentina for longer, you can apply for a 90-day extension (*prórroga*) to your tourist visa at the Dirección Nacional de Migraciones. The process takes a morning and costs about 300 pesos. Alternatively, you can exit the country (by taking a boat trip to Uruguay from Buenos Aires, or crossing into Brazil near Iguazú, for example); upon reentering Argentina, your passport will be stamped allowing an additional 90 days.

Overstaying your tourist visa is illegal, and incurs a fine of 300 pesos, which you must pay at the Dirección Nacional de Migraciones before leaving Argentina. Once you have done so, you must leave the country within 10 days.

Officially, children visiting Argentina with only one parent do not need a signed and notarized permission-to-travel letter from the other parent to visit Argentina. However, as Argentine citizens *are* required to have such documentation, it's worth carrying a letter just in case laws change or border officials get confused. Single Parent Travel is a useful online resource that provides advice and downloadable sample permission letters.

Contacts Dirección Nacional de Migraciones ✉ *Av. Antártida Argentina 1355* ☎ *11/4317–0234* ⊕ *www.migraciones. gov.ar.* **Embassy of Argentina** ⊕ *www. embassyofargentina.us.* **Single Parent Travel** ⊕ *www.singleparenttravel.net.*

U.S. Passport Information U.S. Department of State ☎ *877/487–2778* ⊕ *travel.state.gov/ passport.*

∎ RESTROOMS

Argentine restrooms have regular Western-style toilets, but cleanliness standards of public facilities vary hugely. You can find public restrooms in shopping centers, gas stations, bus stations, and some subway stations. Restaurant proprietors often don't complain if you ask to use the facilities without patronizing the establishment, but buying a coffee or a drink is a nice gesture.

There's no guarantee of toilet paper, so carry tissues in your day pack. Alcohol gel and antibacterial hand wipes are also useful for sanitizing you or the facilities.

Restrooms are usually labeled *baño* or *toilette*. Men's toilets are typically labeled *hombres,* often shortened to "H" (men), *caballeros* (gentlemen) or *ellos*. Don't get caught out by an "M" on a door: it's short for *mujeres* (women), not "men."*Damas* (ladies) and *ellas* are other labels for female facilities.

Find a Loo The Bathroom Diaries ⊕ *www. thebathroomdiaries.com.* **Sit or Squat** ⊕ *www. sitorsquat.com.*

∎ SAFETY

CRIME

Argentina is safer than many Latin American countries. However, there has been an increase in street crime—mainly pickpocketing, bag-snatching, and occasionally mugging—especially in Buenos Aires. Taking a few precautions when traveling in the region is usually enough to avoid being a target.

Attitude is essential: strive to look aware and purposeful at all times. Don't wear any jewelry you're not willing to lose. Even imitation jewelry and small items can attract attention and are best left behind. Keep a very firm hold on purses and cameras when out and about, and keep them on your lap in restaurants, not dangling off the back of your chair.

Always remain alert for pickpockets. Try to keep your cash and credit cards in different places, so that if one gets stolen you can fall back on the other. Tickets and other valuables are best left in hotel safes. Avoid carrying large sums of money around, but always keep enough to have something to hand over if you do get mugged. Another time-honored tactic is to keep a dummy wallet (an old one containing an expired credit card and a small amount of cash) in your pocket, with your real cash in an inside or vest pocket.

Women can expect pointed looks, the occasional *piropo* (a flirtatious remark, usually alluding to some physical aspect), and some advances. These catcalls rarely escalate into actual physical harassment—the best reaction is to ignore it as local women do. Going to a bar alone will be seen as an open invitation for attention. If you're heading out for the night, it's wise to take a taxi.

There's a notable police presence in barrios popular with visitors, such as San Telmo and Palermo, and this seems to deter potential pickpockets and hustlers. However, porteños have little faith in their police forces: many officers are corrupt and involved in protection rackets or dealing in stolen goods. At best the police are well-meaning but under-equipped, so don't count on them to come to your rescue in a difficult situation. Reporting crimes is usually ineffectual, and is only worth the time it takes if you need the report for insurance.

The most important advice we can give you is that you should not put up a struggle in the unlikely event that you are mugged or robbed. Nearly all physical attacks on tourists are the direct result of their resisting would-be pickpockets or muggers. Comply with demands, hand over your stuff, and try to get the situation over with as quickly as possible—then let your travel insurance take care of it.

PROTESTS AND RALLIES

Argentines like to speak their minds, and there has been a huge increase in strikes and street protests since the economic crisis of 2001–02. Protesters frequently block streets and squares in downtown Buenos Aires, causing major traffic jams. Some are protesting government policies, others may be showing support for these. Either way, trigger-happy local police have historically proved themselves more of a worry than the demonstrators. Although protests are usually peaceful, exercise caution if you happen across one.

SCAMS

Beware scams such as the offer by a seemingly kindly passerby to help you clean the mustard/ketchup/cream that has somehow appeared on your clothes: while your attention is occupied, an accomplice picks your pocket or snatches your bag.

Taxi drivers in Buenos Aires are usually honest, but occasionally they decide to take people for a ride, literally. All official cabs have meters, so make sure this is turned on. Some scam artists have hidden switches that make the meter tick over more quickly, but simply driving a circuitous route is a more common ploy. It helps to have an idea where you're going and how long it will take. Local lore says that if hailing taxis on the street you are safer with those with lights on top (usually labeled "Radio Taxi"). Late at night, try to call for a cab—all hotels and restaurants, no matter how cheap, have a number and will usually call for you.

When asking for price quotes in touristy areas, always confirm whether the price is in dollars or pesos. Some salespeople, especially street vendors, have found that they can take advantage of confused tourists by charging dollars for goods that are actually priced in pesos. If you're in doubt about that beautiful leather coat, don't be shy about asking whether the number on the tag is in pesos or dollars.

Advisories and Other Information Transportation Security Administration (*TSA*) ⊕ *www.tsa.gov*. **U.S. Department of State** ⊕ *www.travel.state.gov*.

▌ TAXES

Argentina has an international departure tax of $29 and an $8 domestic departure tax, both of which are included in ticket prices. Hotel rooms carry a 21% tax. Cheaper hotels and hostels tend to include this in their quoted rates; more expensive hotels add it to your bill.

Argentina has 21% V.A.T. (known as IVA) on most consumer goods and services. The tax is usually included in the price of goods and noted on your receipt. You can get nearly all the IVA back on locally manufactured goods if you spend more than 70 pesos at stores displaying a Global Blue duty-free sign. You're given a Global Blue check to the value of the IVA, which you get stamped by customs at the airport, and can then cash in at the clearly signed tax refund booths (there's one on the upper floor at Ezeiza). Allow an extra hour to get this done.

Tax refunds Global Blue ☎ *11/5238–1970* ⊕ *www.global-blue.com.*

▌ TIME

Argentina is three hours behind GMT, or three hours ahead of U.S. central standard time.

Time-Zone Information Timeanddate.com ⊕ *www.timeanddate.com/worldclock.*

▌ TIPPING

TIPPING GUIDELINES FOR BUENOS AIRES	
Bellhop at top-end hotels	$1 to $5 per bag, depending on the level of the hotel
Hotel Maid at top-end hotels	$1–$3 a day (either daily or at the end of your stay, in cash)
Hotel Room-Service Waiter	$1 to $2 per delivery, even if a service charge has been added
Taxi Driver	Round up the fare to the next full peso amount
Tour Guide	10% of the cost of the tour if service was good
Waiter	10%–15%, depending on service
Restroom Attendants	Small change, such as 50¢ or 1 peso.

Propinas (tips) are a question of rewarding good service rather than an obligation. Restaurant bills—even those that have a *cubierto* (bread and service charge)—don't include gratuities; locals usually

add 10%–15%. Bellhops and maids expect tips only in the very expensive hotels, where a tip in dollars is appreciated. You can also give a small tip (10% or less) to tour guides. Porteños round off taxi fares, though some cabbies who frequent hotels popular with tourists seem to expect more. Tipping is a nice gesture with beauty and barbershop personnel—5%–10% is fine.

▌ VISITOR INFORMATION

Argentina's official Web portal contains a huge range of detailed up-to-date information in English, including sections on culture, tourism, and business and investment.

The Buenos Aires city government operates tourist information booths around the city. Its extensive Web site includes downloadable maps, free MP3 walking tours, hundreds of listings, and insightful articles on porteño culture, though the English translations of these are often hard to understand.

Each Argentine province operates a tourist office in Buenos Aires, usually called the Casa de [Province Name Here] en Buenos Aires; that is, for information about Salta, you'd go to the Casa de Salta en Buenos Aires, for Mendoza, the Casa de Mendoza en Buenos Aires, and so on.

The government umbrella organization for all regional and city-based tourist offices is the Secretaría de Turismo (Secretariat of Tourism). Their no-frills Web site has links and addresses to these offices, and lots of other practical information.

Limited tourist information is also available at Argentina's embassy and consulates in the United States.

Contacts Argentina (Official Web Portal) ⊕ *www.argentina.ar.* **Argentine Secretariat of Tourism** ☎ *800/555–0016 in Argentina* ⊕ *www.turismo.gov.ar.* **Dirección de Turismo del Gobierno de la Ciudad de Buenos Aires** (*Turismo Buenos Aires*) ☎ *0800/999–2838 in Argentina* ⊕ *www.bue.gov.ar.* **Embassy of Argentina** ⊕ *www.embassyofargentina.us.*

ONLINE RESOURCES

ALL ABOUT BUENOS AIRES

The like-minded travelers on Fodors.com are eager to answer questions and share information.

Several Web sites have information that will supplement or complement that on tourist board sites. Atlas Ambiental de Buenos Aires is part atlas, part environmental encyclopedia. It's a well-designed site that has detailed background information about the city.

Mapa Interactivo de Buenos Aires is an interactive online map run by the city government. It allows you to search for specific addresses, as well as facilities and services such as ATMs, hospitals, and cycle lanes. Welcome Argentina has good overviews of Argentina's different regions, and lots of articles on Buenos Aires. The BA Expats forum and Discover Buenos Aires have lots of insider tips on expat life in Buenos Aires.

CULTURE AND ENTERTAINMENT

Insightful—and often amusing—commentaries on local news and cultural events can be found at *The Argentine Post*. The English-language daily *Buenos Aires Herald* gives a conservative take on local news.

The Web site of English-language monthly newspaper *The Argentina Independent* has traveler-oriented news and cultural information. *What's Up Buenos Aires* is a slick bilingual guide, run by American expats, to contemporary culture and partying in the city.

The Web site of bimonthly English-language magazine *BA Insider* is packed with up-to-date listings on cultural activities such as language exchanges, writing workshops, and volunteering opportunities. It also has a wealth of information and resources aimed at long-term foreign visitors to Buenos Aires.

The Museo Nacional de Bellas Artes, which contains the world's biggest collection of Argentine art, has lots of information about Argentine artists on its Web site.

Todo Tango is a comprehensive bilingual tango site with tango lyrics, history, and free downloads.

All About Buenos Aires Atlas Ambiental de Buenos Aires ⊕ www.atlasdebuenosaires. gov.ar. **Fodors.com** ⊕ www.fodors.com/ forums. **Mapa de Buenos Aires** ⊕ www.mapa. buenosaires.gov.ar. **Welcome Argentina** ⊕ www.welcomeargentina.com.ar.

Culture and Entertainment The Argentine Post ⊕ www.argentinepost.com. **The Argentina Independent** ⊕ www. argentinaindependent.com. **Buenos Aires Herald** ⊕ www.buenosairesherald.com. **Museo Nacional de Bellas Artes** ⊕ www. mnba.org.ar. **Todo Tango** ⊕ www.todotango. com.ar. **What's Up Buenos Aires** ⊕ www. whatsupbuenosaires.com.

Expat Life BA Expats ⊕ www.baexpats. com. **Discover Buenos Aires** ⊕ www. discoverbuenosaires.com.

Travel Agents Argentina Escapes ☏ 11/5032–2938 ⊕ www.argentinaescapes. com. **Buenos Aires Tours** ⊕ www. buenosaires-tours.com.ar. **Limitless Argentina** ☏ 202/536–5812 in U.S., 11/4772–8700 in Buenos Aires ⊕ www.limitlessargentina.com. **Wow! Argentina** ☏ 11/5239–3019 ⊕ www. wowargentina.com.

INDEX

PHOTO CREDITS

1, Silvia Boratti/iStockphoto. 3, Michel Friang/Alamy. **Chapter 1: Experience Buenos Aires:** 6-7, HUGHES Hervé/age fotostock. 8, Christopher Pillitz/Alamy. 9 (top left), Juanderlust, Fodors.com member. 9 (top right), jd_miller, Fodors.com member. 9 (bottom), Diego_3336/Flickr. 12, Jason Friend/ Alamy. 13, Thomas Cockrem/Alamy. 14 (left), Giulio Andreini/age fotostock. 14 (top center), Jon Hicks/Alamy. 14 (top right), P Sinclair, Fodors.com member. 14 (bottom right), Wim Wiskerke/Alamy. 15 (top left), Frank Nowikowski/South American Pictures. 15 (bottom left), Enrique Shore-Woodfin Camp/Aurora Photos. 15(top right), APEIRON-PHOTO/Alamy. 15 (bottom right), Pictorial Press Ltd/ Alamy. 16, Alvaro Leiva/age fotostock. 17 (left), Michel Friang/Alamy. 17 (right), David R. Frazier Photolibrary, Inc./Alamy. 18, edithbruck/Flickr. 19 (left), RH_Miller, Fodors.com member. 19 (right), puroticorico/Flickr. 20, M. Scanel, Fodors.com member. 21 (left), Seamus, Fodors.com member. 21 (right), Rcidte/wikipedia.org. 22, Alvaro Leiva/age fotostock. 23 (left), Maggie Birkner/age fotostock. 23 (right), tercerojista/Flickr. 24, Peter M. Wilson/Alamy. 25, Beatrice Murch/Flickr. 26, El Universal/Newscom. 27, Laura Brunow Miner/Flickr. 28, VinoFamily/Flickr. 29 (left), by Rivard/Flickr. 29 (right), feserc/Flickr. 30, Beverly Logan/SuperStock. 31 (top left), Michael Obert/age fotostock. 31 (top right), AFP PHOTO/ALI BURAFI/Newscom. 31 (bottom), South American Pictures. 32, Christine Yuan, Fodors.com member. 33 (left), Jeremy Hoare/Alamy. 33 (right), Tony Morrison/South American Pictures. 34, Amado Group. 35, TravelStockCollection - Homer Sykes/Alamy. 36, Eduardo Dreizzen/ age fotostock. 37 (left), Image Asset Management/age fotostock. 37 (right), José Francisco Ruiz/age fotostock. 38 (left), Eduardo M. Rivero/age fotostock. 38 (top right), Public domain. 38 (bottom right), Jordi Camí/age fotostock. 39 (left), Public domain. 39 (right), Apeiron-Photo/Alamy. 40 (left and top right), A.H.C./age fotostock. 40 (bottom right), Pictorial Press Ltd/Alamy. 41 (left), Archivo Gráfico de Clarín (Argentina)/Wikimedia Commons/Public domain. 41 (top right), Tramonto/age fotostock. 41 (bottom right), Griffiths911/wikipedia.org. 42 (left), Christopher Pillitz/Alamy. 42 (top right), Nikada/ iStockphoto. 42 (bottom right), DYN/Getty Images/Newscom. 43 (top), Roberto Fiadone/wikipedia. org. 43 (bottom left), wikipedia.org. 44, fortes/Flickr. **Chapter 2: Buenos Aires Neighborhoods:** 45, caron malecki, Fodors.com member. 46, KE1TH, Fodors.com member. 47, by 2litros > raimundo illanes/Flickr. 48, berhbs, Fodors.com member. 51, lilap/Flickr. 52, blmurch/Flickr. 54-55, iStockphoto. 59, Amanda Bullock. 63, Kobi Israel/Alamy. 64, Julian Rotela Rosow/Flickr. 67, James Wong, Fodors. com member. 68, Alfredo Maiquez/age fotostock. 70, Picasa 2.7/Flickr. 73, Frank Nowikowski/South American Pictures. 74, Sara Nixon, Fodors.com member. 77, Dan DeLuca/wikipedia.org. 78, caron malecki, Fodors.com member. 80, Amanda Bullock. 82, giulio andreini/age fotostock. 84, Michele Molinari/Alamy. 85, Martin Byrne, Fodors.com member. 87, wabauer, Fodors.com member. 89, Beth/ Queen/ZUMA Press/Newscom. 90, wim wiskerke/Alamy. 93 (top), Network Photographers/Alamy. 93 (bottom), Shinichi Yamada/AFLO SPORT/Icon SMI. 94 (top), Visual Arts Library (London)/Alamy. 94 (bottom), P. Narayan/age fotostock. 95 (top), Tramonto/age fotostock. 95 (bottom), A.H.C./age fotostock. 96 (top), Keystone/Getty Images/Newscom. 96 (bottom), Public domain. 97 (left), Bruno Perousse/age fotostock. 97 (right), Beth/Queen/Zuma Press/Newscom. 98 (top), Christopher Pillitz/ Alamy. 99 (top left), Odile Montserrat/Sygma/Corbis. 99 (top right), Universal/Newscom. 100 (top left), Interfoto Pressebildagentur/Alamy. 100 (top right), SuperStock/age fotostock. 100 (bottom), G. Sioen/DEA/age fotostock. 101 (top), Shinichi Yamada/AFLO SPORT/Icon SMI. 101 (bottom), Picture-Alliance/DPA/Newscom. **Chapter 3: Shopping:** 103, NL, Fodors.com member. 104, Jochem Wijnands/ age fotostock. 108, Alexander Hafemann/iStockphoto. 110, P. Narayan/age fotostock. 111, Jeremy Hoare/Alamy. 116, Susan Seubert/drr.net. 117, Jon Hicks/Alamy. 119, Flickr. 121, Courtesy of Marcelo Toledo, Silversmith/www.marcelotoledo.net. 122, Joel Mann/Flickr. 124, Luis Argerich/wikipedia.org. 125, Jeremy Hoare/age fotostock. 132, Yadid Levy/age fotostock. 133, nick baylis/Alamy. 134, Pablo Abuliak. **Chapter 4: After Dark:** 151, Jorge Royan/Alamy. 152, AFP PHOTO/Miguel MENDEZ/Newscom. 162, laubenthal, Fodors.com member. 165, Ernesto Ríos Lanz/age fotostock. 166, wikipedia. org. 167, eyalos.com/Shutterstock. 168 (top), *Picture Contact/Alamy.* 168 (2nd from top), *Christina Wilson/Alamy.* 168 (3rd from top), *Michel Friang/Alamy.* 168 (bottom), *Jason Howe/South American Pictures.* 169 (top), Archivo General de la Nación/wikipedia.org. 169 (bottom), Danita Delimont/ Alamy. 170, christina wilson/Alamy. 172, blmurch/Flickr. 176, Demetrio Carrasco/age fotostock. 179, Libertinus/Flickr. **Chapter 5: Where to Eat:** 183, wim wiskerke/Alamy. 184, nick baylis/Alamy. 188, Fabricio Di Dio. 189 (top), Alan Howden - Argentina Stock Photography/Alamy. 189 (bottom), Church of emacs/wikipedia.org. 190, Sergio Pitamitz/age fotostock. 191, Picture Contact/Alamy. 192, Orient-Express Hotels, Trains, & Cruises. 193 (top), Jeremy Hoare/age fotostock. 193 (bottom), Hyatt. 194, Angel Terry/Alamy. 195 (top), blmurch/Flickr. 195 (bottom), Harriet Cummings/Alamy. 196 and 197 (top), Fabricio Di Dio. 197 (bottom), mashe/Shutterstock. 205, einalem/Flickr. 209, Hyatt Hotels & Resorts. 210, Alvear Hotel. 212, Casa Cruz. 218, Osaka. **Chapter 6: Where to Stay:** 229, jd_miller,

NOTES

NOTES

NOTES

NOTES

NOTES

NOTES

ABOUT OUR WRITERS

Karina Martinez-Carter lives in Buenos Aires, the city she moved to after graduating college in 2010. She contributes regularly to BBC Travel and also has written for *The Atlantic, The Huffington Post,* and *Time Out Buenos Aires,* among other publications. Karina updated the Where to Stay chapter for this edition.

A British journalist working on the Buenos Aires Herald's economy desk, Sorrel Moseley-Williams first visited Argentina as a year-abroad student in 1998 and has been in a long-term with the relationship with the country since 2006. She contributes to *Time Out Buenos Aires, The Real Argentina, Wallpaper*, DK Eyewitness Argentina, Screen International,* and *ON Mag* (in Spanish), and writes the weekly Wining On food and drink column found on ⊕ *www.sorrelmw.com.* She updated the After Dark and Shopping chapters for this edition.

Victoria Patience first came to Argentina to spend a year studying Latin American literature. Eleven years later, she still hasn't managed to leave. She lives in Buenos Aires province with her Argentinian husband, daughter, dogs, and cats. She is a freelance contributor to many Fodor's guidebooks and also runs her own editing and translation company, Nativa Wordcraft. Victoria updated the Experience, Travel Smart, and Neighborhoods chapters of this book, as well as Tango sections of the After Dark chapter and portions of the Side Trips chapter.

Dan Perlman is a trained chef and sommelier, and an internationally published food, wine, and travel writer with some 30 years experience under his whisk and pen. Currently he's living and working in Buenos Aires, where he runs the wildly popular Casa SaltShaker underground restaurant. Dan updated the Where to Eat chapter.

Jessica Pollack, a Buenos Aires–based writer, updated portions of the Side Trips chapter for this edition.